CUBE ARTS

1

story & art
TOMOMI USUI

Cube Arts

Play

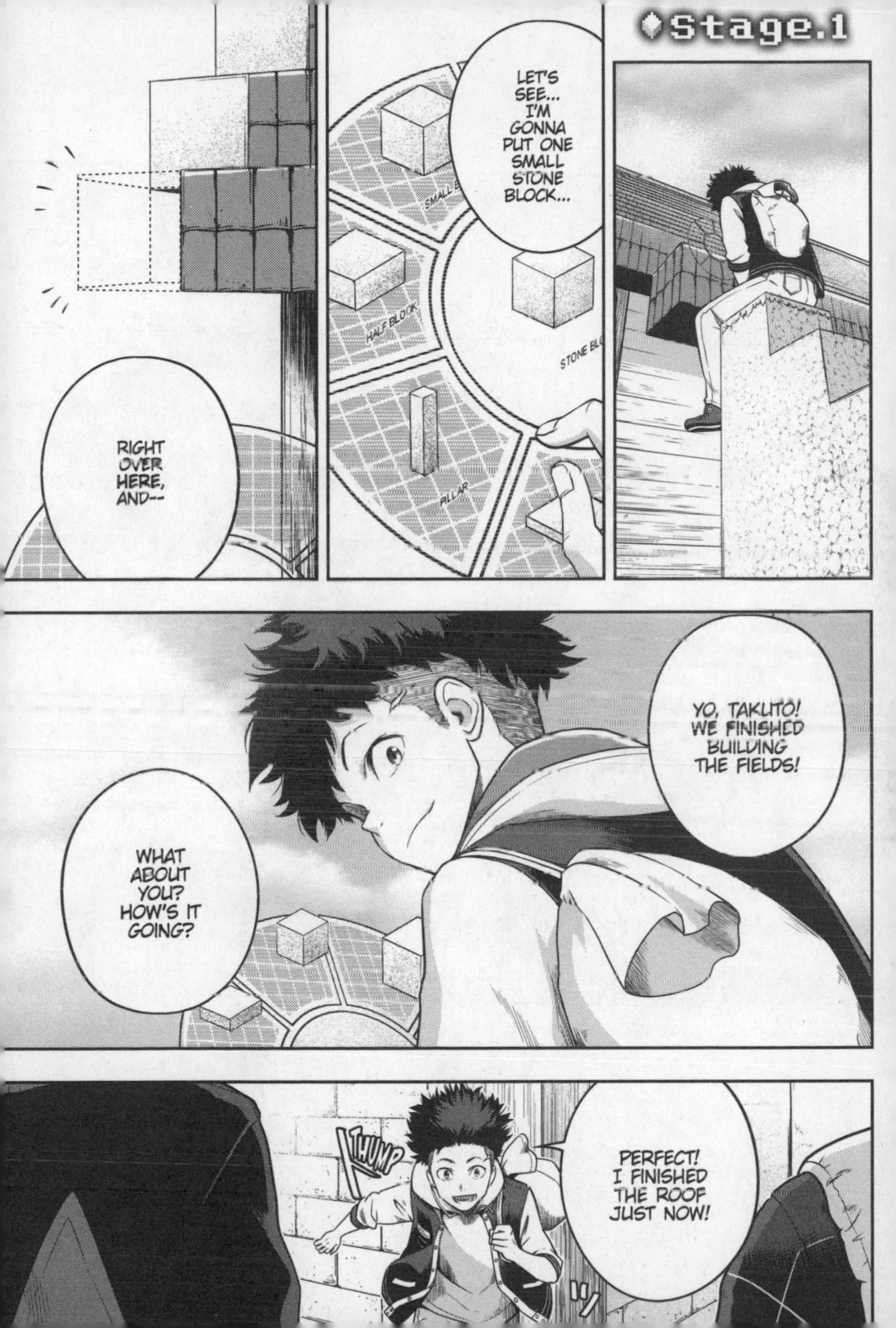
LET'S SEE... I'M GONNA PUT ONE SMALL STONE BLOCK...
HALF BLOCK
PILLAR
RIGHT OVER HERE, AND--
YO, TAKUTO! WE FINISHED BUILDING THE FIELDS!
WHAT ABOUT YOU? HOW'S IT GOING?
PERFECT! I FINISHED THE ROOF JUST NOW!
THUMP

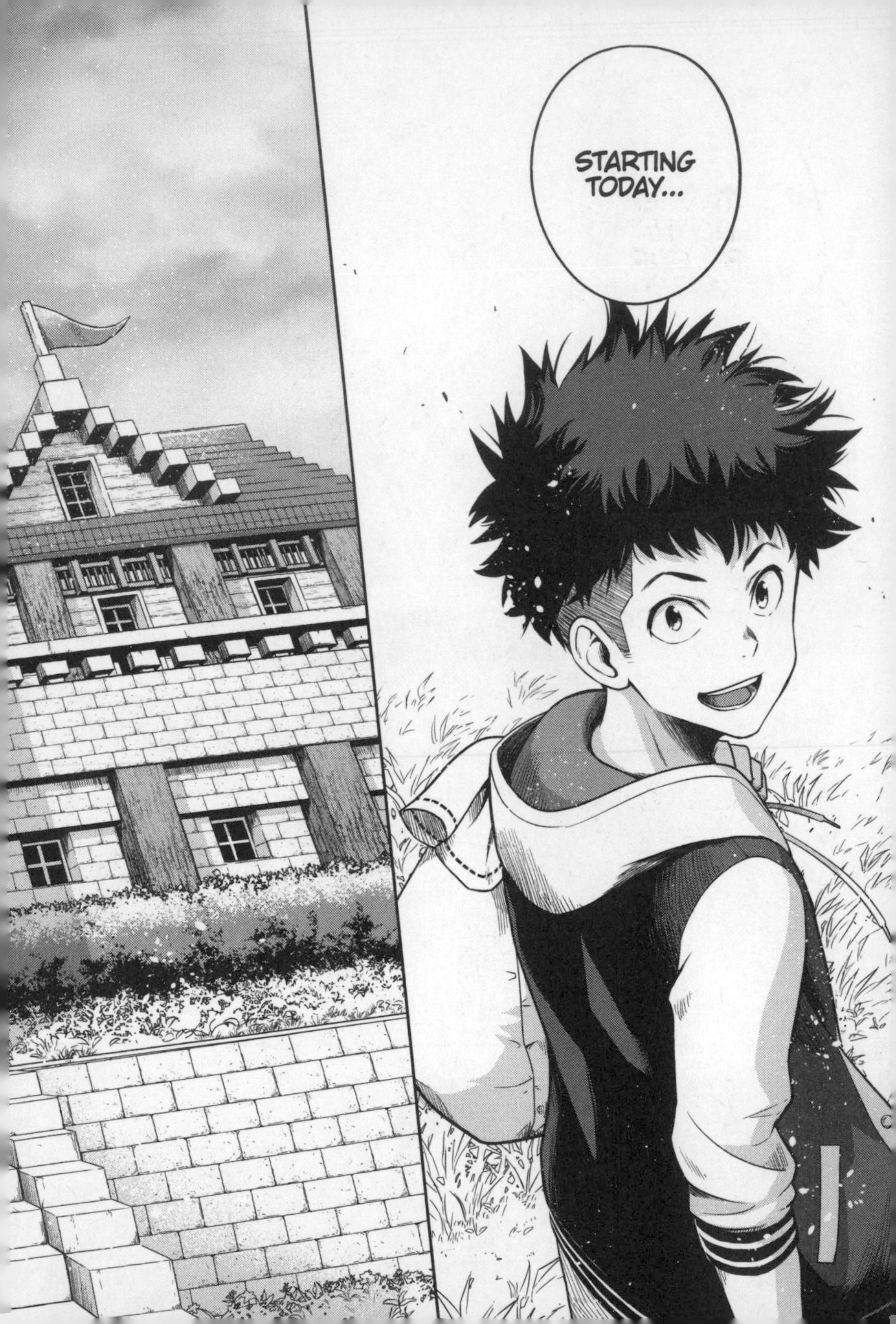
STARTING TODAY...

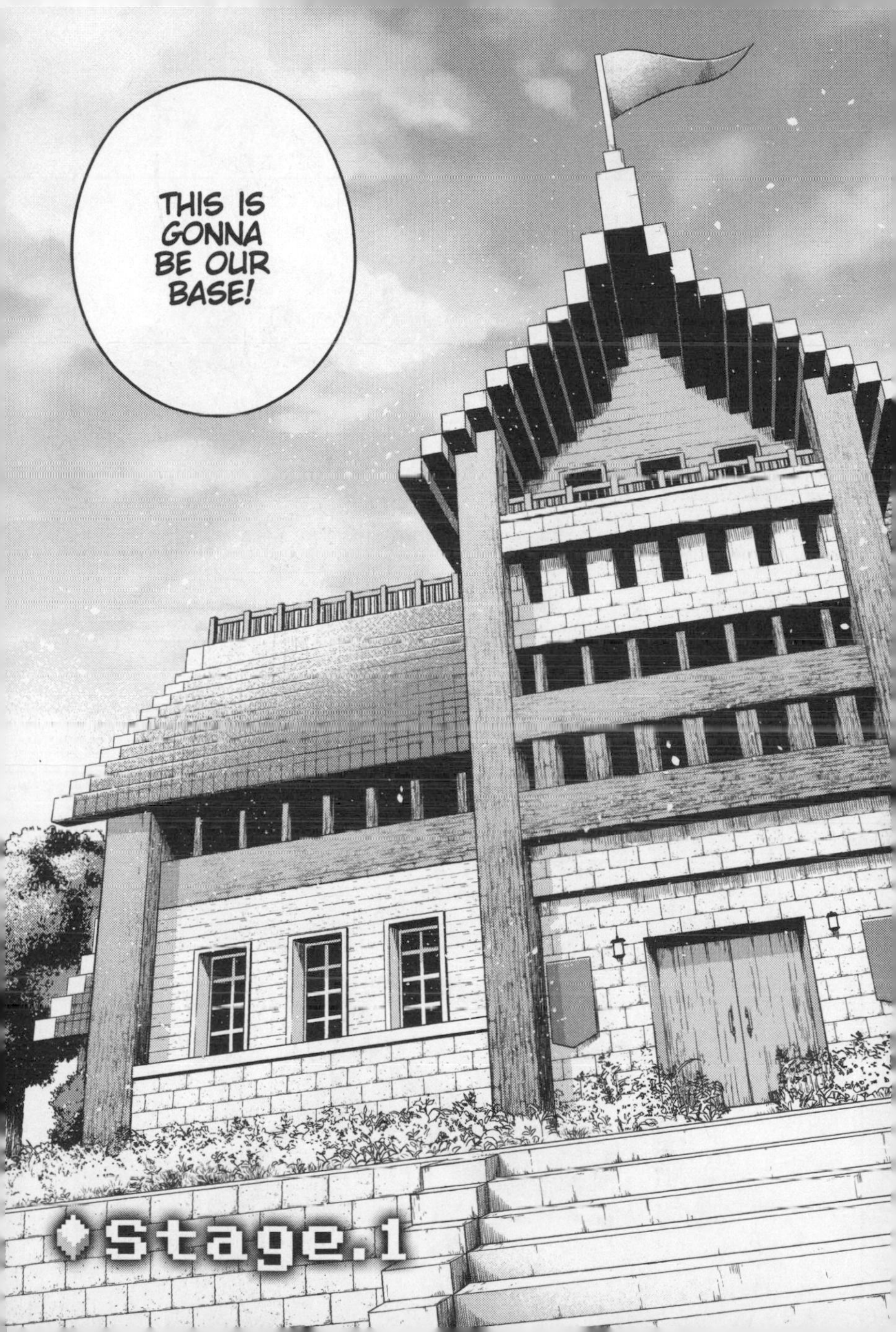
THIS IS GONNA BE OUR BASE!
Stage.1

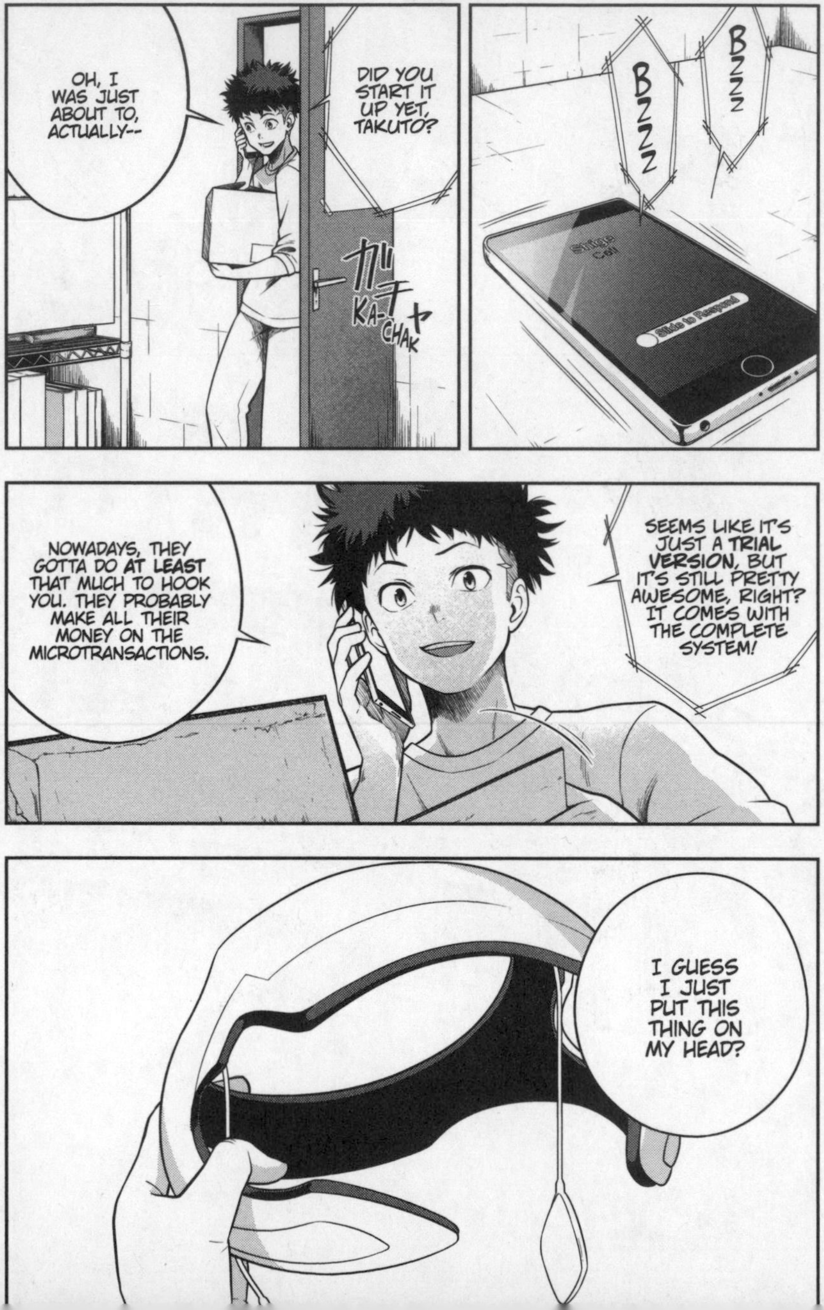
BZZZ
BZZZ
Slide to Respond
DID YOU START IT UP YET, TAKUTO?
OH, I WAS JUST ABOUT TO, ACTUALLY--
ガチャ
KA-CHAK
SEEMS LIKE IT'S JUST A TRIAL VERSION, BUT IT'S STILL PRETTY AWESOME, RIGHT? IT COMES WITH THE COMPLETE SYSTEM!
NOWADAYS, THEY GOTTA DO AT LEAST THAT MUCH TO HOOK YOU. THEY PROBABLY MAKE ALL THEIR MONEY ON THE MICROTRANSACTIONS.
I GUESS I JUST PUT THIS THING ON MY HEAD?

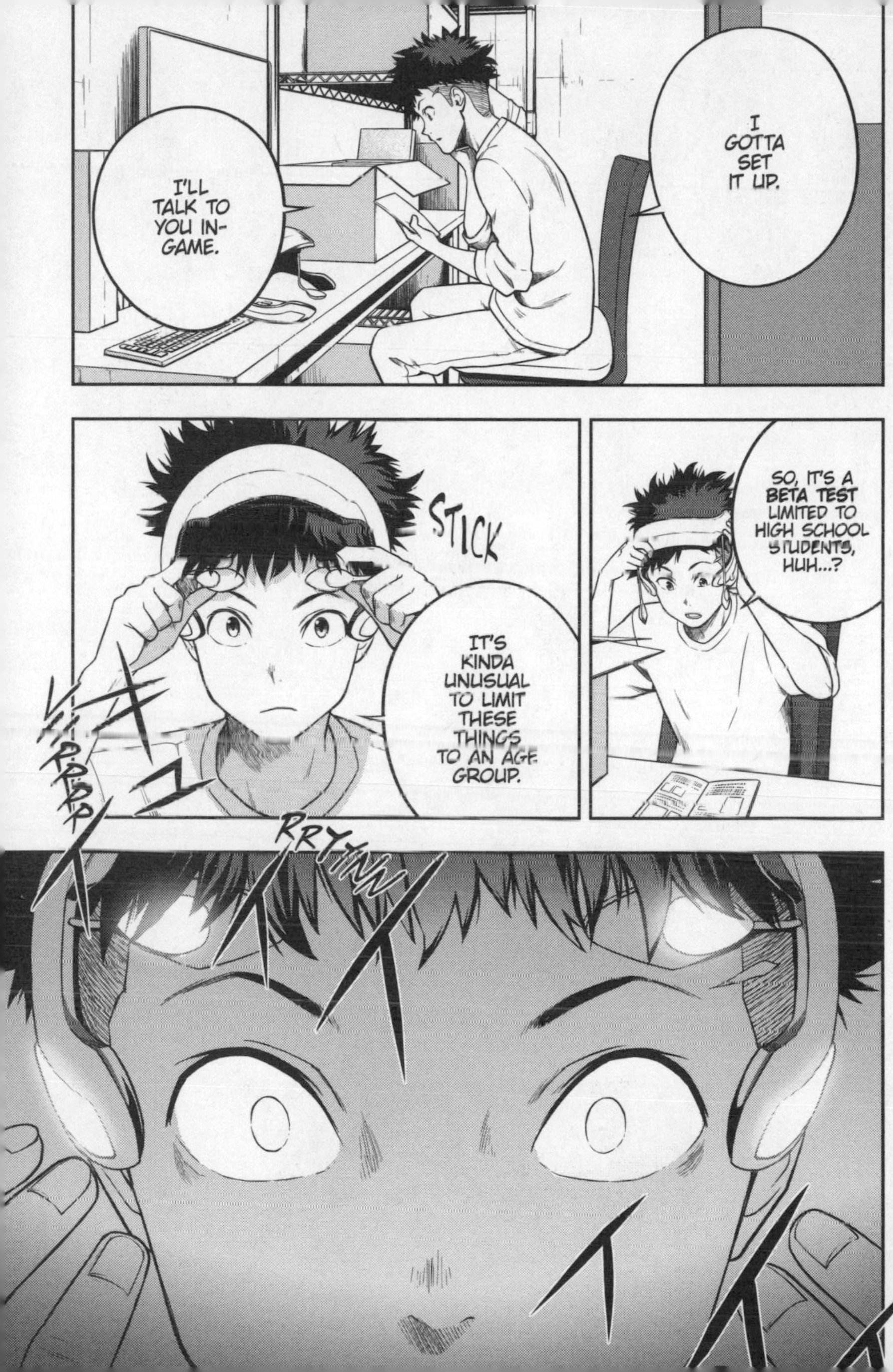
I GOTTA SET IT UP.
I'LL TALK TO YOU IN-GAME.
SO, IT'S A BETA TEST LIMITED TO HIGH SCHOOL STUDENTS, HUH...?
STICK
IT'S KINDA UNUSUAL TO LIMIT THESE THINGS TO AN AGE GROUP.
VRRRR
RRYINN

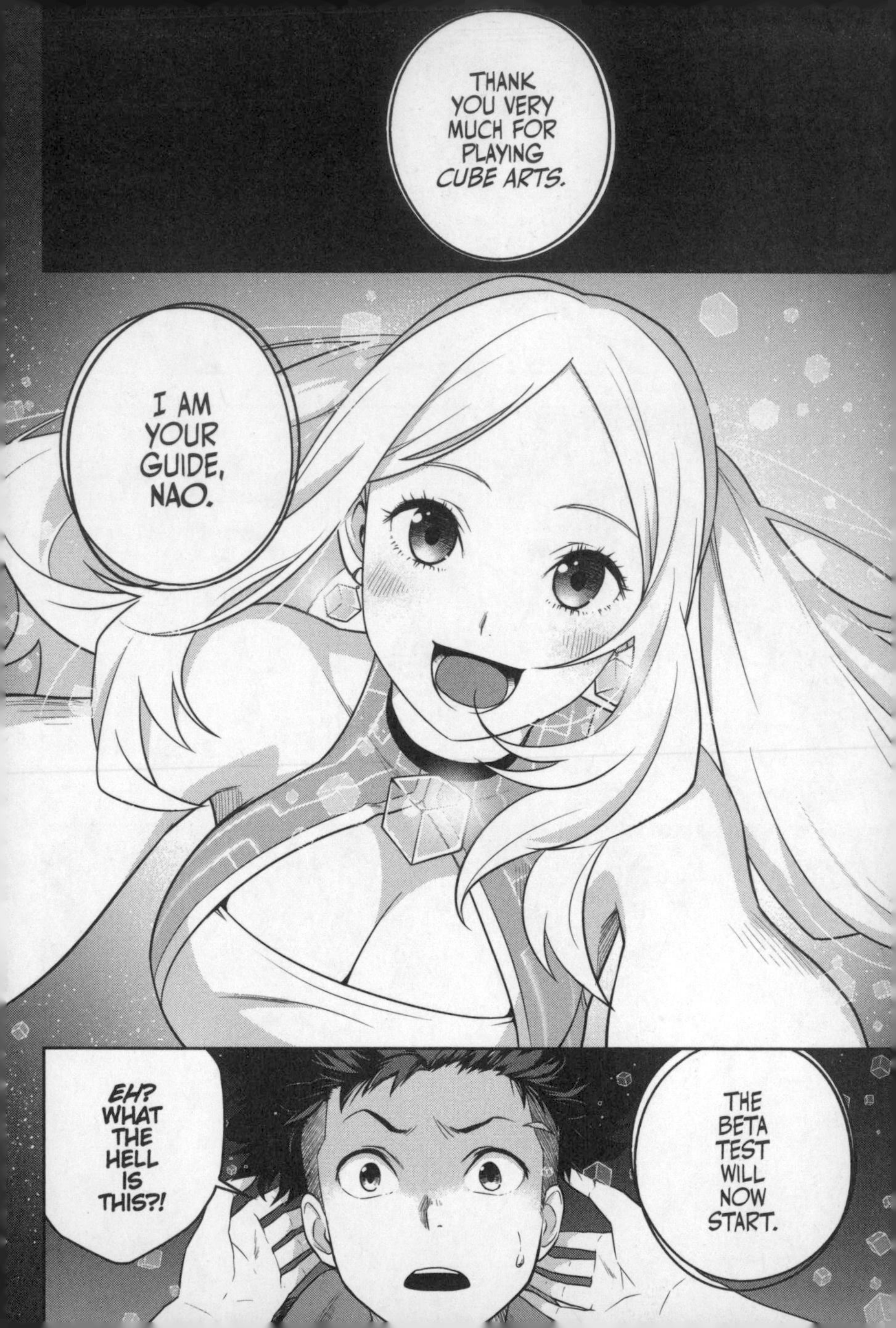
THANK YOU VERY MUCH FOR PLAYING CUBE ARTS.
I AM YOUR GUIDE, NAO.
THE BETA TEST WILL NOW START.
EH? WHAT THE HELL IS THIS?!

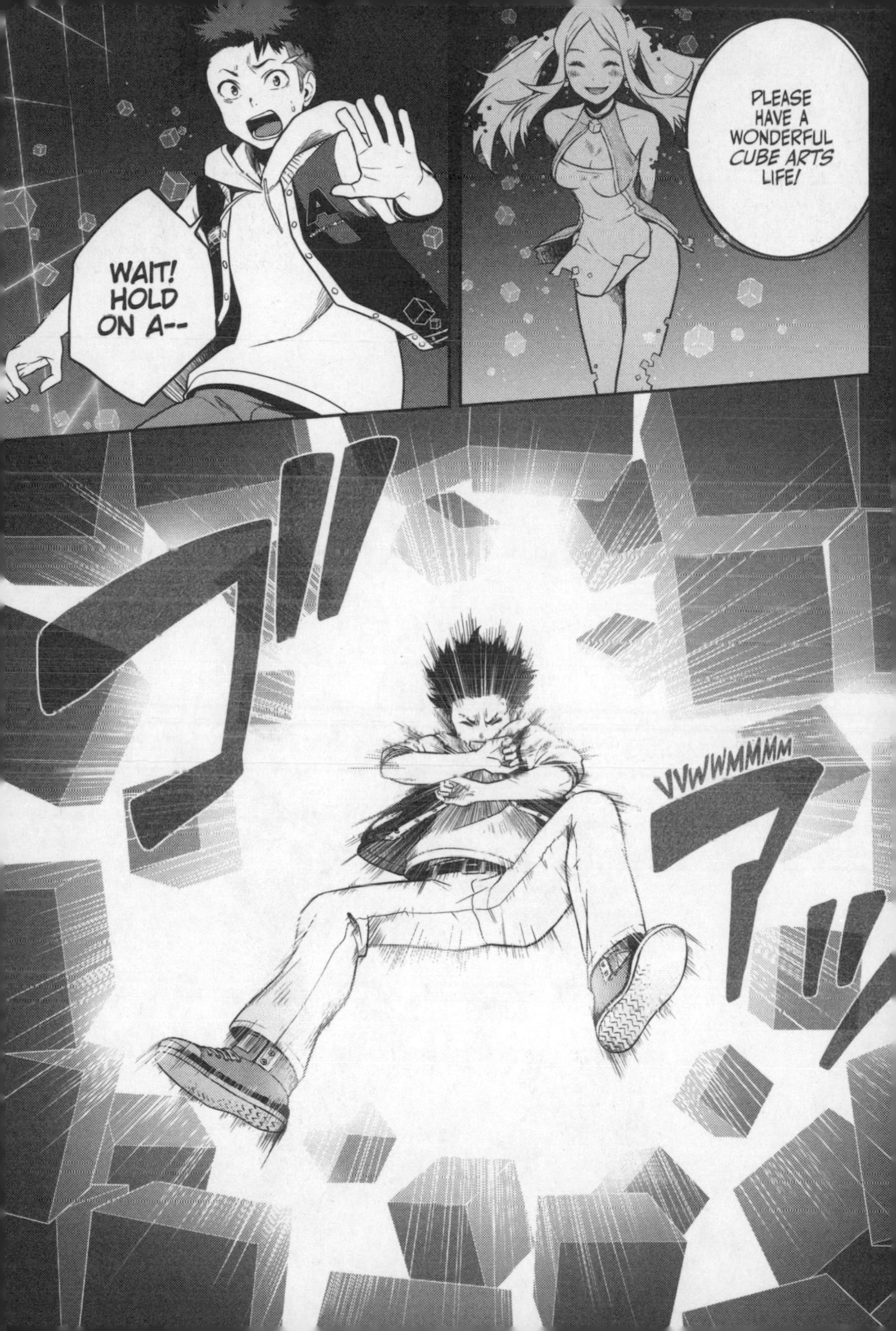
PLEASE HAVE A WONDERFUL CUBE ARTS LIFE!
WAIT! HOLD ON A--
VVWWMMMM

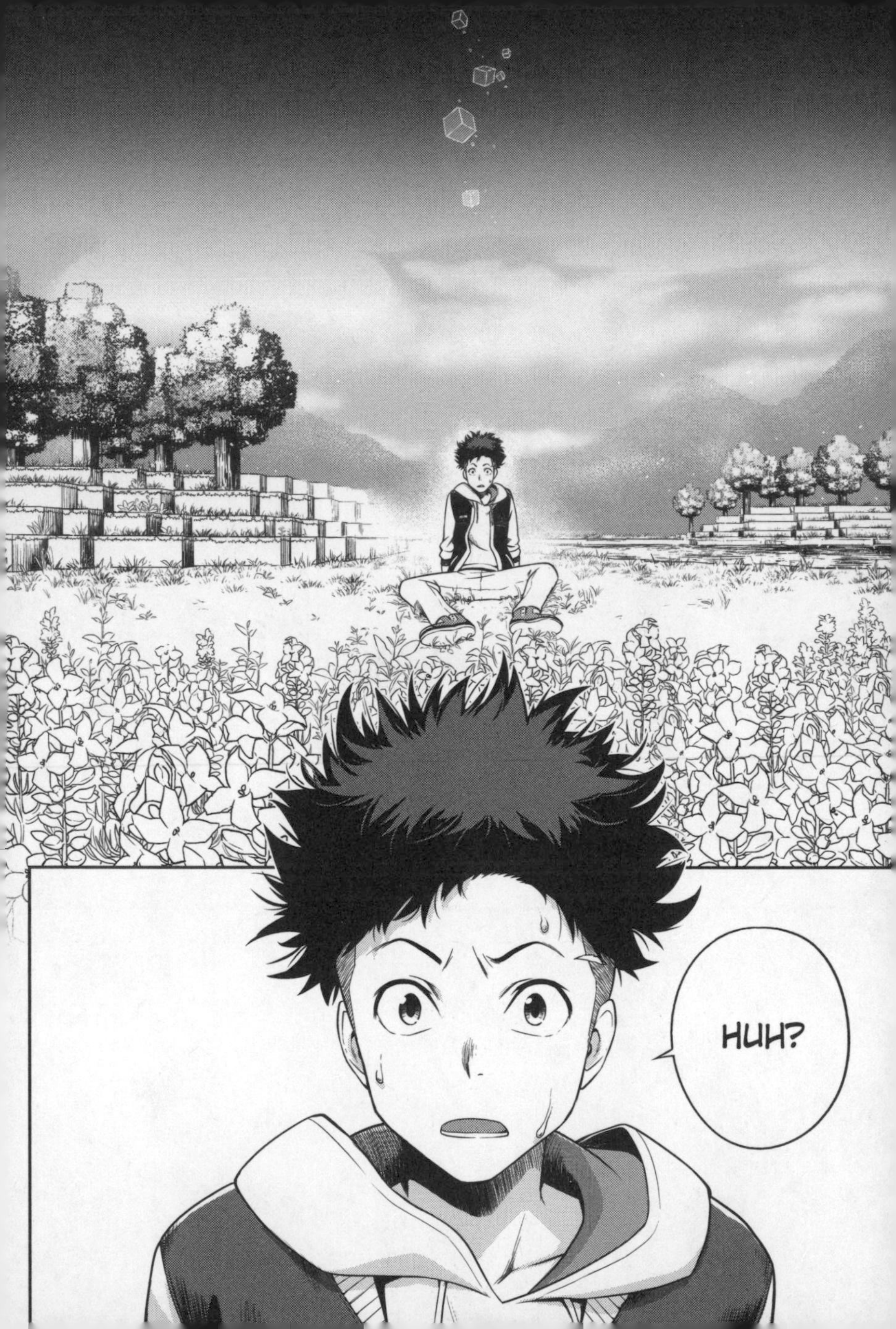
HUH?

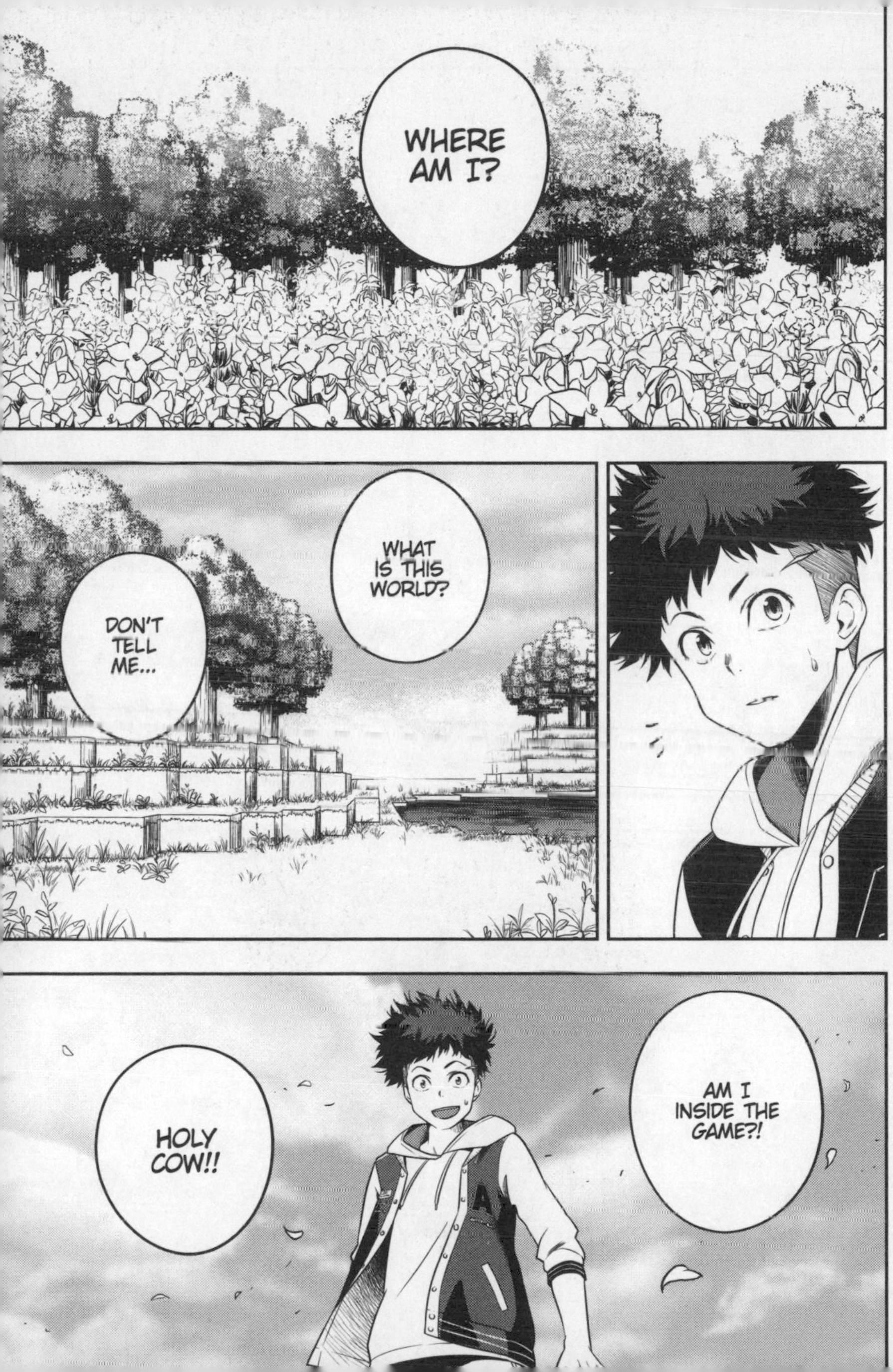
WHERE AM I?
WHAT IS THIS WORLD?
DON'T TELL ME...
AM I INSIDE THE GAME?!
HOLY COW!!

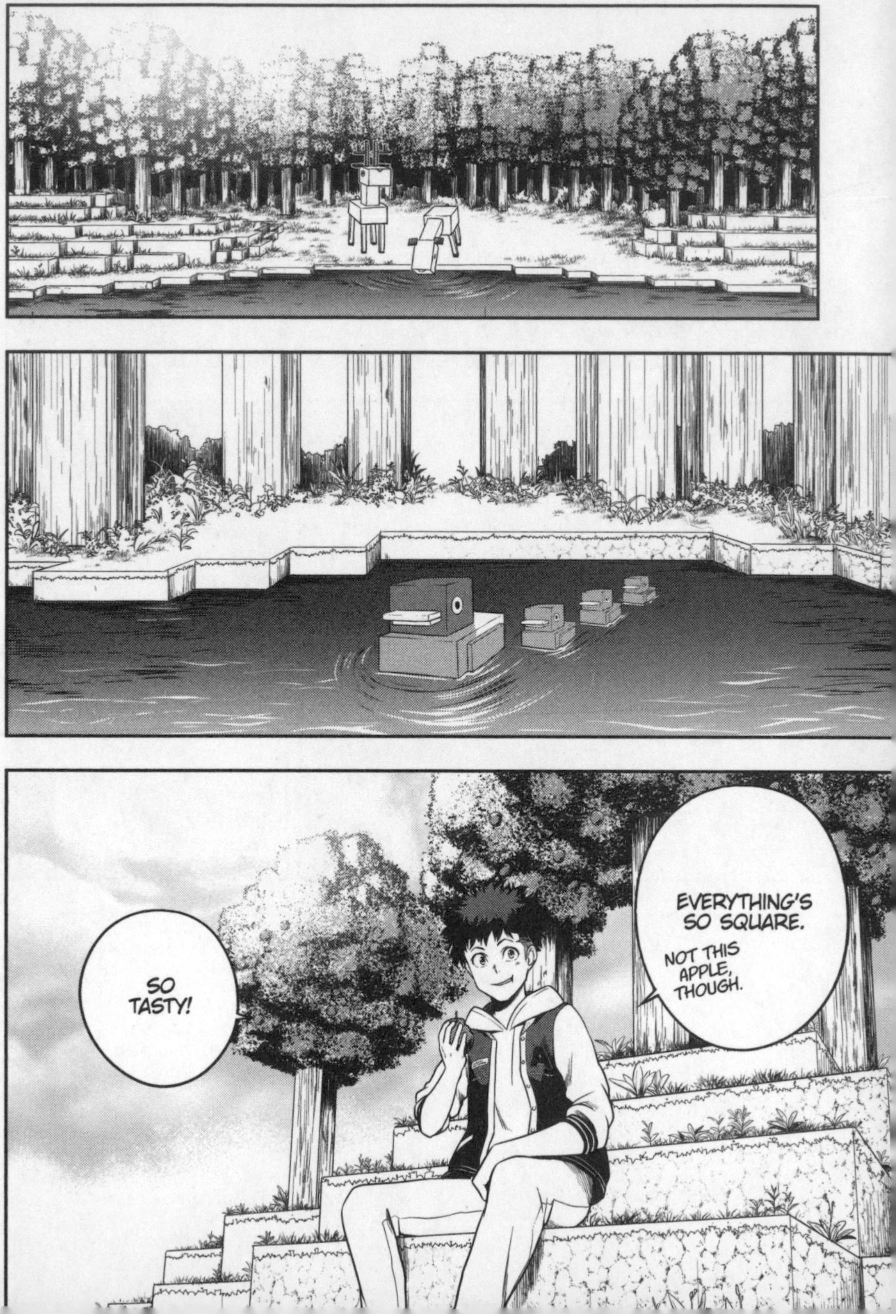
EVERYTHING'S SO SQUARE.
NOT THIS APPLE, THOUGH.
SO TASTY!

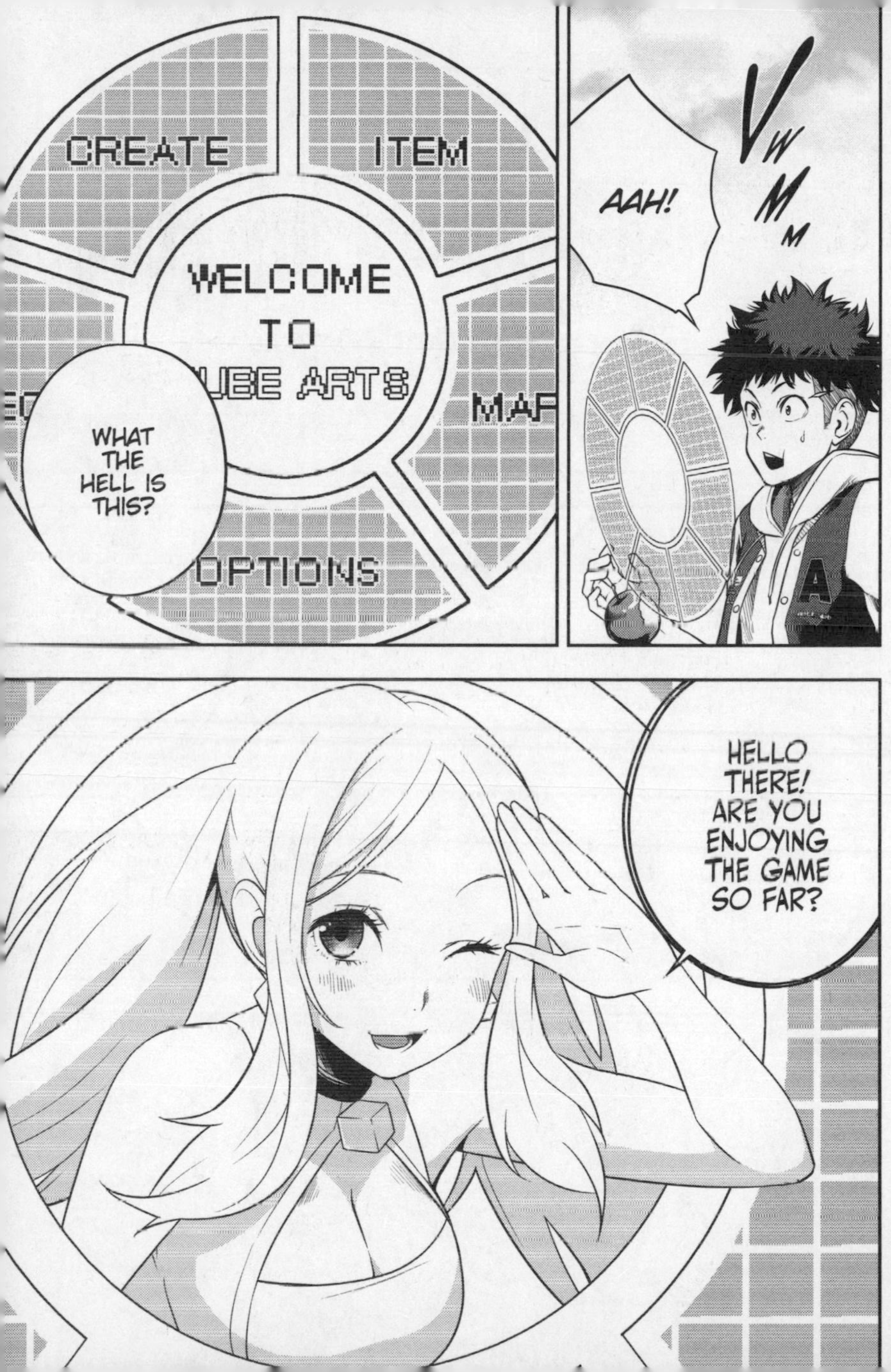
VWMM
AAH!
CREATE
ITEM
WELCOME TO
OPTIONS
WHAT THE HELL IS THIS?
HELLO THERE! ARE YOU ENJOYING THE GAME SO FAR?

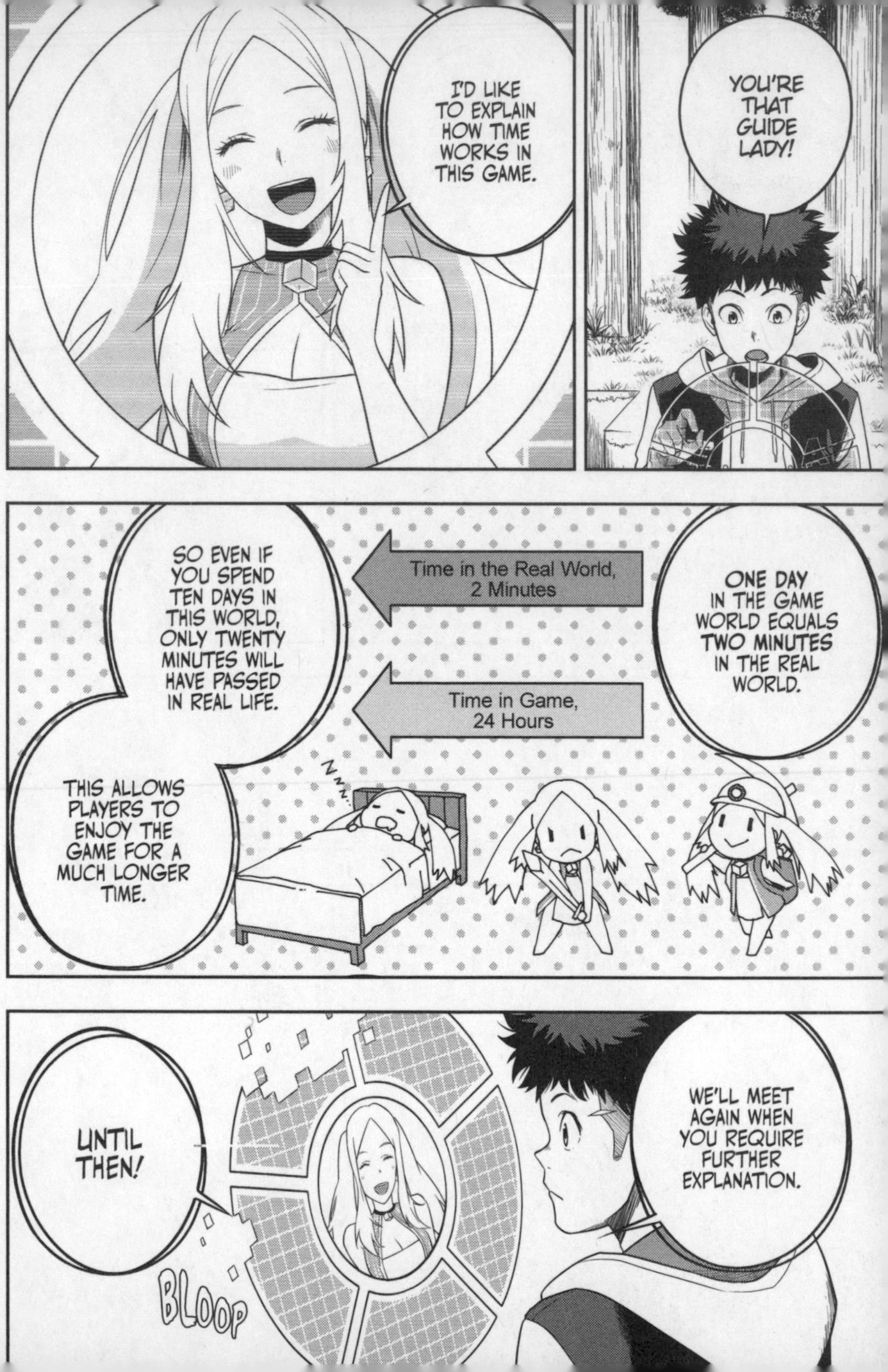
YOU'RE THAT GUIDE LADY!
I'D LIKE TO EXPLAIN HOW TIME WORKS IN THIS GAME.
ONE DAY IN THE GAME WORLD EQUALS TWO MINUTES IN THE REAL WORLD.
Time in the Real World, 2 Minutes
Time in Game, 24 Hours
SO EVEN IF YOU SPEND TEN DAYS IN THIS WORLD, ONLY TWENTY MINUTES WILL HAVE PASSED IN REAL LIFE.
THIS ALLOWS PLAYERS TO ENJOY THE GAME FOR A MUCH LONGER TIME.
WE'LL MEET AGAIN WHEN YOU REQUIRE FURTHER EXPLANATION.
UNTIL THEN!
BLOOP

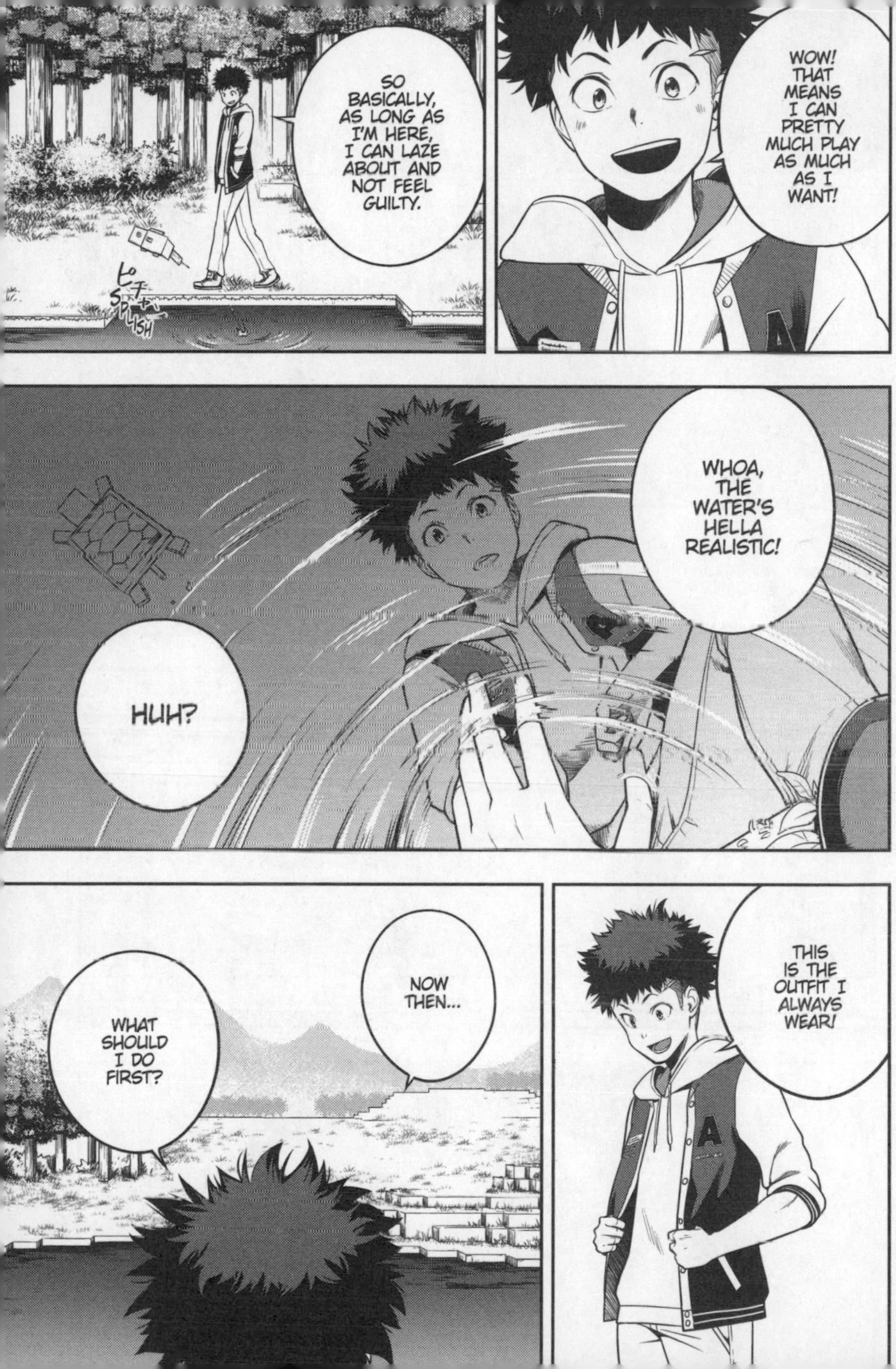
WOW! THAT MEANS I CAN PRETTY MUCH PLAY AS MUCH AS I WANT!
SO BASICALLY, AS LONG AS I'M HERE, I CAN LAZE ABOUT AND NOT FEEL GUILTY.
ピチャ
SPLISH
WHOA, THE WATER'S HELLA REALISTIC!
HUH?
THIS IS THE OUTFIT I ALWAYS WEAR!
NOW THEN...
WHAT SHOULD I DO FIRST?

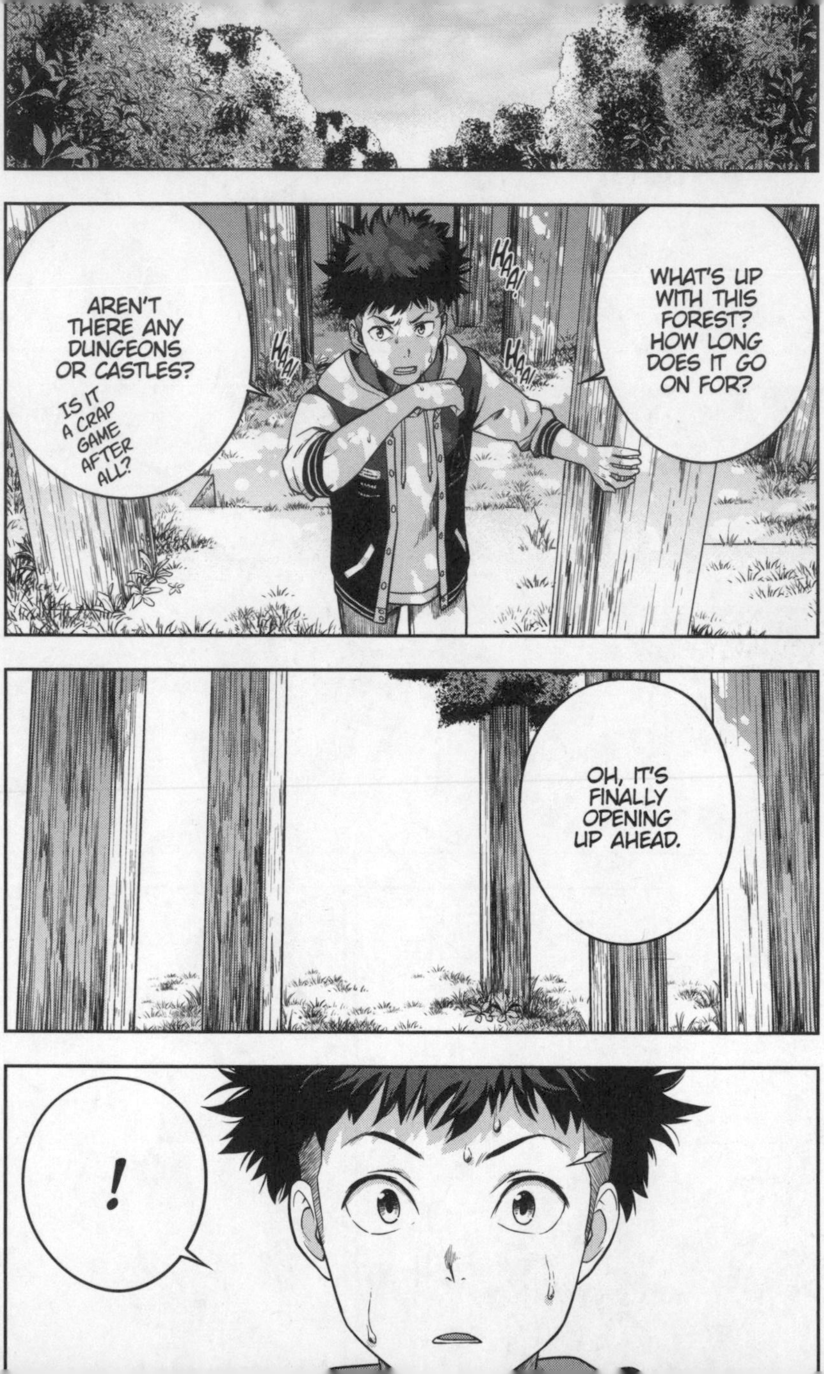
WHAT'S UP WITH THIS FOREST? HOW LONG DOES IT GO ON FOR?
HAAA!
HAAA!
HAAA!
AREN'T THERE ANY DUNGEONS OR CASTLES?
IS IT A CRAP GAME AFTER ALL?
OH, IT'S FINALLY OPENING UP AHEAD.
!

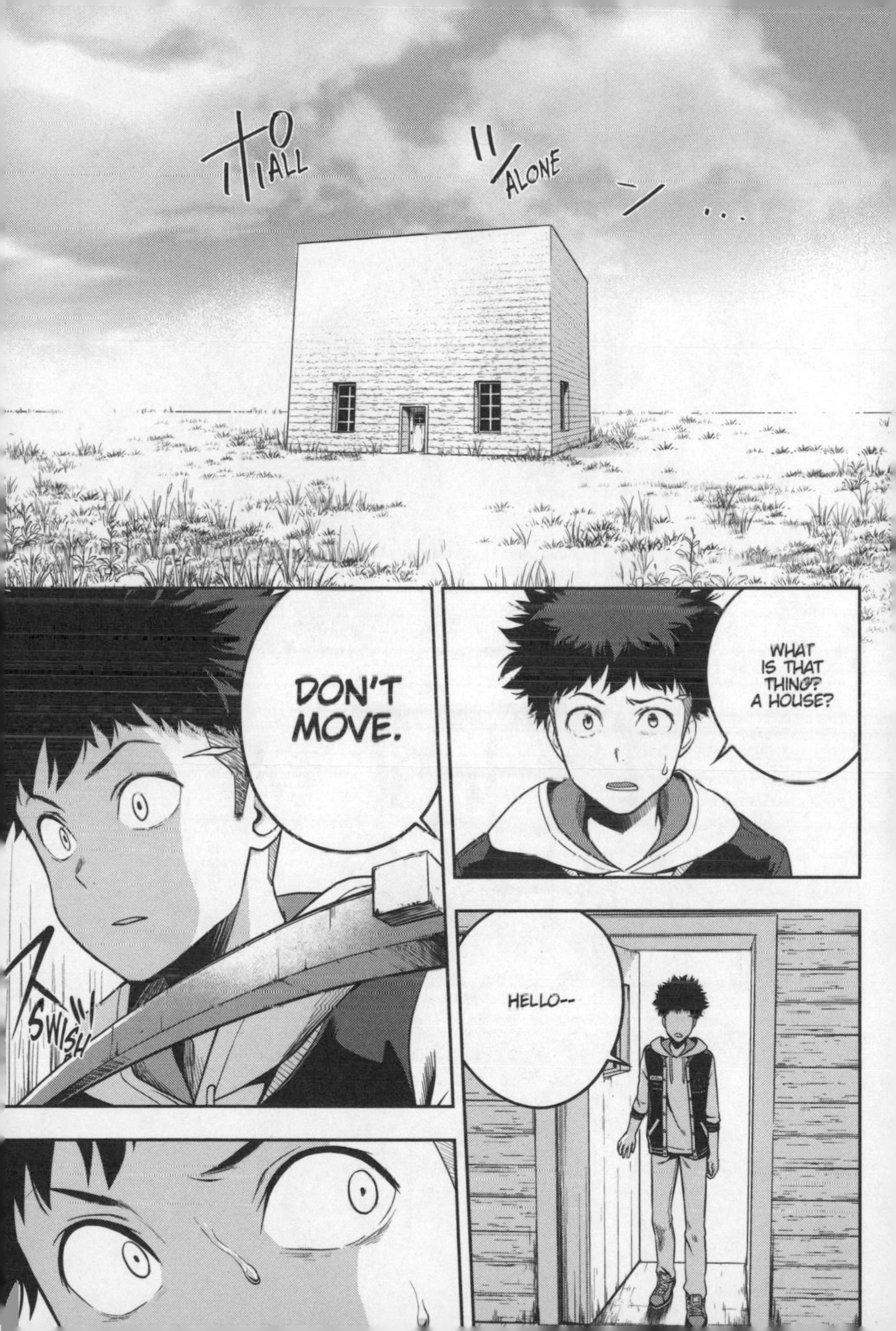
ALL
ALONE
...
WHAT IS THAT THING? A HOUSE?
HELLO--
DON'T MOVE.
SWISH

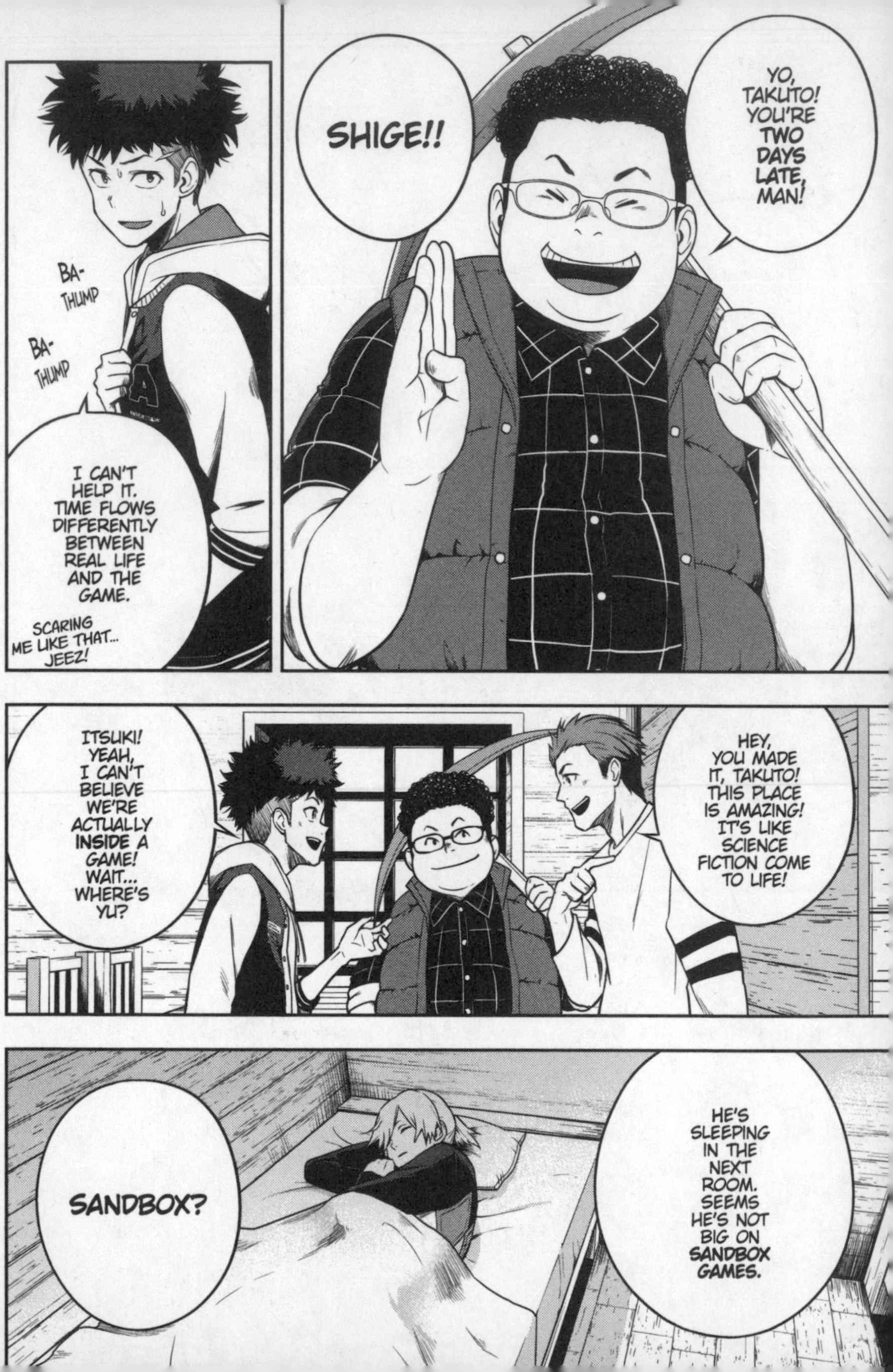
YO, TAKUTO! YOU'RE TWO DAYS LATE, MAN!
SHIGE!!
BA-THUMP
BA-THUMP
I CAN'T HELP IT. TIME FLOWS DIFFERENTLY BETWEEN REAL LIFE AND THE GAME.
SCARING ME LIKE THAT... JEEZ!
HEY, YOU MADE IT, TAKUTO! THIS PLACE IS AMAZING! IT'S LIKE SCIENCE FICTION COME TO LIFE!
ITSUKI! YEAH, I CAN'T BELIEVE WE'RE ACTUALLY INSIDE A GAME! WAIT... WHERE'S YU?
HE'S SLEEPING IN THE NEXT ROOM. SEEMS HE'S NOT BIG ON SANDBOX GAMES.
SANDBOX?

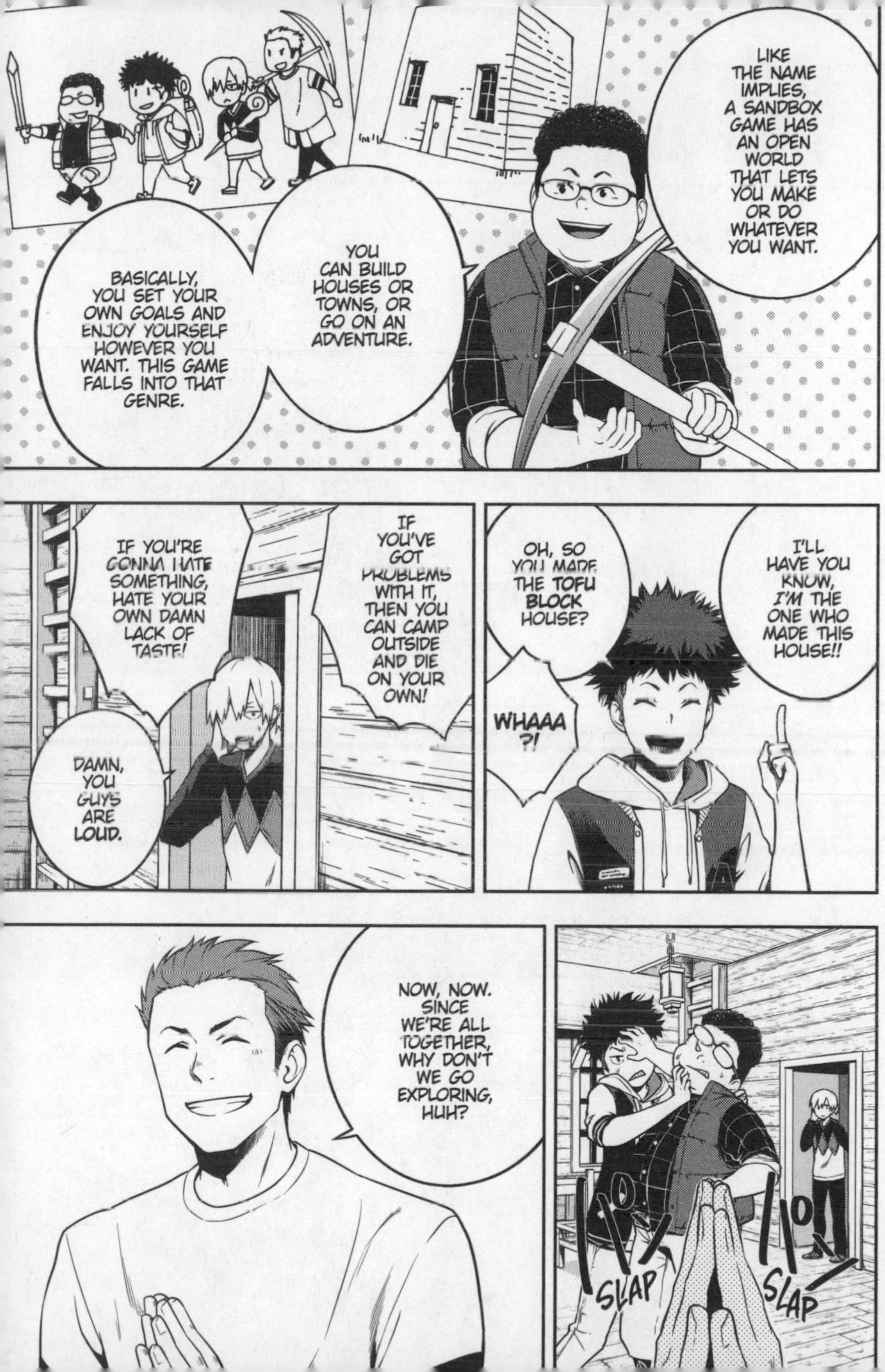
LIKE THE NAME IMPLIES, A SANDBOX GAME HAS AN OPEN WORLD THAT LETS YOU MAKE OR DO WHATEVER YOU WANT.
YOU CAN BUILD HOUSES OR TOWNS, OR GO ON AN ADVENTURE.
BASICALLY, YOU SET YOUR OWN GOALS AND ENJOY YOURSELF HOWEVER YOU WANT. THIS GAME FALLS INTO THAT GENRE.
I'LL HAVE YOU KNOW, *I'M* THE ONE WHO MADE THIS HOUSE!!
OH, SO YOU MADE THE TOFU BLOCK HOUSE?
WHAAA?!
IF YOU'VE GOT PROBLEMS WITH IT, THEN YOU CAN CAMP OUTSIDE AND DIE ON YOUR OWN!
IF YOU'RE GONNA HATE SOMETHING, HATE YOUR OWN DAMN LACK OF TASTE!
DAMN, YOU GUYS ARE LOUD.
SLAP
SLAP
NOW, NOW. SINCE WE'RE ALL TOGETHER, WHY DON'T WE GO EXPLORING, HUH?

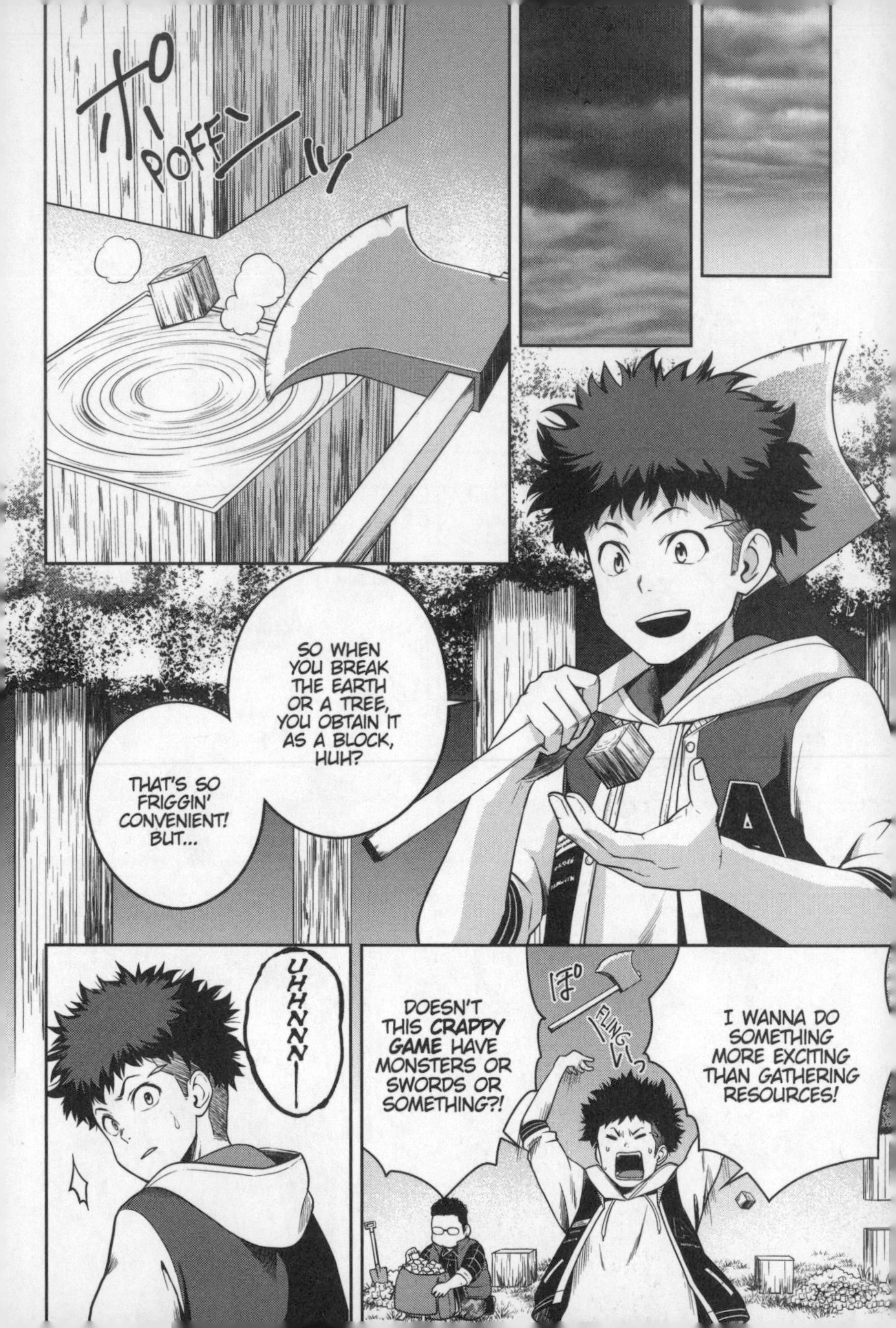
POFF
SO WHEN YOU BREAK THE EARTH OR A TREE, YOU OBTAIN IT AS A BLOCK, HUH?
THAT'S SO FRIGGIN' CONVENIENT! BUT...
I WANNA DO SOMETHING MORE EXCITING THAN GATHERING RESOURCES!
FLING
DOESN'T THIS **CRAPPY GAME** HAVE MONSTERS OR SWORDS OR SOMETHING?!
UHHNNN—

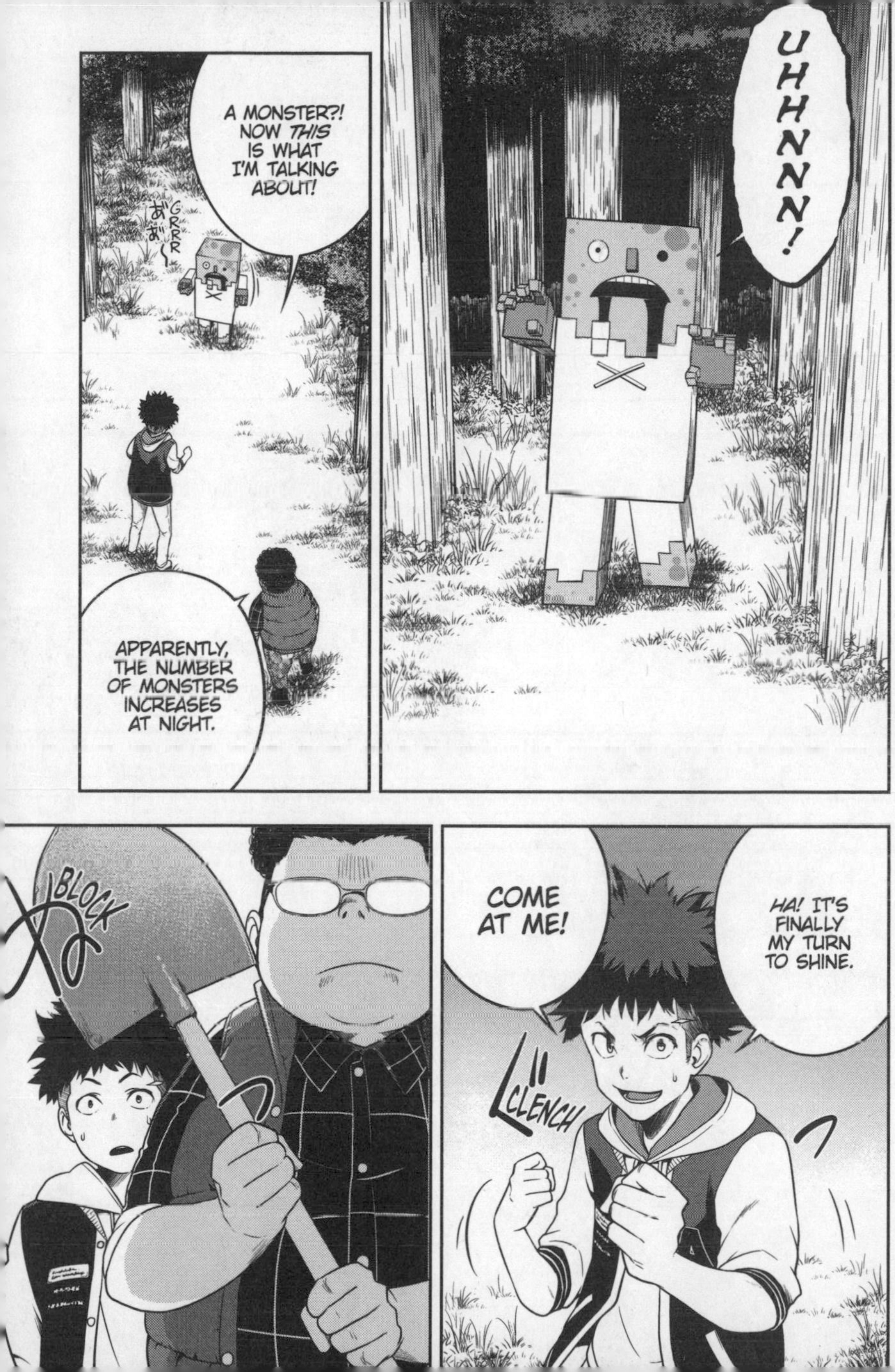
UHHNNN!
A MONSTER?! NOW THIS IS WHAT I'M TALKING ABOUT!
GRRR
APPARENTLY, THE NUMBER OF MONSTERS INCREASES AT NIGHT.
HA! IT'S FINALLY MY TURN TO SHINE.
COME AT ME!
CLENCH
BLOCK

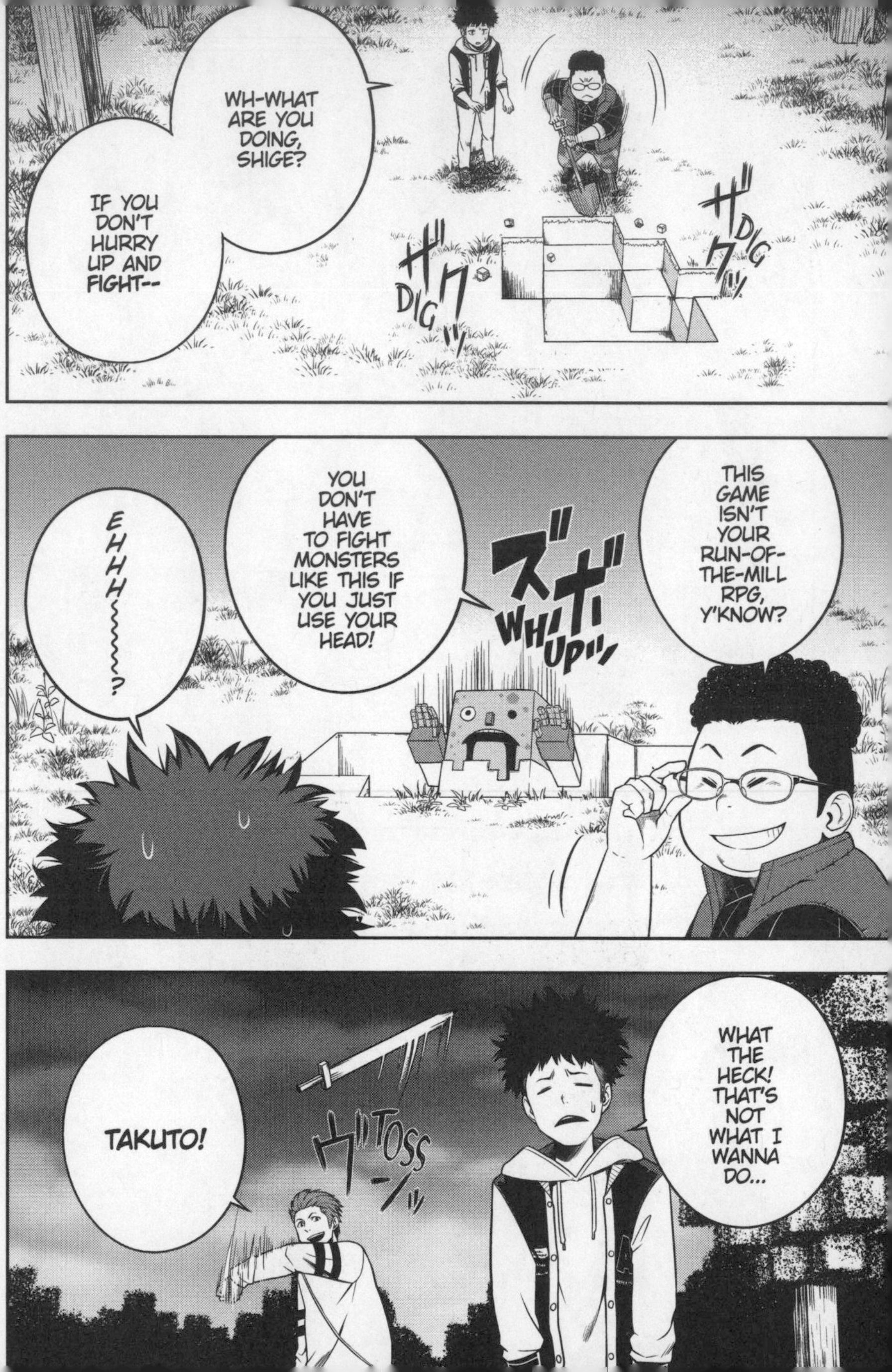
WH-WHAT ARE YOU DOING, SHIGE?
IF YOU DON'T HURRY UP AND FIGHT--
DIG
DIG
THIS GAME ISN'T YOUR RUN-OF-THE-MILL RPG, Y'KNOW?
WHUP
YOU DON'T HAVE TO FIGHT MONSTERS LIKE THIS IF YOU JUST USE YOUR HEAD!
EHHH~~~?
WHAT THE HECK! THAT'S NOT WHAT I WANNA DO...
TOSS
TAKUTO!

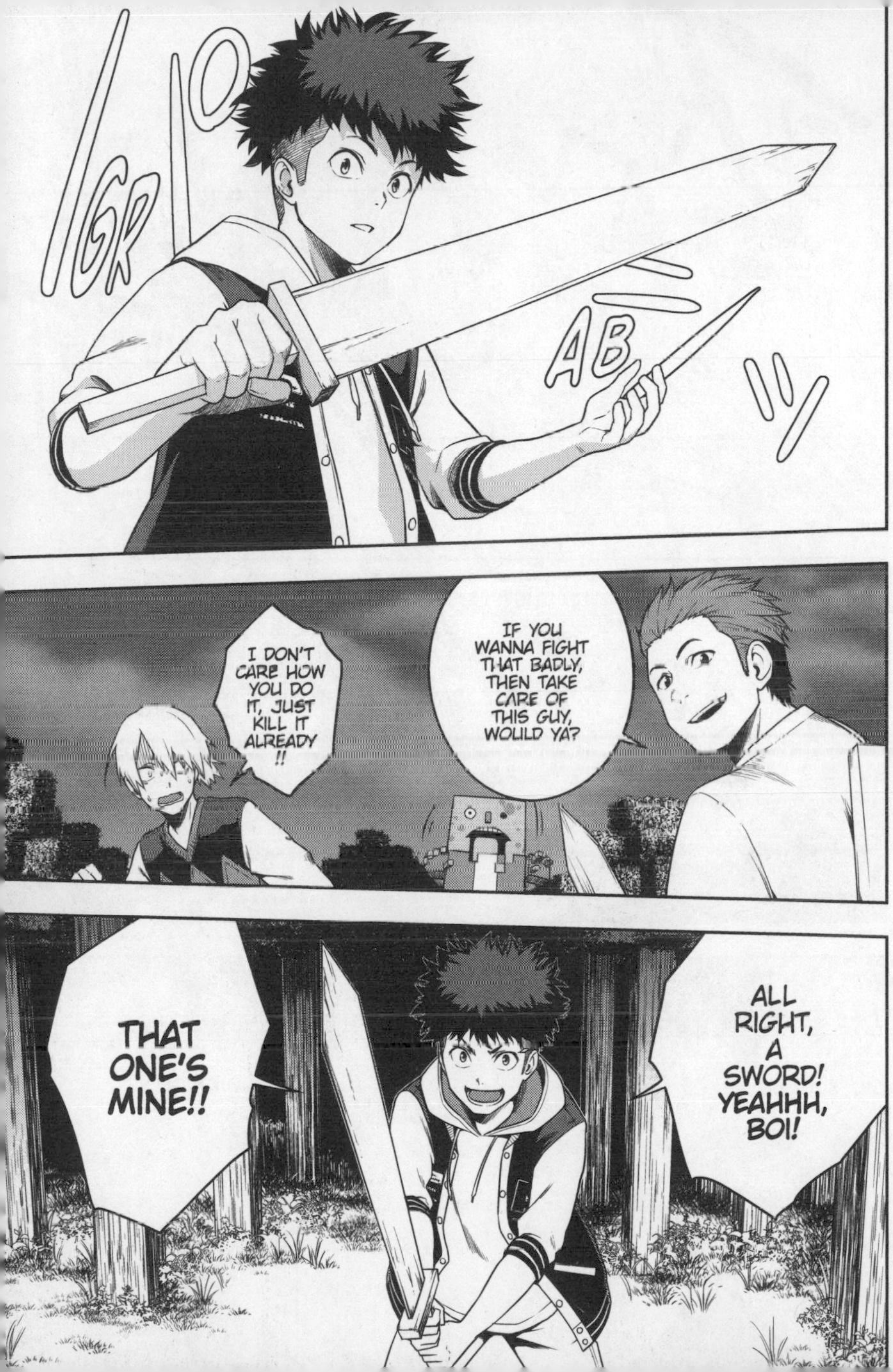
GRAB
IF YOU WANNA FIGHT THAT BADLY, THEN TAKE CARE OF THIS GUY, WOULD YA?
I DON'T CARE HOW YOU DO IT, JUST KILL IT ALREADY!!
ALL RIGHT, A SWORD! YEAHHH, BOI!
THAT ONE'S MINE!!

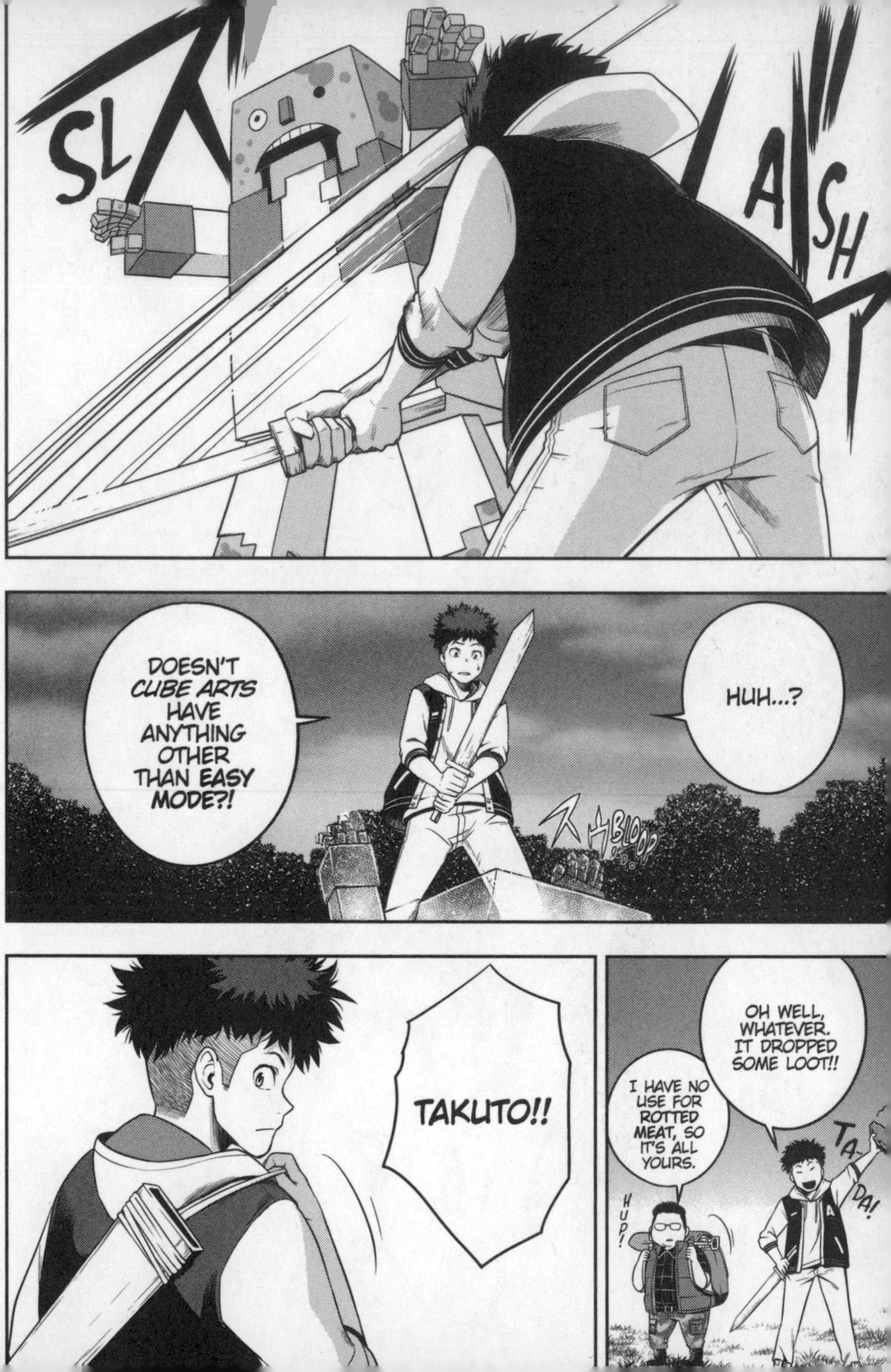
SLASH
HUH...?
BLOOP
DOESN'T CUBE ARTS HAVE ANYTHING OTHER THAN EASY MODE?!
OH WELL, WHATEVER. IT DROPPED SOME LOOT!!
TA-DA!
I HAVE NO USE FOR ROTTED MEAT, SO IT'S ALL YOURS.
HUP!
TAKUTO!!

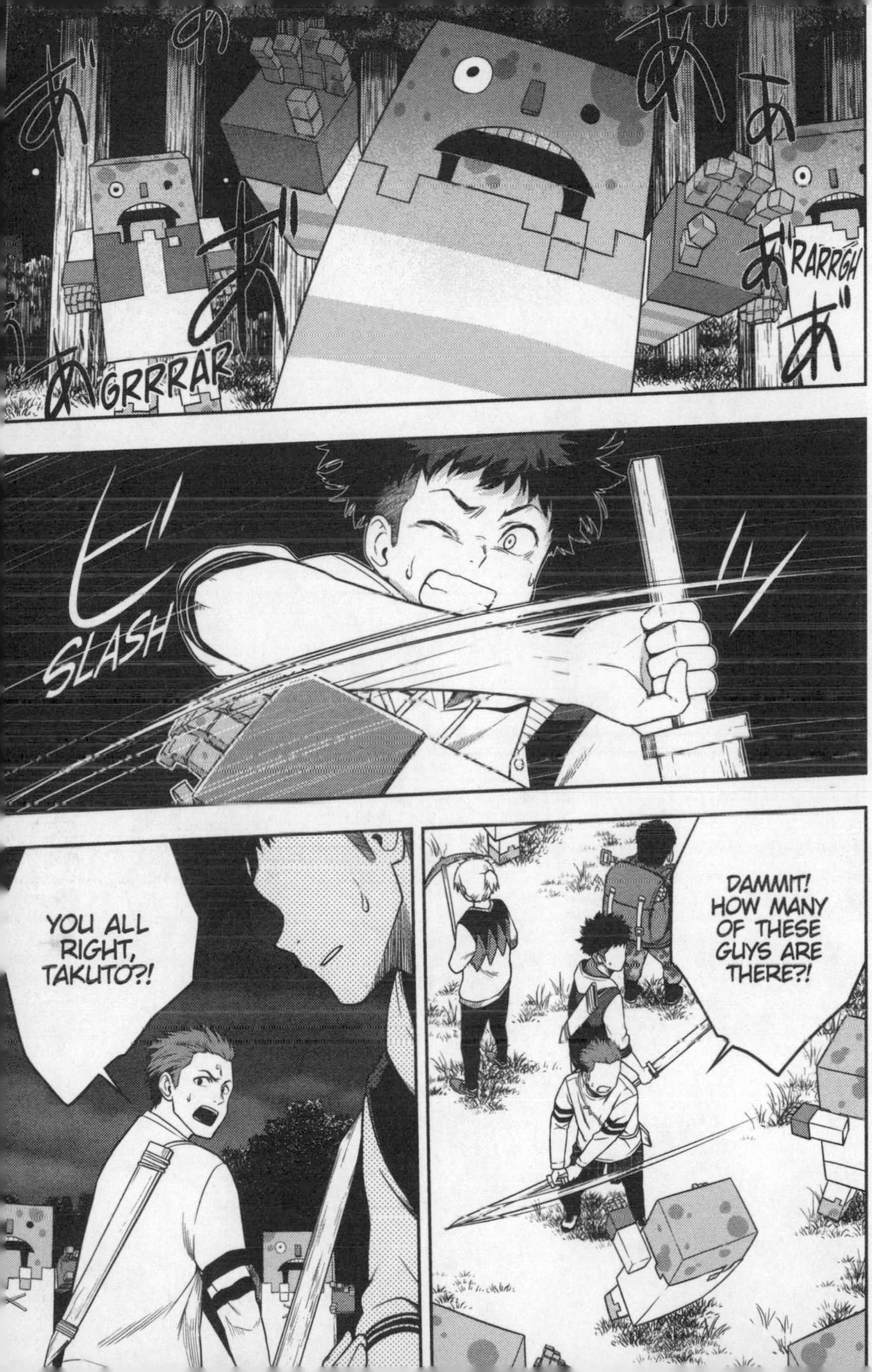
RARRGH
GRRRAR
SLASH
DAMMIT! HOW MANY OF THESE GUYS ARE THERE?!
YOU ALL RIGHT, TAKUTO?!

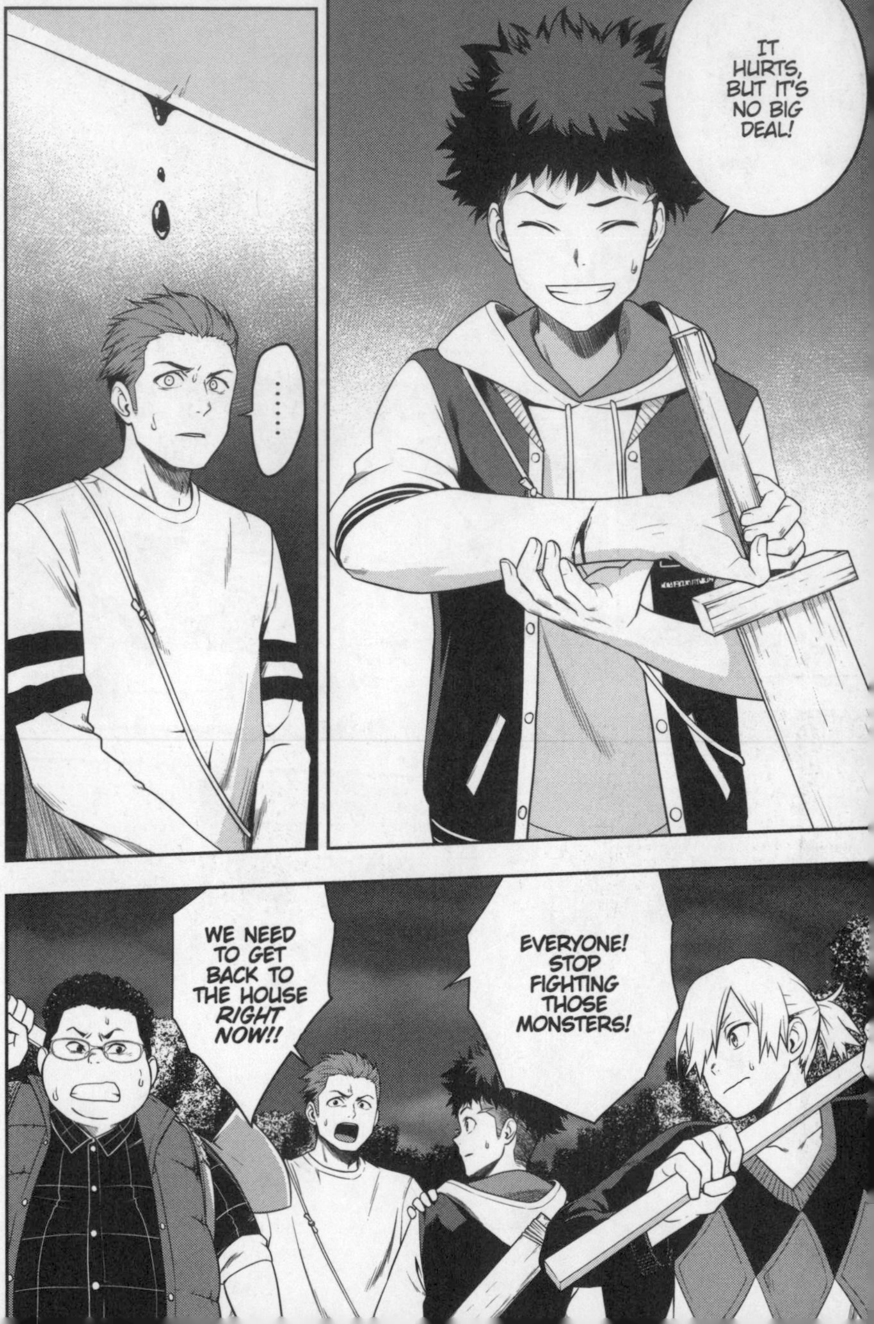
IT HURTS, BUT IT'S NO BIG DEAL!
......
EVERYONE! STOP FIGHTING THOSE MONSTERS!
WE NEED TO GET BACK TO THE HOUSE *RIGHT NOW!!*

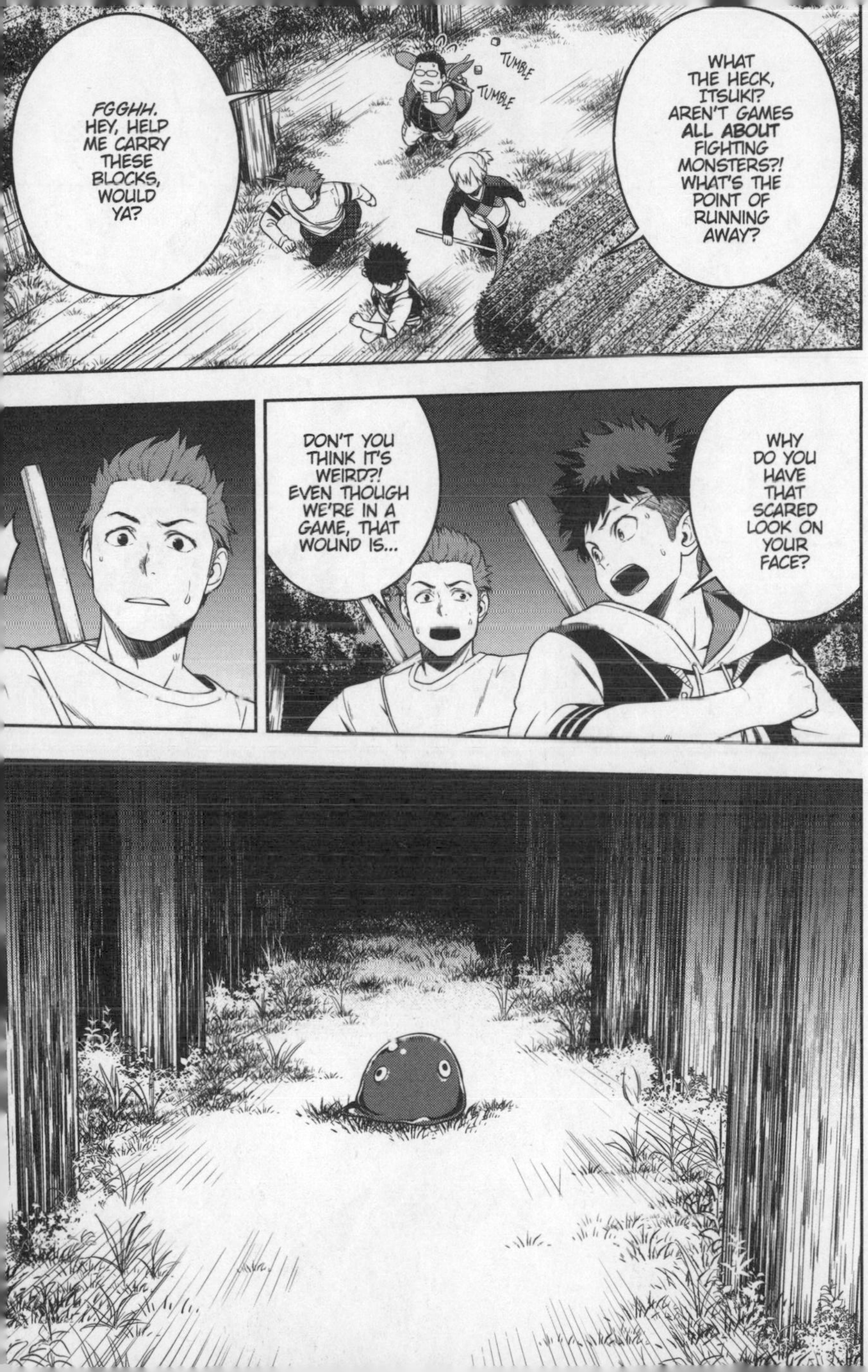
WHAT THE HECK, ITSUKI? AREN'T GAMES ALL ABOUT FIGHTING MONSTERS?! WHAT'S THE POINT OF RUNNING AWAY?
TUMBLE
TUMBLE
FGGHH. HEY, HELP ME CARRY THESE BLOCKS, WOULD YA?
WHY DO YOU HAVE THAT SCARED LOOK ON YOUR FACE?
DON'T YOU THINK IT'S WEIRD?! EVEN THOUGH WE'RE IN A GAME, THAT WOUND IS...

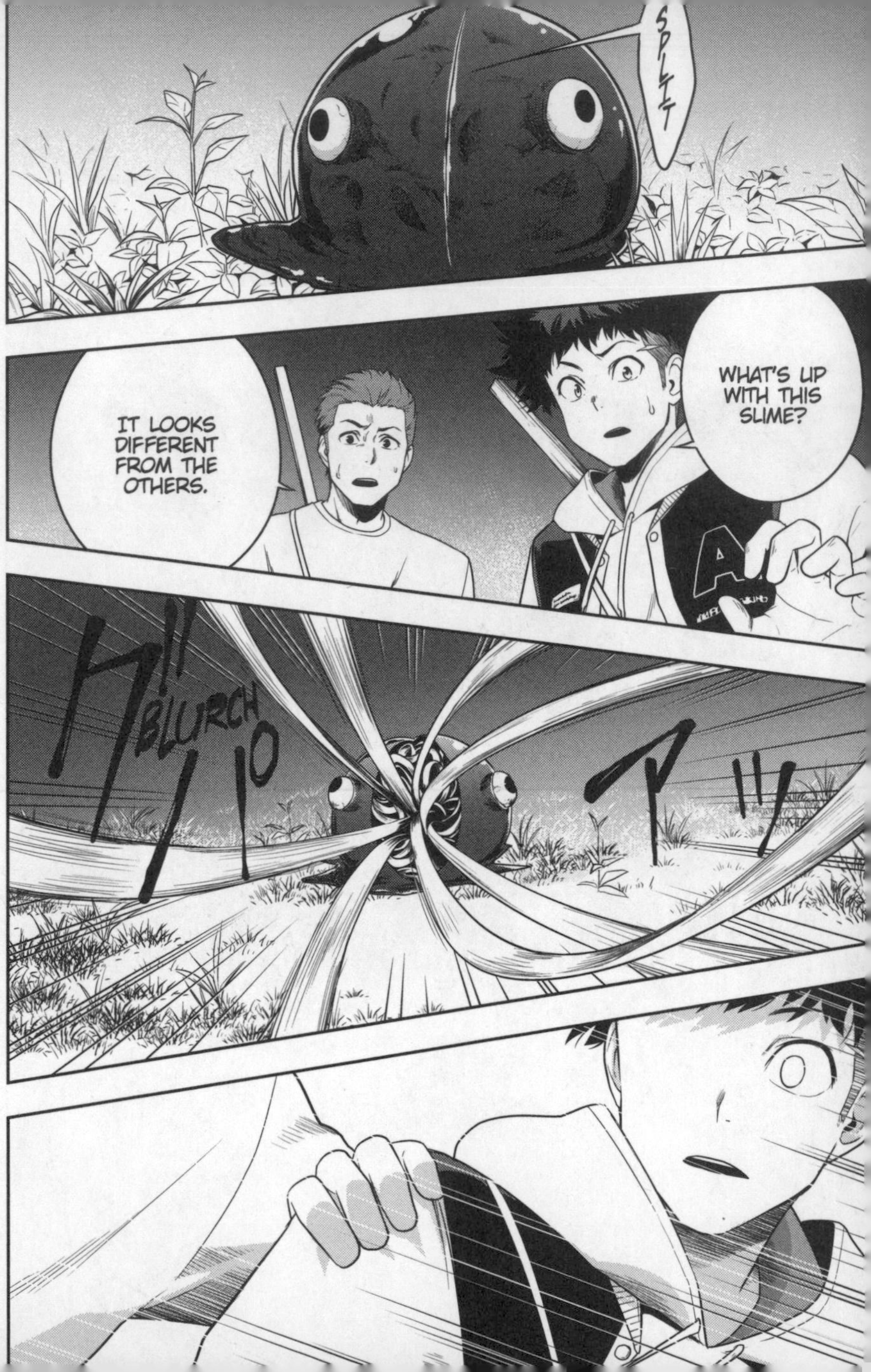
SPLIT
WHAT'S UP WITH THIS SLIME?
IT LOOKS DIFFERENT FROM THE OTHERS.
BLURCH

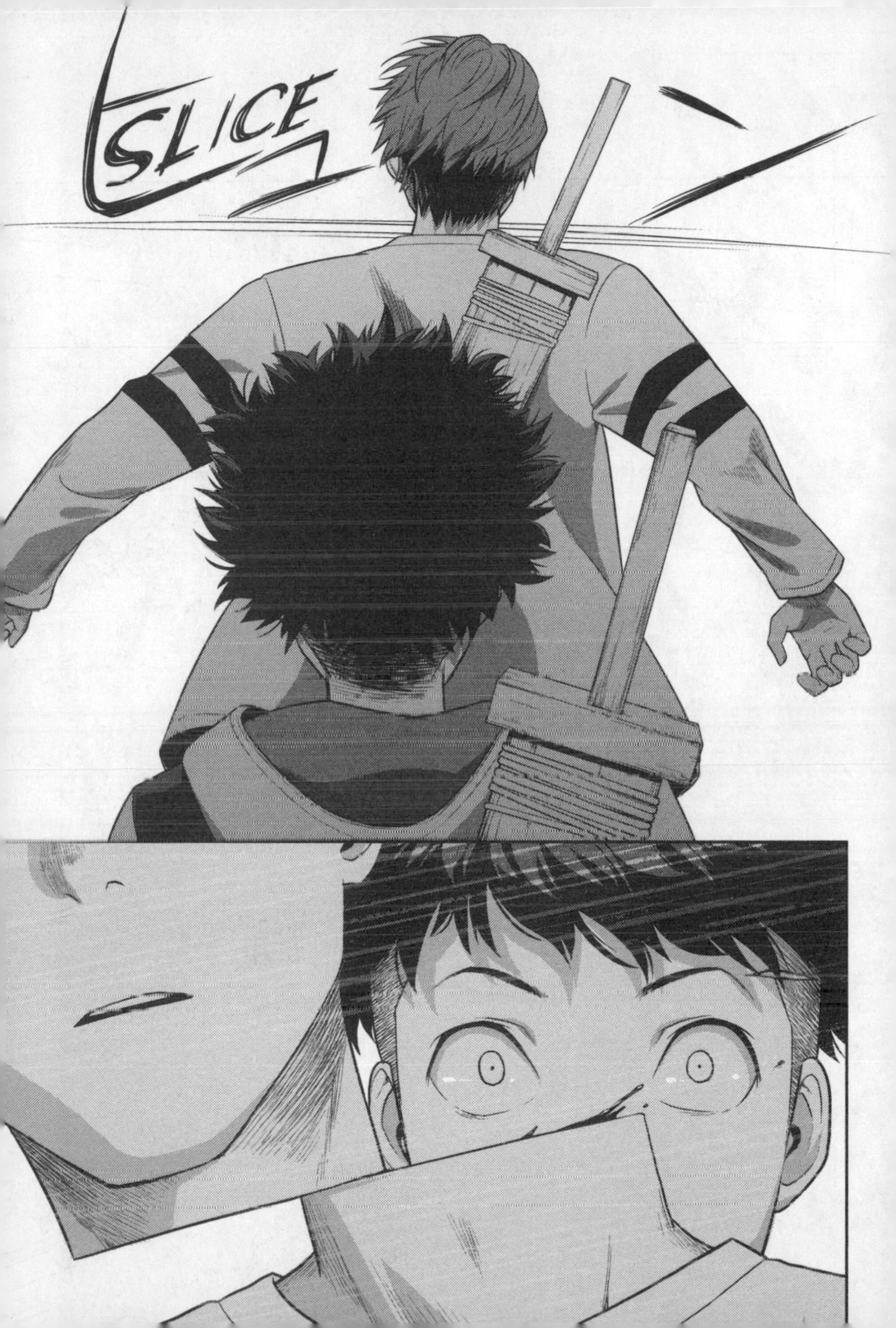
SLICE

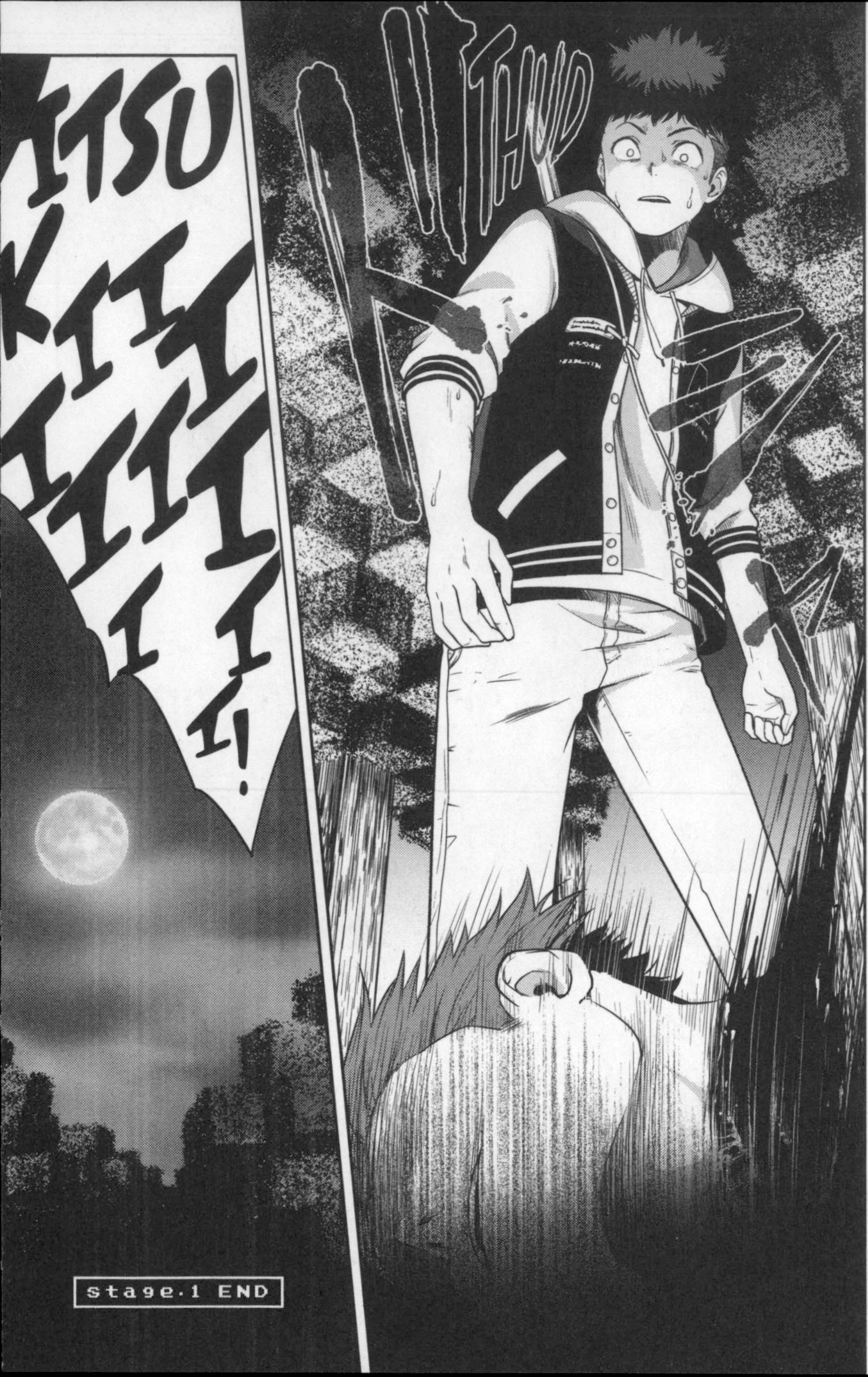
THUD
...ITSU
KIIIIIIIIII!
stage.1 END

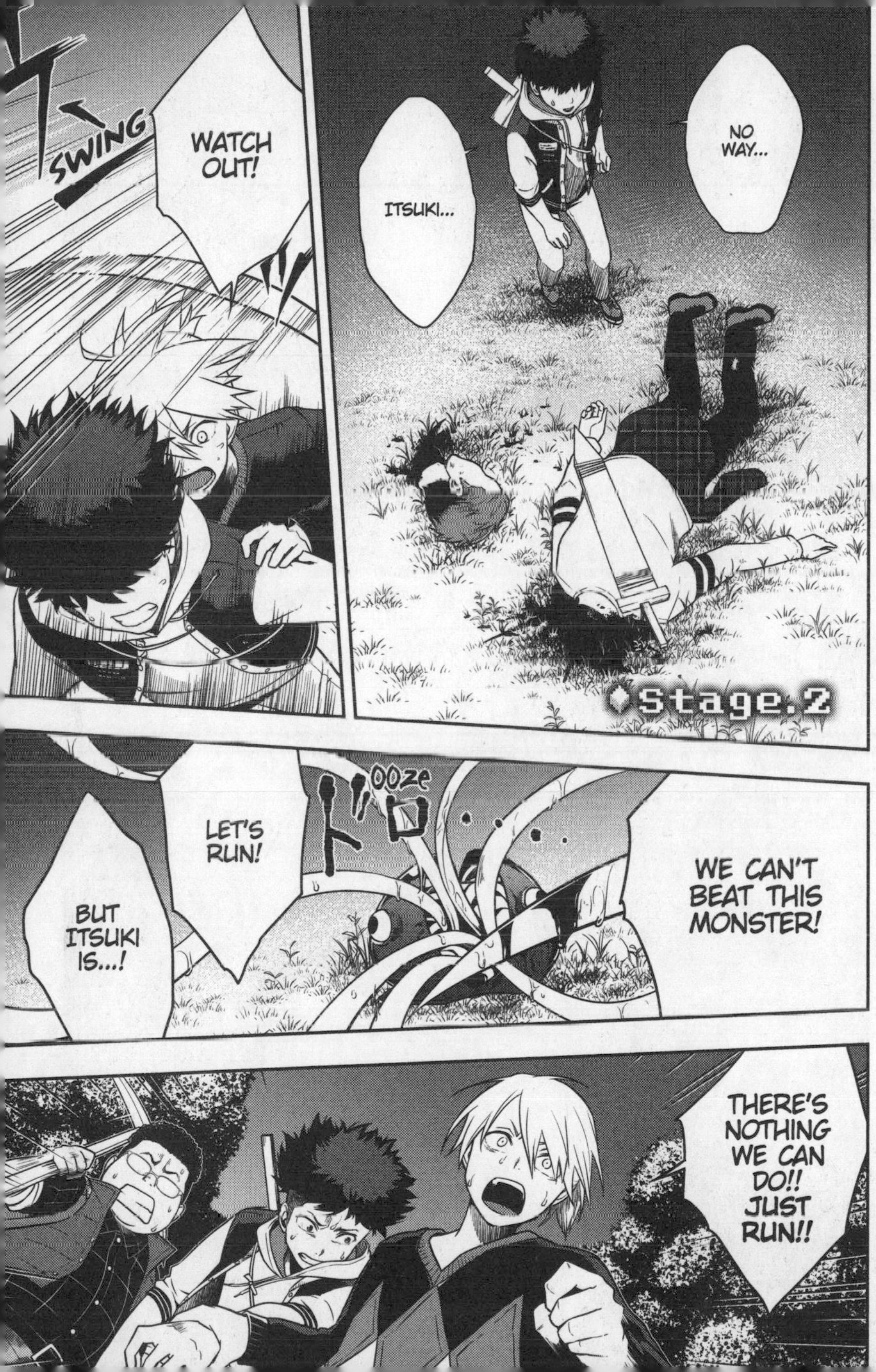
NO WAY...
ITSUKI...
Stage.2
SWING
WATCH OUT!
WE CAN'T BEAT THIS MONSTER!
OOZE
LET'S RUN!
BUT ITSUKI IS...!
THERE'S NOTHING WE CAN DO!! JUST RUN!!

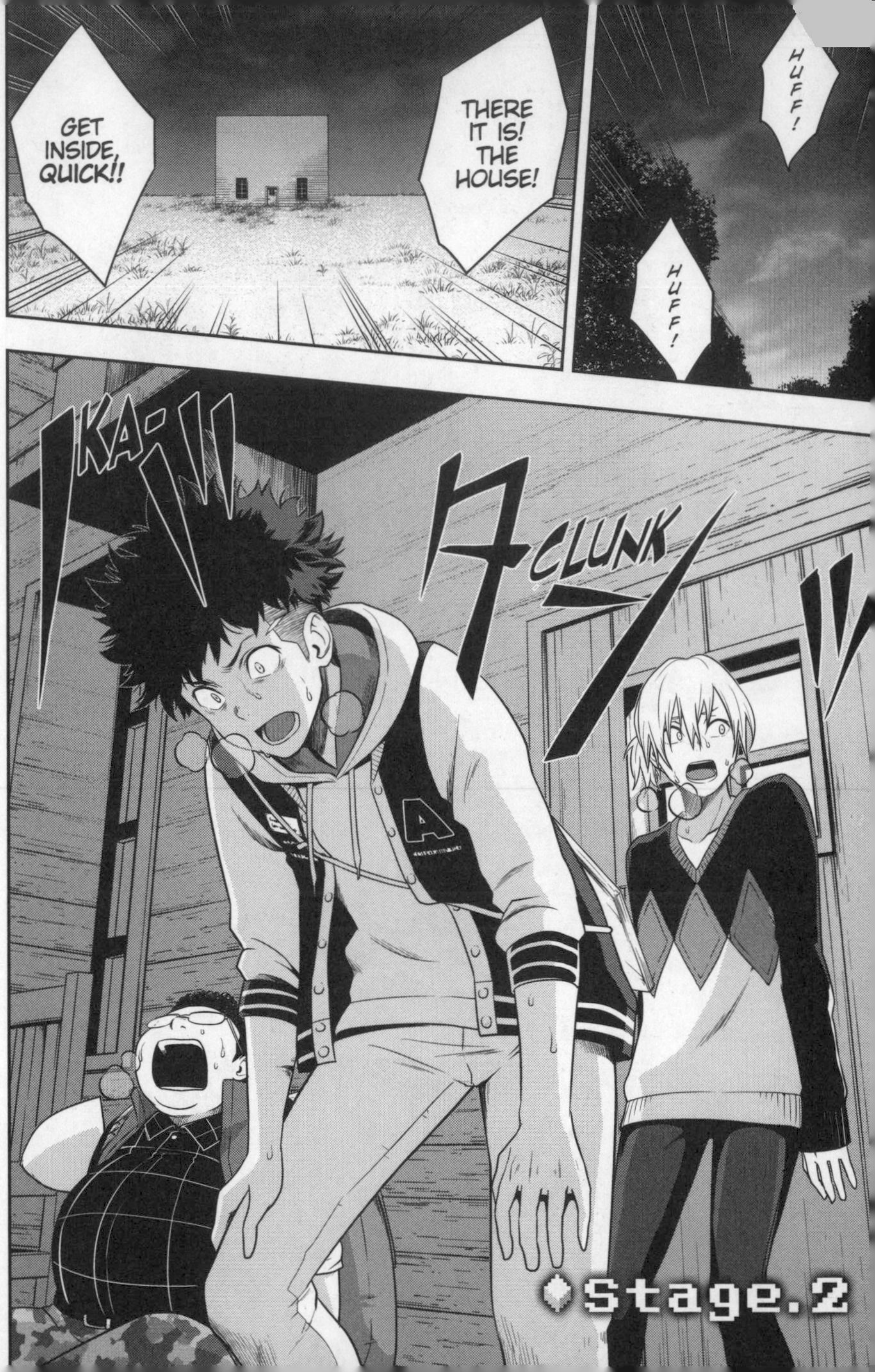
HUFF!
HUFF!
THERE IT IS! THE HOUSE!
GET INSIDE, QUICK!!
CLUNK
KA-
Stage.2

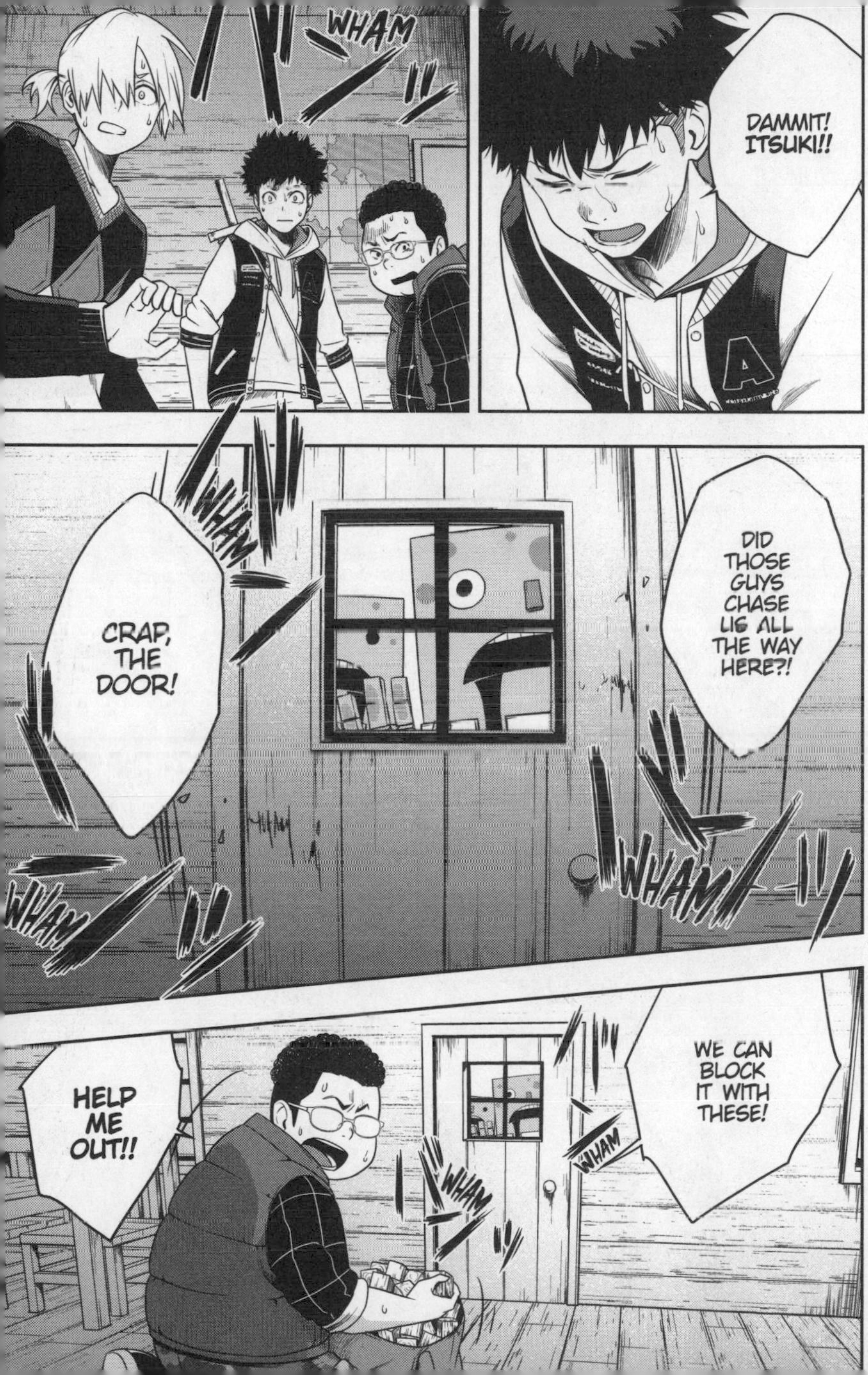
DAMMIT! ITSUKI!!
WHAM
DID THOSE GUYS CHASE US ALL THE WAY HERE?!
WHAM
WHAM
CRAP, THE DOOR!
WHAM
WE CAN BLOCK IT WITH THESE!
WHAM
WHAM
HELP ME OUT!!

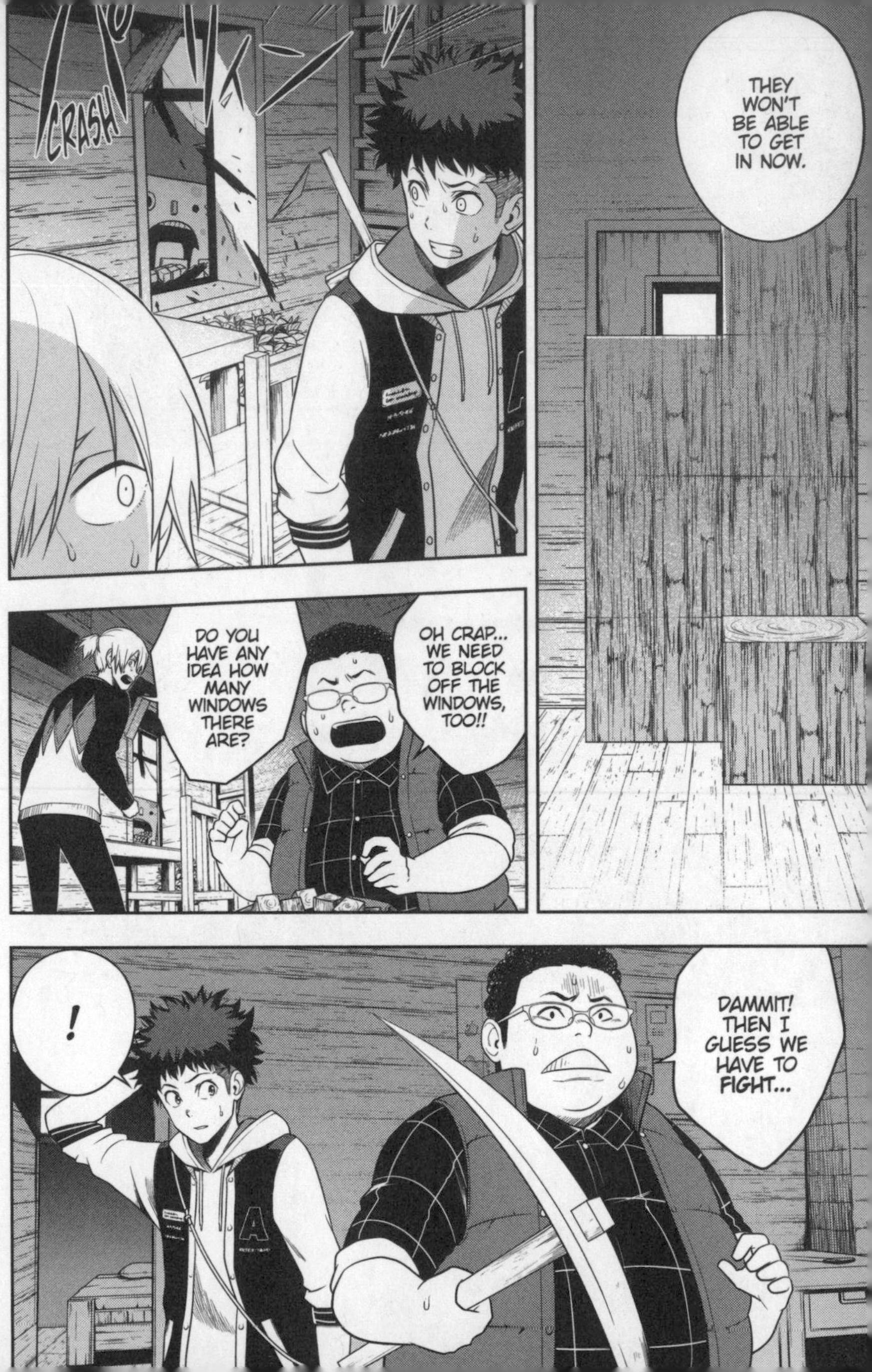
THEY WON'T BE ABLE TO GET IN NOW.
CRASH
OH CRAP... WE NEED TO BLOCK OFF THE WINDOWS, TOO!!
DO YOU HAVE ANY IDEA HOW MANY WINDOWS THERE ARE?
DAMMIT! THEN I GUESS WE HAVE TO FIGHT...
!

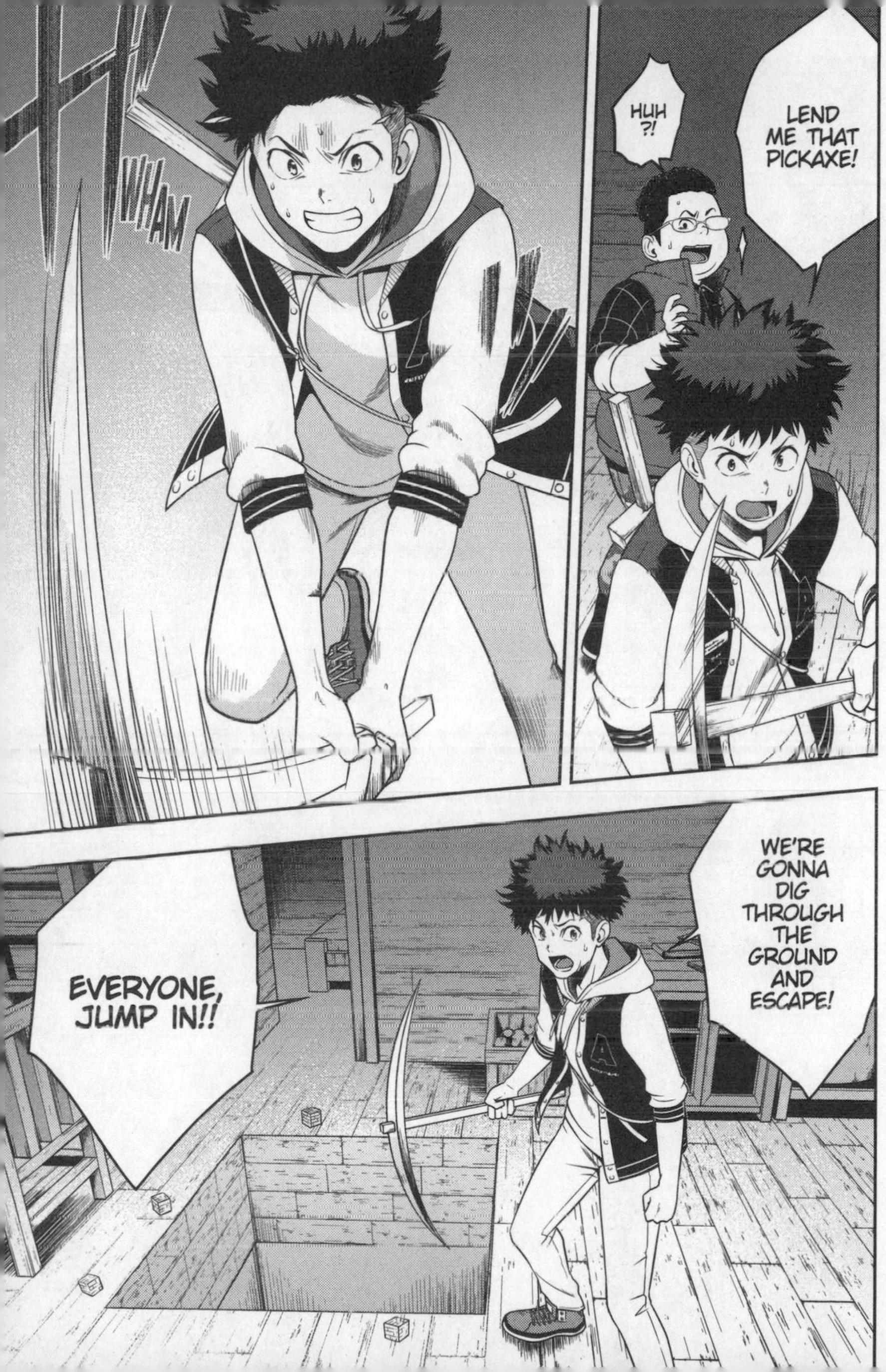
LEND ME THAT PICKAXE!
HUH?!
WHAM
WE'RE GONNA DIG THROUGH THE GROUND AND ESCAPE!
EVERYONE, JUMP IN!!

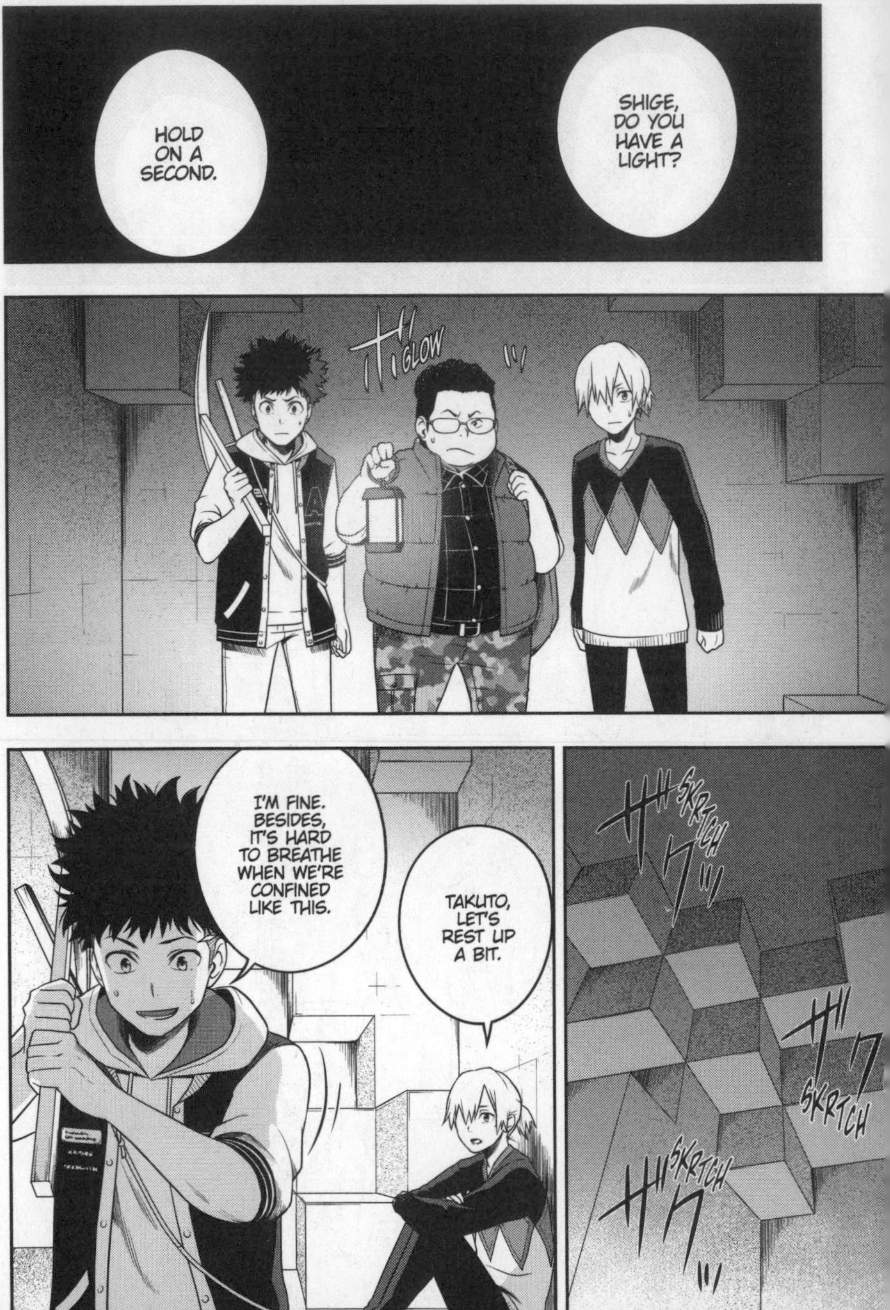
SHIGE, DO YOU HAVE A LIGHT?
HOLD ON A SECOND.
GLOW
SKRTCH
SKRTCH
SKRTCH
TAKUTO, LET'S REST UP A BIT.
I'M FINE. BESIDES, IT'S HARD TO BREATHE WHEN WE'RE CONFINED LIKE THIS.

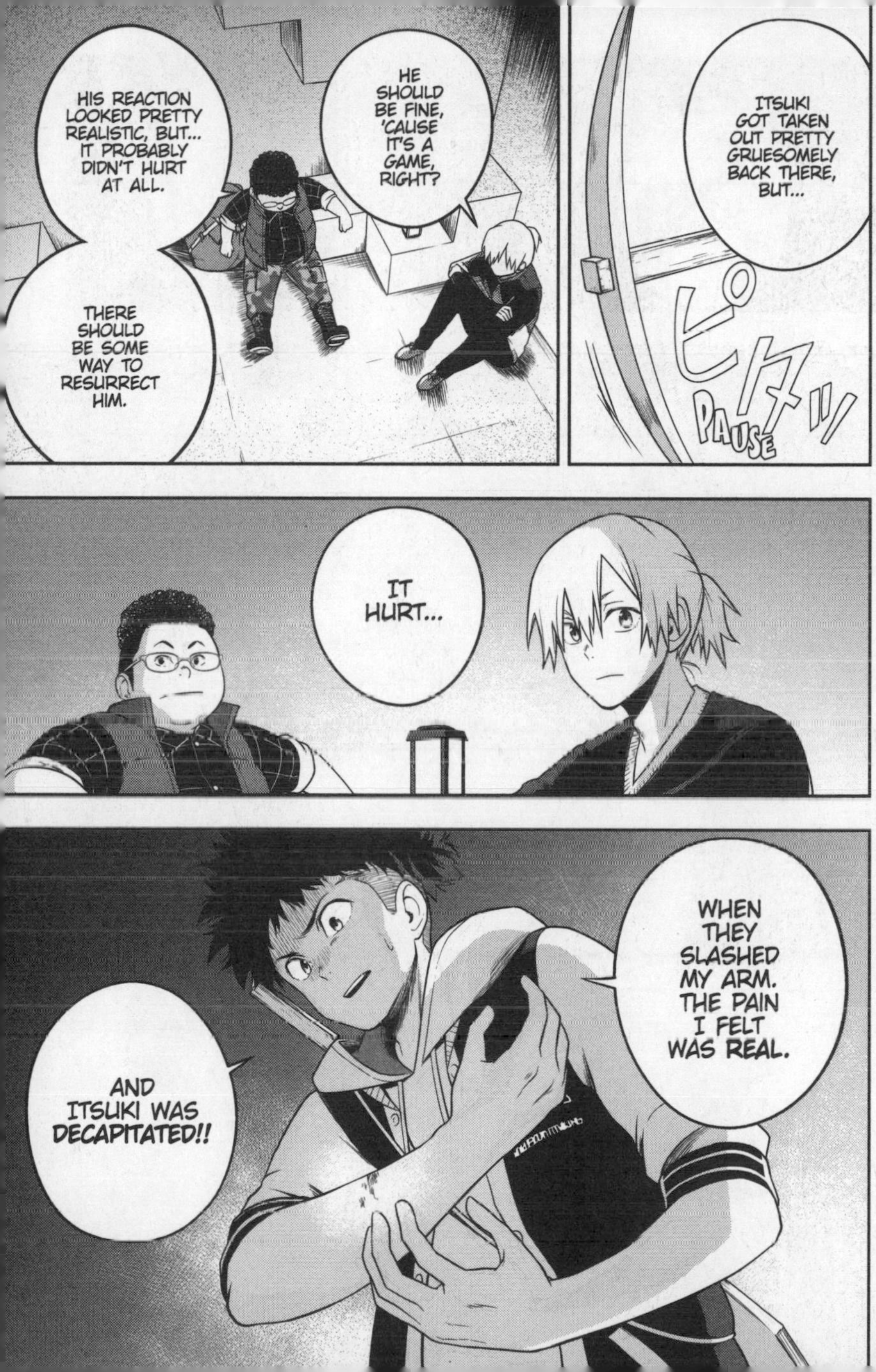
ITSUKI GOT TAKEN OUT PRETTY GRUESOMELY BACK THERE, BUT...
ピカッ
PAUSE
HE SHOULD BE FINE, 'CAUSE IT'S A GAME, RIGHT?
HIS REACTION LOOKED PRETTY REALISTIC, BUT... IT PROBABLY DIDN'T HURT AT ALL.
THERE SHOULD BE SOME WAY TO RESURRECT HIM.
IT HURT...
WHEN THEY SLASHED MY ARM. THE PAIN I FELT WAS REAL.
AND ITSUKI WAS DECAPITATED!!

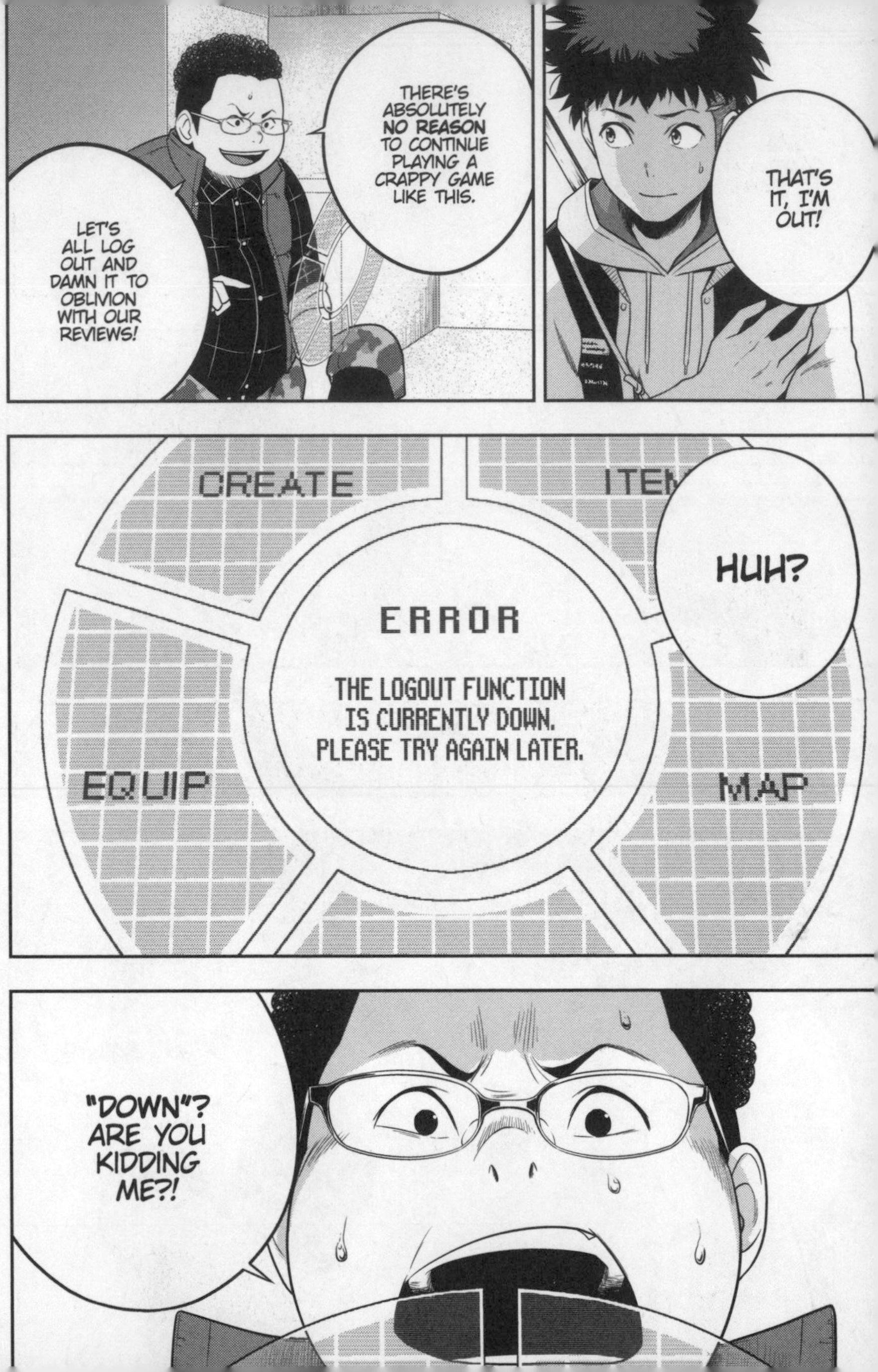
THAT'S IT, I'M OUT!
THERE'S ABSOLUTELY NO REASON TO CONTINUE PLAYING A CRAPPY GAME LIKE THIS.
LET'S ALL LOG OUT AND DAMN IT TO OBLIVION WITH OUR REVIEWS!
HUH?
CREATE
ERROR
THE LOGOUT FUNCTION IS CURRENTLY DOWN. PLEASE TRY AGAIN LATER.
MAP
EQUIP
"DOWN"? ARE YOU KIDDING ME?!

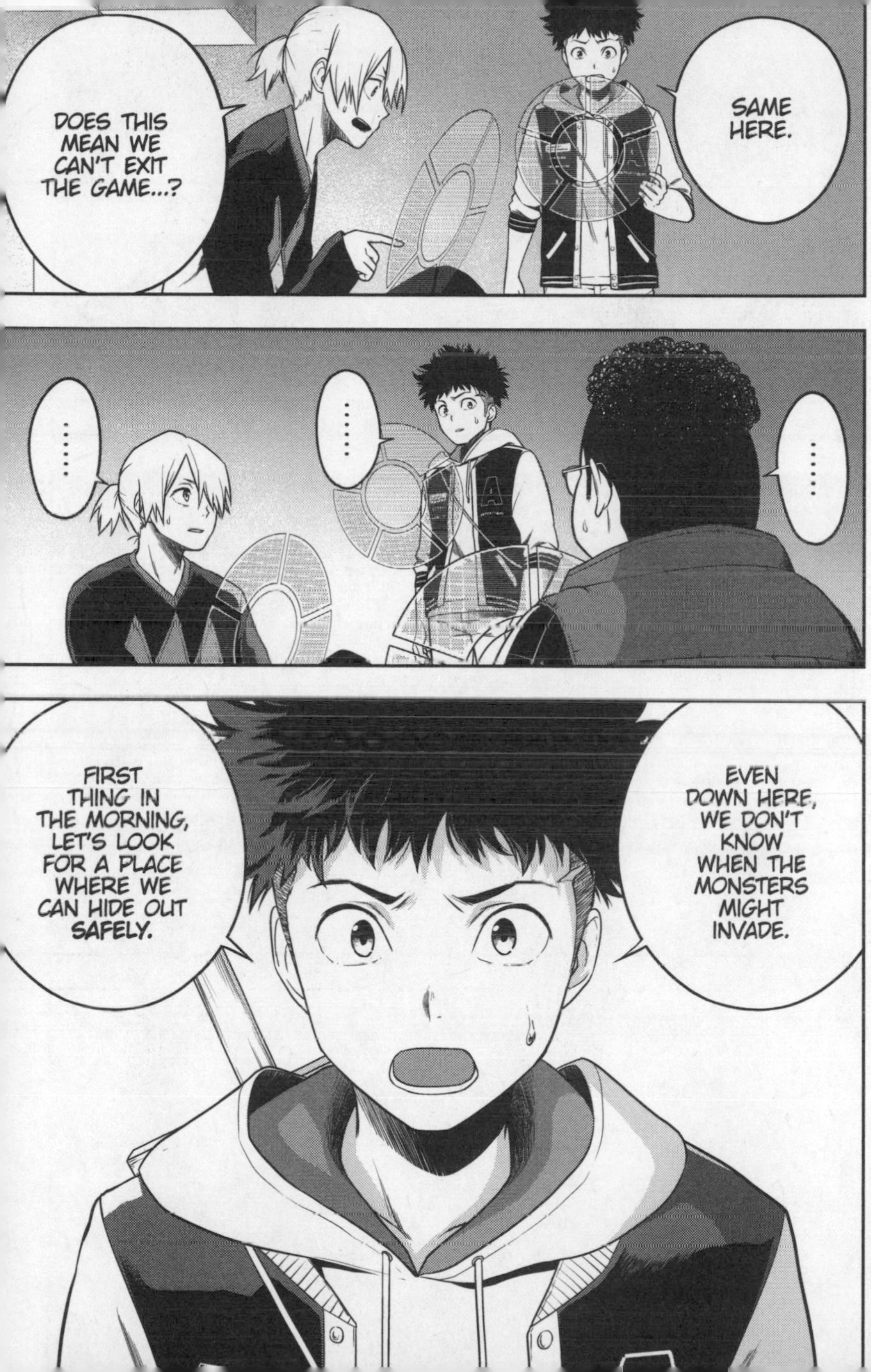
SAME HERE.
DOES THIS MEAN WE CAN'T EXIT THE GAME...?
......
......
......
EVEN DOWN HERE, WE DON'T KNOW WHEN THE MONSTERS MIGHT INVADE.
FIRST THING IN THE MORNING, LET'S LOOK FOR A PLACE WHERE WE CAN HIDE OUT SAFELY.

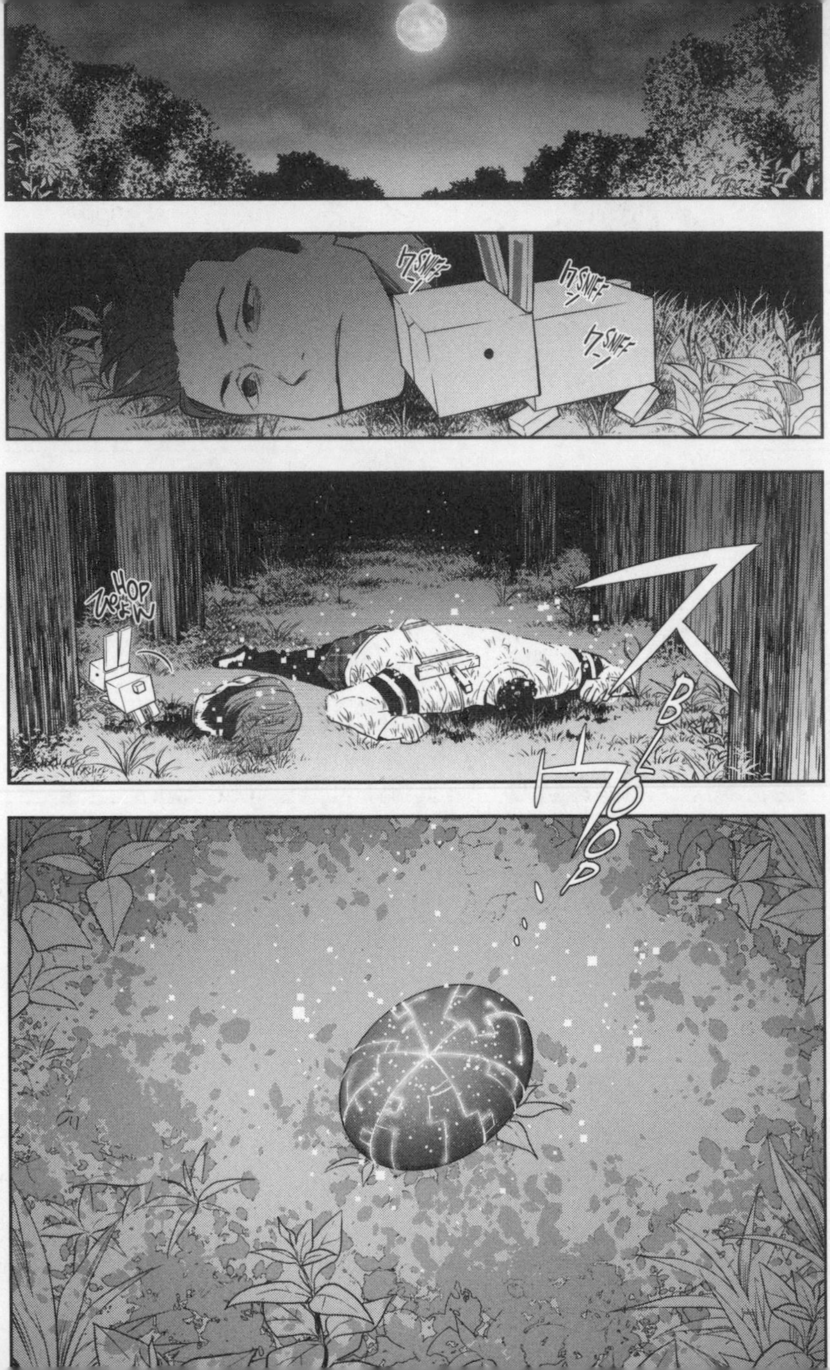
SNIFF
SNIFF
SNIFF
HOP
BLOOOP

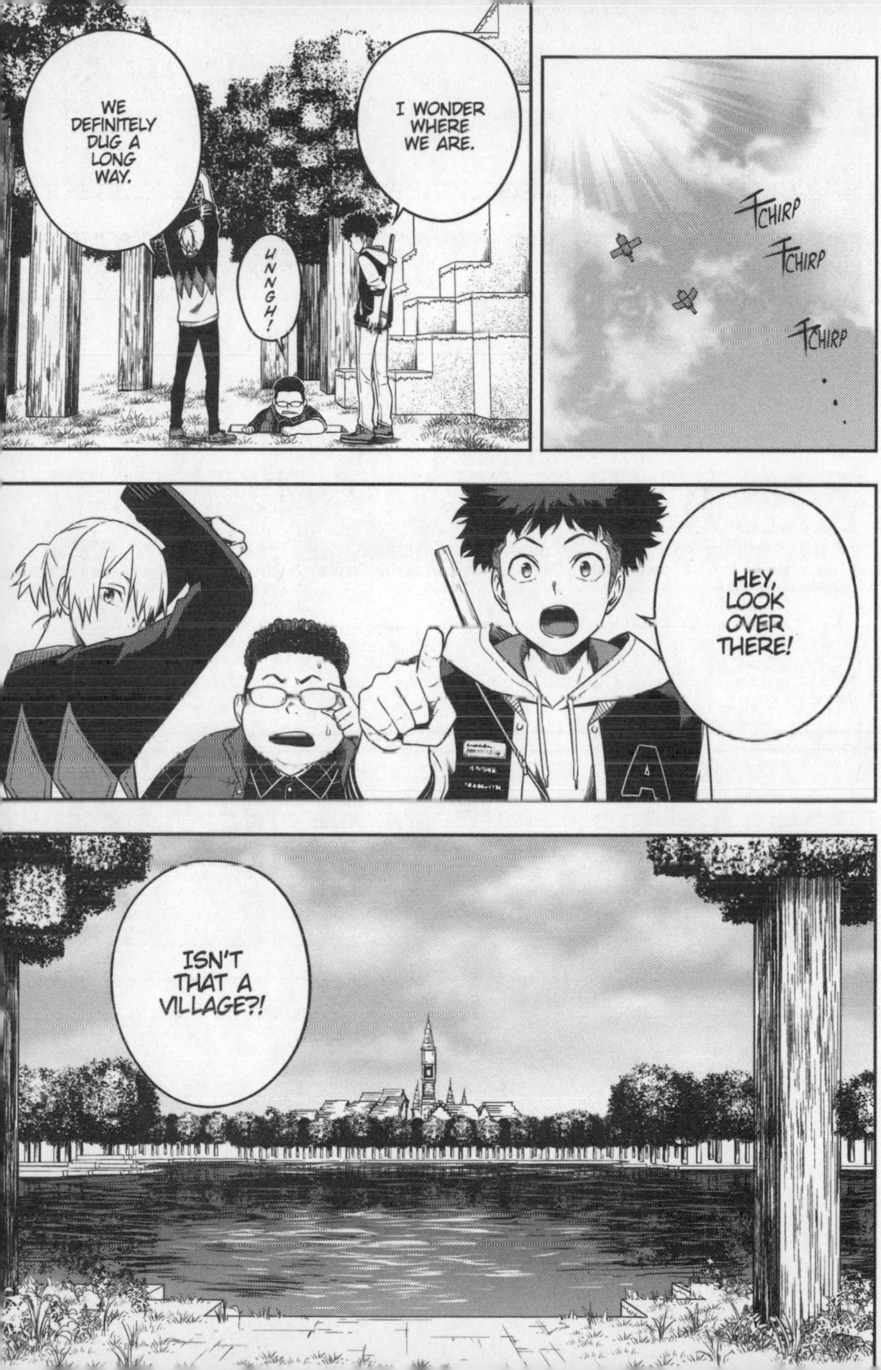
CHIRP
CHIRP
CHIRP
I WONDER WHERE WE ARE.
WE DEFINITELY DUG A LONG WAY.
UNNGH!
HEY, LOOK OVER THERE!
ISN'T THAT A VILLAGE?!

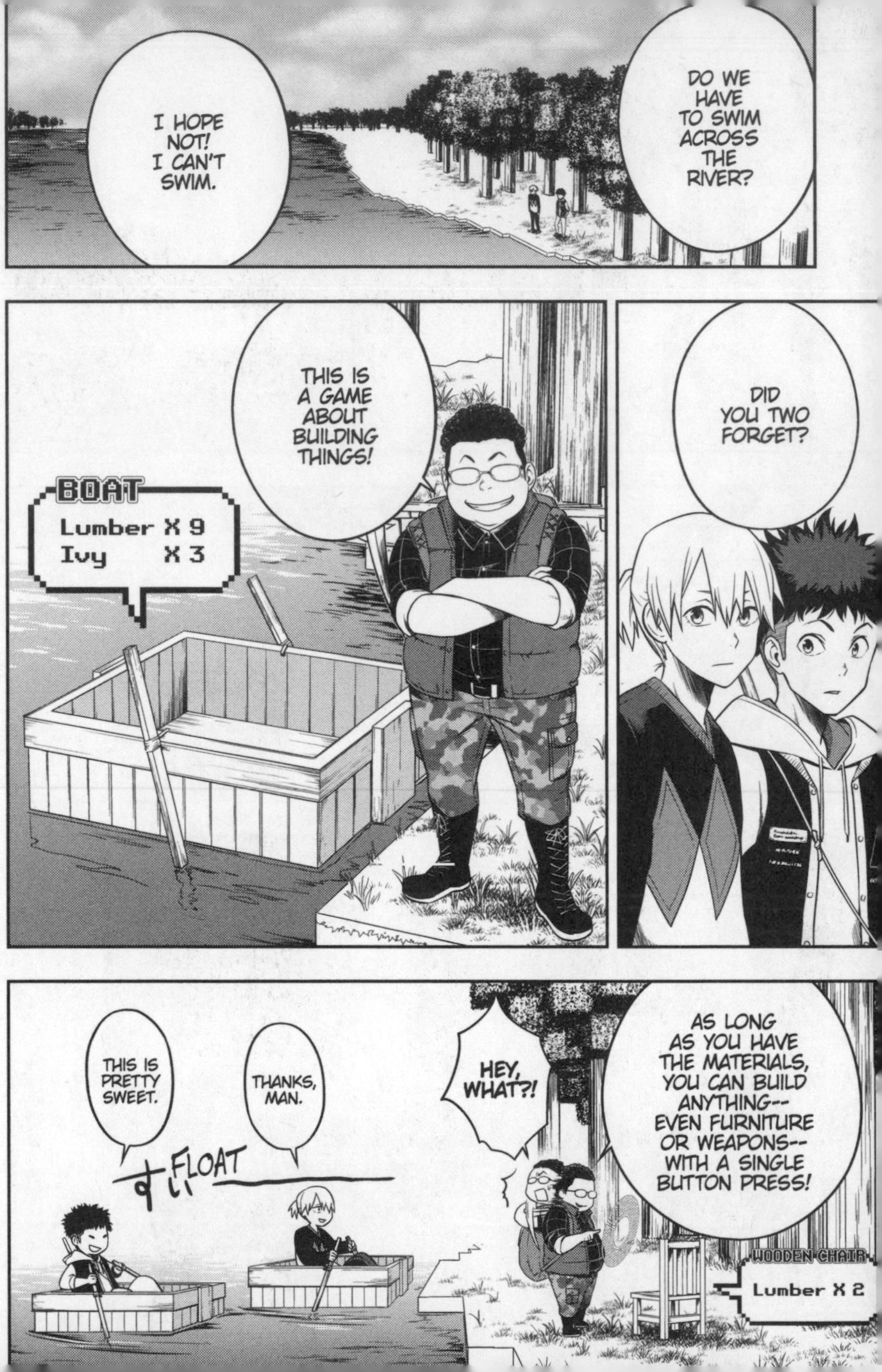
DO WE HAVE TO SWIM ACROSS THE RIVER?
I HOPE NOT! I CAN'T SWIM.
DID YOU TWO FORGET?
THIS IS A GAME ABOUT BUILDING THINGS!
BOAT
Lumber X 9
Ivy X 3
AS LONG AS YOU HAVE THE MATERIALS, YOU CAN BUILD ANYTHING-- EVEN FURNITURE OR WEAPONS-- WITH A SINGLE BUTTON PRESS!
WOODEN CHAIR
Lumber X 2
HEY, WHAT?!
THANKS, MAN.
THIS IS PRETTY SWEET.
すい FLOAT

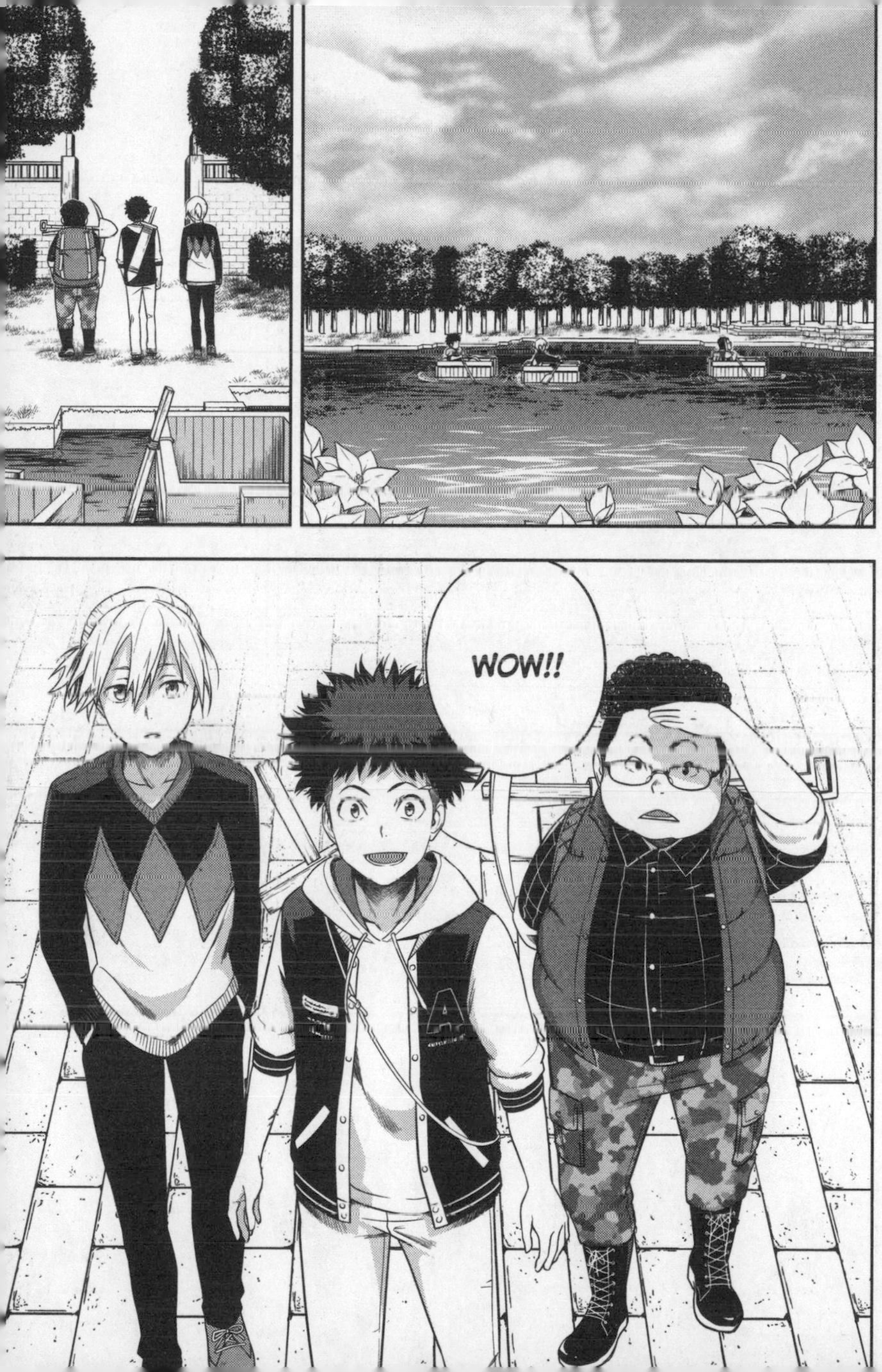
WOW!!

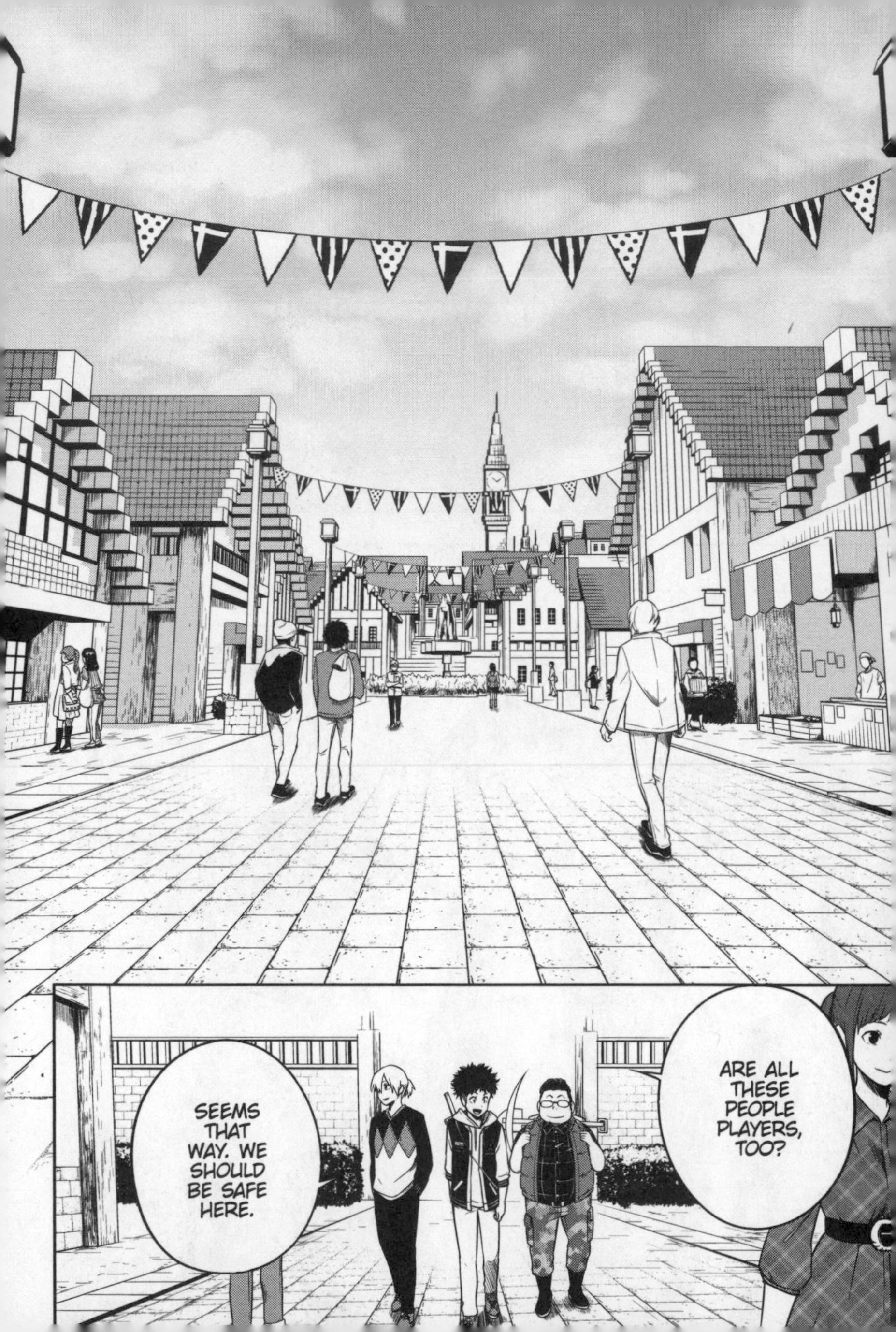
ARE ALL THESE PEOPLE PLAYERS, TOO?
SEEMS THAT WAY. WE SHOULD BE SAFE HERE.

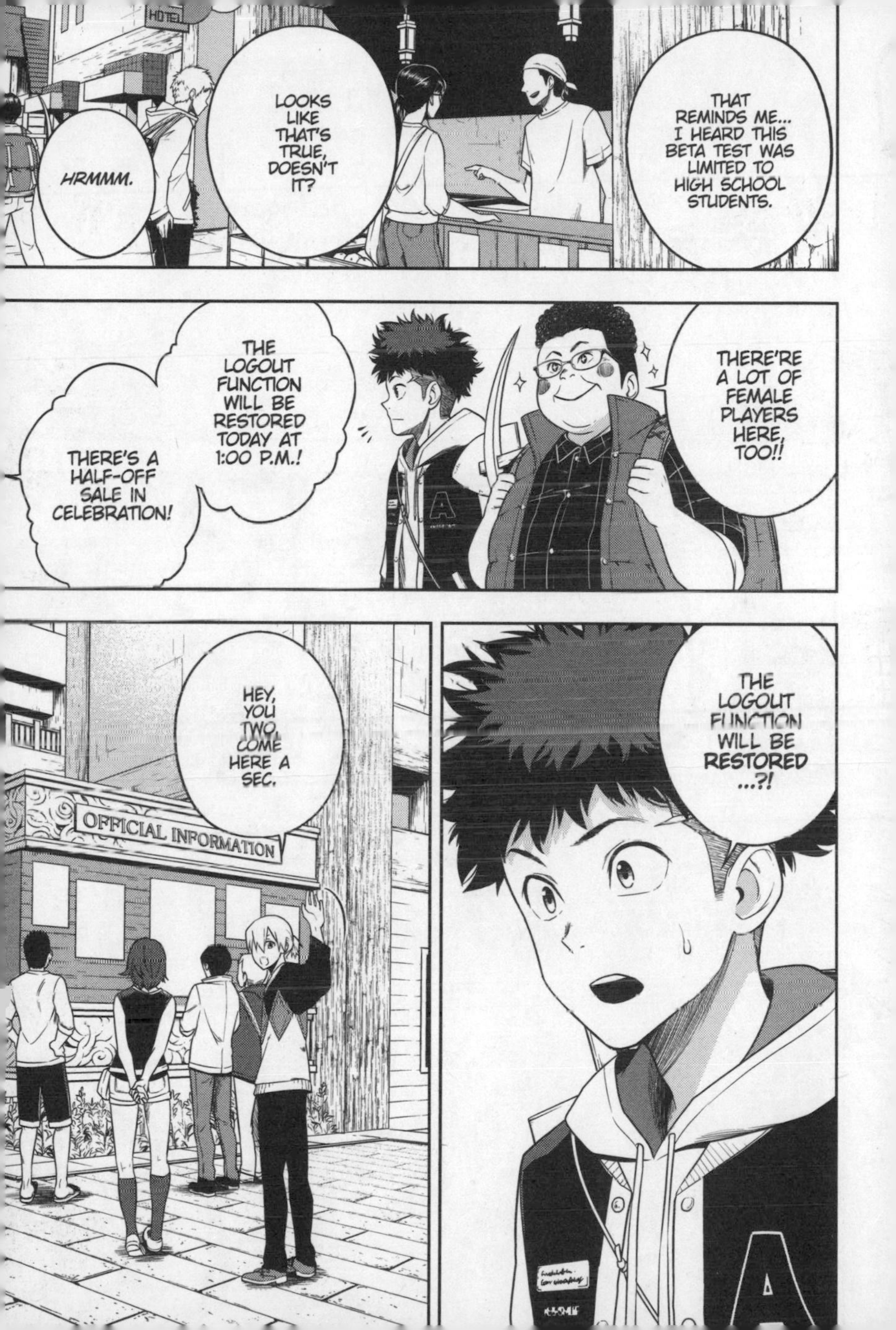
THAT REMINDS ME... I HEARD THIS BETA TEST WAS LIMITED TO HIGH SCHOOL STUDENTS.
LOOKS LIKE THAT'S TRUE, DOESN'T IT?
HOTEL
HRMMM.
THERE'RE A LOT OF FEMALE PLAYERS HERE, TOO!!
THE LOGOUT FUNCTION WILL BE RESTORED TODAY AT 1:00 P.M.!
THERE'S A HALF-OFF SALE IN CELEBRATION!
THE LOGOUT FUNCTION WILL BE RESTORED ...?!
HEY, YOU TWO, COME HERE A SEC.
OFFICIAL INFORMATION

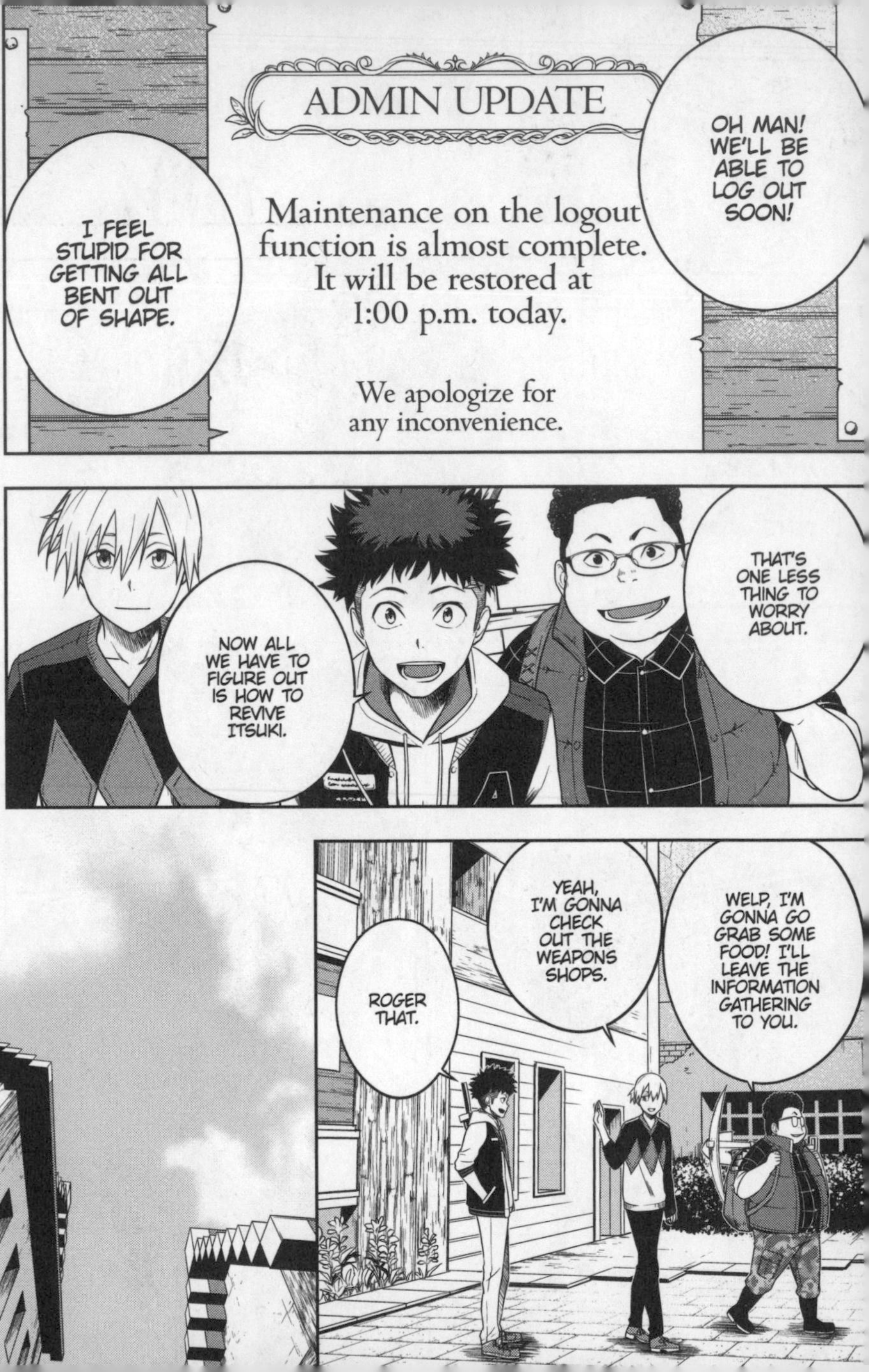
ADMIN UPDATE
Maintenance on the logout function is almost complete. It will be restored at 1:00 p.m. today.
We apologize for any inconvenience.
OH MAN! WE'LL BE ABLE TO LOG OUT SOON!
I FEEL STUPID FOR GETTING ALL BENT OUT OF SHAPE.
THAT'S ONE LESS THING TO WORRY ABOUT.
NOW ALL WE HAVE TO FIGURE OUT IS HOW TO REVIVE ITSUKI.
WELP, I'M GONNA GO GRAB SOME FOOD! I'LL LEAVE THE INFORMATION GATHERING TO YOU.
YEAH, I'M GONNA CHECK OUT THE WEAPONS SHOPS.
ROGER THAT.

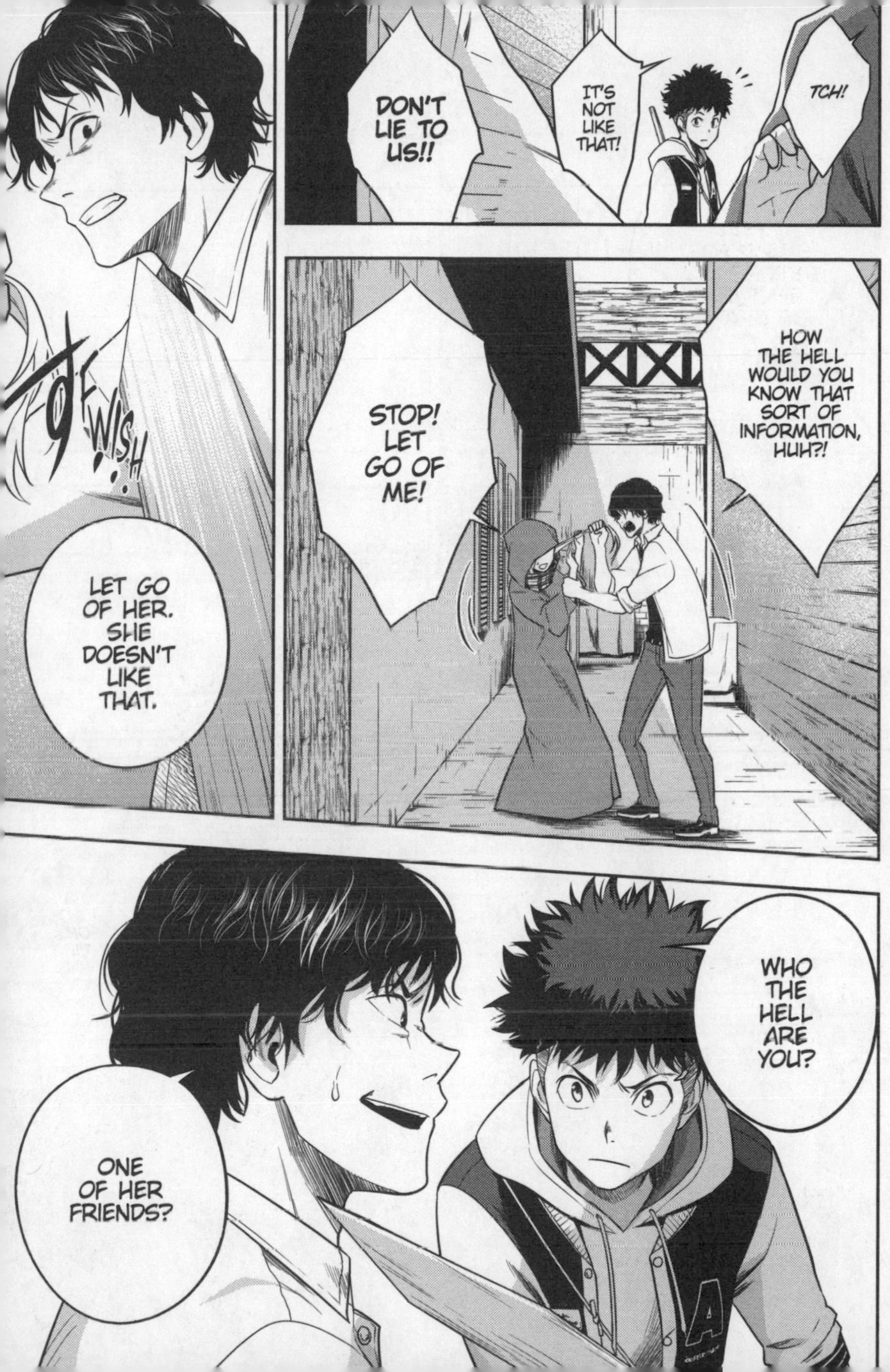
TCH!
IT'S NOT LIKE THAT!
DON'T LIE TO US!!
HOW THE HELL WOULD YOU KNOW THAT SORT OF INFORMATION, HUH?!
STOP! LET GO OF ME!
FWISH
LET GO OF HER. SHE DOESN'T LIKE THAT.
WHO THE HELL ARE YOU?
ONE OF HER FRIENDS?

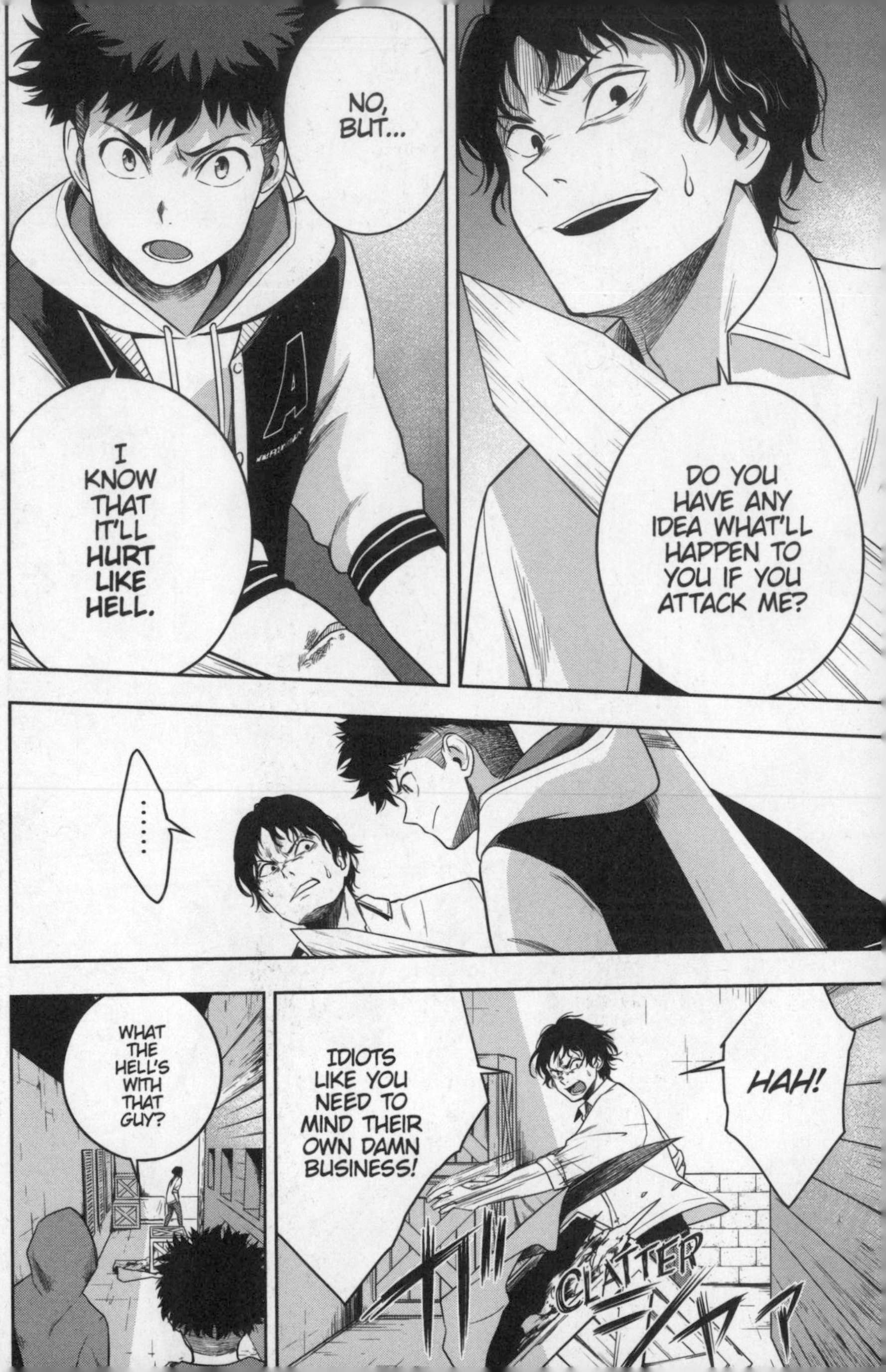
DO YOU HAVE ANY IDEA WHAT'LL HAPPEN TO YOU IF YOU ATTACK ME?
NO, BUT...
I KNOW THAT IT'LL HURT LIKE HELL.
......
HAH!
IDIOTS LIKE YOU NEED TO MIND THEIR OWN DAMN BUSINESS!
CLATTER
WHAT THE HELL'S WITH THAT GUY?

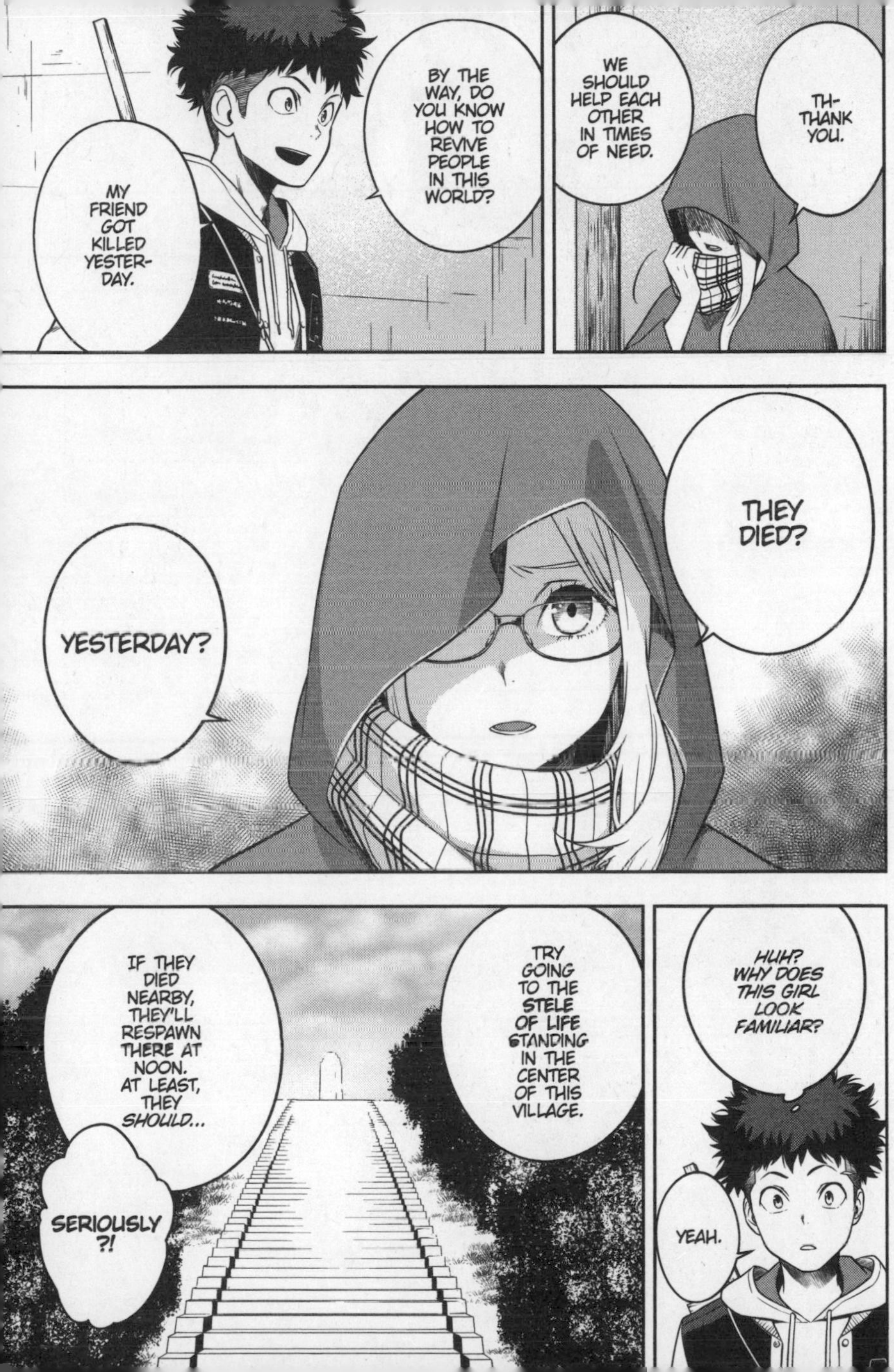
TH-THANK YOU.
WE SHOULD HELP EACH OTHER IN TIMES OF NEED.
BY THE WAY, DO YOU KNOW HOW TO REVIVE PEOPLE IN THIS WORLD?
MY FRIEND GOT KILLED YESTERDAY.
THEY DIED?
YESTERDAY?
HUH? WHY DOES THIS GIRL LOOK FAMILIAR?
YEAH.
TRY GOING TO THE STELE OF LIFE STANDING IN THE CENTER OF THIS VILLAGE.
IF THEY DIED NEARBY, THEY'LL RESPAWN THERE AT NOON. AT LEAST, THEY SHOULD...
SERIOUSLY?!

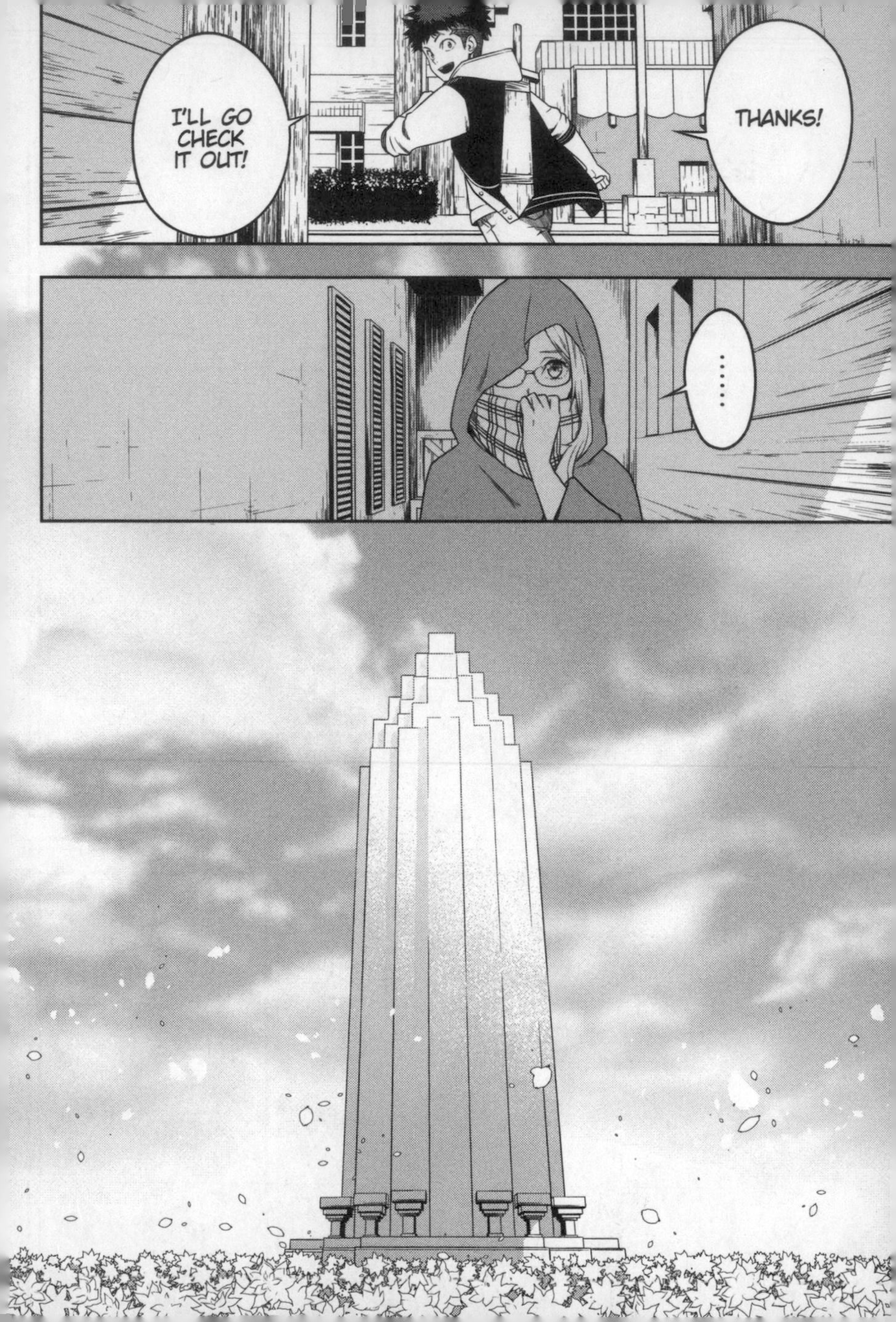
THANKS!
I'LL GO CHECK IT OUT!
......

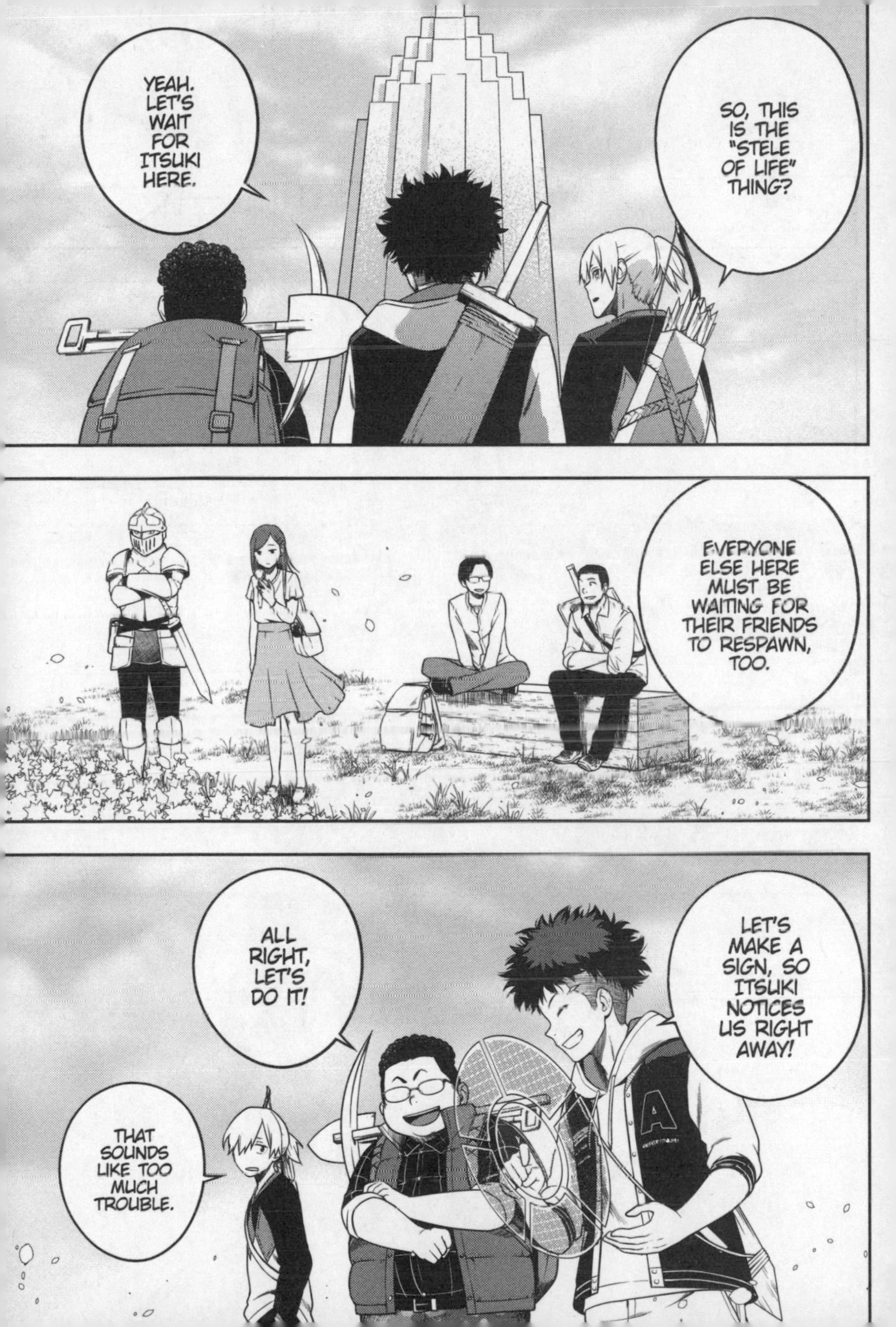
SO, THIS IS THE "STELE OF LIFE" THING?
YEAH. LET'S WAIT FOR ITSUKI HERE.
EVERYONE ELSE HERE MUST BE WAITING FOR THEIR FRIENDS TO RESPAWN, TOO.
LET'S MAKE A SIGN, SO ITSUKI NOTICES US RIGHT AWAY!
ALL RIGHT, LET'S DO IT!
THAT SOUNDS LIKE TOO MUCH TROUBLE.

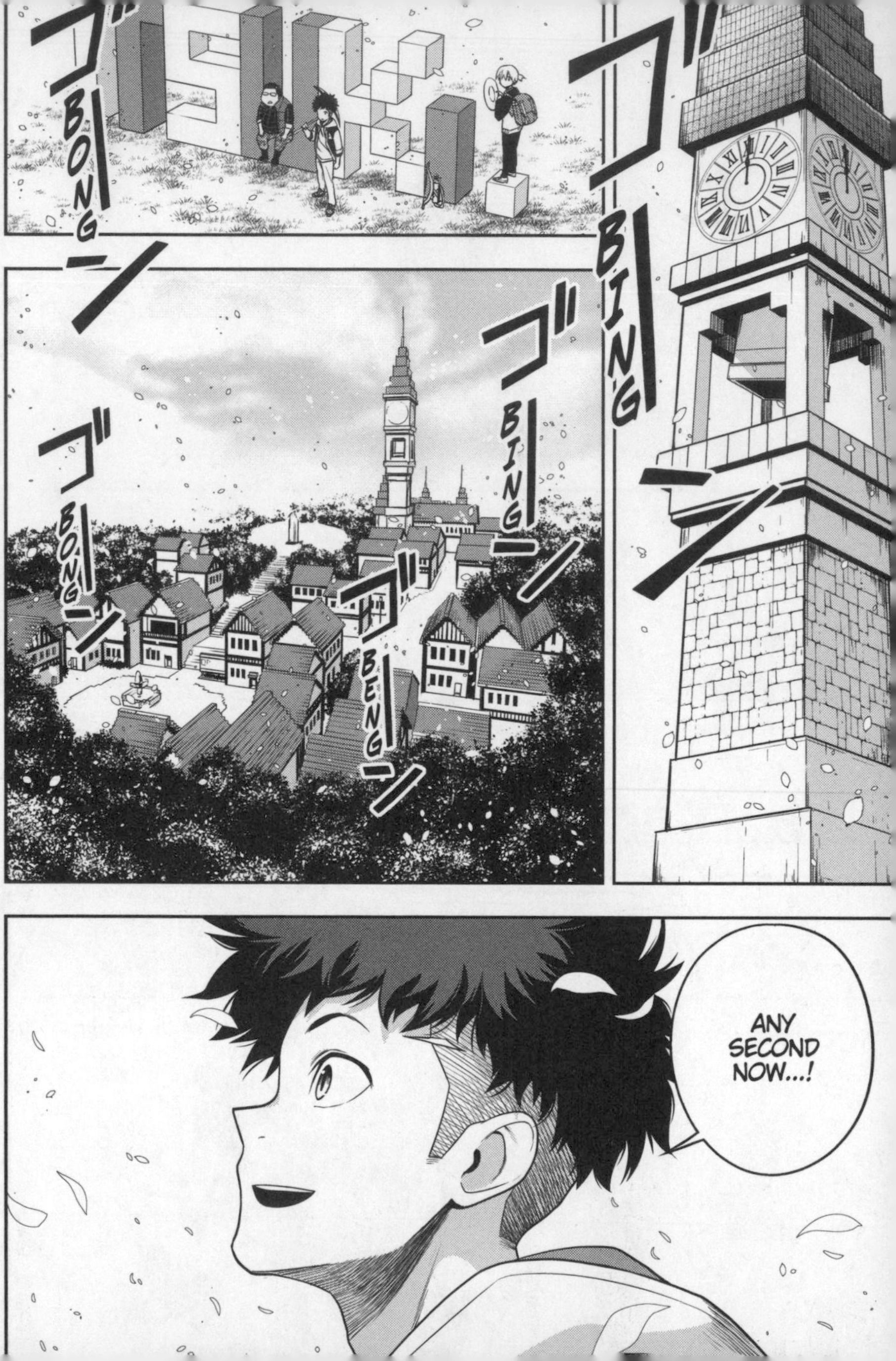
ゴーン BING
ゴーン BONG
ゴーン BING
ゴーン BONG
ゴーン BENG
ANY SECOND NOW...!

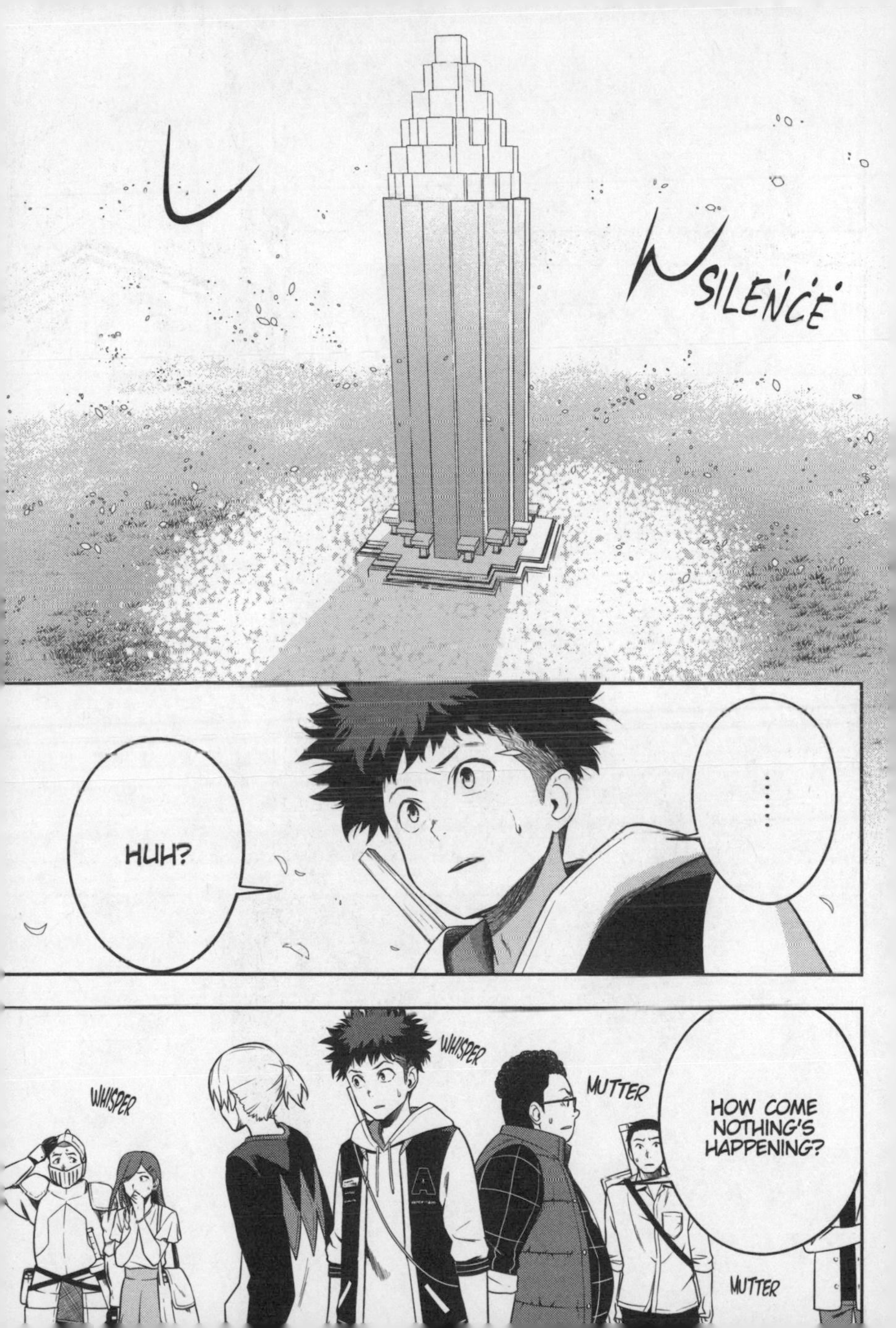
SILENCE
......
HUH?
HOW COME NOTHING'S HAPPENING?
MUTTER
WHISPER
WHISPER
MUTTER

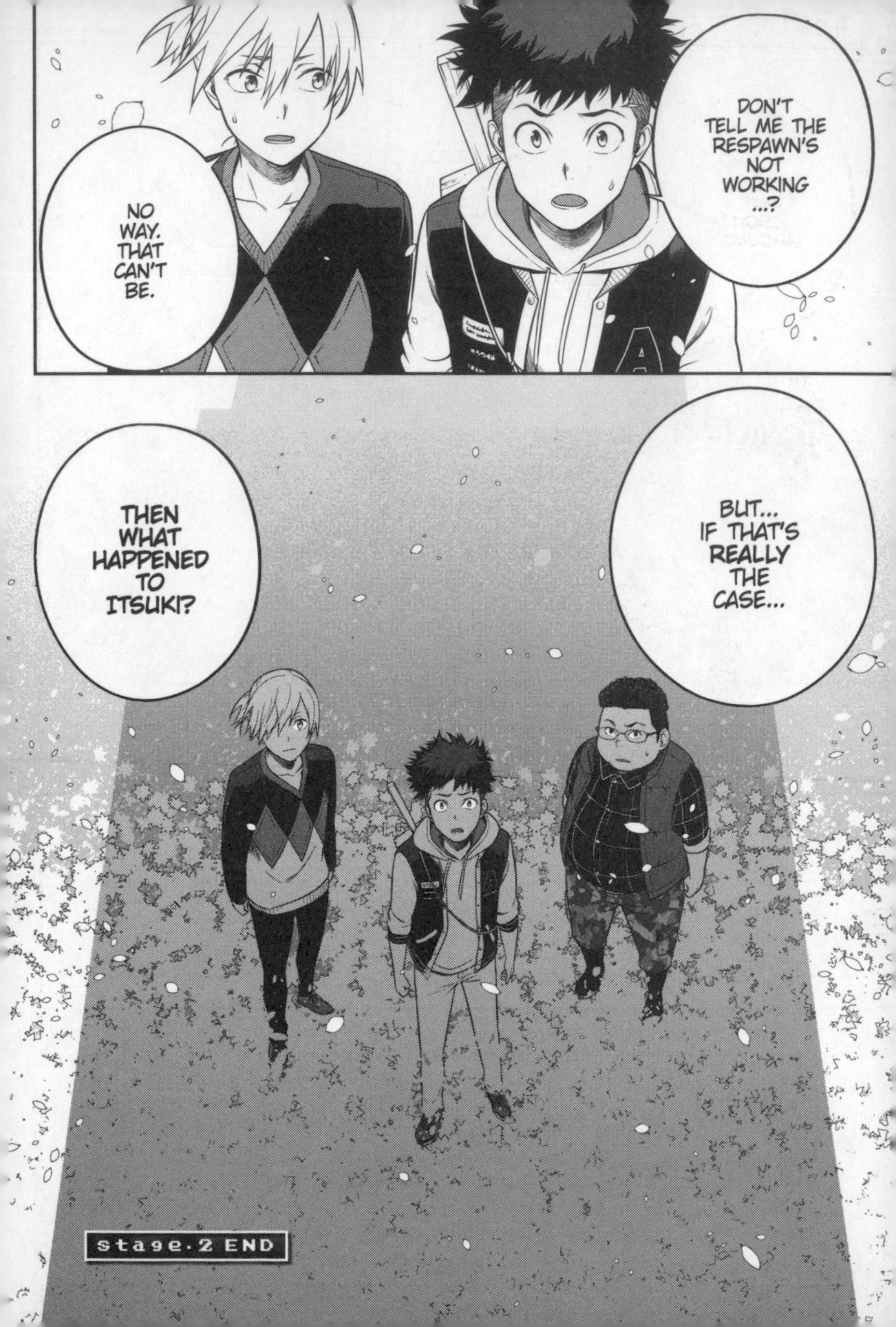
DON'T TELL ME THE RESPAWN'S NOT WORKING ...?
NO WAY. THAT CAN'T BE.
BUT... IF THAT'S REALLY THE CASE...
THEN WHAT HAPPENED TO ITSUKI?
stage.2 END

Stage.3

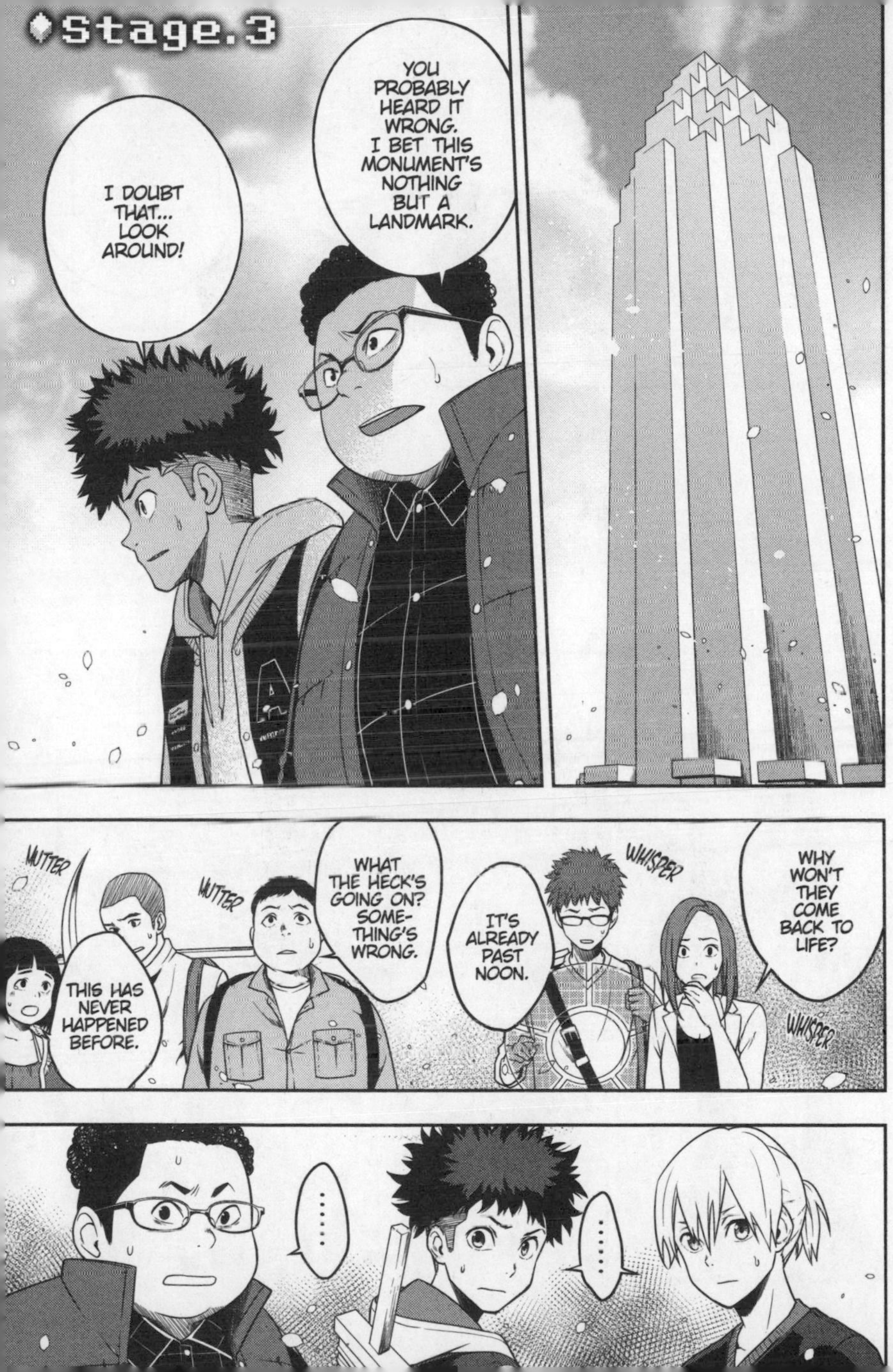
YOU PROBABLY HEARD IT WRONG. I BET THIS MONUMENT'S NOTHING BUT A LANDMARK.
I DOUBT THAT... LOOK AROUND!
WHISPER
WHY WON'T THEY COME BACK TO LIFE?
WHISPER
IT'S ALREADY PAST NOON.
WHAT THE HECK'S GOING ON? SOME-THING'S WRONG.
MUTTER
MUTTER
THIS HAS NEVER HAPPENED BEFORE.
......
......

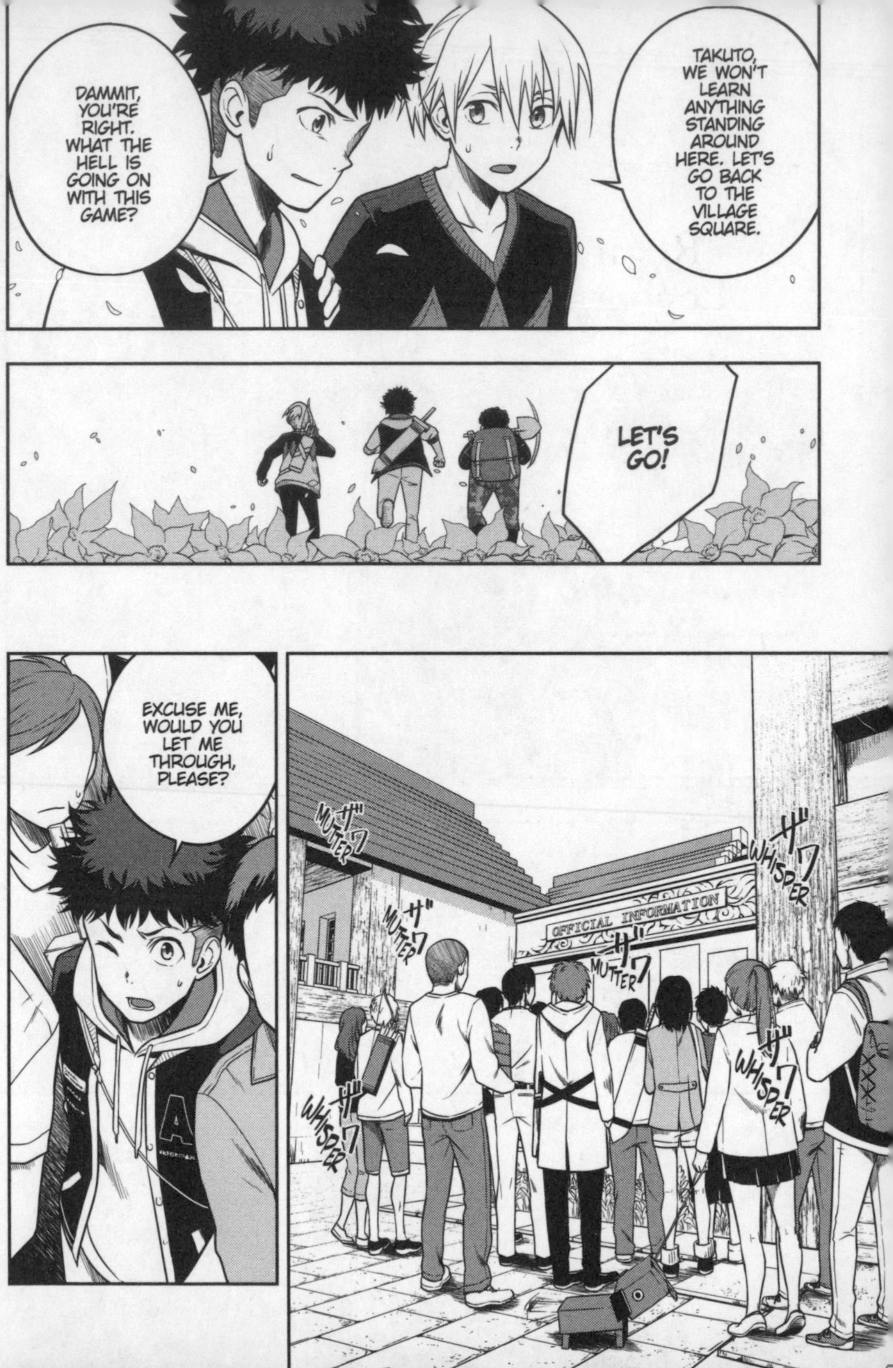
TAKUTO, WE WON'T LEARN ANYTHING STANDING AROUND HERE. LET'S GO BACK TO THE VILLAGE SQUARE.
DAMMIT, YOU'RE RIGHT. WHAT THE HELL IS GOING ON WITH THIS GAME?
LET'S GO!
ザワ WHISPER
ザワ MUTTER
OFFICIAL INFORMATION
ザワ MUTTER
ザワ MUTTER
ザワ WHISPER
ザワ WHISPER
EXCUSE ME, WOULD YOU LET ME THROUGH, PLEASE?

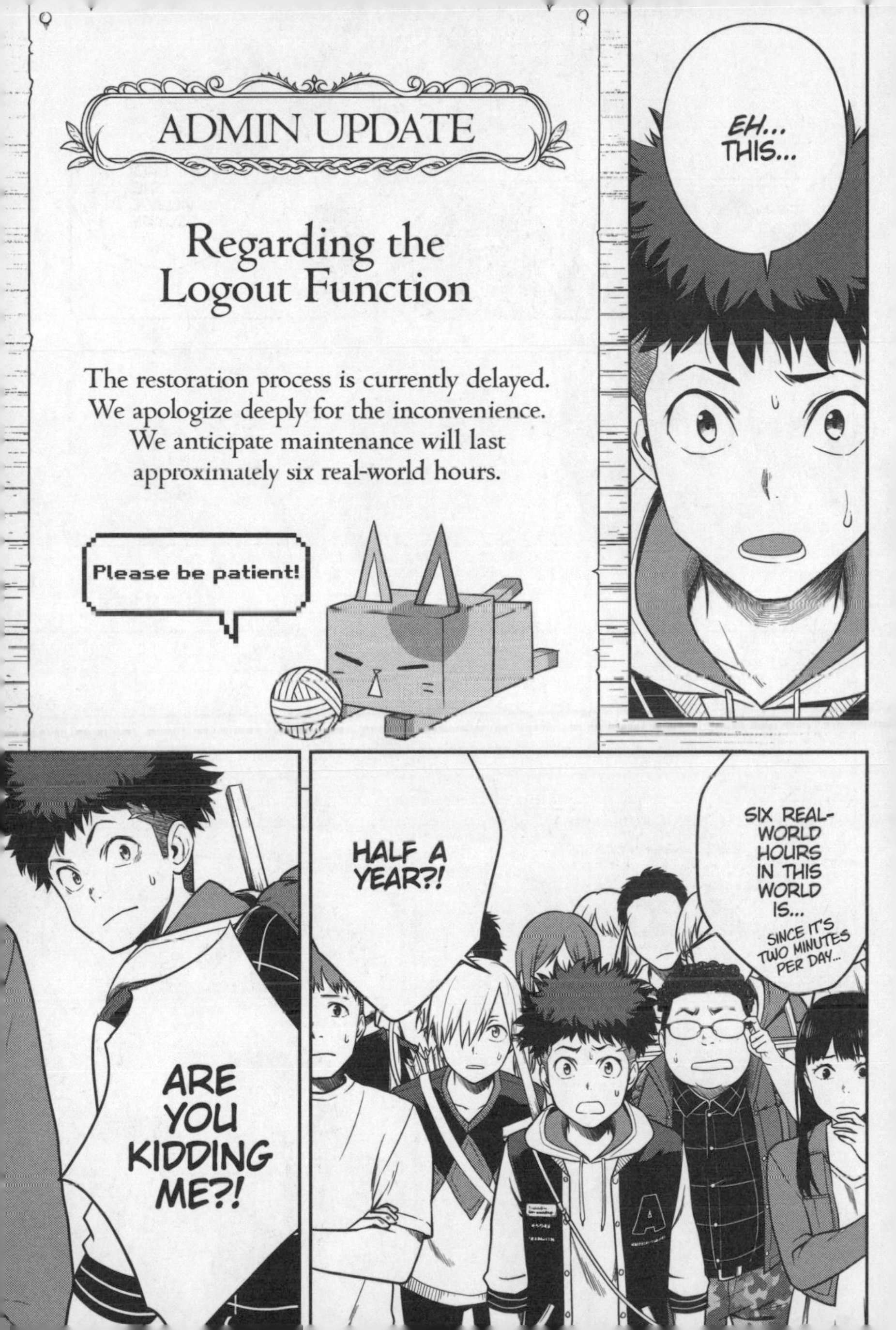
EH... THIS...
ADMIN UPDATE
Regarding the Logout Function
The restoration process is currently delayed. We apologize deeply for the inconvenience. We anticipate maintenance will last approximately six real-world hours.
Please be patient!
SIX REAL-WORLD HOURS IN THIS WORLD IS...
SINCE IT'S TWO MINUTES PER DAY...
HALF A YEAR?!
ARE YOU KIDDING ME?!

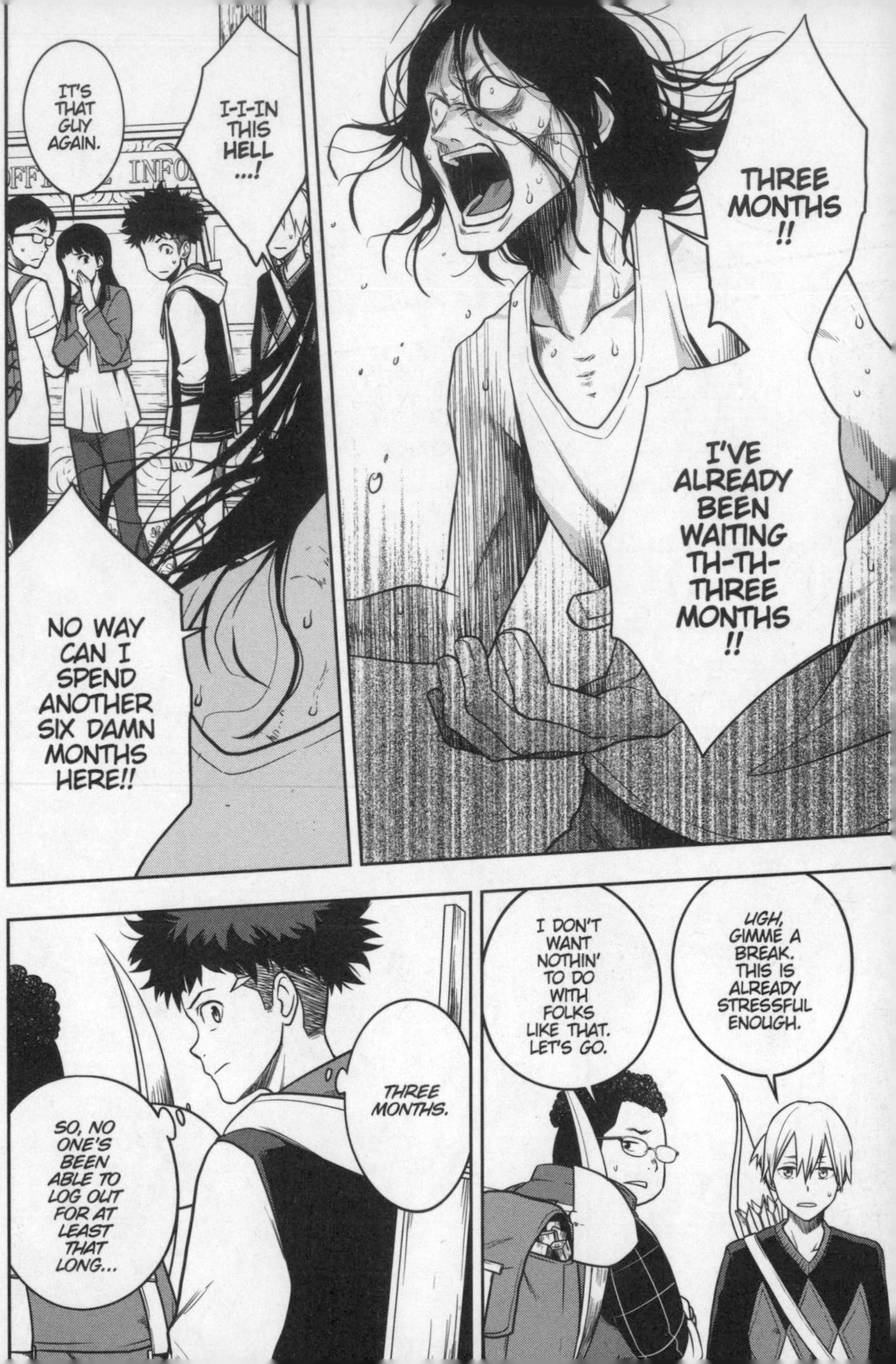
THREE MONTHS!!
I'VE ALREADY BEEN WAITING TH-TH-THREE MONTHS!!
I-I-IN THIS HELL ...!
IT'S THAT GUY AGAIN.
NO WAY CAN I SPEND ANOTHER SIX DAMN MONTHS HERE!!
UGH, GIMME A BREAK. THIS IS ALREADY STRESSFUL ENOUGH.
I DON'T WANT NOTHIN' TO DO WITH FOLKS LIKE THAT. LET'S GO.
THREE MONTHS.
SO, NO ONE'S BEEN ABLE TO LOG OUT FOR AT LEAST THAT LONG...

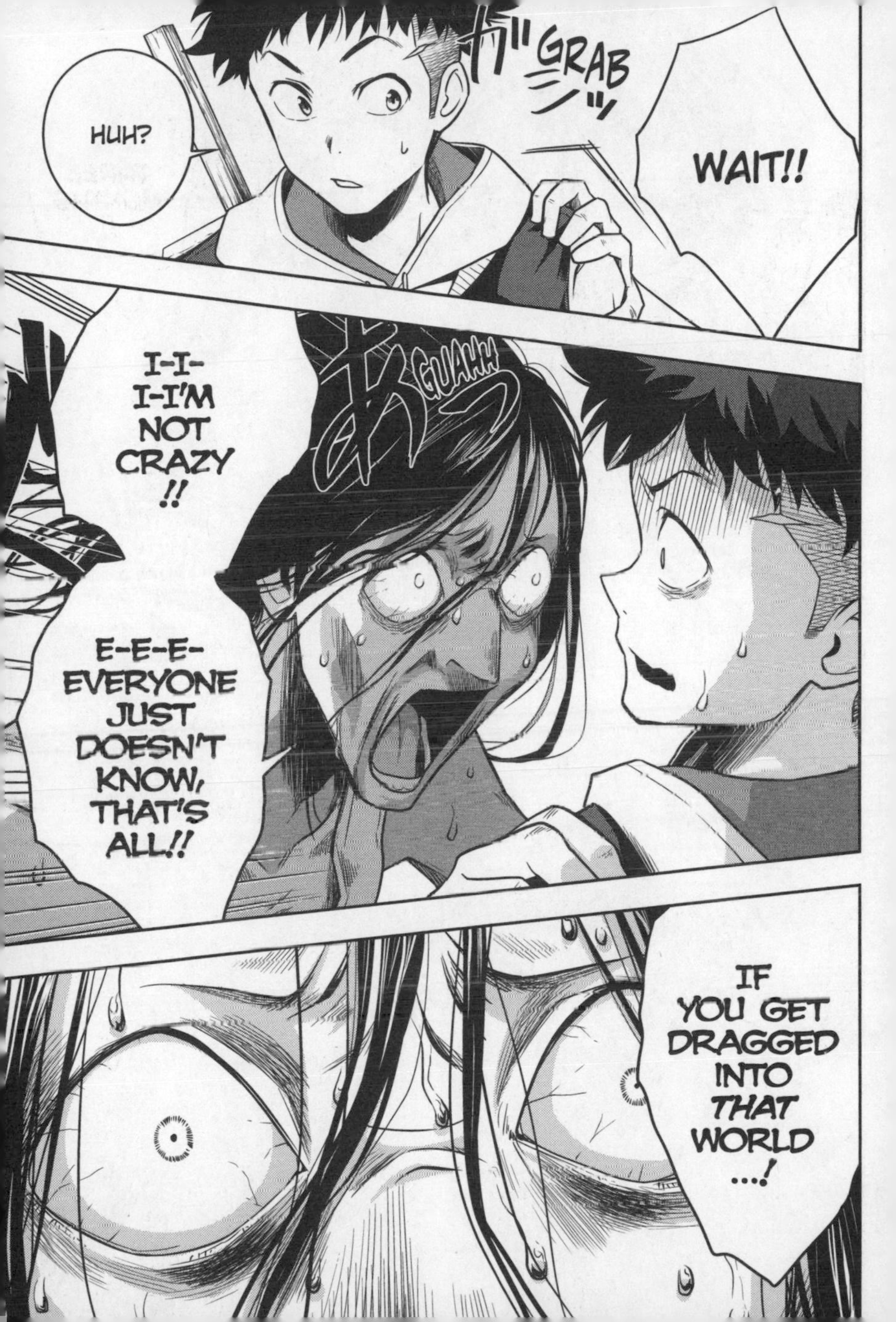
WAIT!!
GRAB
HUH?
GUAHH
I-I-I-I'M NOT CRAZY!!
E-E-E-EVERYONE JUST DOESN'T KNOW, THAT'S ALL!!
IF YOU GET DRAGGED INTO THAT WORLD ...!

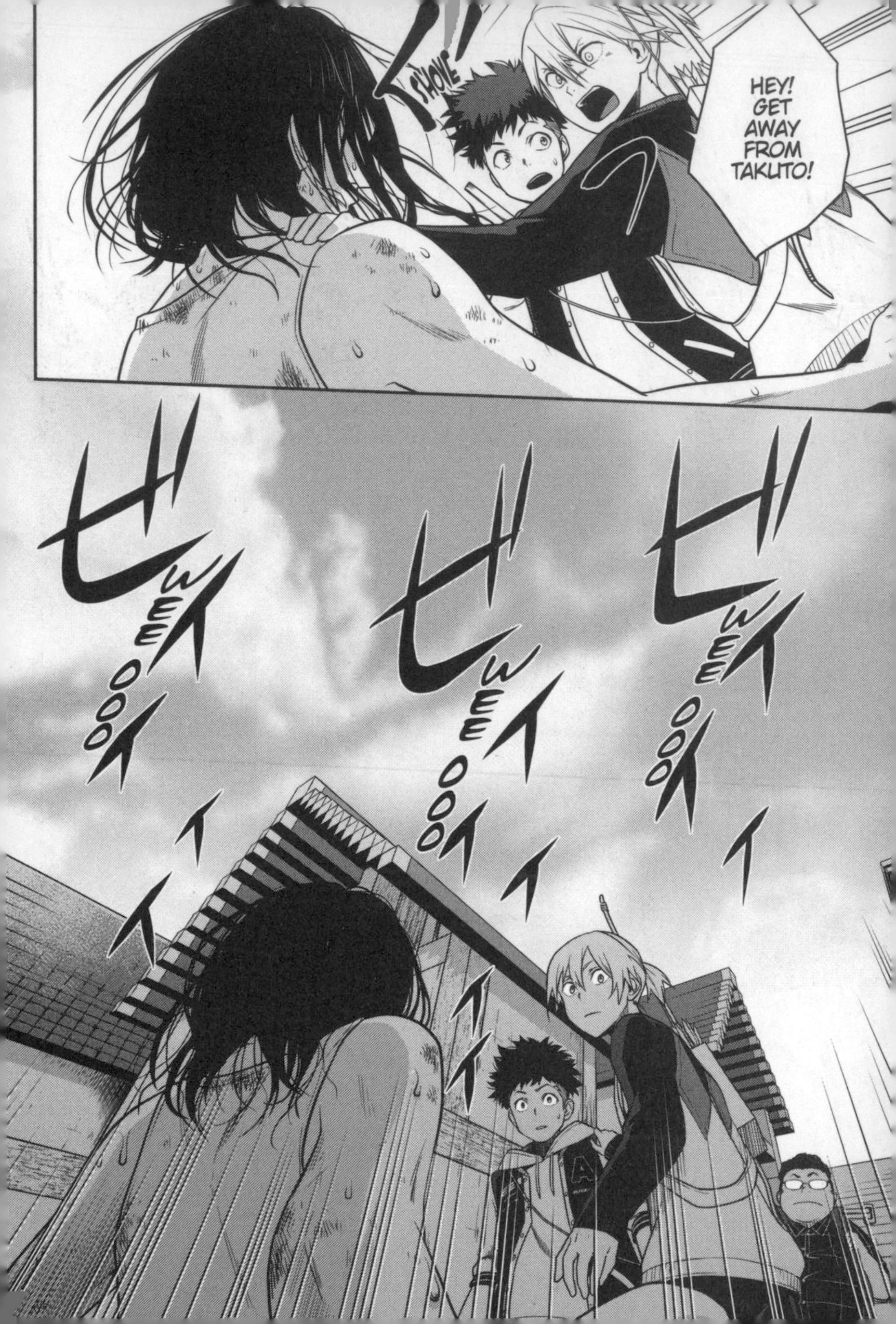
HEY! GET AWAY FROM TAKUTO!
SHOVE!
WEEOOO
WEEOOO
WEEOOO

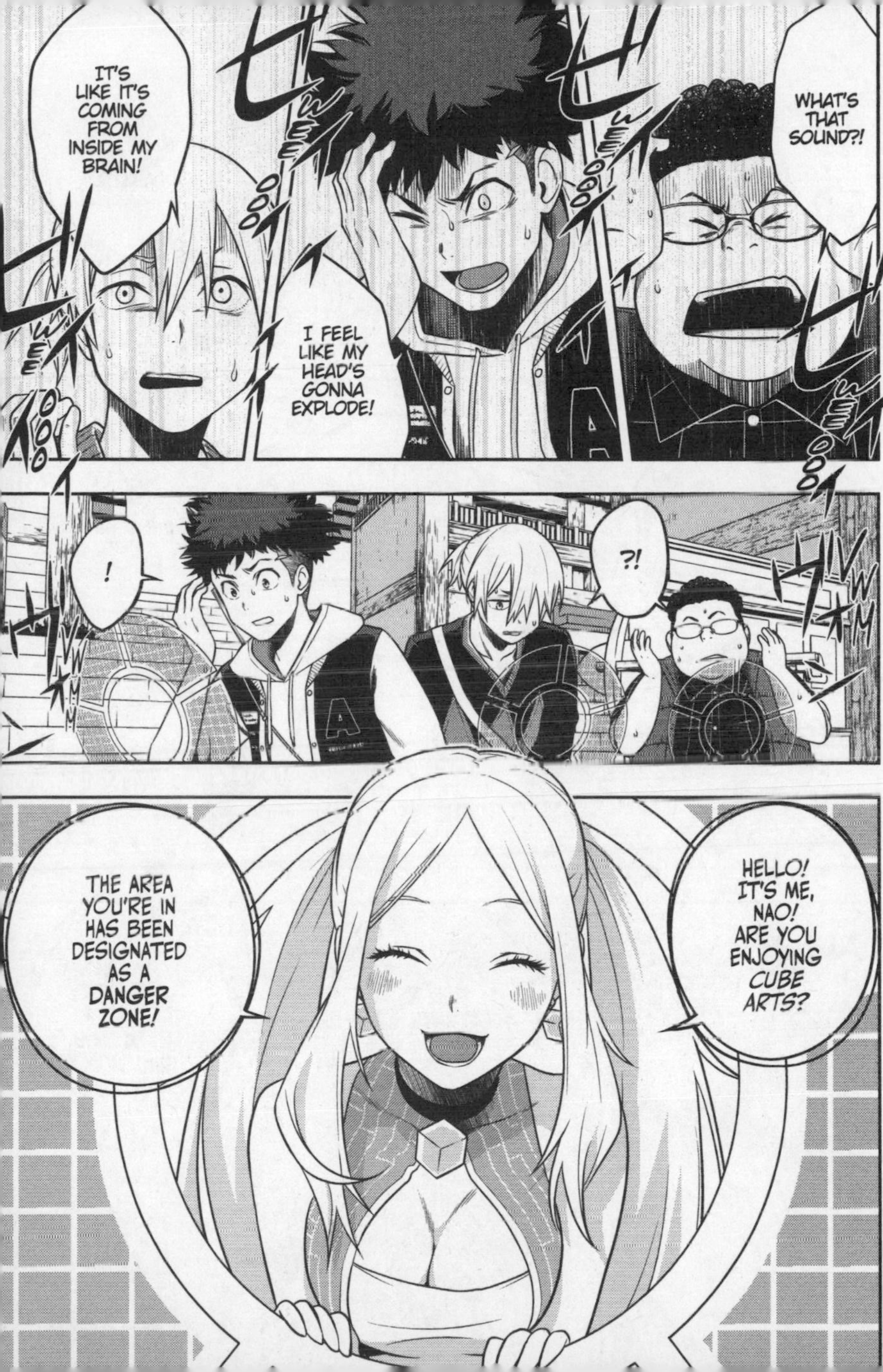
WHAT'S THAT SOUND?!
I FEEL LIKE MY HEAD'S GONNA EXPLODE!
IT'S LIKE IT'S COMING FROM INSIDE MY BRAIN!
?!
!
HELLO! IT'S ME, NAO! ARE YOU ENJOYING *CUBE ARTS*?
THE AREA YOU'RE IN HAS BEEN DESIGNATED AS A DANGER ZONE!

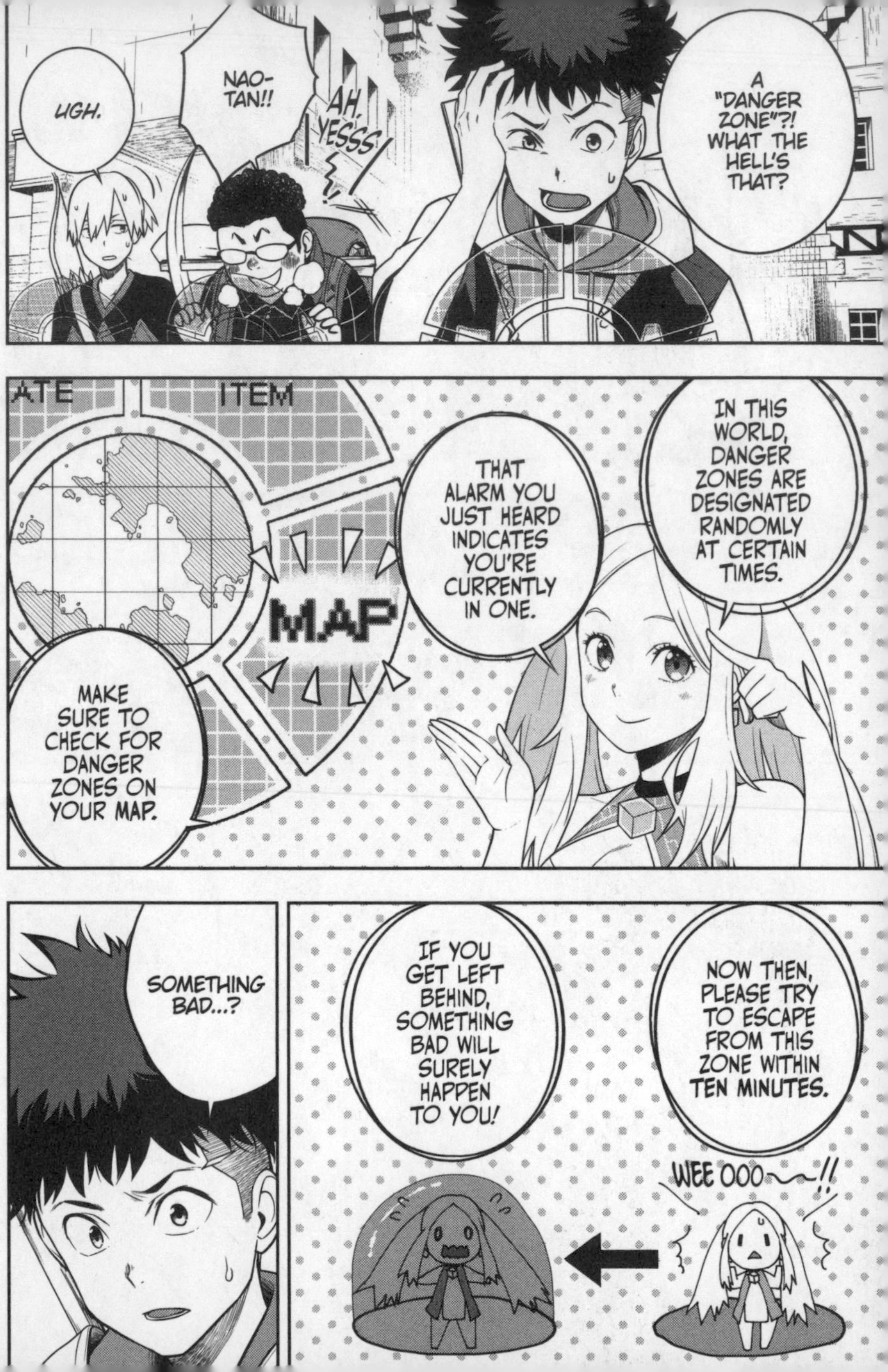
A "DANGER ZONE"?! WHAT THE HELL'S THAT?
AH, YESSS
NAO-TAN!!
UGH.
ITEM
ATE
IN THIS WORLD, DANGER ZONES ARE DESIGNATED RANDOMLY AT CERTAIN TIMES.
THAT ALARM YOU JUST HEARD INDICATES YOU'RE CURRENTLY IN ONE.
MAP
MAKE SURE TO CHECK FOR DANGER ZONES ON YOUR MAP.
NOW THEN, PLEASE TRY TO ESCAPE FROM THIS ZONE WITHIN TEN MINUTES.
IF YOU GET LEFT BEHIND, SOMETHING BAD WILL SURELY HAPPEN TO YOU!
WEE OOO~~!!
SOMETHING BAD...?

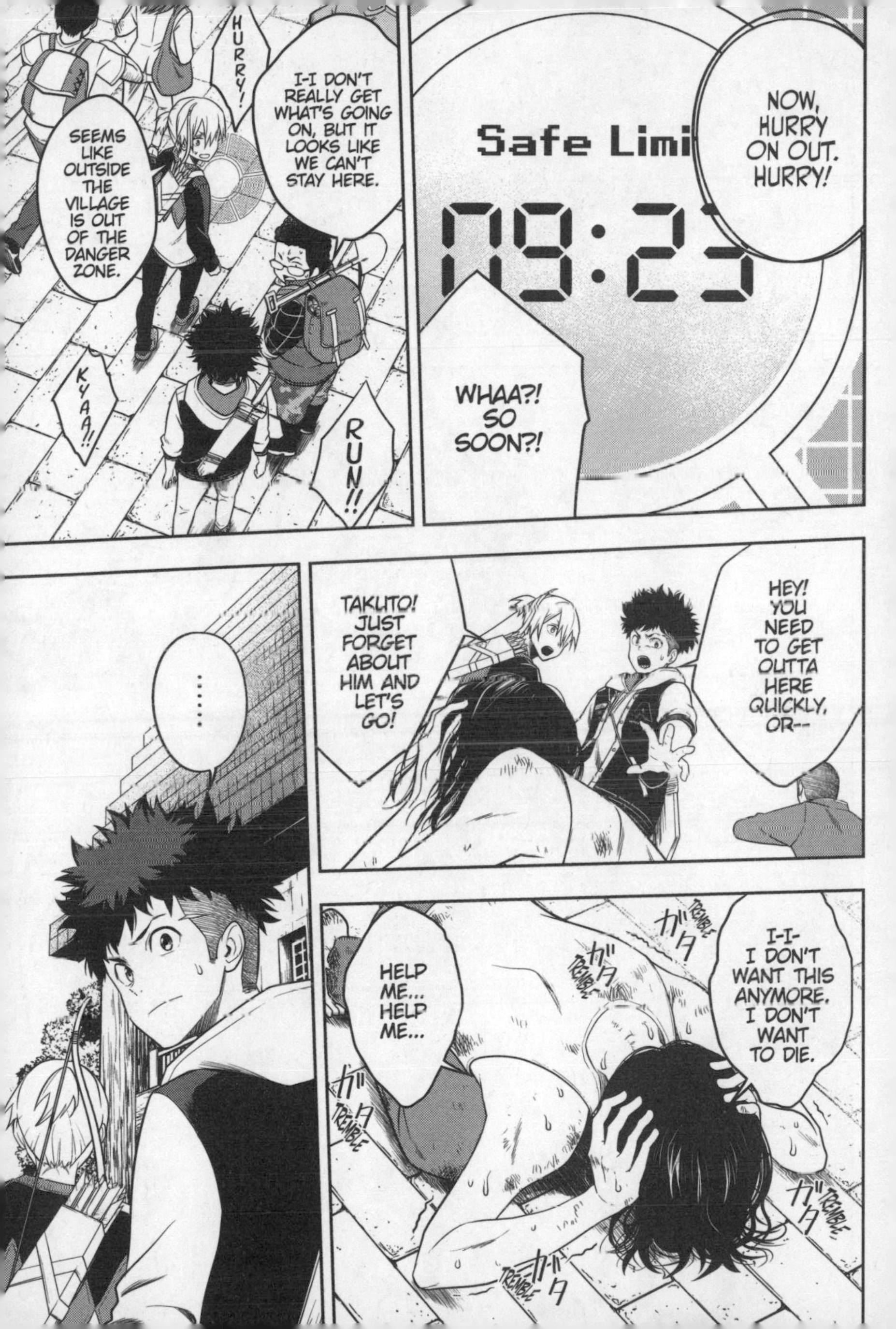
Safe Limi
09:23
NOW, HURRY ON OUT. HURRY!
WHAA?! SO SOON?!
HURRY!
I-I DON'T REALLY GET WHAT'S GOING ON, BUT IT LOOKS LIKE WE CAN'T STAY HERE.
SEEMS LIKE OUTSIDE THE VILLAGE IS OUT OF THE DANGER ZONE.
RUN!!
KYAA?!!
HEY! YOU NEED TO GET OUTTA HERE QUICKLY, OR--
TAKUTO! JUST FORGET ABOUT HIM AND LET'S GO!
ガタ TREMBLE
ガタ TREMBLE
I-I- I DON'T WANT THIS ANYMORE. I DON'T WANT TO DIE.
HELP ME... HELP ME...
ガタ TREMBLE
ガタ TREMBLE
ガタガタ TREMBLE
......

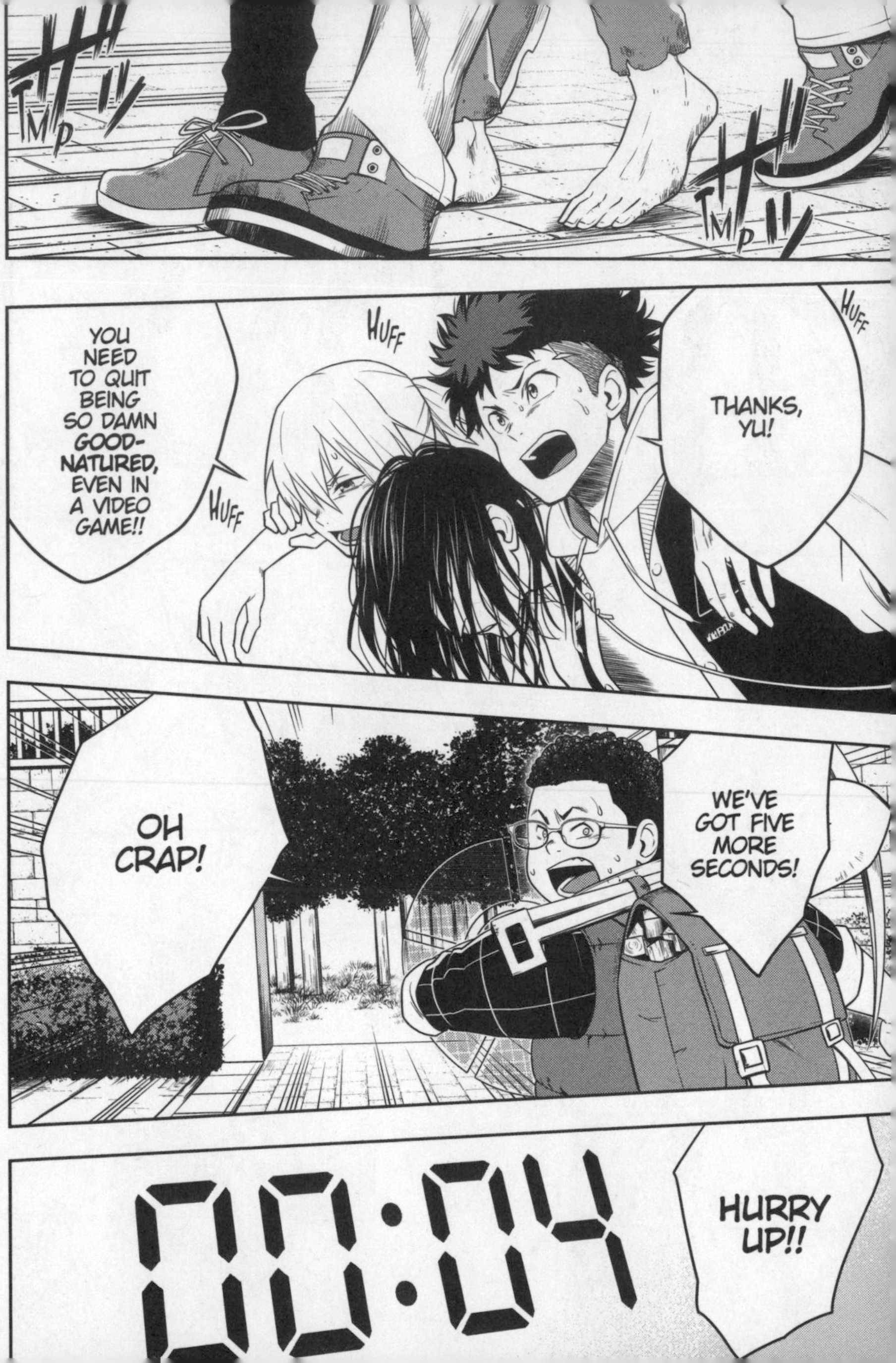
TMP
TMP
HUFF
THANKS, YU!
HUFF
HUFF
YOU NEED TO QUIT BEING SO DAMN GOOD-NATURED, EVEN IN A VIDEO GAME!!
WE'VE GOT FIVE MORE SECONDS!
OH CRAP!
HURRY UP!!
00:04

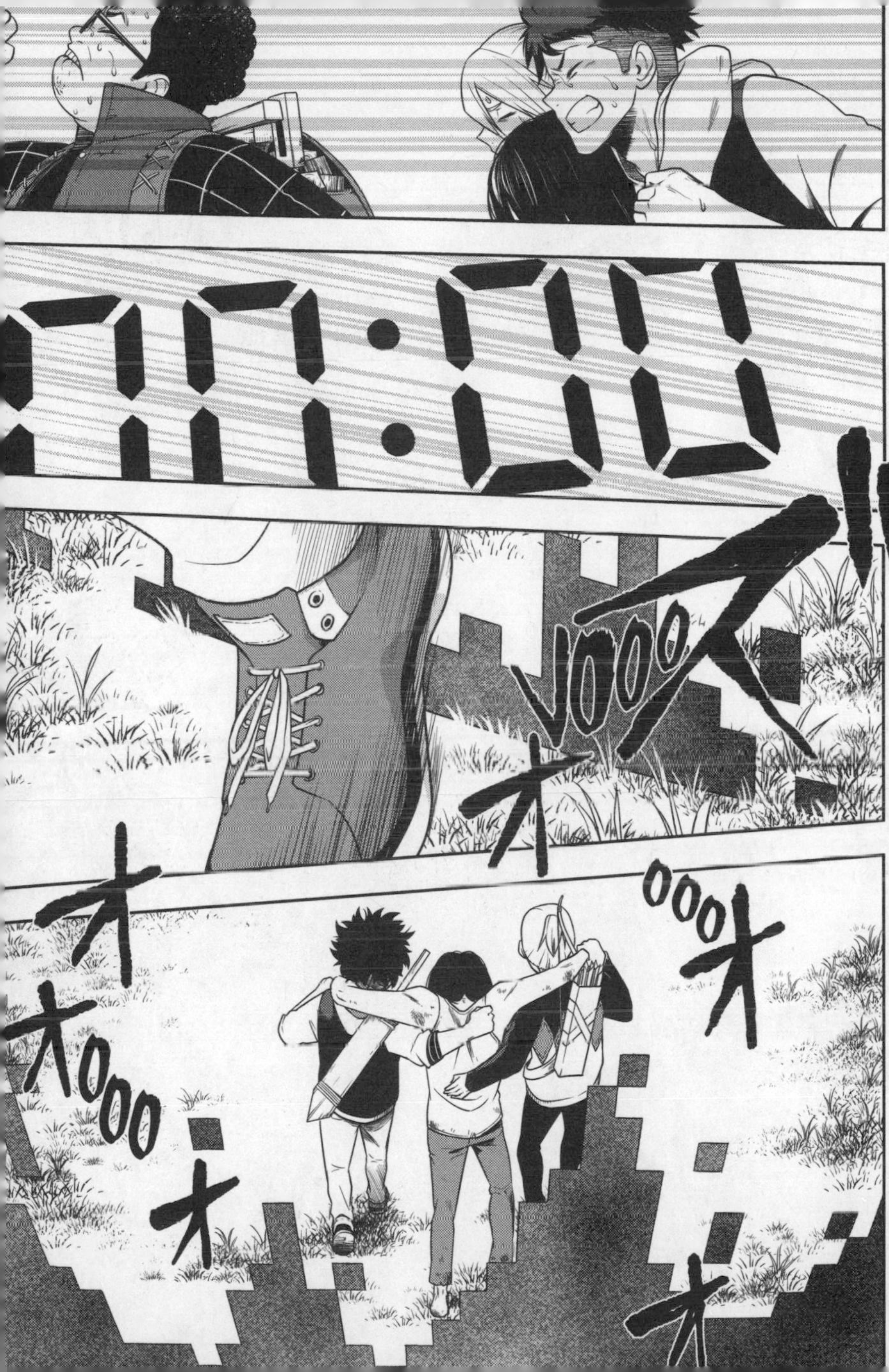
00:00
VOOOズッ
オ
OOOオ
オ
オ
オOOO
オ

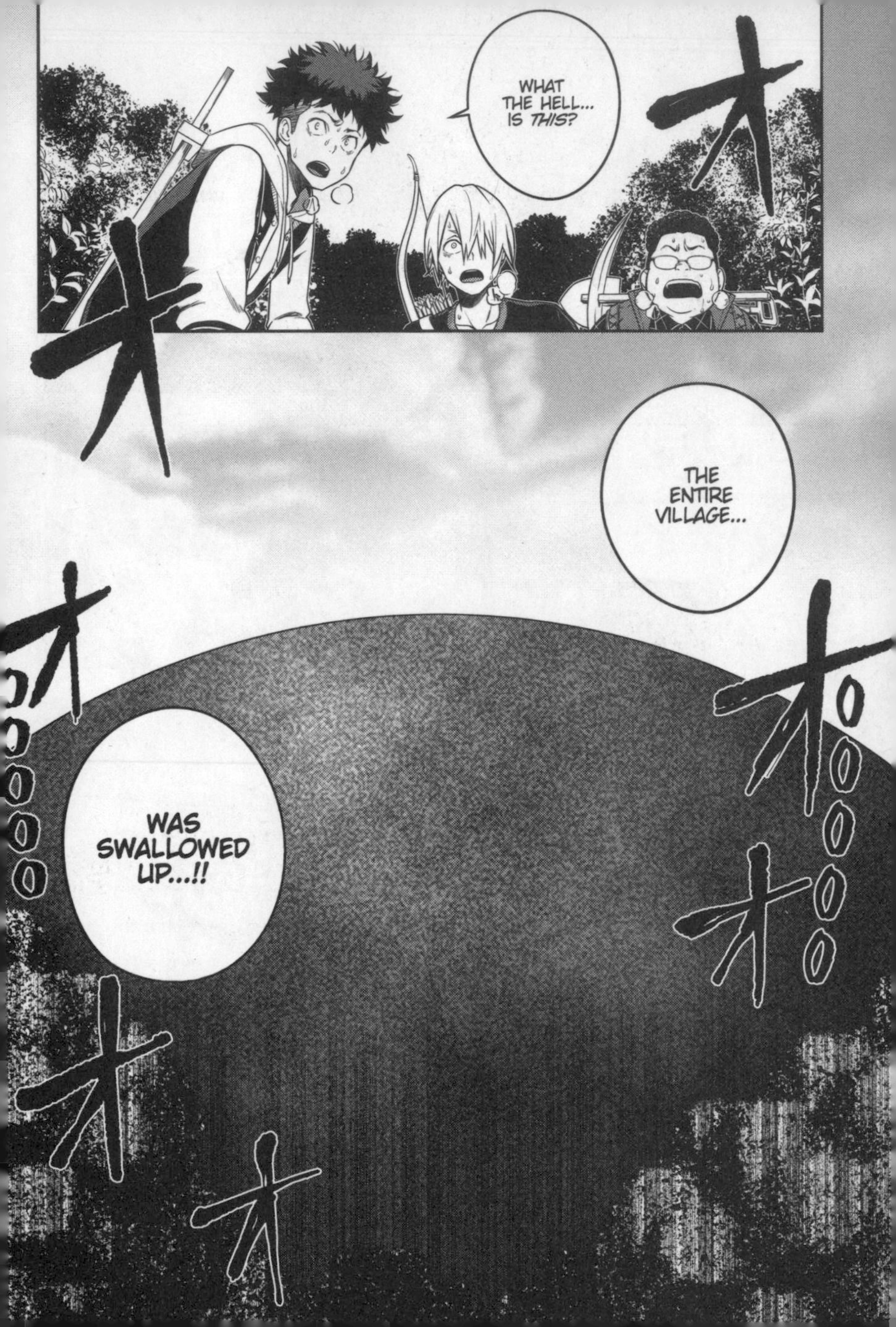
WHAT THE HELL... IS *THIS?*
THE ENTIRE VILLAGE...
WAS SWALLOWED UP...!!

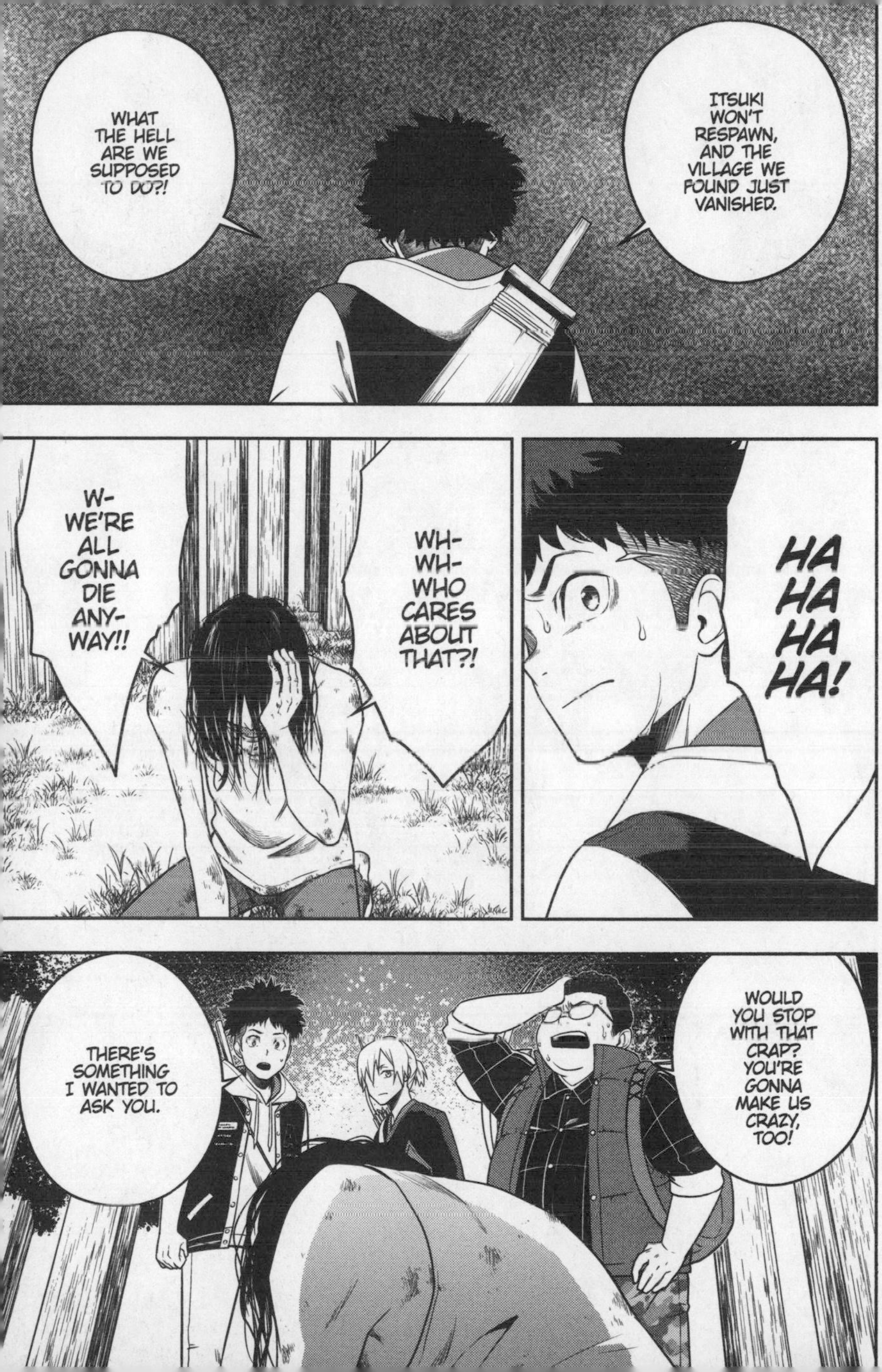
ITSUKI WON'T RESPAWN, AND THE VILLAGE WE FOUND JUST VANISHED.
WHAT THE HELL ARE WE SUPPOSED TO DO?!
HA HA HA HA!
WH- WH- WHO CARES ABOUT THAT?!
W- WE'RE ALL GONNA DIE ANY- WAY!!
WOULD YOU STOP WITH THAT CRAP? YOU'RE GONNA MAKE US CRAZY, TOO!
THERE'S SOMETHING I WANTED TO ASK YOU.

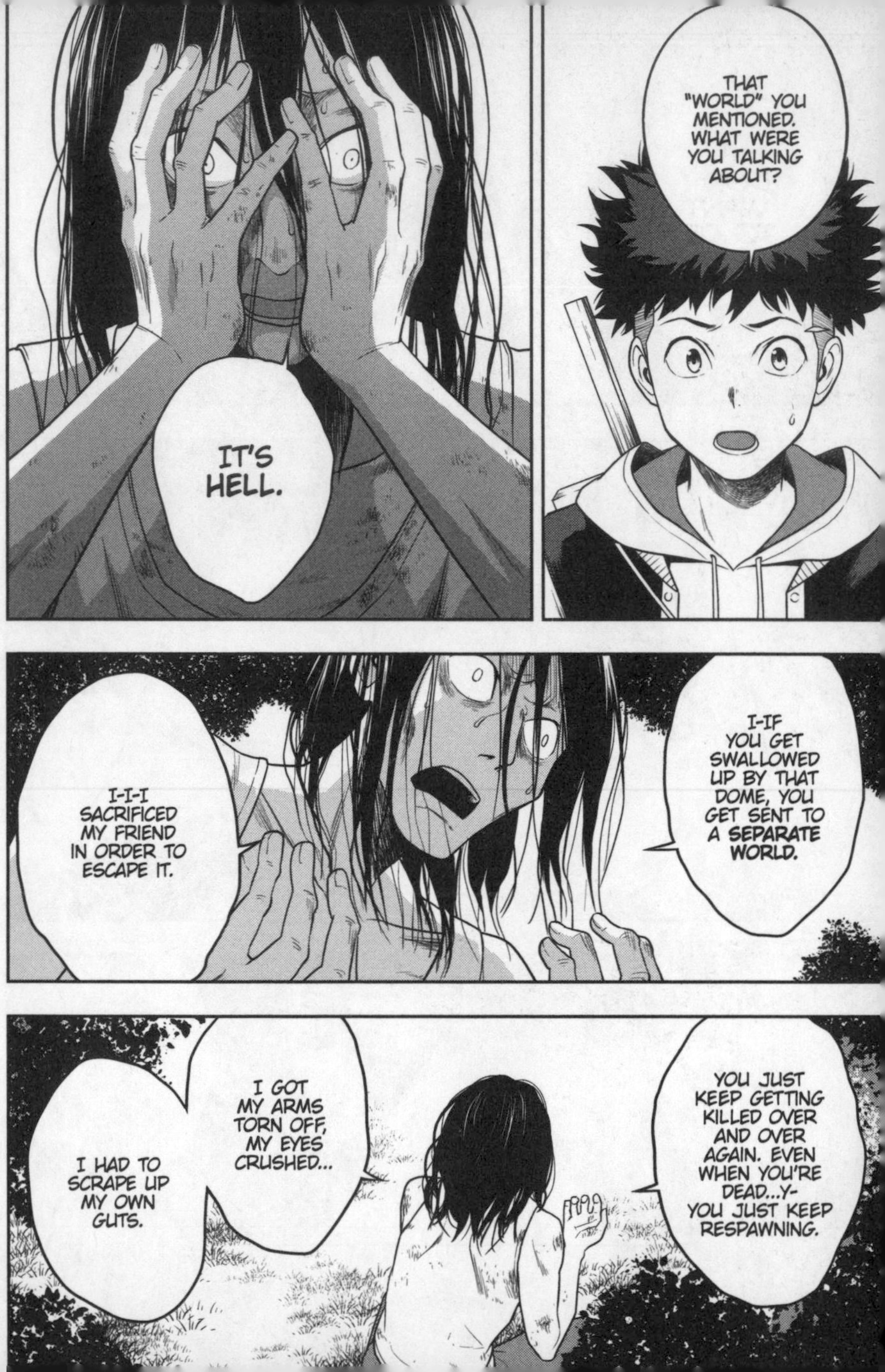
THAT "WORLD" YOU MENTIONED. WHAT WERE YOU TALKING ABOUT?
IT'S HELL.
I-IF YOU GET SWALLOWED UP BY THAT DOME, YOU GET SENT TO A SEPARATE WORLD.
I-I-I SACRIFICED MY FRIEND IN ORDER TO ESCAPE IT.
YOU JUST KEEP GETTING KILLED OVER AND OVER AGAIN. EVEN WHEN YOU'RE DEAD...Y-YOU JUST KEEP RESPAWNING.
I GOT MY ARMS TORN OFF, MY EYES CRUSHED...
I HAD TO SCRAPE UP MY OWN GUTS.

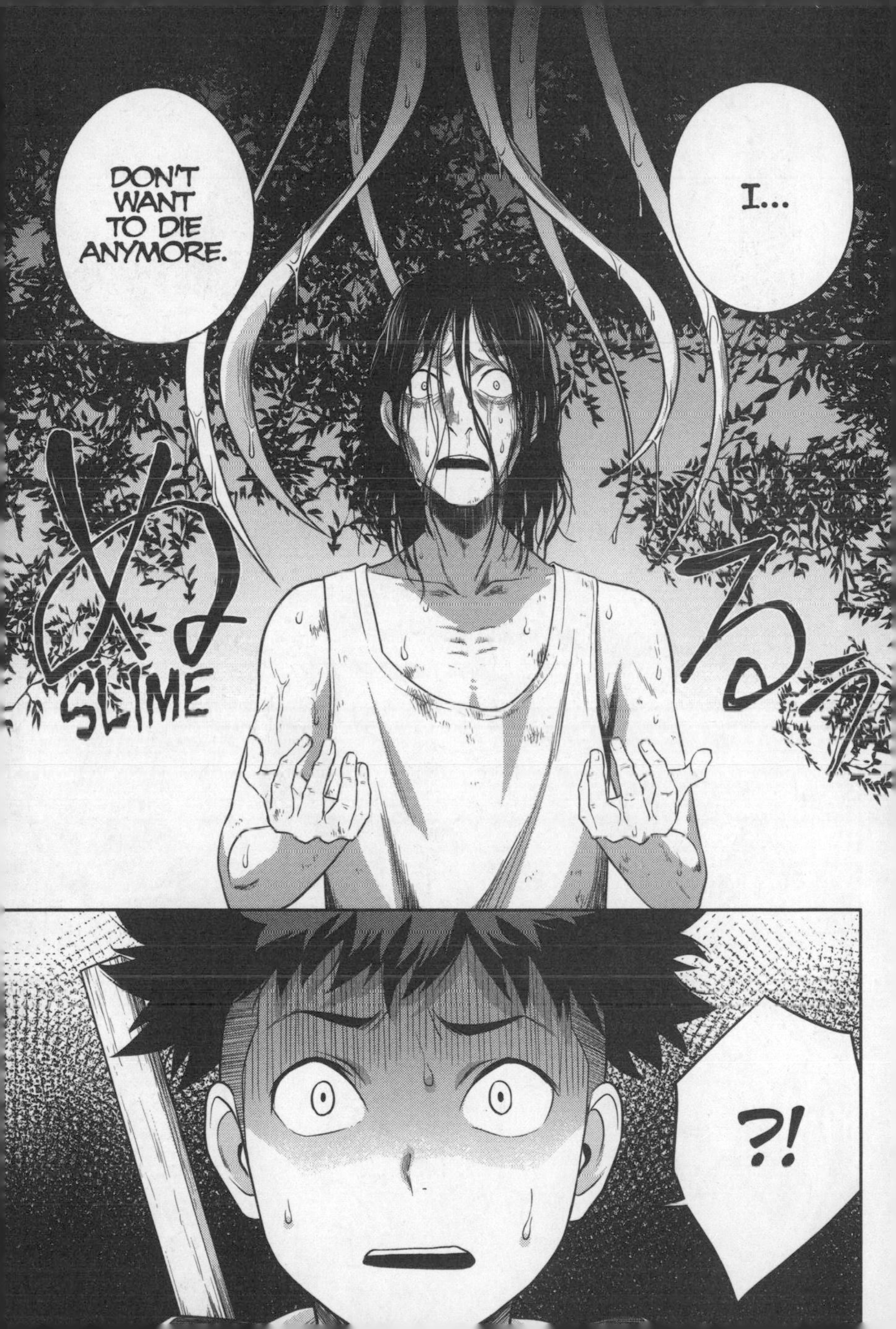
I...
DON'T WANT TO DIE ANYMORE.
SLIME
?!

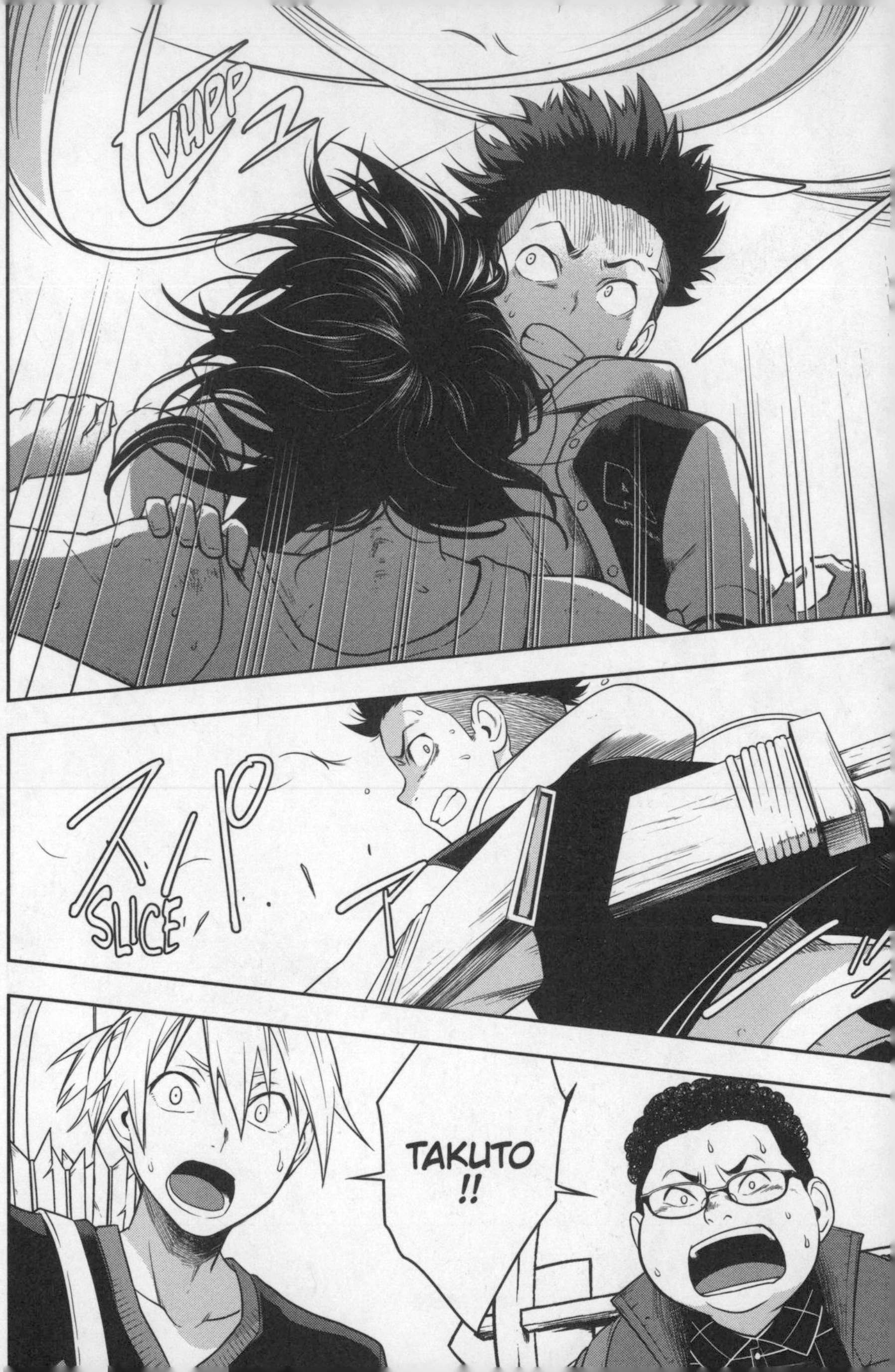
VHPP
SLICE
TAKUTO !!

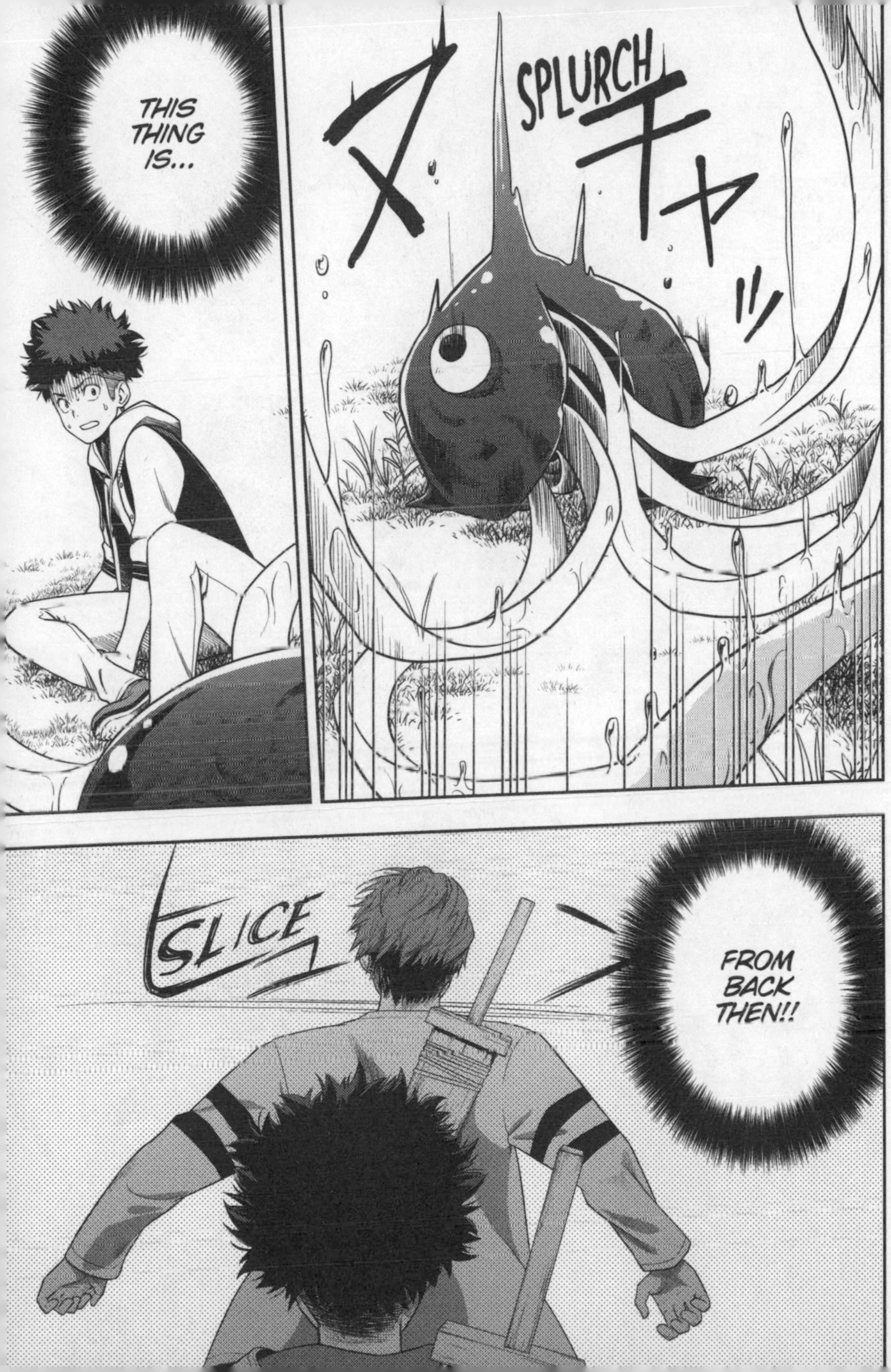
SPLURCH
ヌチャッ
THIS THING IS...
FROM BACK THEN!!
SLICE

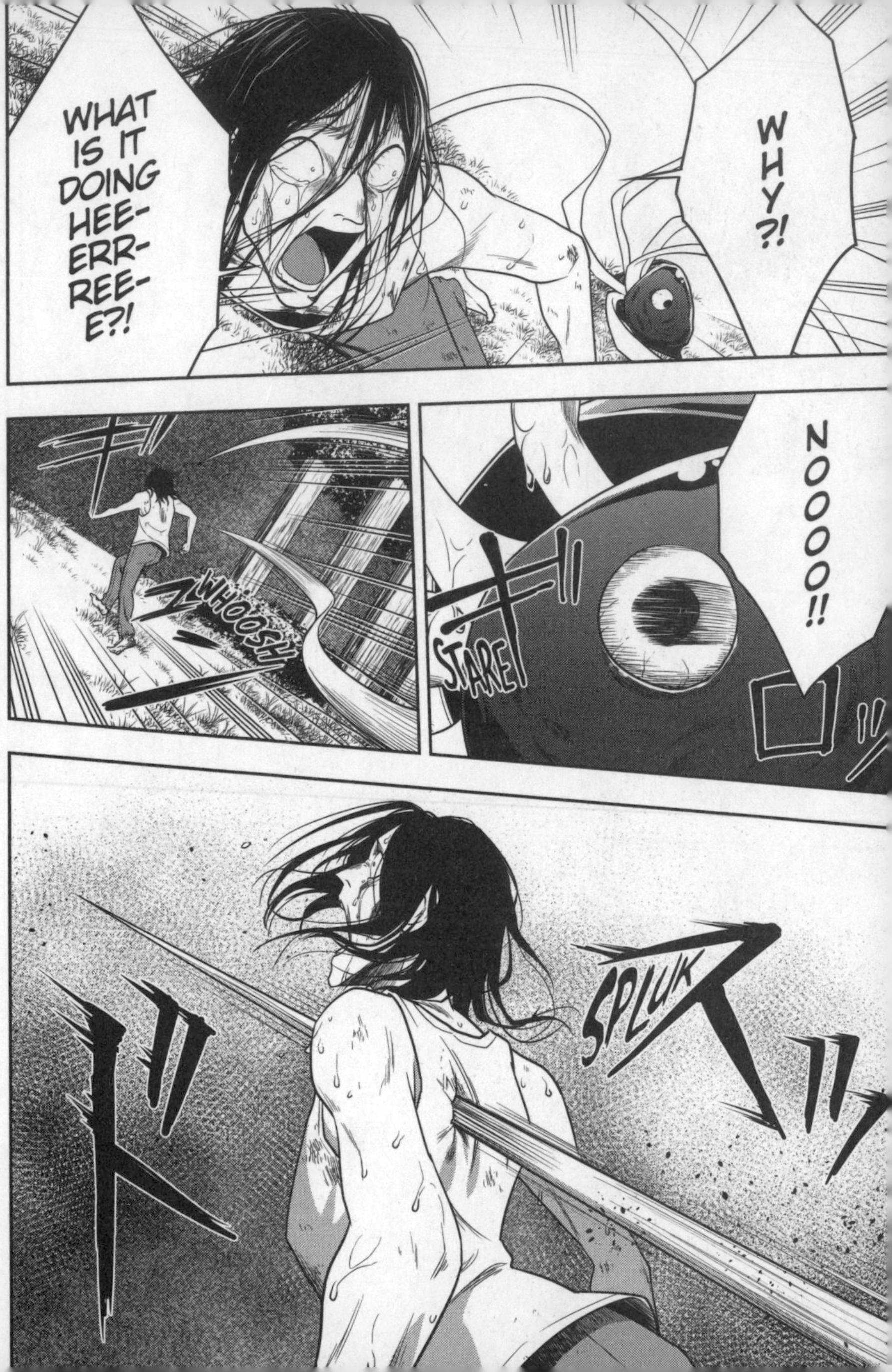
WHY?!
WHAT IS IT DOING HEE-ERR-REE-E?!
NOOOOO!!
STARE
WHOOSH
SPLUK

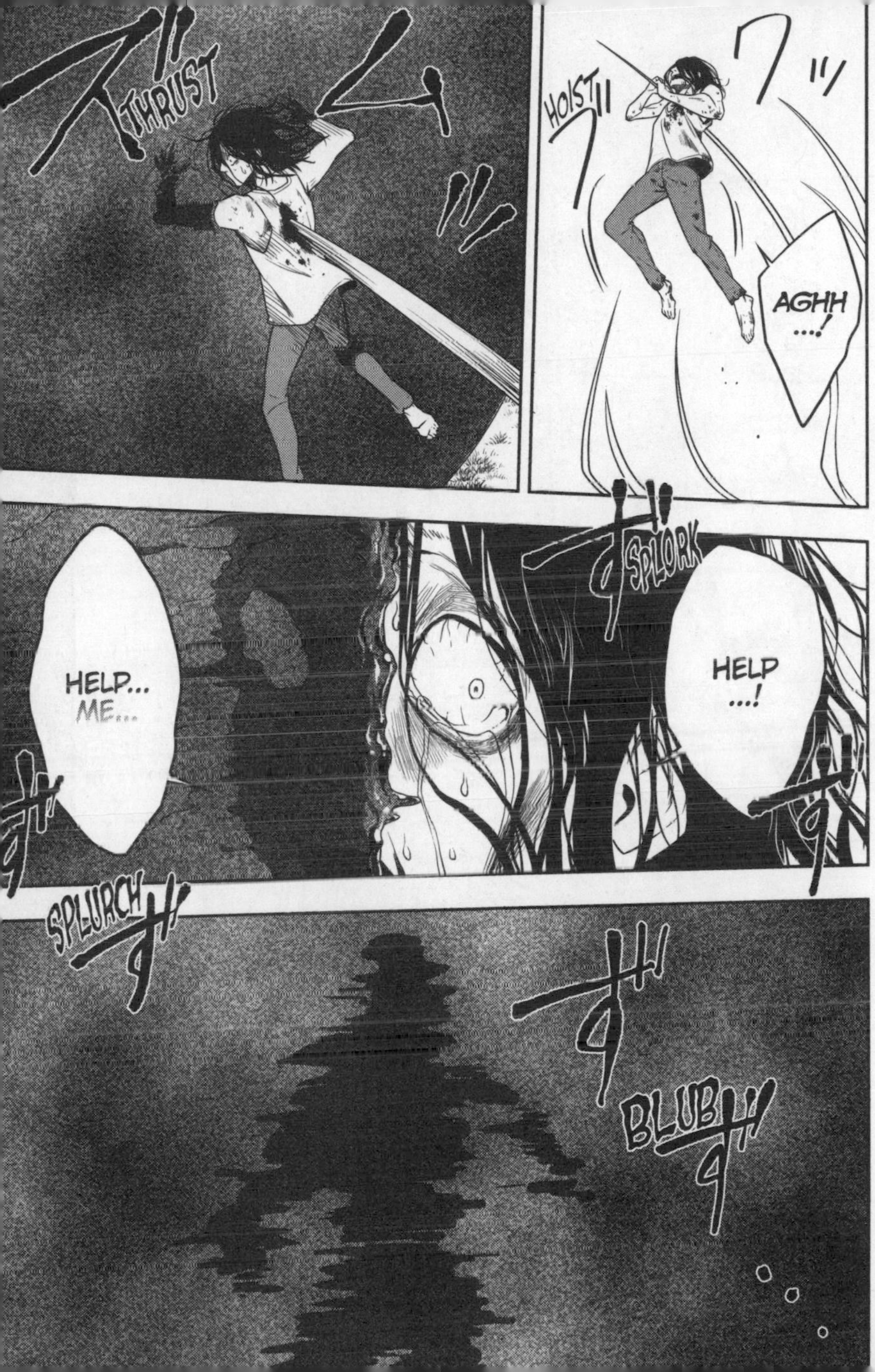
HOIST
AGHH ...!
THRUST
SPLORK
HELP ...!
HELP... ME...
SPLURCH
BLUB

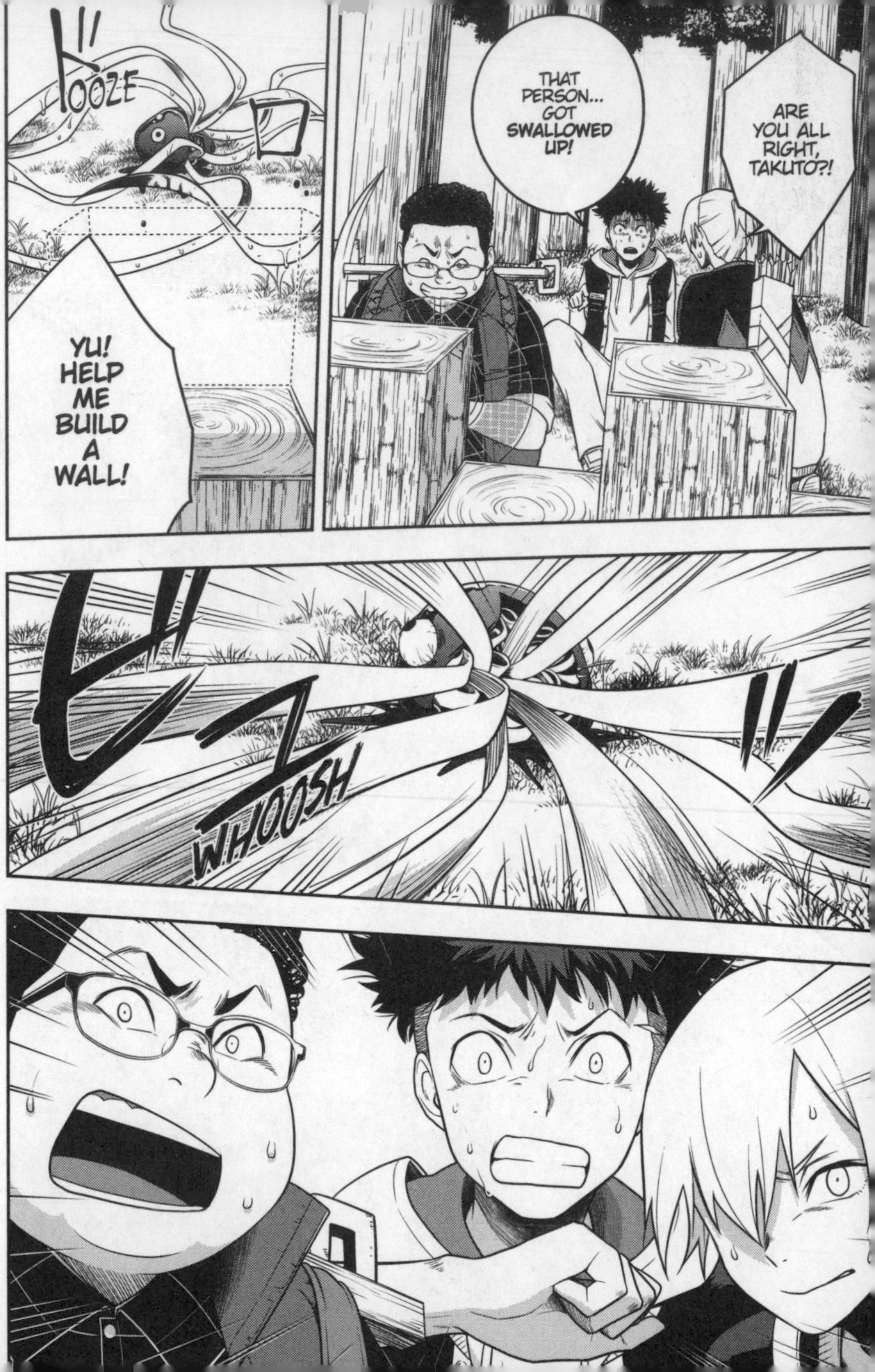
ARE YOU ALL RIGHT, TAKUTO?!
THAT PERSON... GOT SWALLOWED UP!
OOZE
YU! HELP ME BUILD A WALL!
WHOOSH

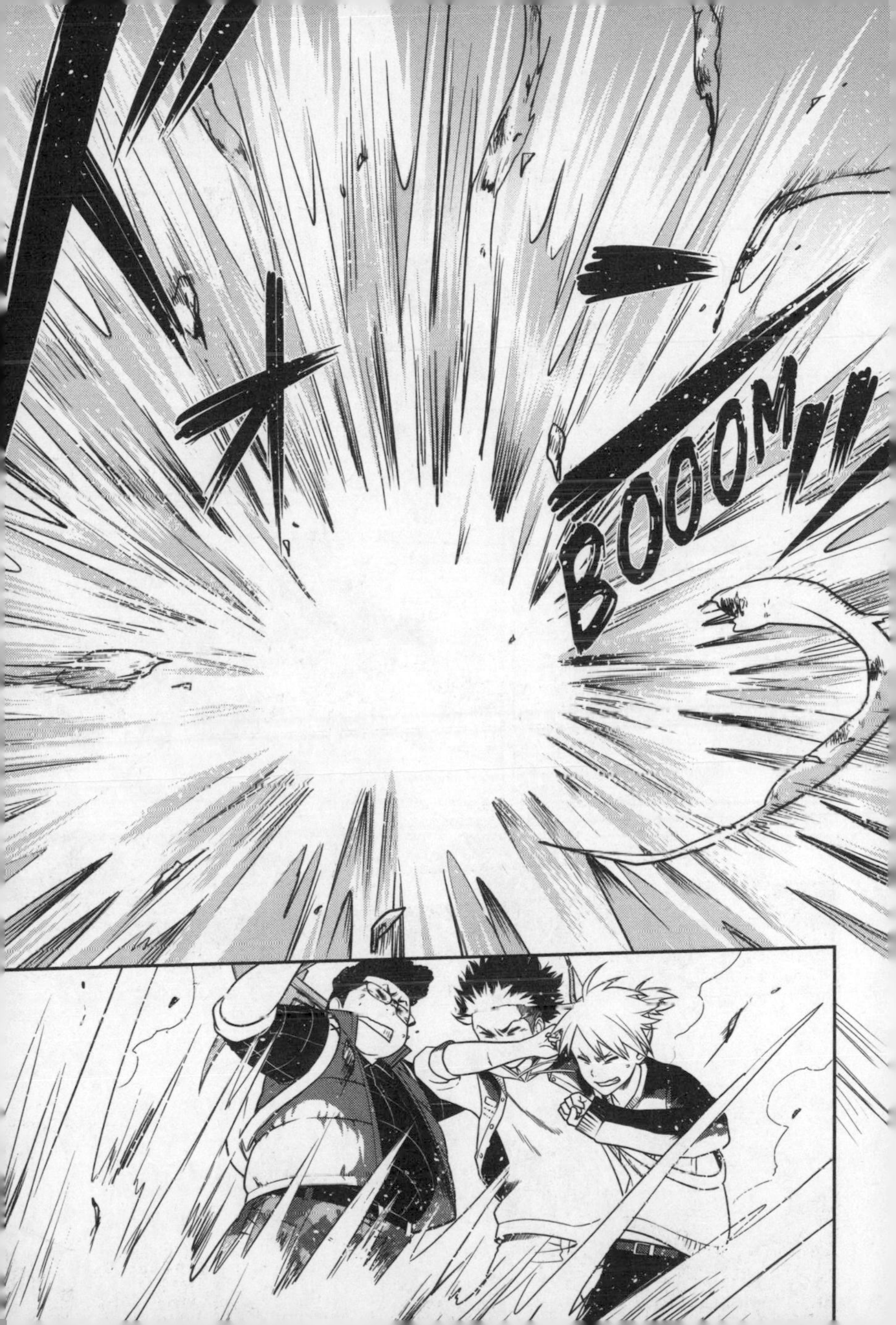
BOOOM!!

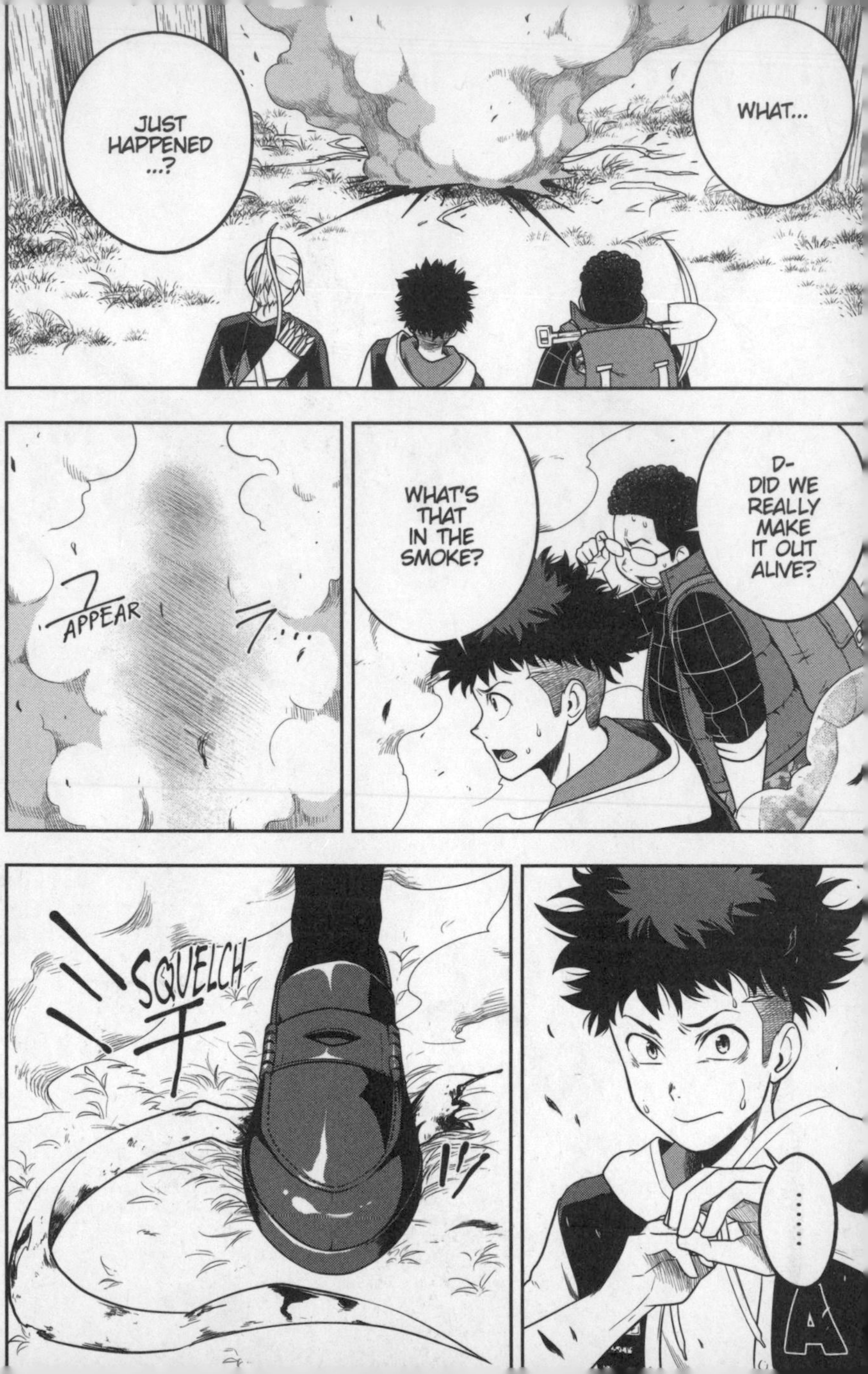
WHAT...
JUST HAPPENED ...?
D- DID WE REALLY MAKE IT OUT ALIVE?
WHAT'S THAT IN THE SMOKE?
APPEAR
......
SQUELCH

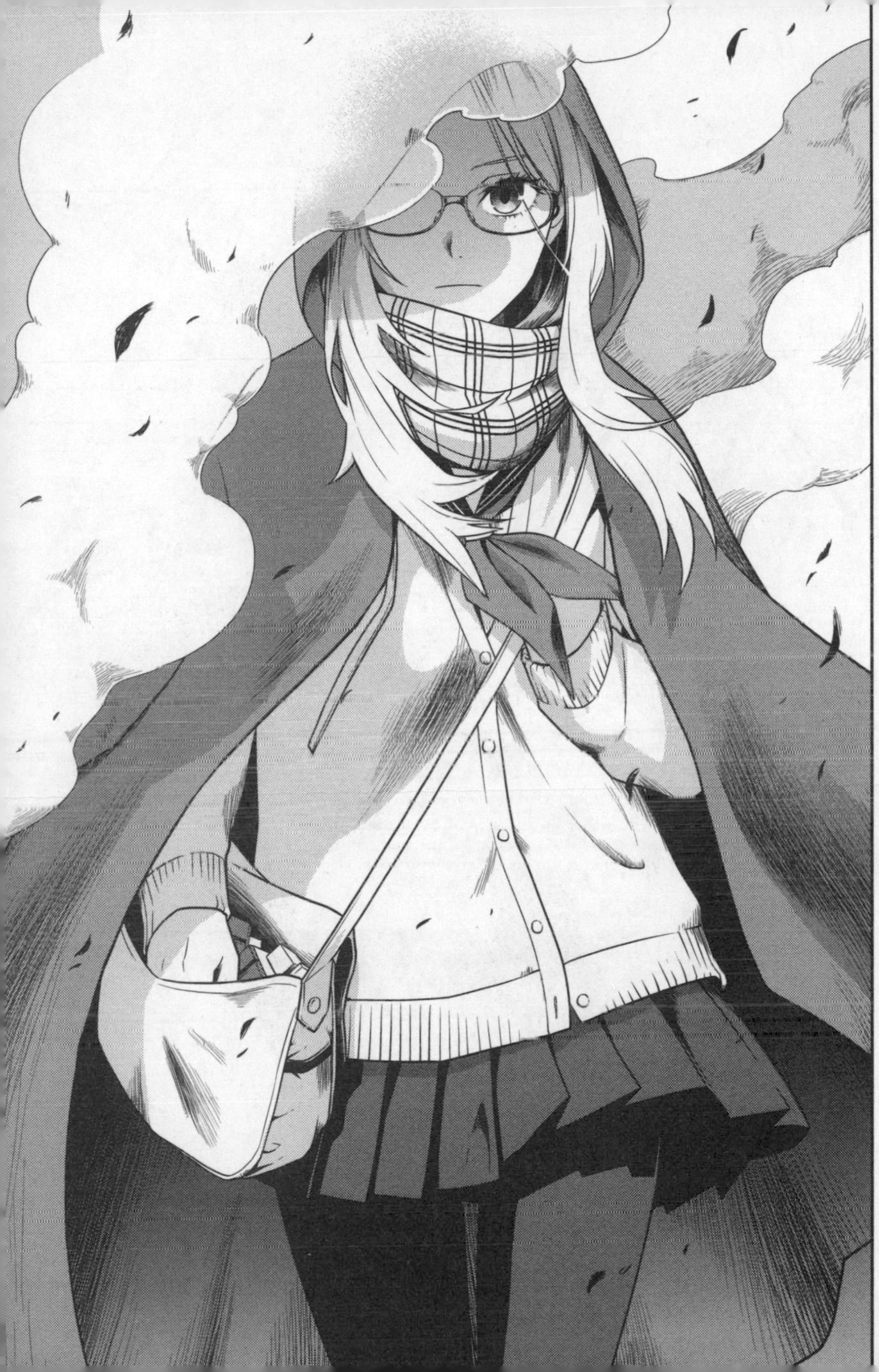

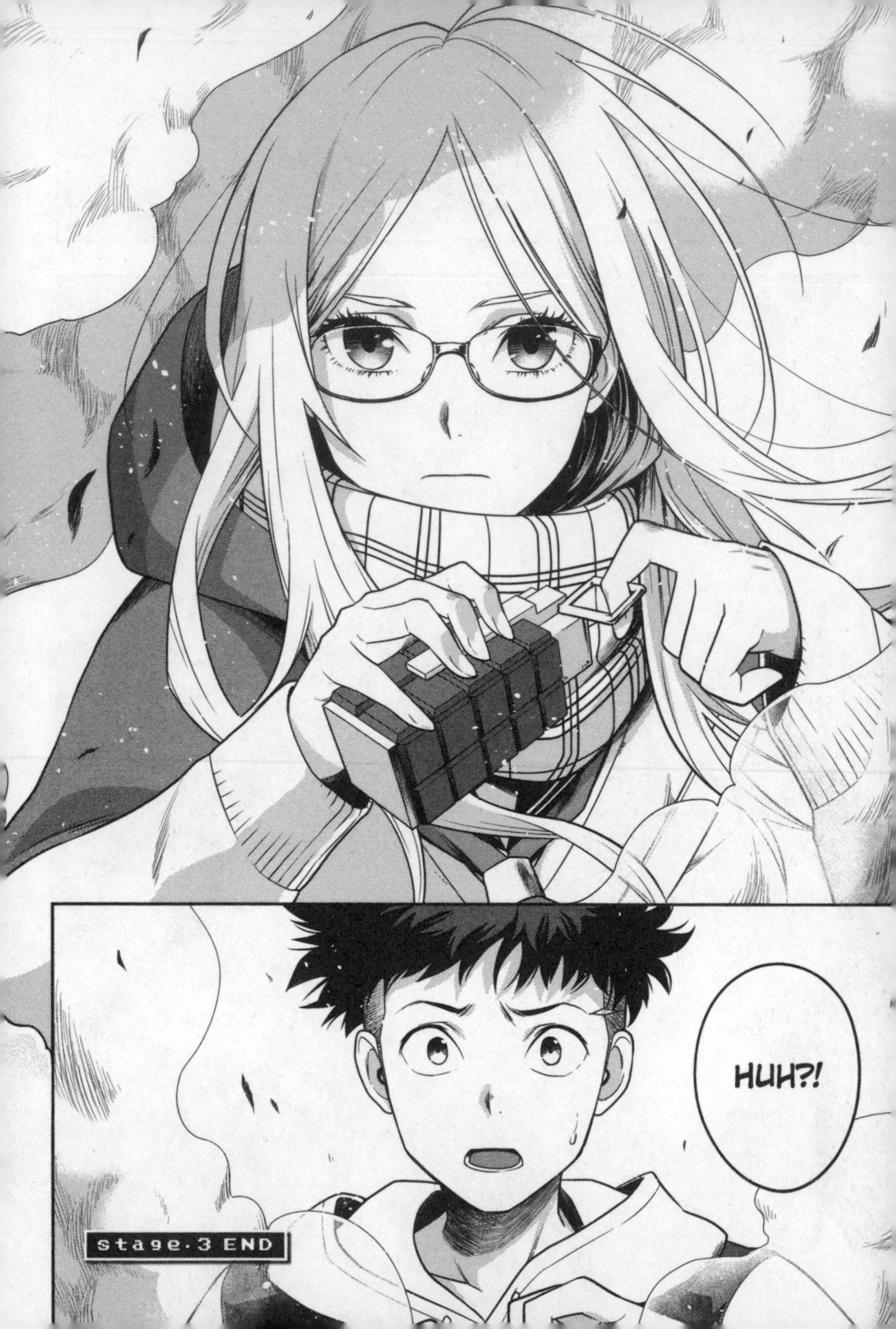
HUH?!
stage.3 END

Stage.4

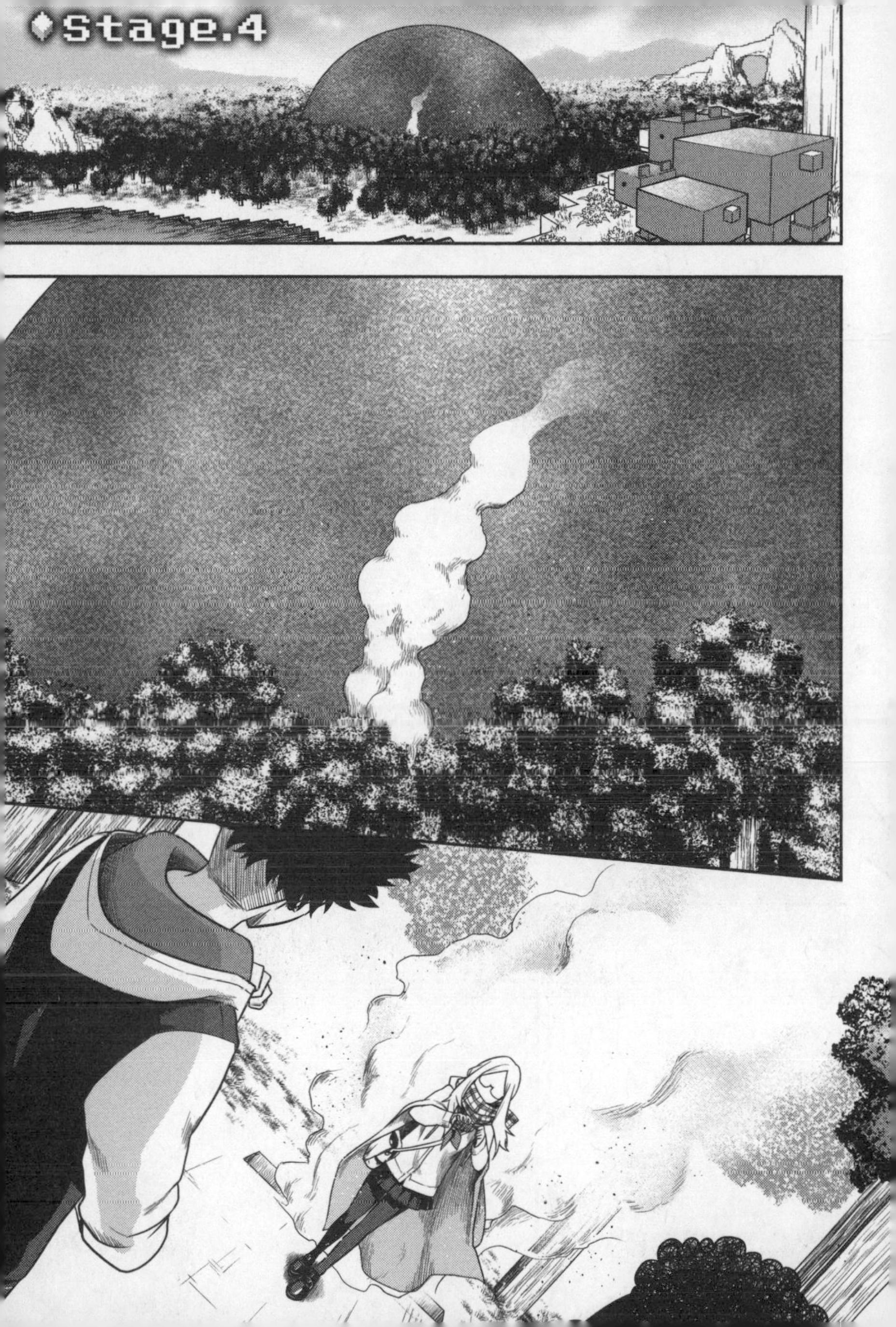

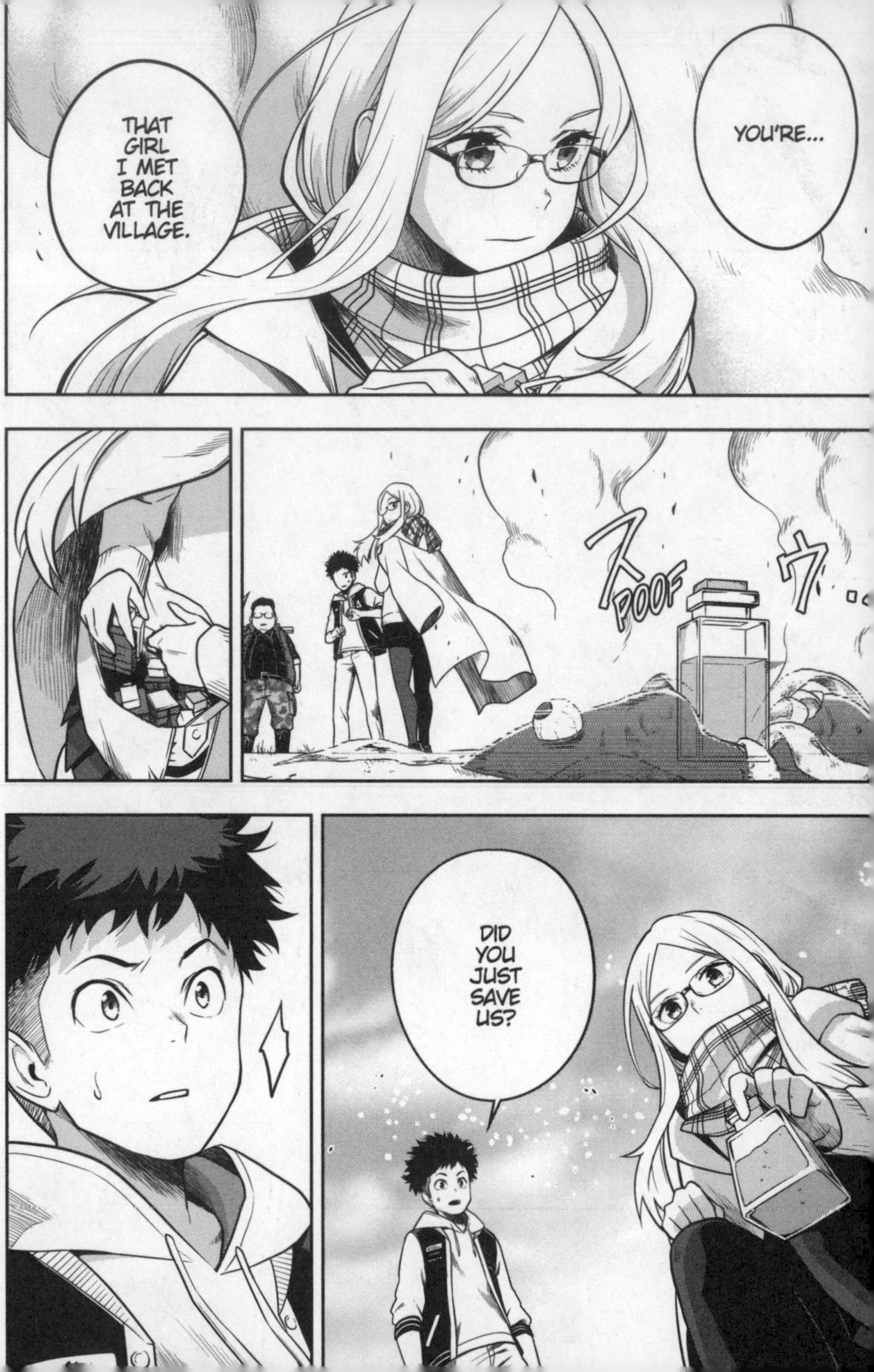
YOU'RE...
THAT GIRL I MET BACK AT THE VILLAGE.
POOF
DID YOU JUST SAVE US?

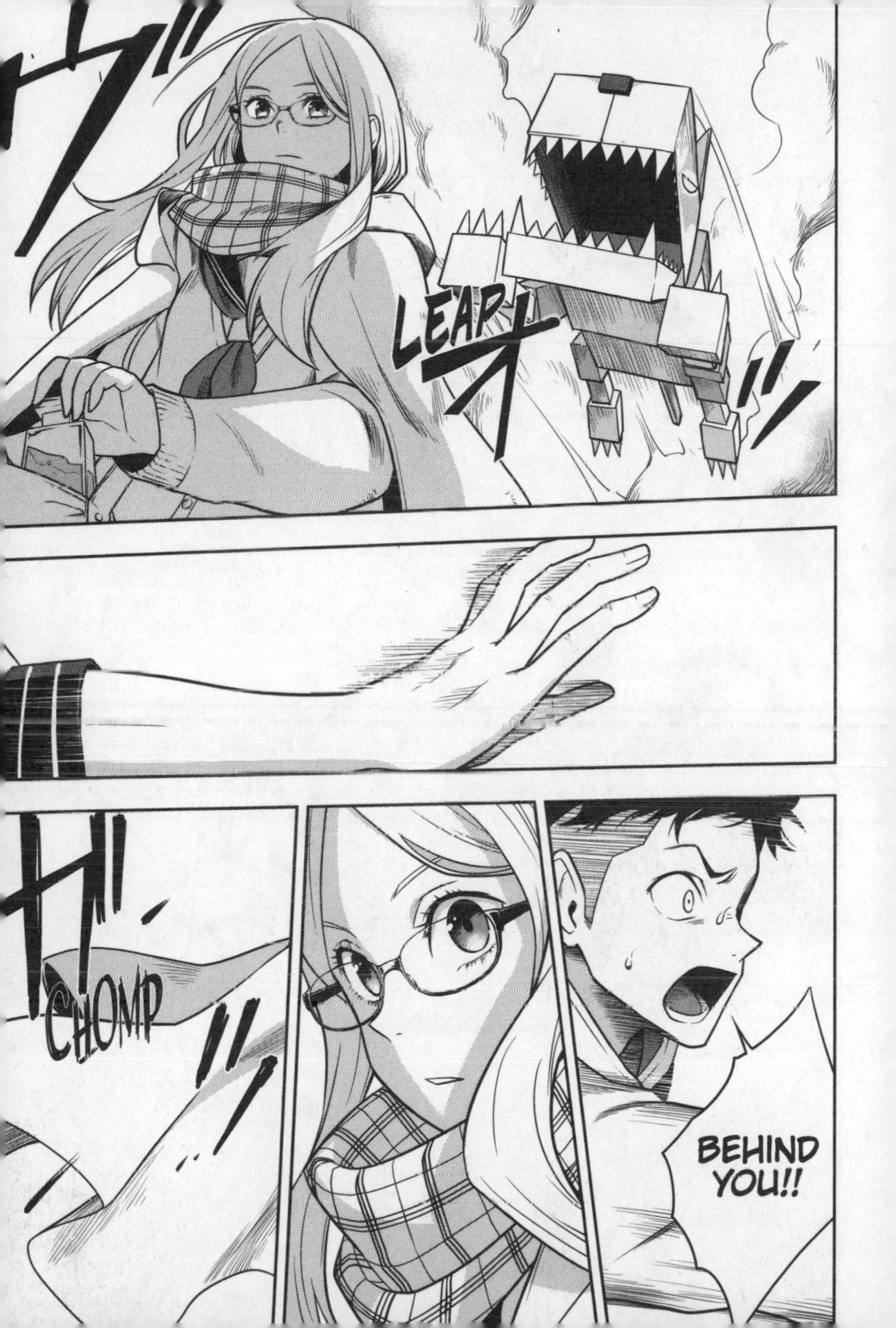
LEAP
CHOMP
BEHIND YOU!!

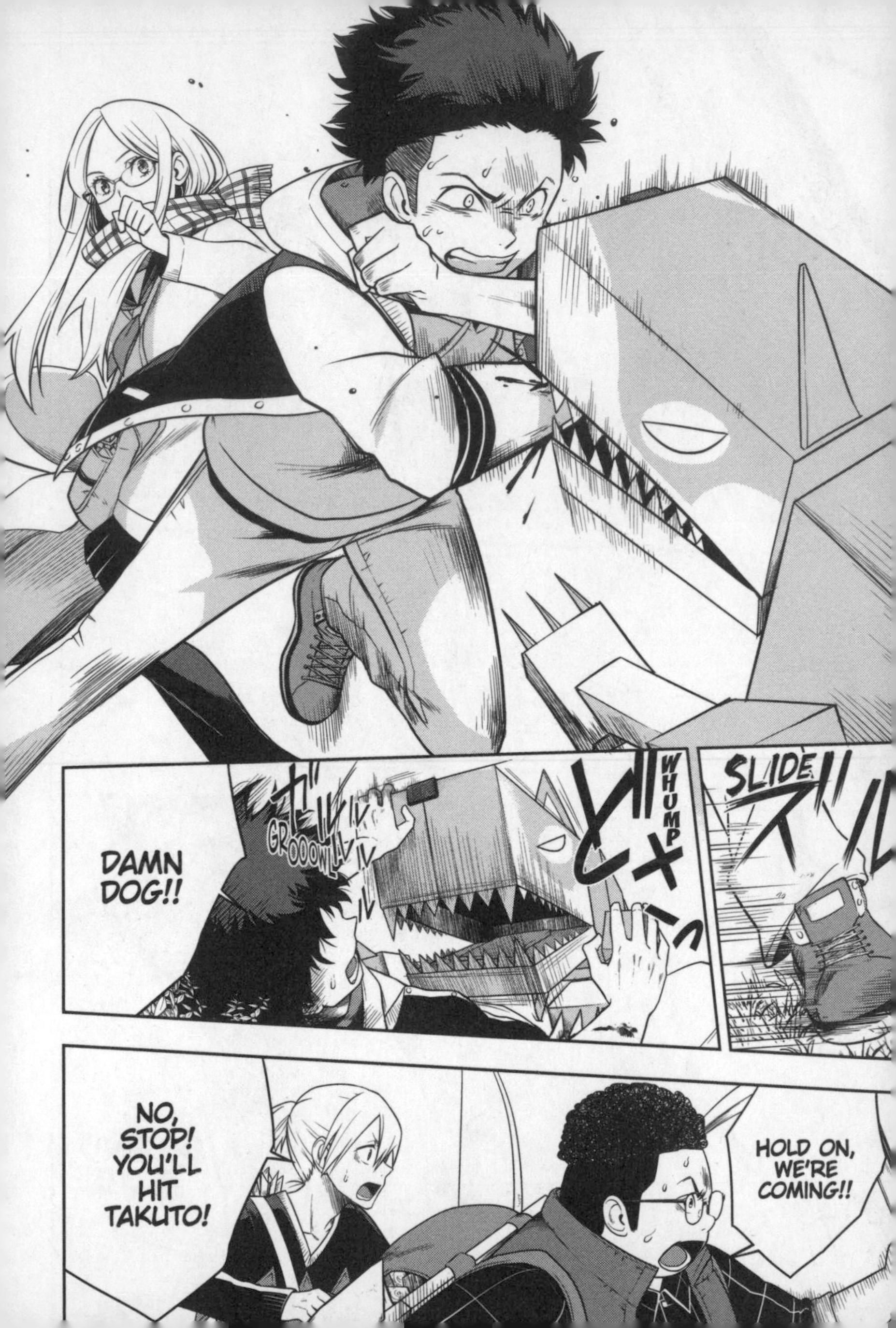
SLIDE
WHUMP
GROOOWL
DAMN DOG!!
HOLD ON, WE'RE COMING!!
NO, STOP! YOU'LL HIT TAKUTO!

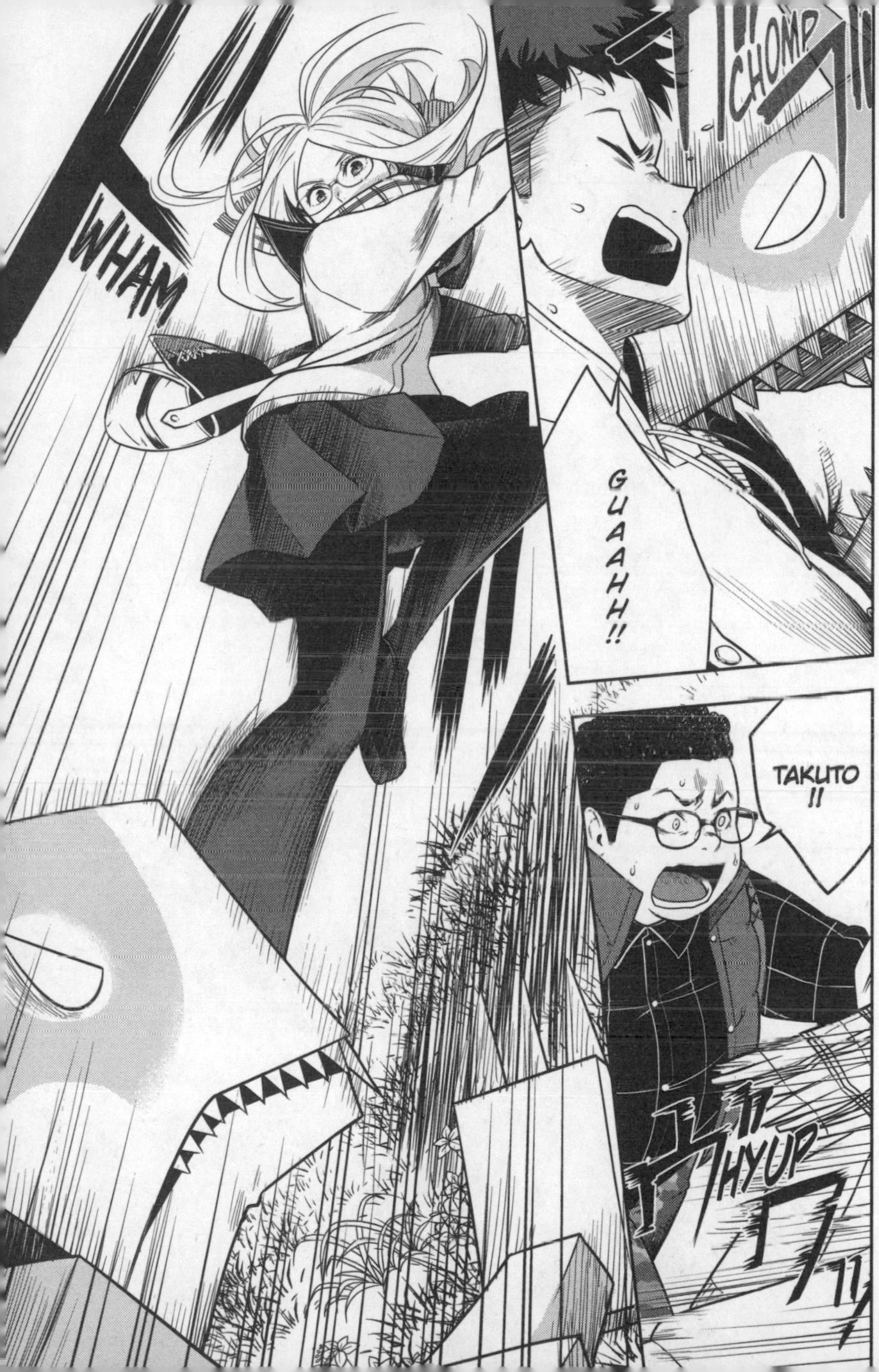
CHOMP
GUAAAHH!!
WHAM
TAKUTO !!
HYUP

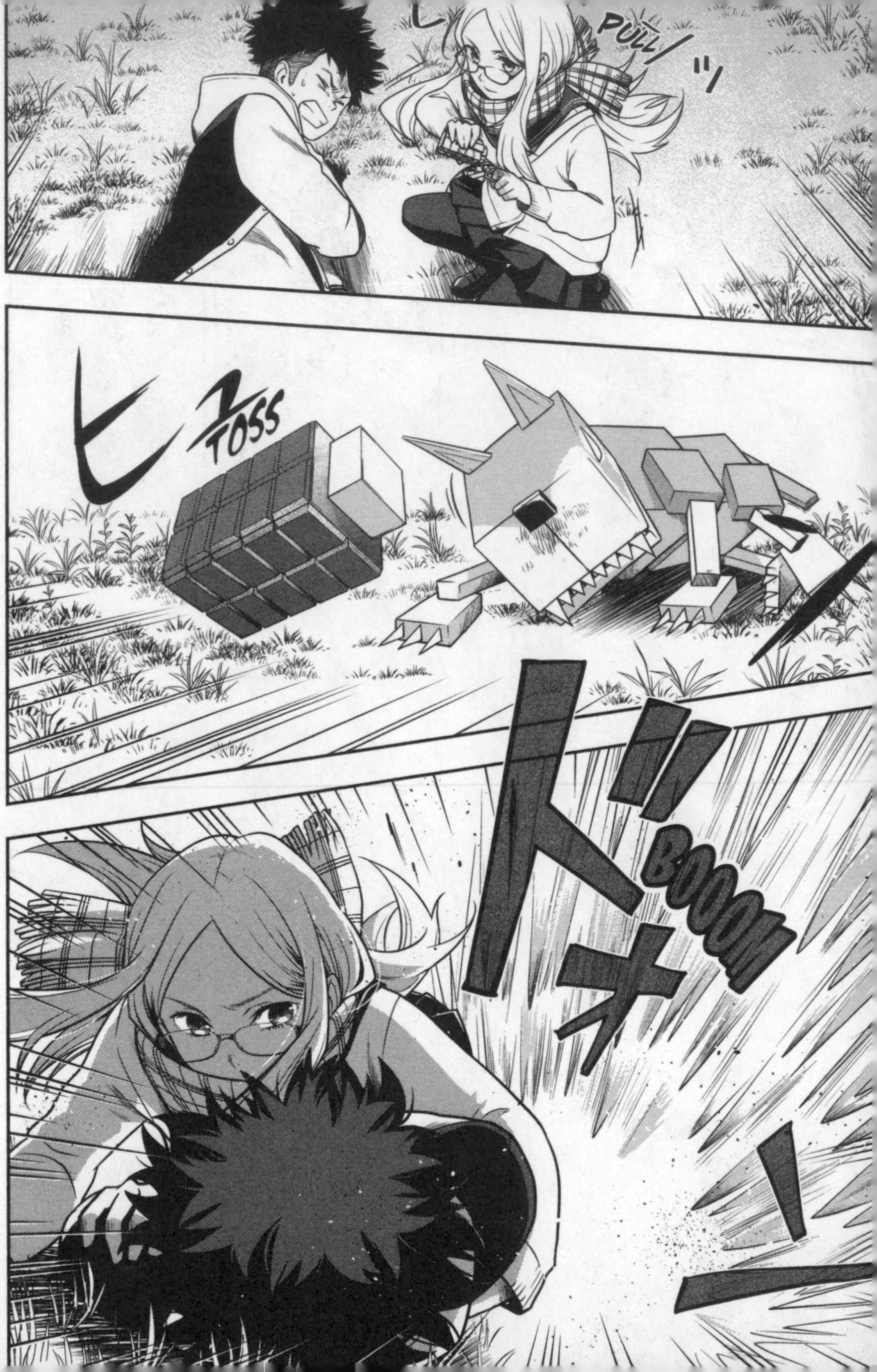
PULL
TOSS
BOOOM

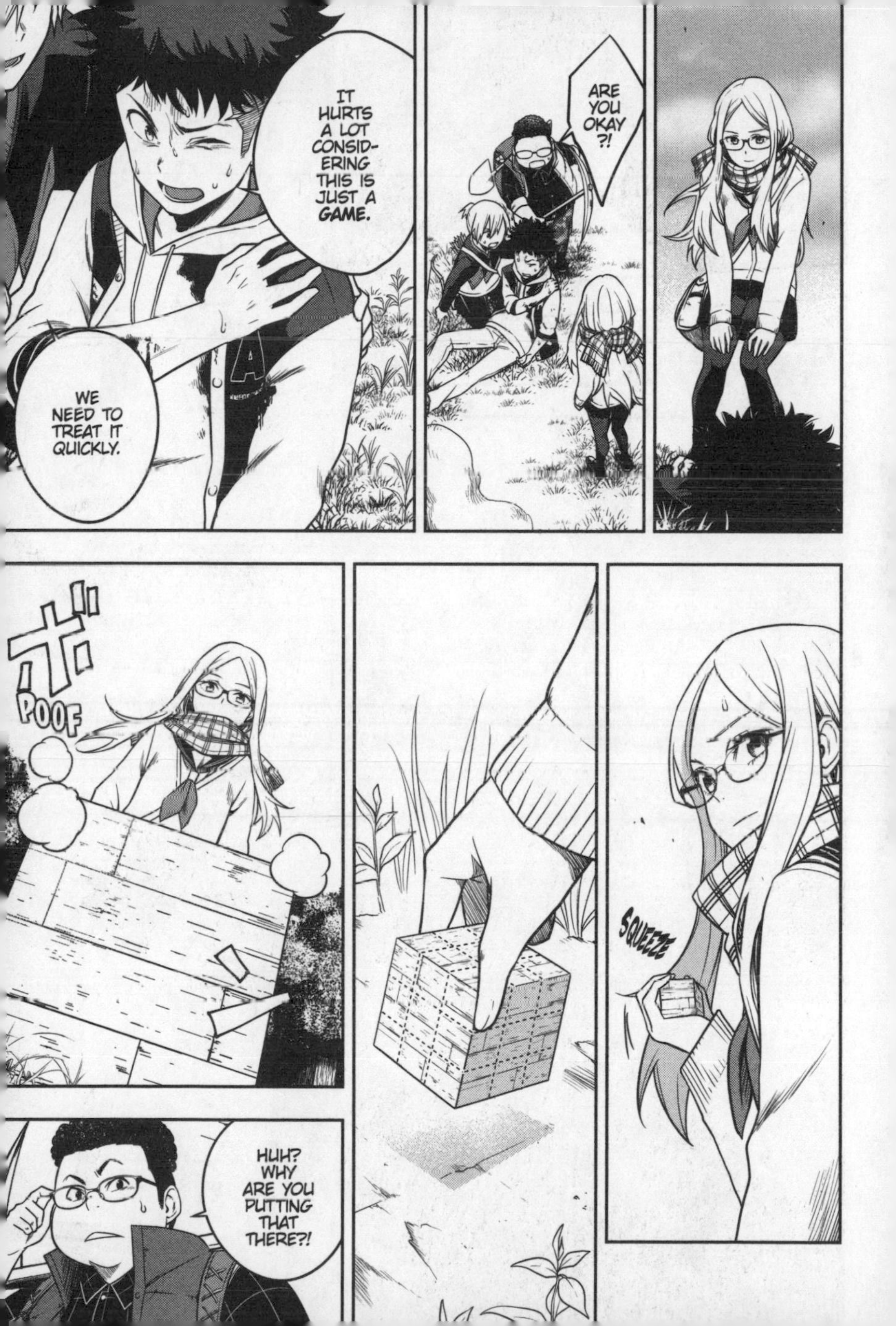
ARE YOU OKAY?!
IT HURTS A LOT CONSIDERING THIS IS JUST A GAME.
WE NEED TO TREAT IT QUICKLY.
SQUEEZE
POOF
HUH? WHY ARE YOU PUTTING THAT THERE?!

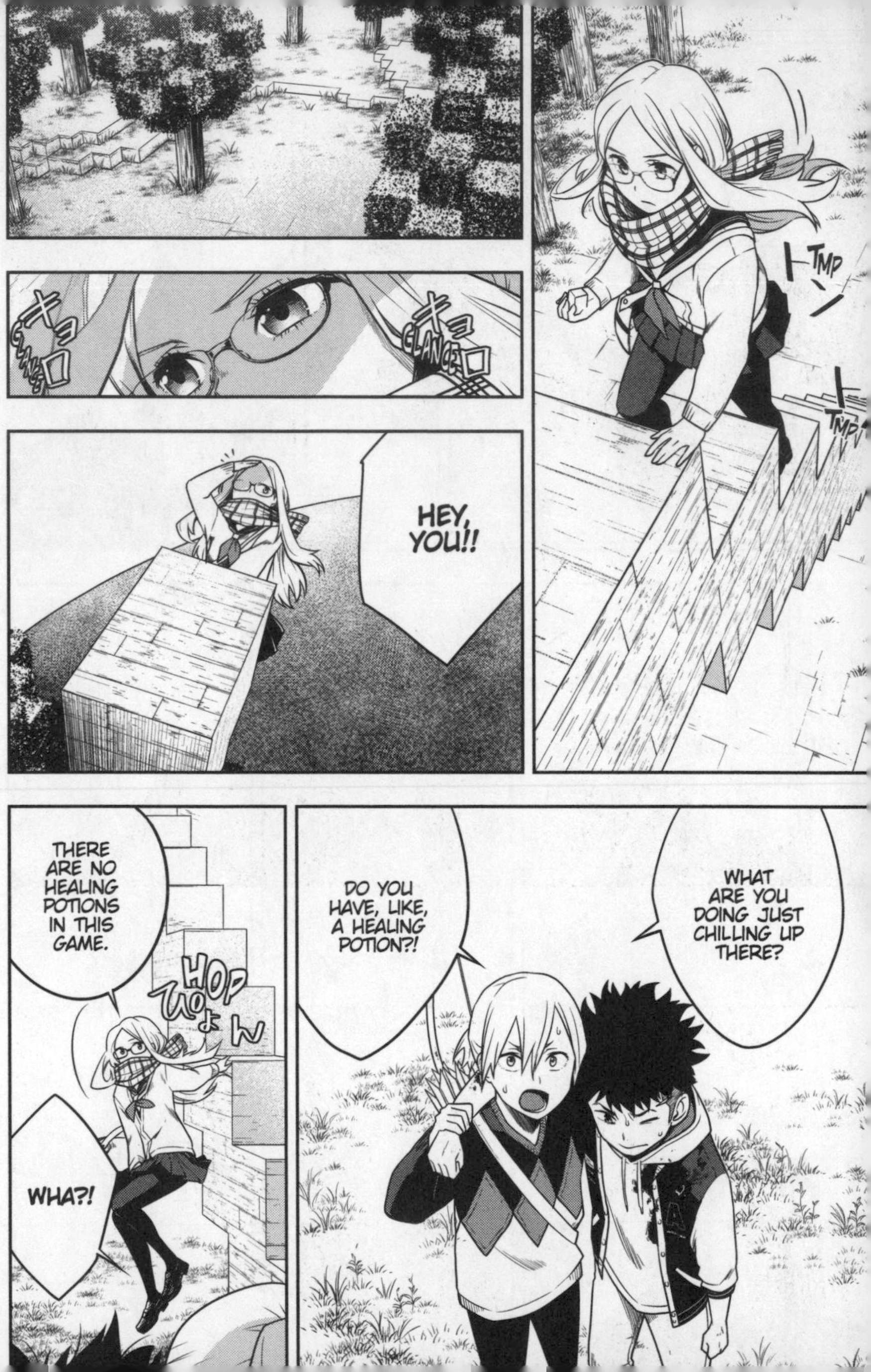

TMP
TMP
GLANCE
GLANCE
HEY, YOU!!
WHAT ARE YOU DOING JUST CHILLING UP THERE?
DO YOU HAVE, LIKE, A HEALING POTION?!
THERE ARE NO HEALING POTIONS IN THIS GAME.
HOP
WHA?!

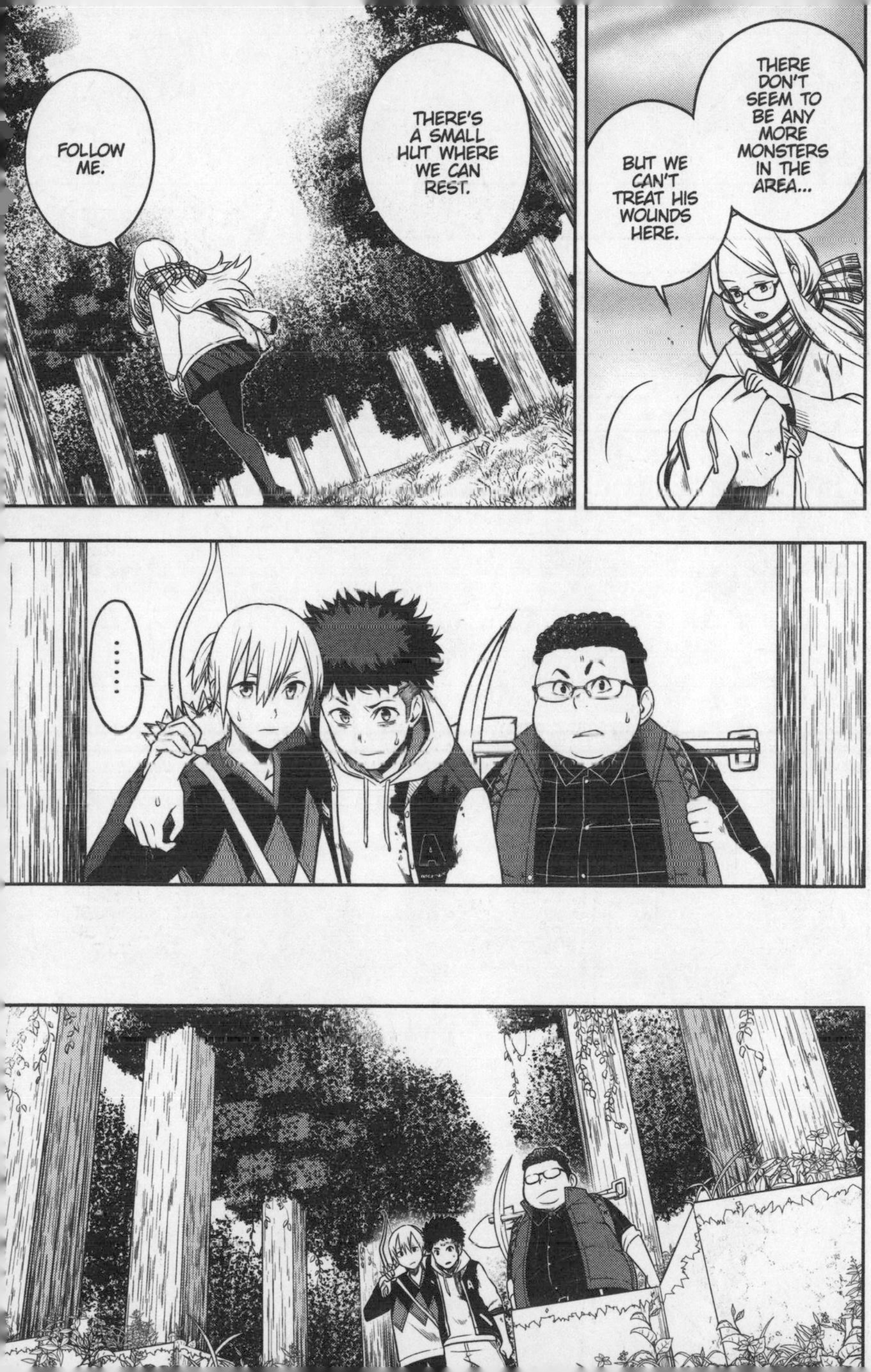
THERE DON'T SEEM TO BE ANY MORE MONSTERS IN THE AREA...
BUT WE CAN'T TREAT HIS WOUNDS HERE.
THERE'S A SMALL HUT WHERE WE CAN REST.
FOLLOW ME.
......

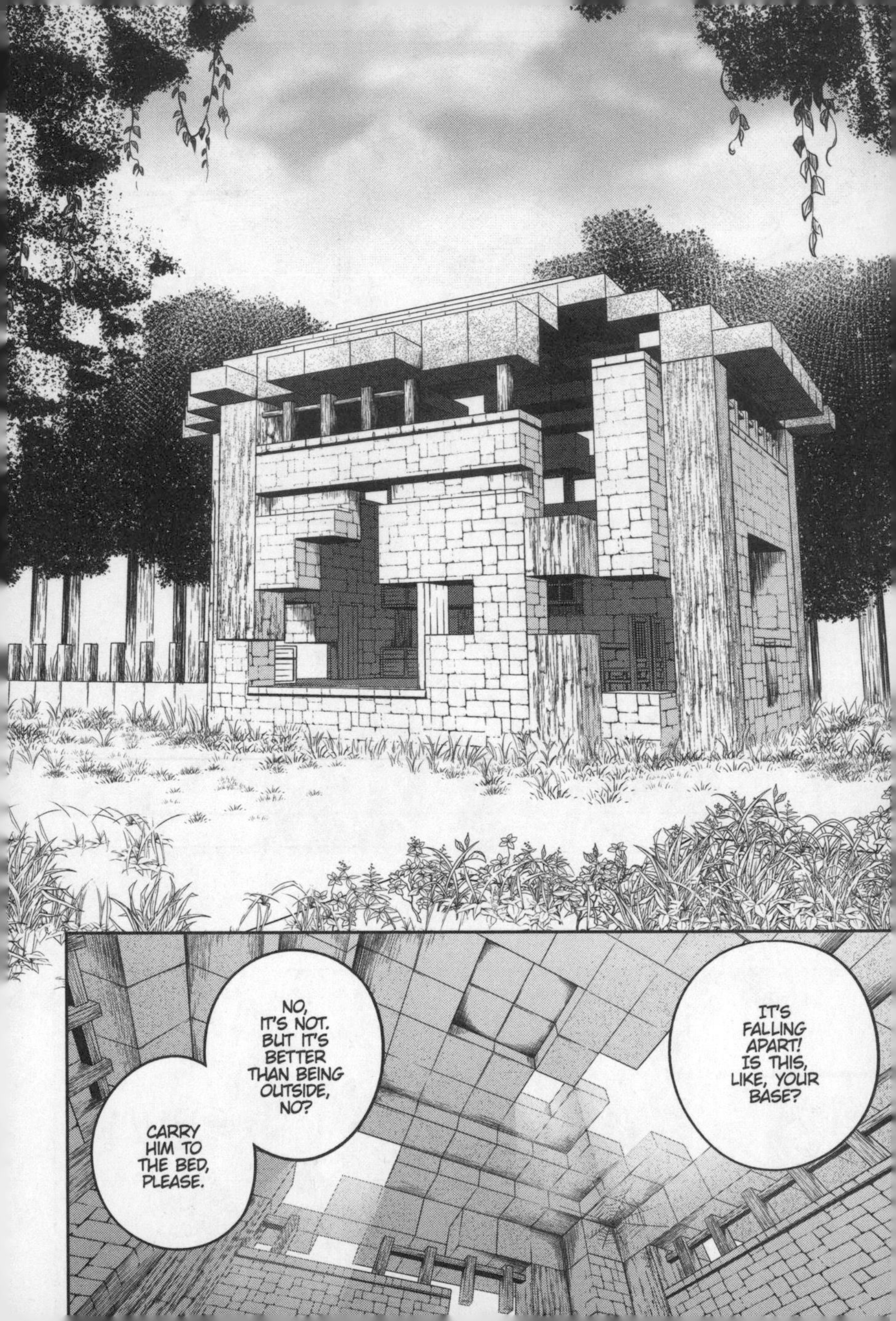
IT'S FALLING APART! IS THIS, LIKE, YOUR BASE?
NO, IT'S NOT. BUT IT'S BETTER THAN BEING OUTSIDE, NO?
CARRY HIM TO THE BED, PLEASE.

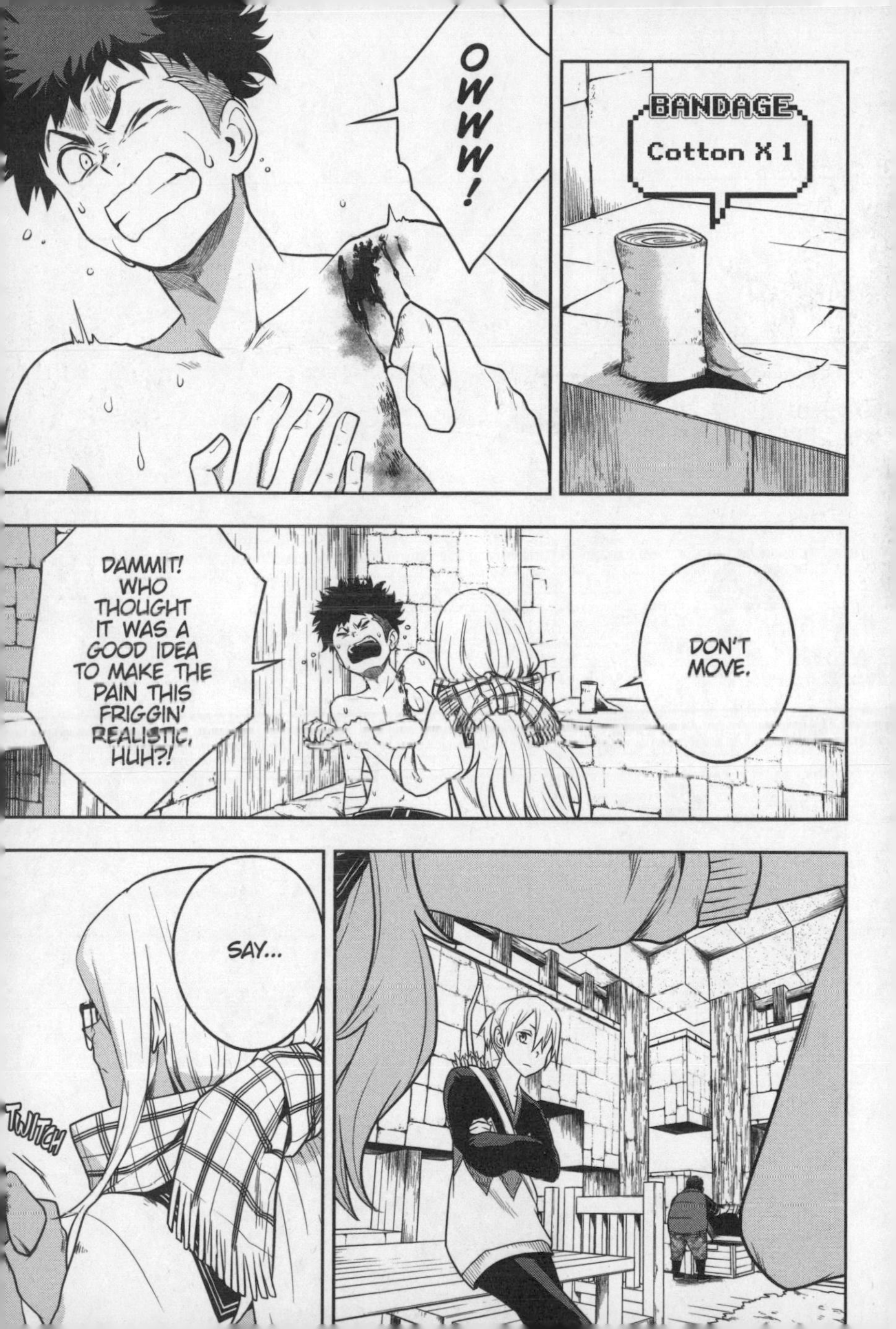
BANDAGE
Cotton X 1
OWWW!
DAMMIT! WHO THOUGHT IT WAS A GOOD IDEA TO MAKE THE PAIN THIS FRIGGIN' REALISTIC, HUH?!
DON'T MOVE.
SAY...
TWITCH

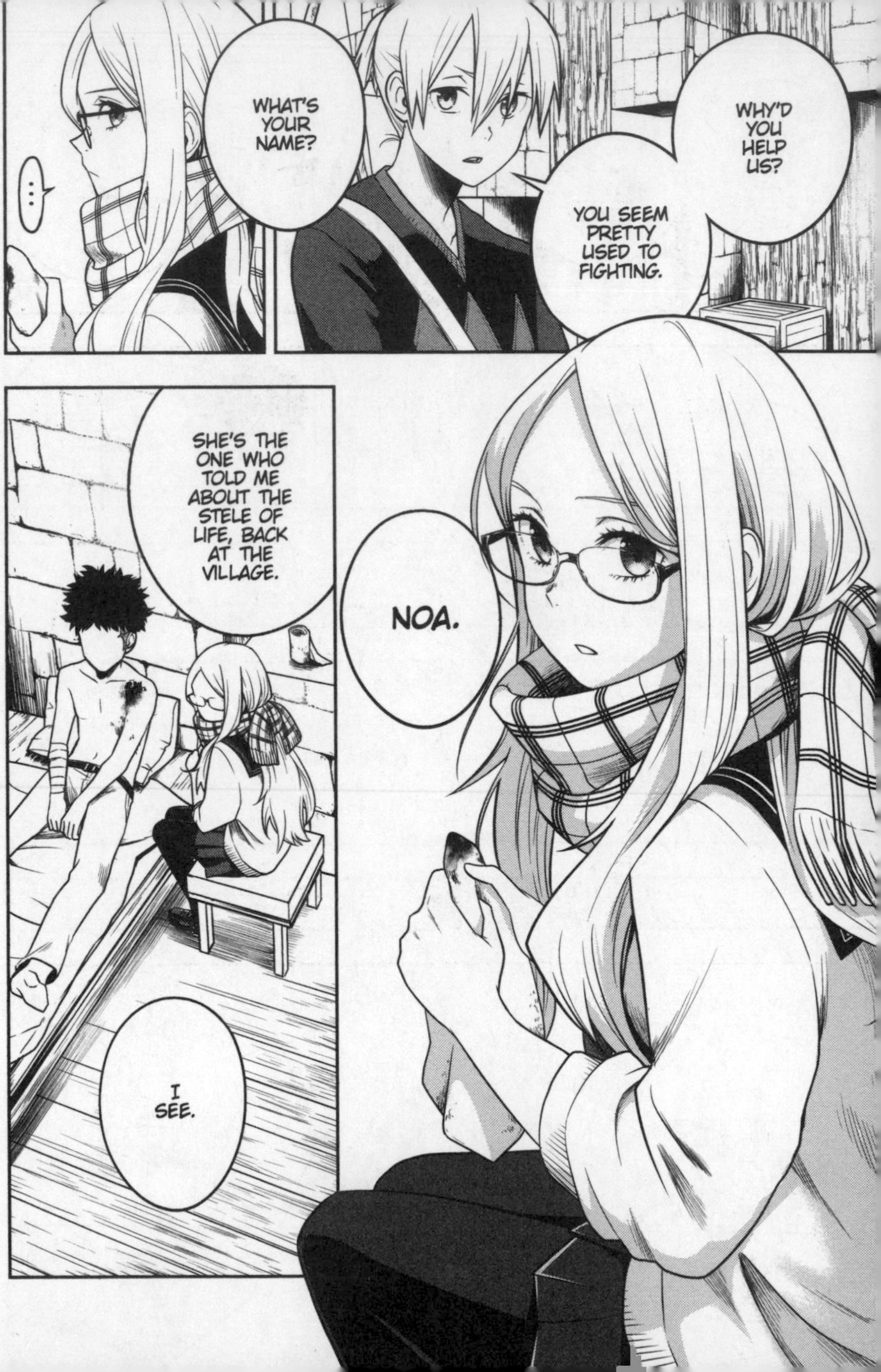
WHY'D YOU HELP US?
YOU SEEM PRETTY USED TO FIGHTING.
WHAT'S YOUR NAME?
...
NOA.
SHE'S THE ONE WHO TOLD ME ABOUT THE STELE OF LIFE, BACK AT THE VILLAGE.
I SEE.

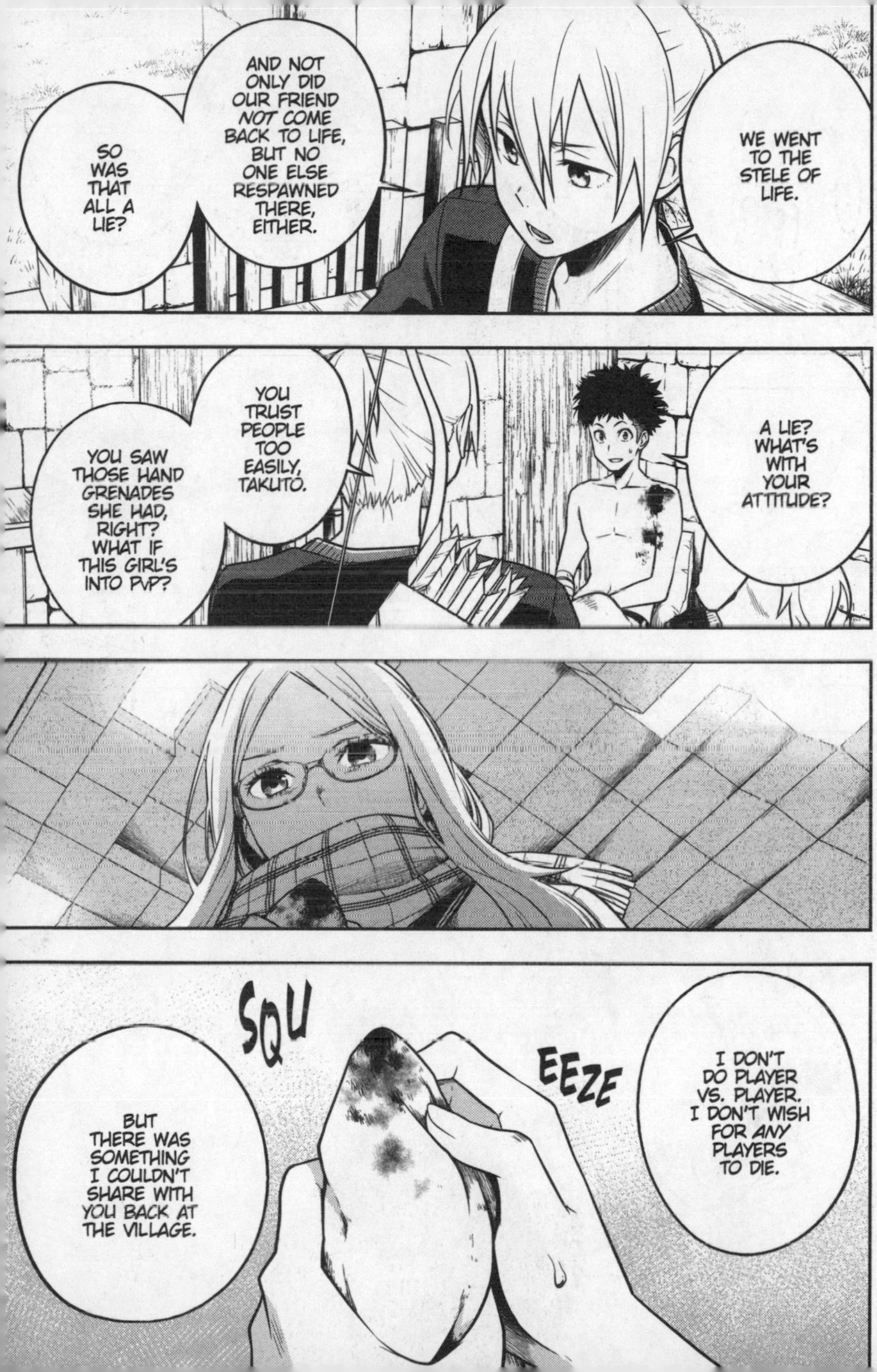
WE WENT TO THE STELE OF LIFE.
AND NOT ONLY DID OUR FRIEND *NOT* COME BACK TO LIFE, BUT NO ONE ELSE RESPAWNED THERE, EITHER.
SO WAS THAT ALL A LIE?
A LIE? WHAT'S WITH YOUR ATTITUDE?
YOU TRUST PEOPLE TOO EASILY, TAKUTO.
YOU SAW THOSE HAND GRENADES SHE HAD, RIGHT? WHAT IF THIS GIRL'S INTO PVP?
I DON'T DO PLAYER VS. PLAYER. I DON'T WISH FOR *ANY* PLAYERS TO DIE.
SQU
EEZE
BUT THERE WAS SOMETHING I COULDN'T SHARE WITH YOU BACK AT THE VILLAGE.

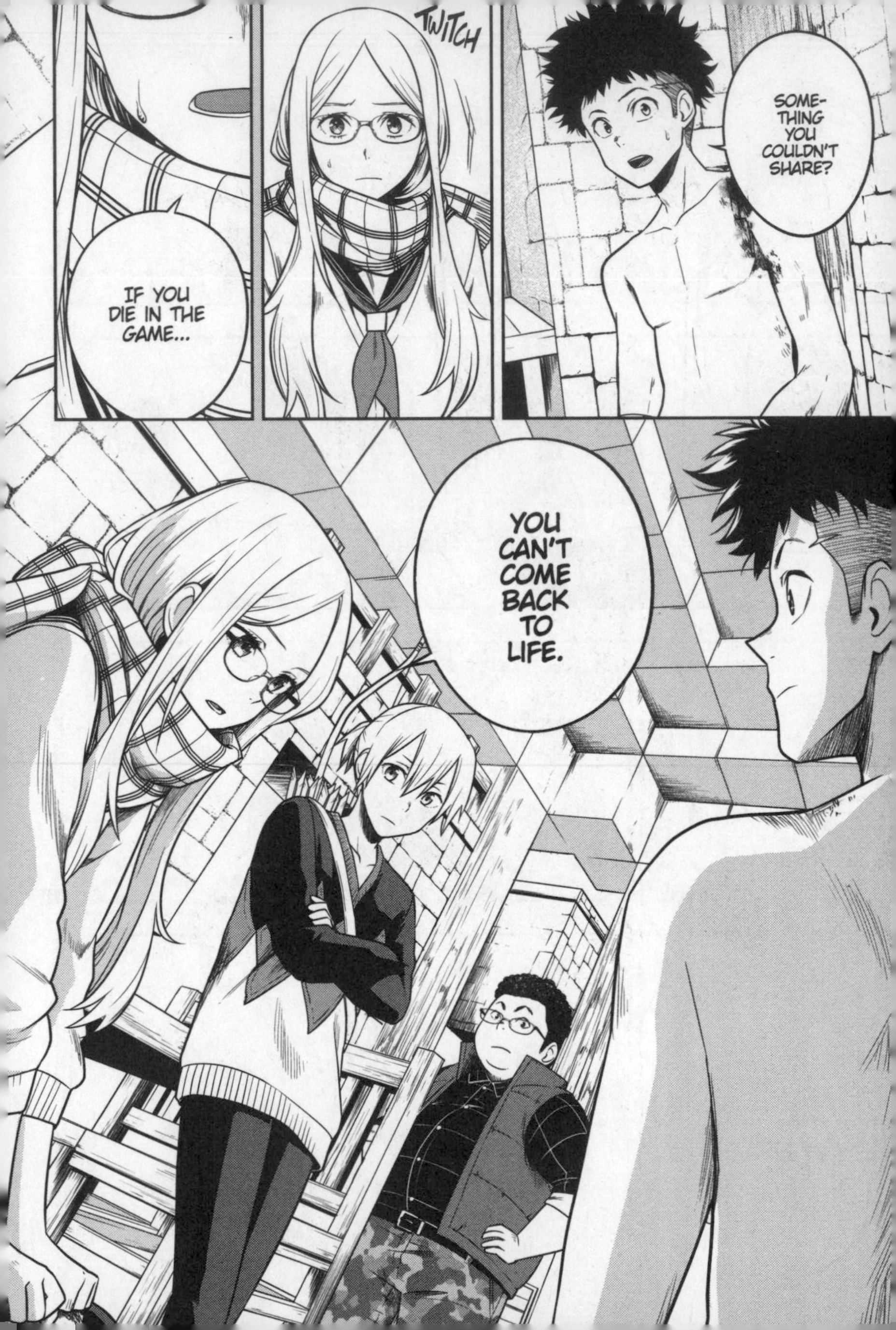
SOME-THING YOU COULDN'T SHARE?
TWITCH
IF YOU DIE IN THE GAME...
YOU CAN'T COME BACK TO LIFE.

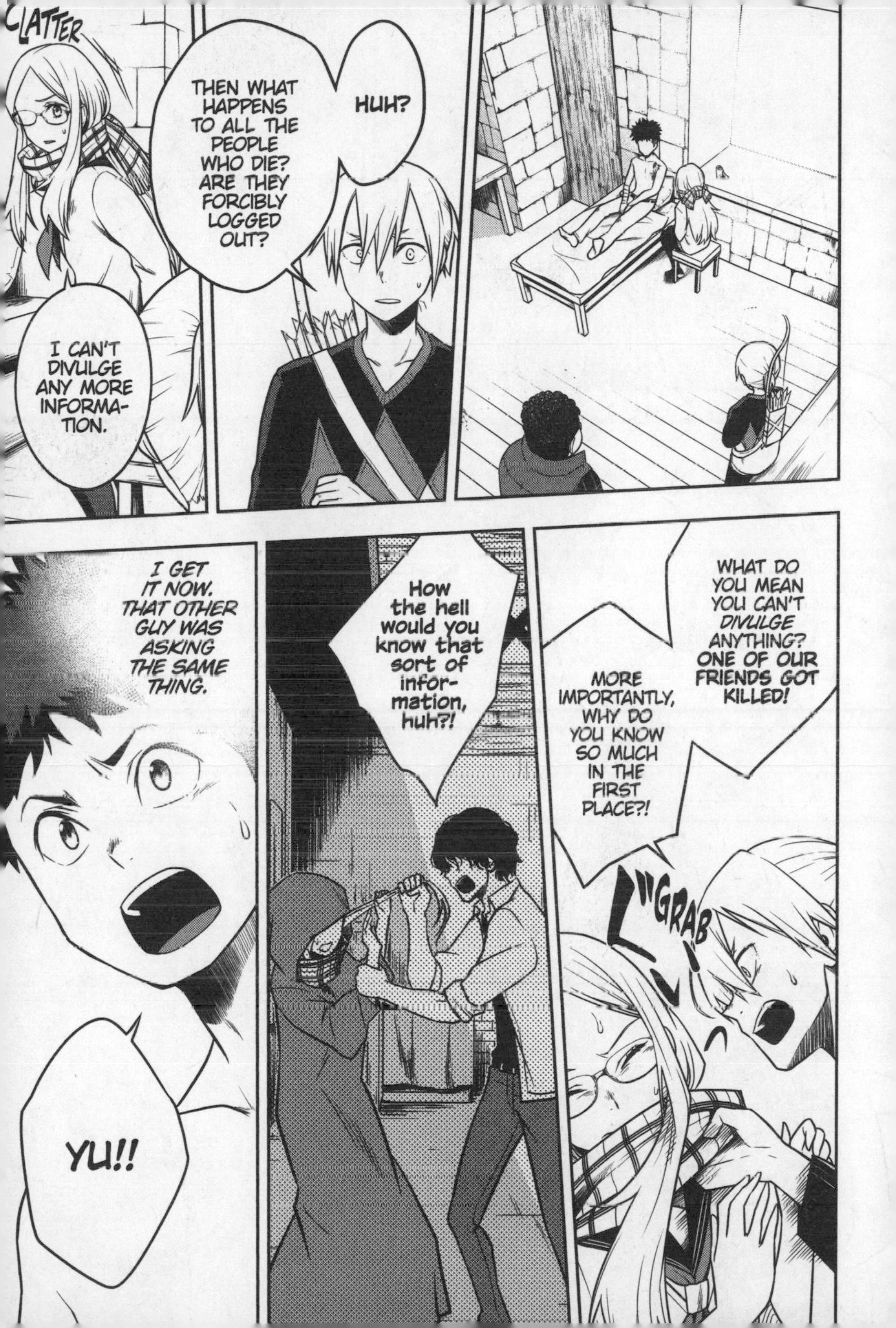
HUH?
THEN WHAT HAPPENS TO ALL THE PEOPLE WHO DIE? ARE THEY FORCIBLY LOGGED OUT?
CLATTER
I CAN'T DIVULGE ANY MORE INFORMATION.
WHAT DO YOU MEAN YOU CAN'T DIVULGE ANYTHING? ONE OF OUR FRIENDS GOT KILLED!
MORE IMPORTANTLY, WHY DO YOU KNOW SO MUCH IN THE FIRST PLACE?!
GRAB
How the hell would you know that sort of information, huh?!
I GET IT NOW. THAT OTHER GUY WAS ASKING THE SAME THING.
YU!!

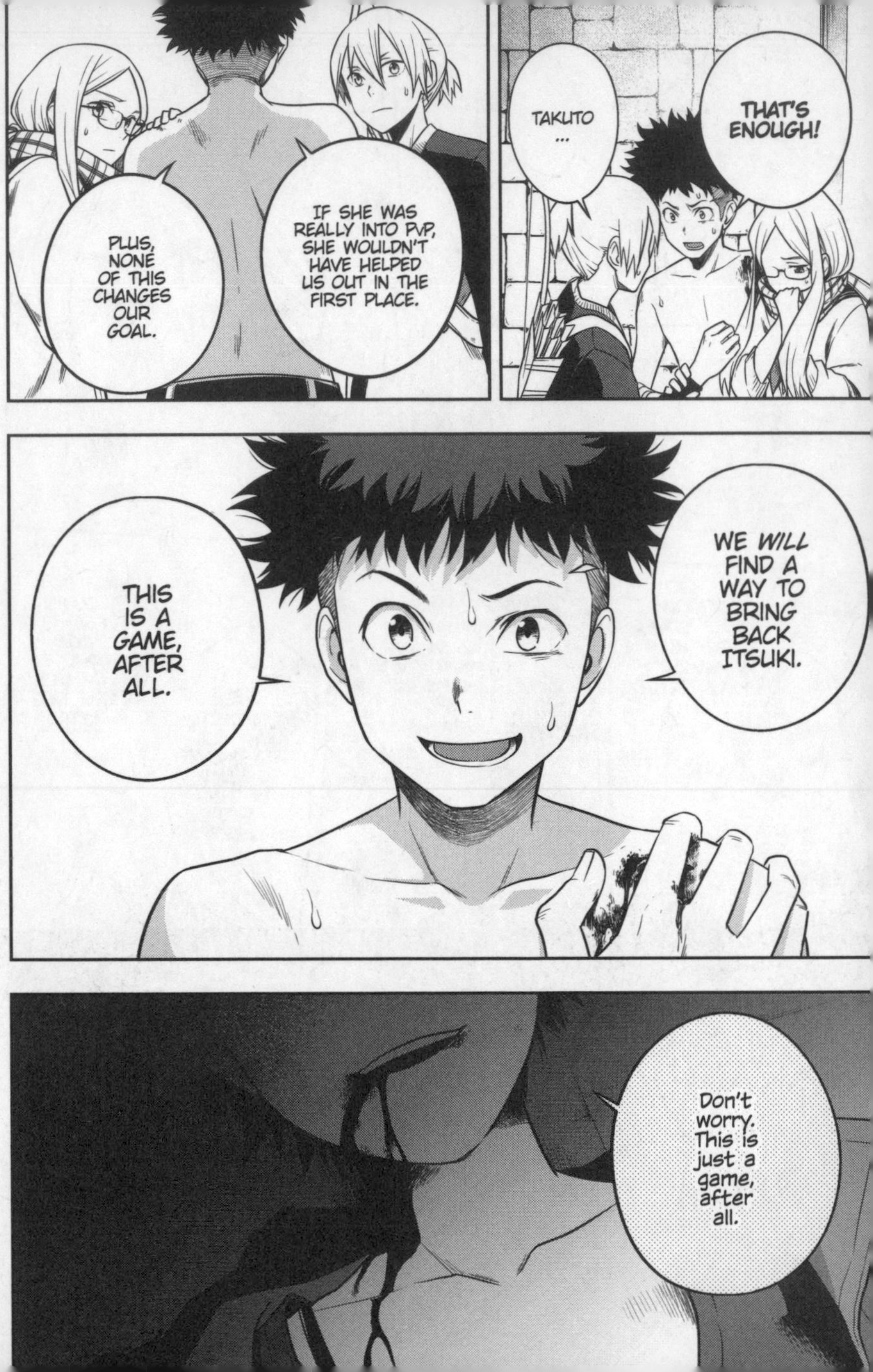
THAT'S ENOUGH!
TAKUTO ...
IF SHE WAS REALLY INTO PvP, SHE WOULDN'T HAVE HELPED US OUT IN THE FIRST PLACE.
PLUS, NONE OF THIS CHANGES OUR GOAL.
WE *WILL* FIND A WAY TO BRING BACK ITSUKI.
THIS IS A GAME, AFTER ALL.
Don't worry. This is just a game, after all.

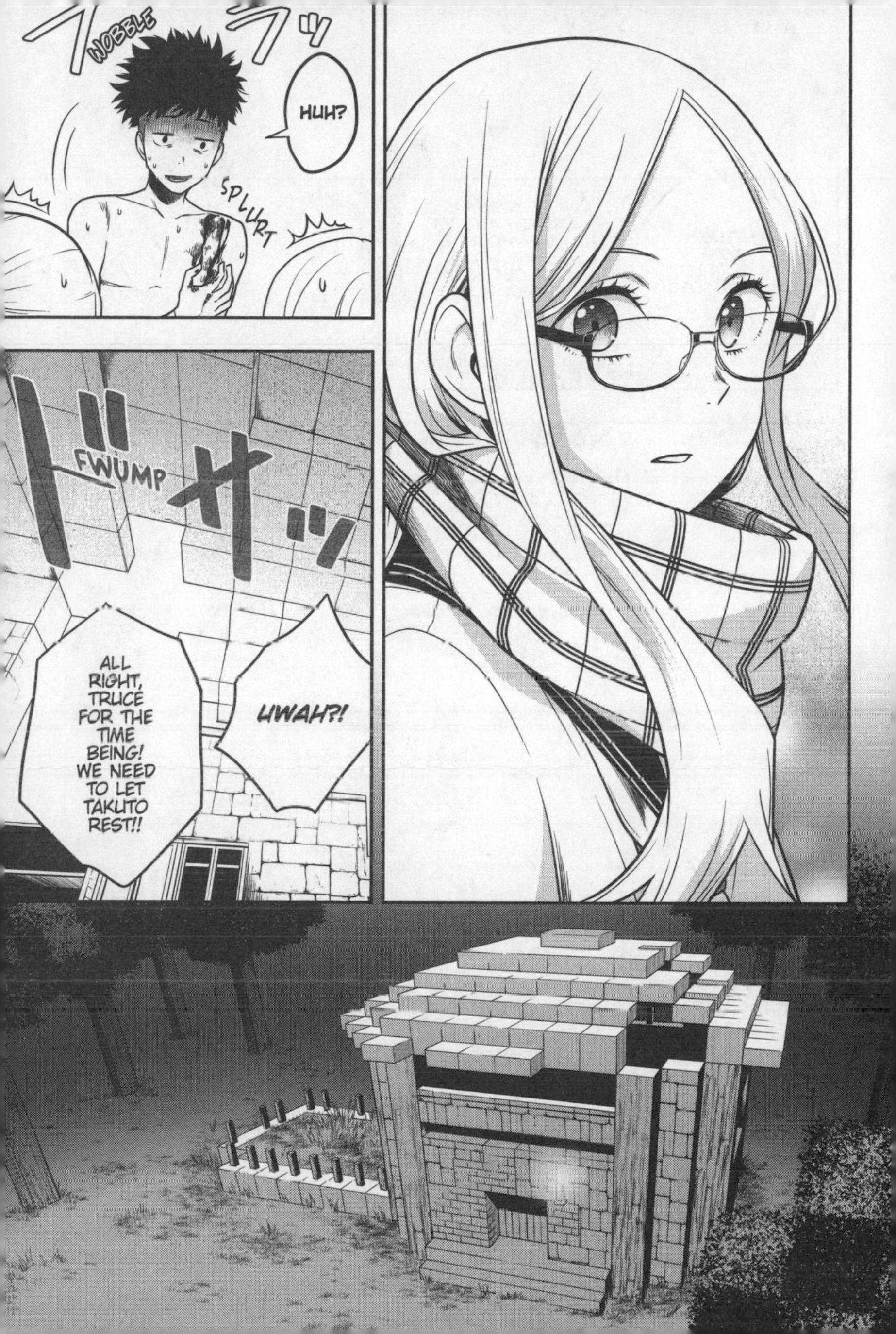
WOBBLE
HUH?
SPLURT
FWUMP
UWAH?!
ALL RIGHT, TRUCE FOR THE TIME BEING! WE NEED TO LET TAKUTO REST!!

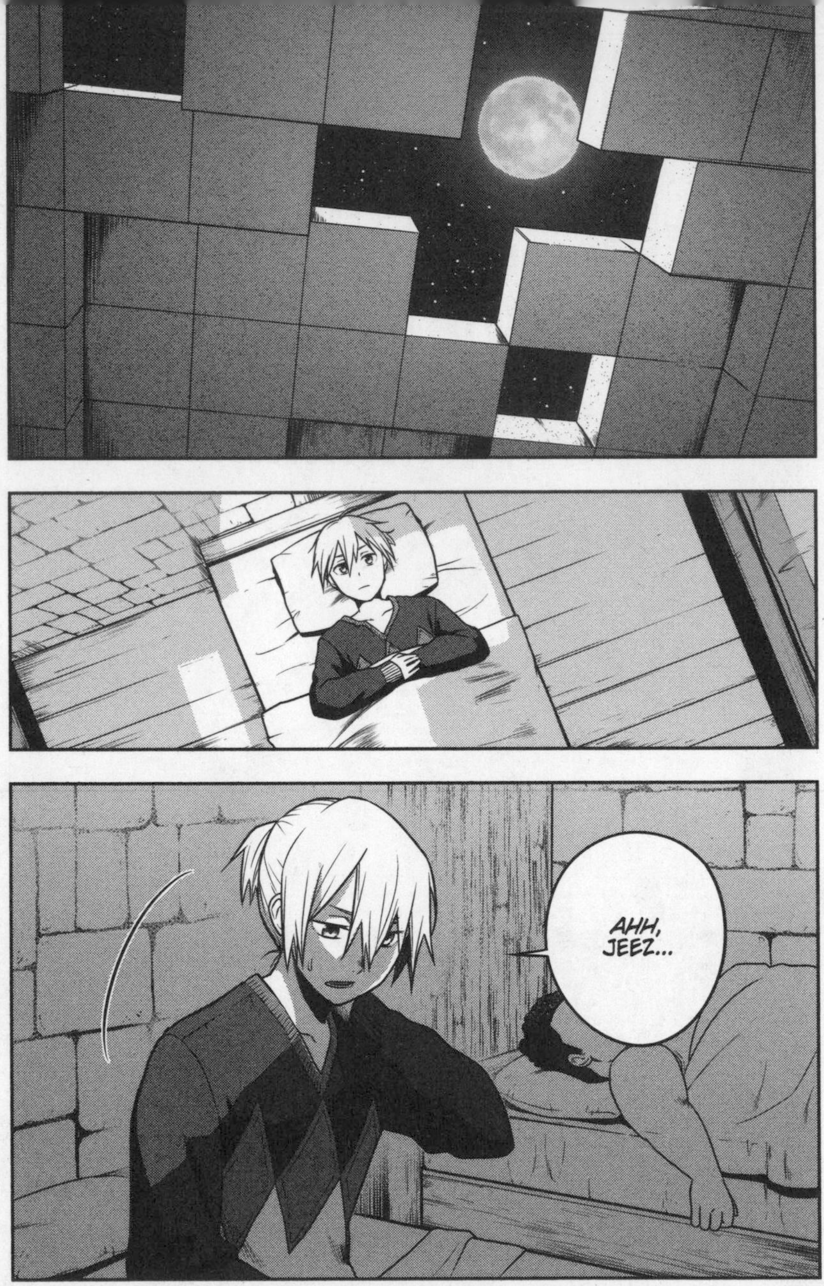
AHH, JEEZ...

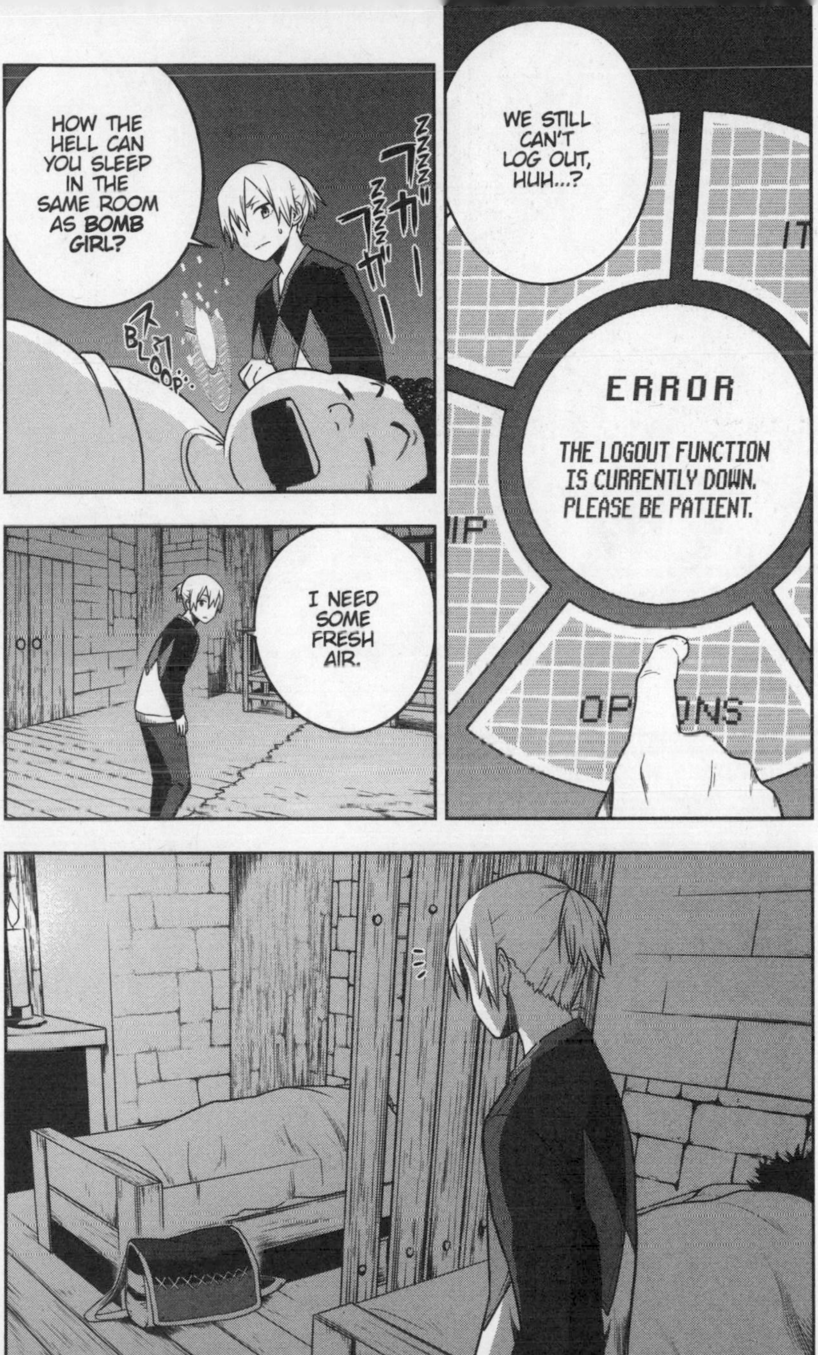
WE STILL CAN'T LOG OUT, HUH...?
ERROR
THE LOGOUT FUNCTION IS CURRENTLY DOWN. PLEASE BE PATIENT.
ZZZZ
ZZZZ
HOW THE HELL CAN YOU SLEEP IN THE SAME ROOM AS BOMB GIRL?
BLOOP..
I NEED SOME FRESH AIR.

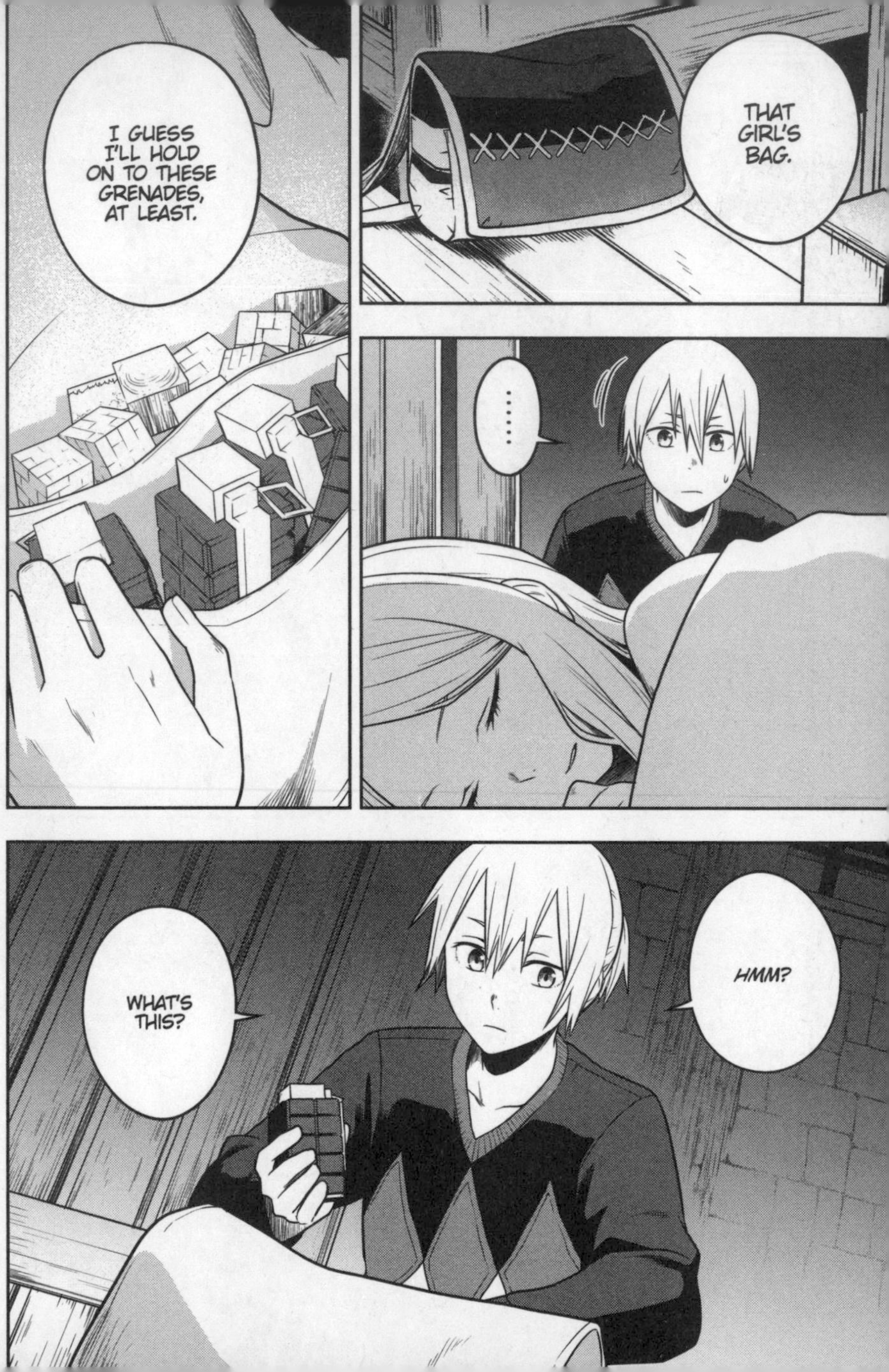
THAT GIRL'S BAG.
......
I GUESS I'LL HOLD ON TO THESE GRENADES, AT LEAST.
HMM?
WHAT'S THIS?

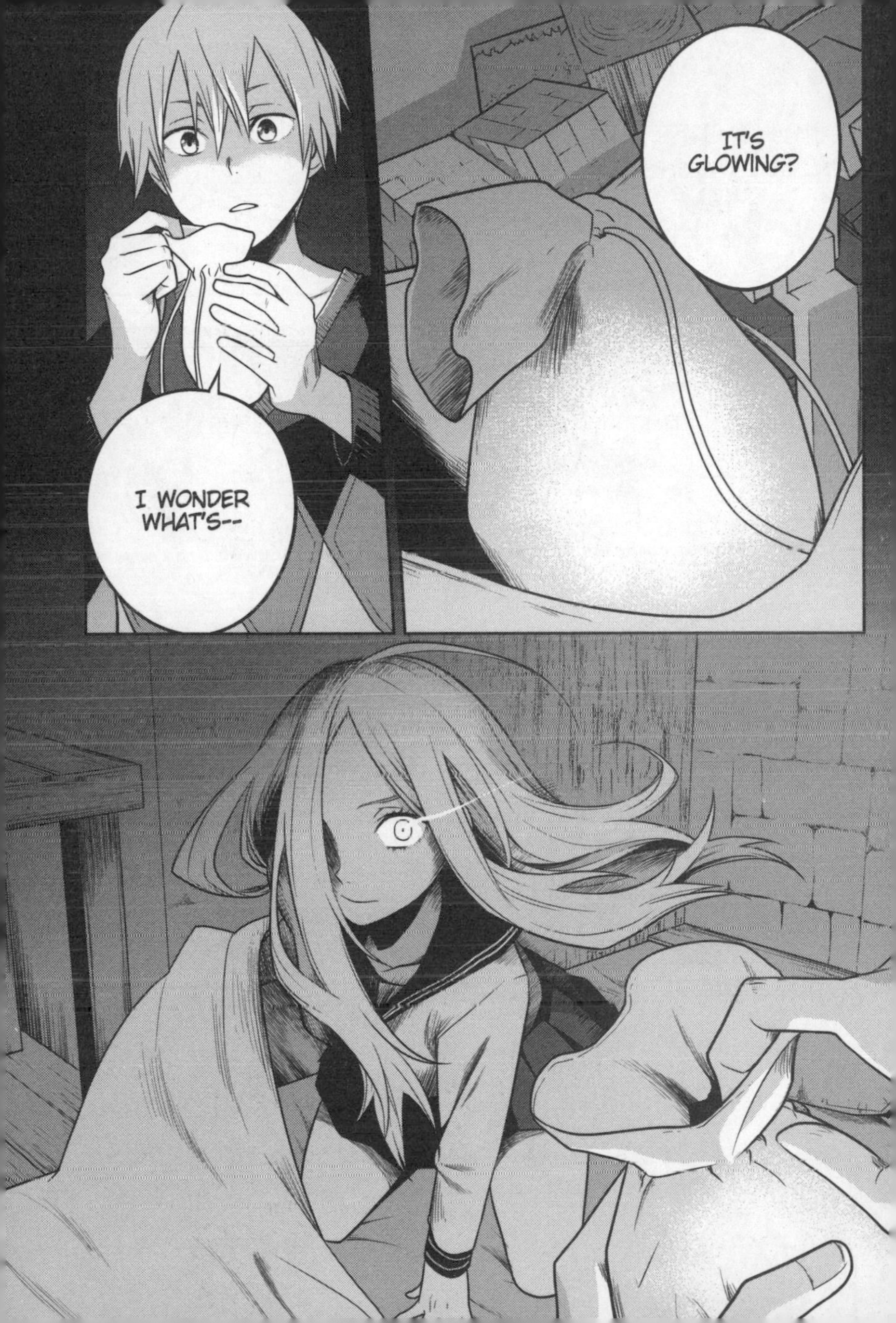
IT'S GLOWING?
I WONDER WHAT'S--

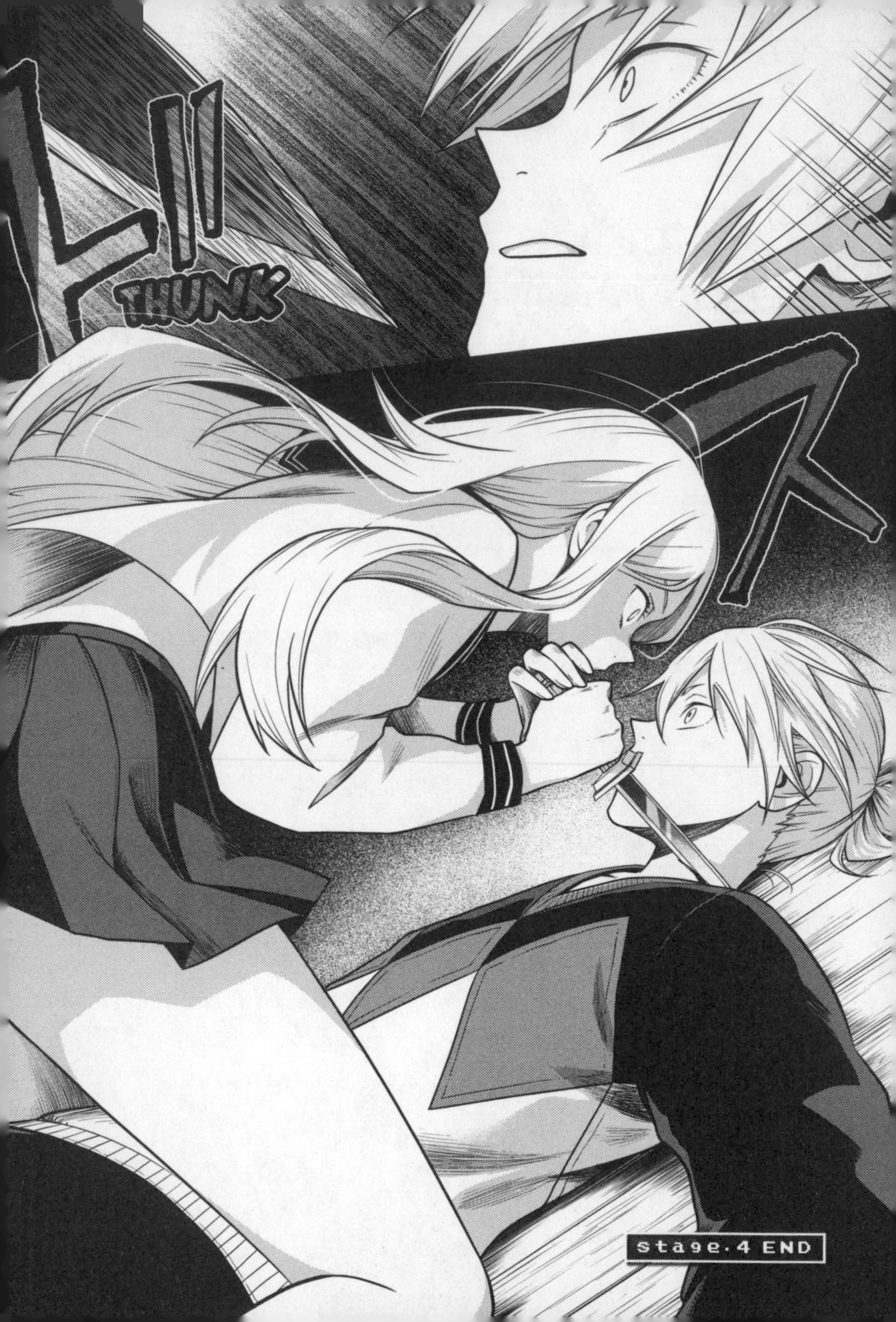
THUNK
stage.4 END

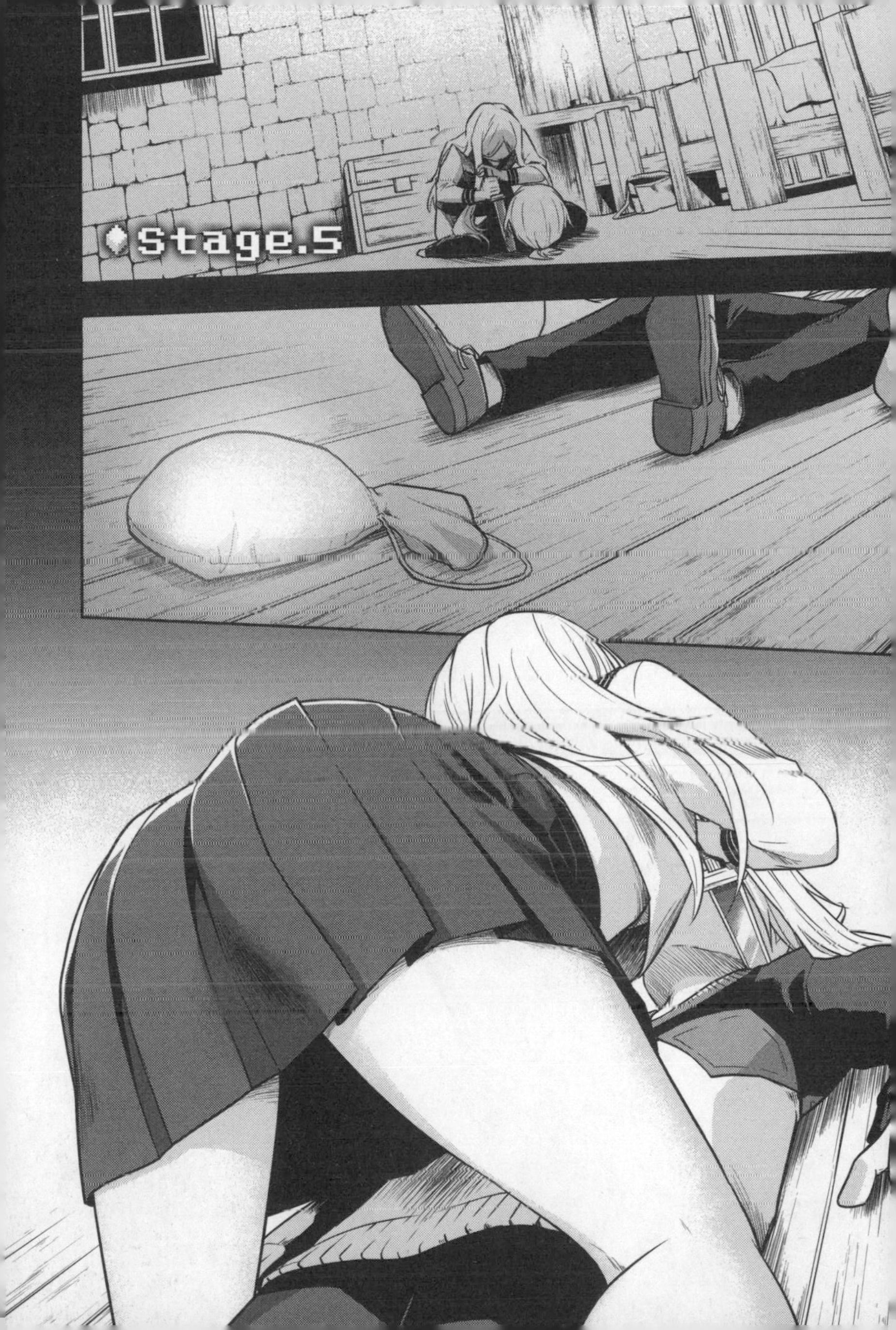
Stage.5

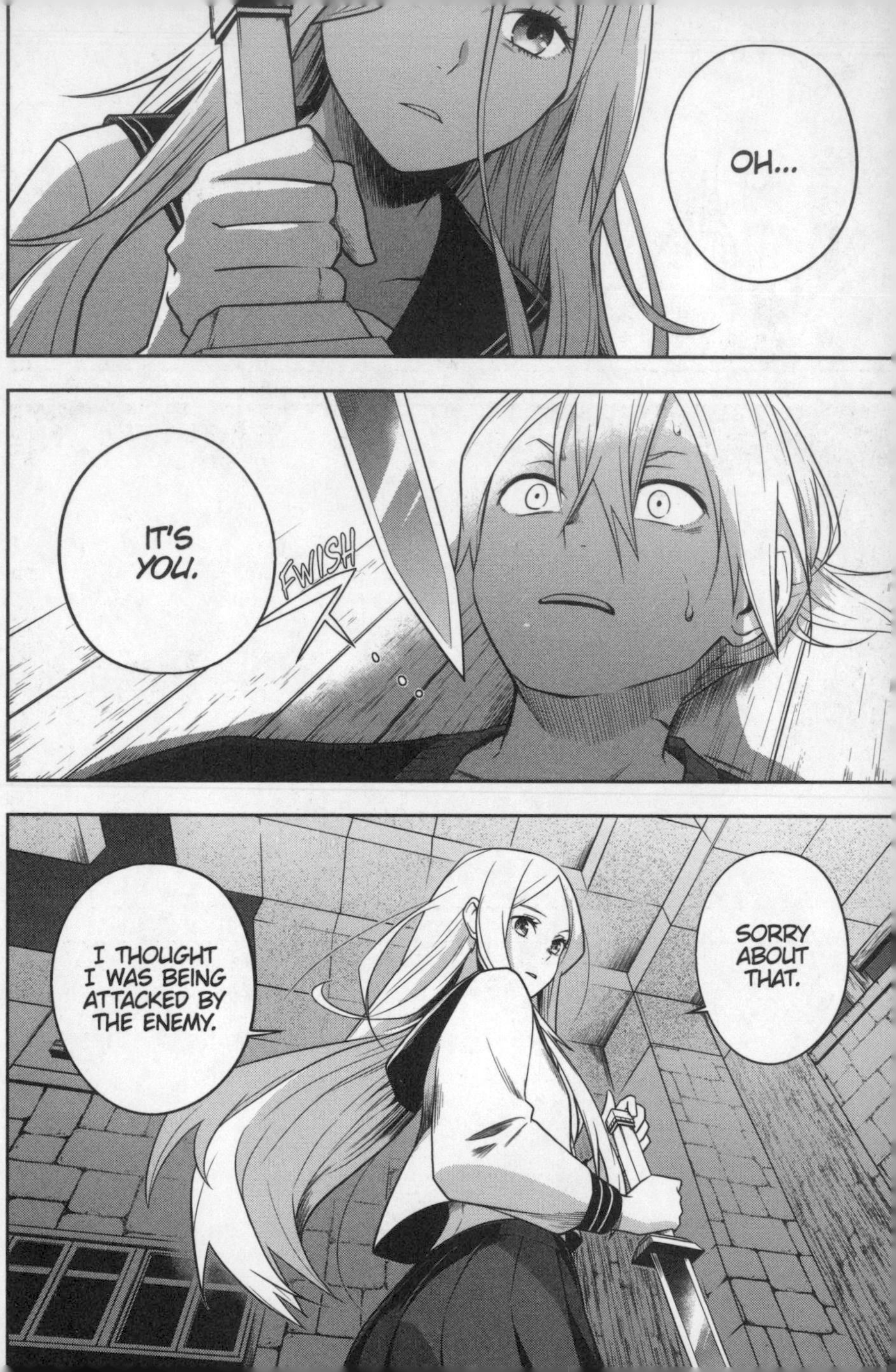
OH...
FWISH
IT'S YOU.
SORRY ABOUT THAT.
I THOUGHT I WAS BEING ATTACKED BY THE ENEMY.

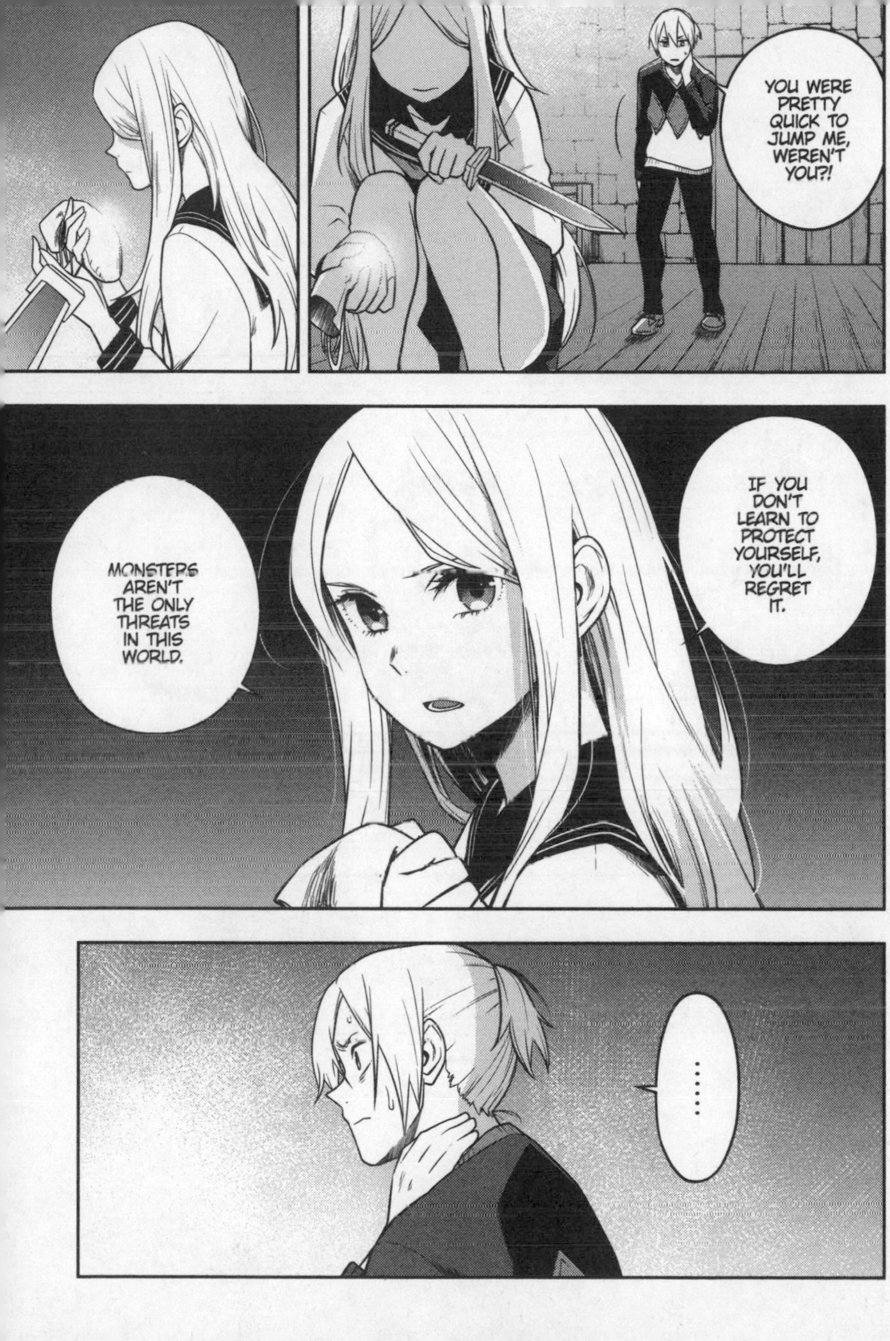
YOU WERE PRETTY QUICK TO JUMP ME, WEREN'T YOU?!
IF YOU DON'T LEARN TO PROTECT YOURSELF, YOU'LL REGRET IT.
MONSTERS AREN'T THE ONLY THREATS IN THIS WORLD.
......

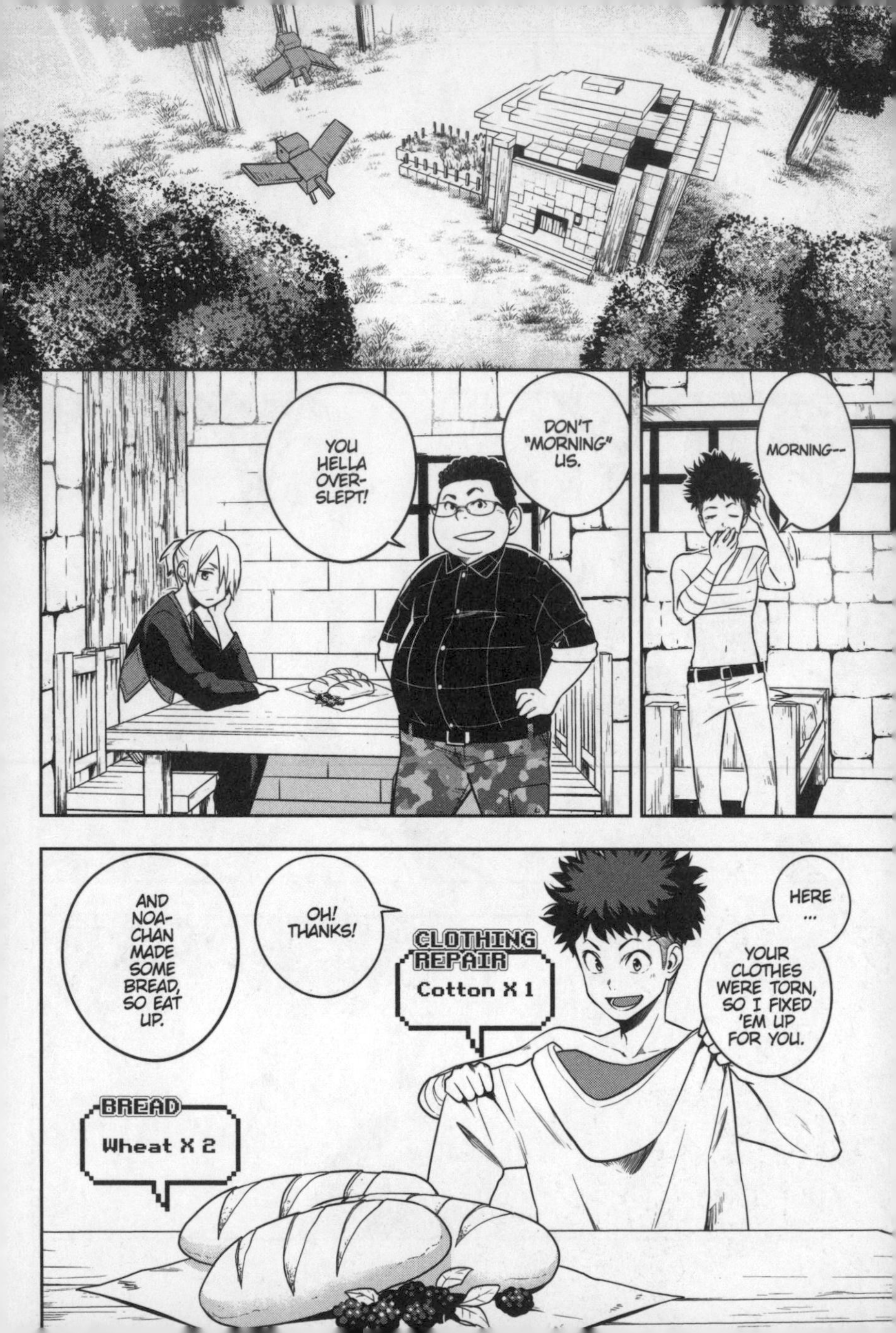
MORNING--
DON'T "MORNING" US.
YOU HELLA OVER-SLEPT!
HERE...
YOUR CLOTHES WERE TORN, SO I FIXED 'EM UP FOR YOU.
CLOTHING REPAIR
Cotton X 1
OH! THANKS!
AND NOA-CHAN MADE SOME BREAD, SO EAT UP.
BREAD
Wheat X 2

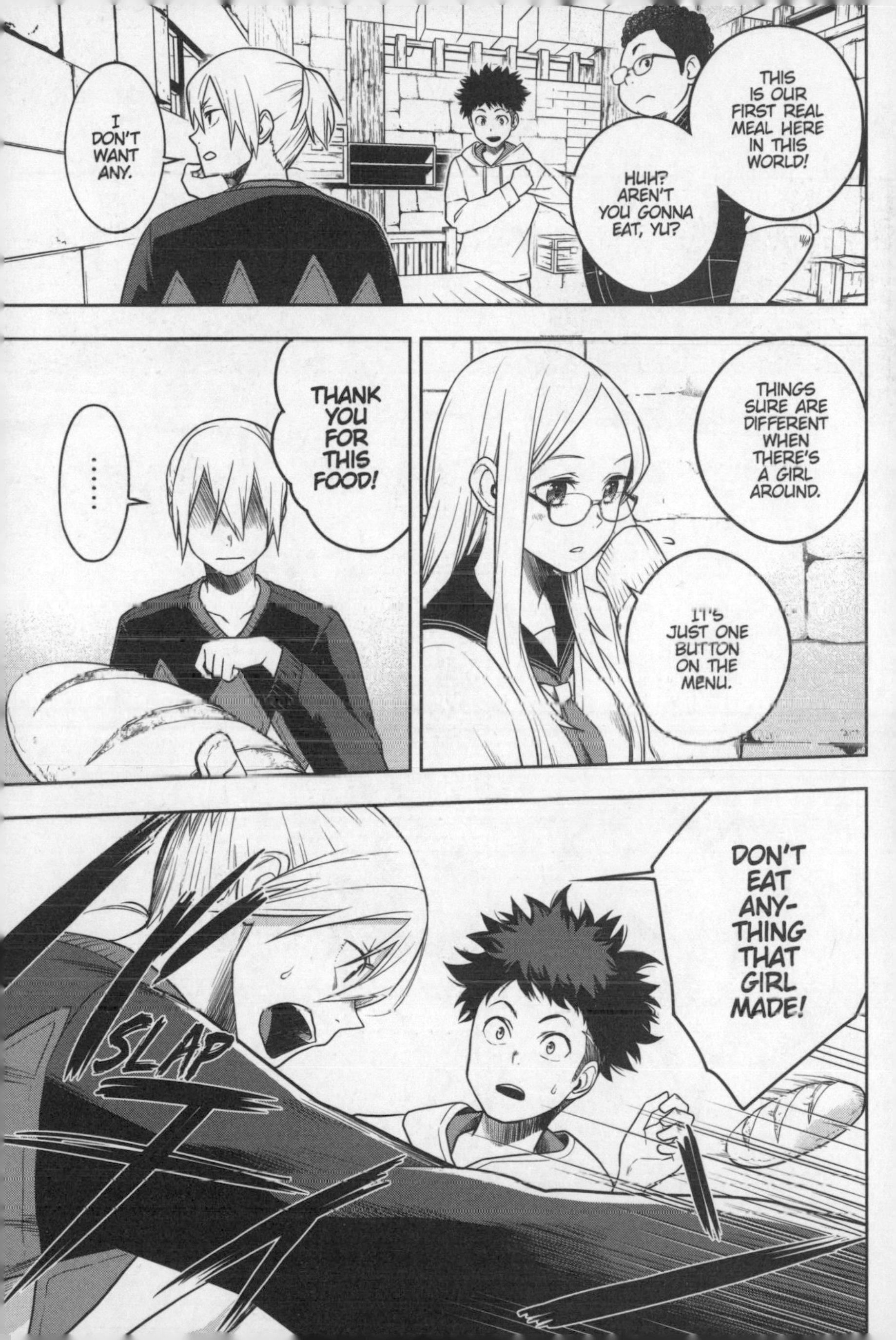
THIS IS OUR FIRST REAL MEAL HERE IN THIS WORLD!
HUH? AREN'T YOU GONNA EAT, YU?
I DON'T WANT ANY.
THINGS SURE ARE DIFFERENT WHEN THERE'S A GIRL AROUND.
IT'S JUST ONE BUTTON ON THE MENU.
THANK YOU FOR THIS FOOD!
......
DON'T EAT ANY-THING THAT GIRL MADE!
SLAP

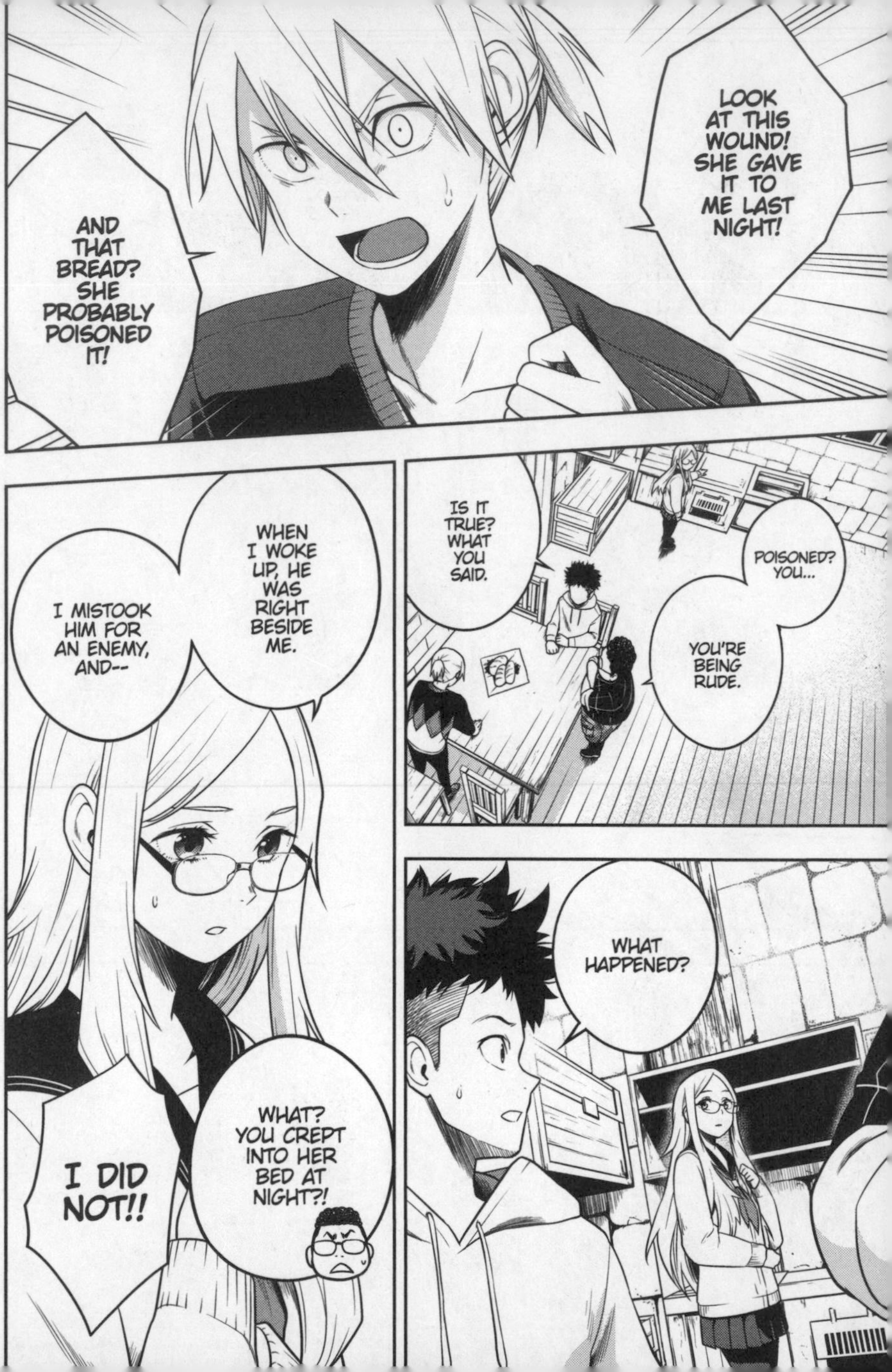
LOOK AT THIS WOUND! SHE GAVE IT TO ME LAST NIGHT!
AND THAT BREAD? SHE PROBABLY POISONED IT!
POISONED? YOU...
YOU'RE BEING RUDE.
IS IT TRUE? WHAT YOU SAID.
WHAT HAPPENED?
WHEN I WOKE UP, HE WAS RIGHT BESIDE ME.
I MISTOOK HIM FOR AN ENEMY, AND--
WHAT? YOU CREPT INTO HER BED AT NIGHT?!
I DID NOT!!

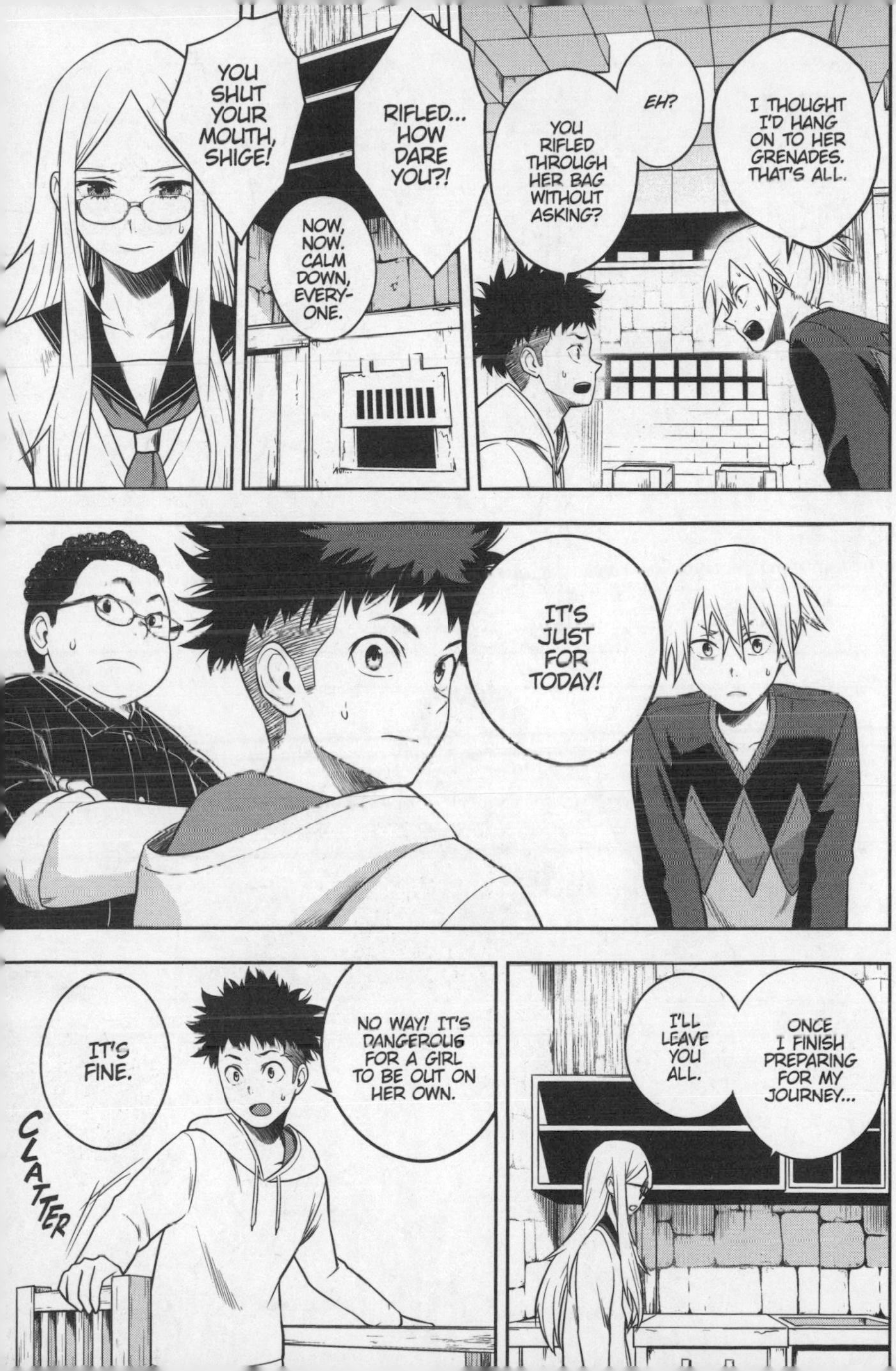
I THOUGHT I'D HANG ON TO HER GRENADES. THAT'S ALL.
EH?
YOU RIFLED THROUGH HER BAG WITHOUT ASKING?
RIFLED... HOW DARE YOU?!
NOW, NOW. CALM DOWN, EVERYONE.
YOU SHUT YOUR MOUTH, SHIGE!
IT'S JUST FOR TODAY!
ONCE I FINISH PREPARING FOR MY JOURNEY...
I'LL LEAVE YOU ALL.
NO WAY! IT'S DANGEROUS FOR A GIRL TO BE OUT ON HER OWN.
IT'S FINE.
CLATTER

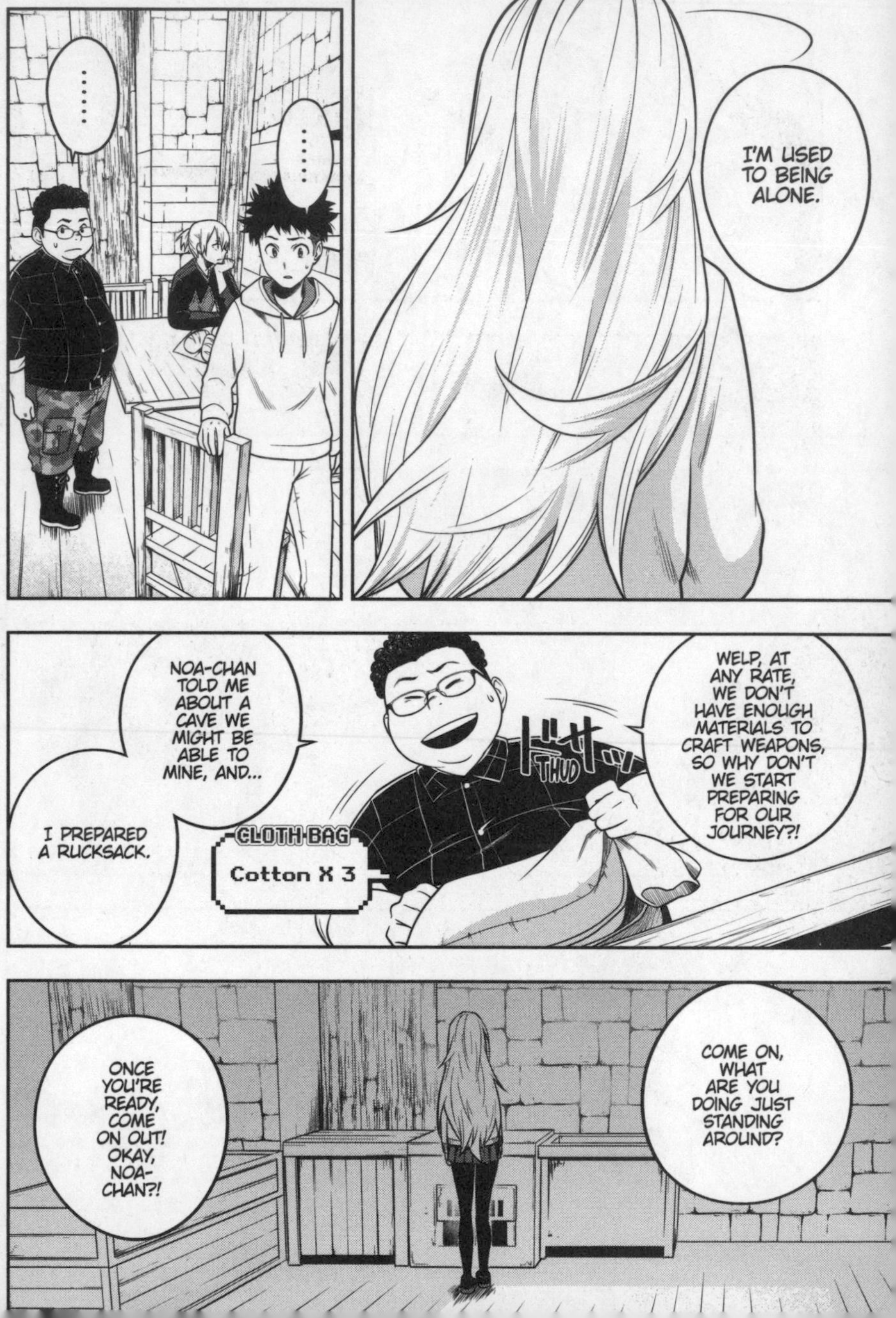
I'M USED TO BEING ALONE.
......
......
WELP, AT ANY RATE, WE DON'T HAVE ENOUGH MATERIALS TO CRAFT WEAPONS, SO WHY DON'T WE START PREPARING FOR OUR JOURNEY?!
THUD
NOA-CHAN TOLD ME ABOUT A CAVE WE MIGHT BE ABLE TO MINE, AND...
I PREPARED A RUCKSACK.
CLOTH BAG
Cotton X 3
COME ON, WHAT ARE YOU DOING JUST STANDING AROUND?
ONCE YOU'RE READY, COME ON OUT! OKAY, NOA-CHAN?!

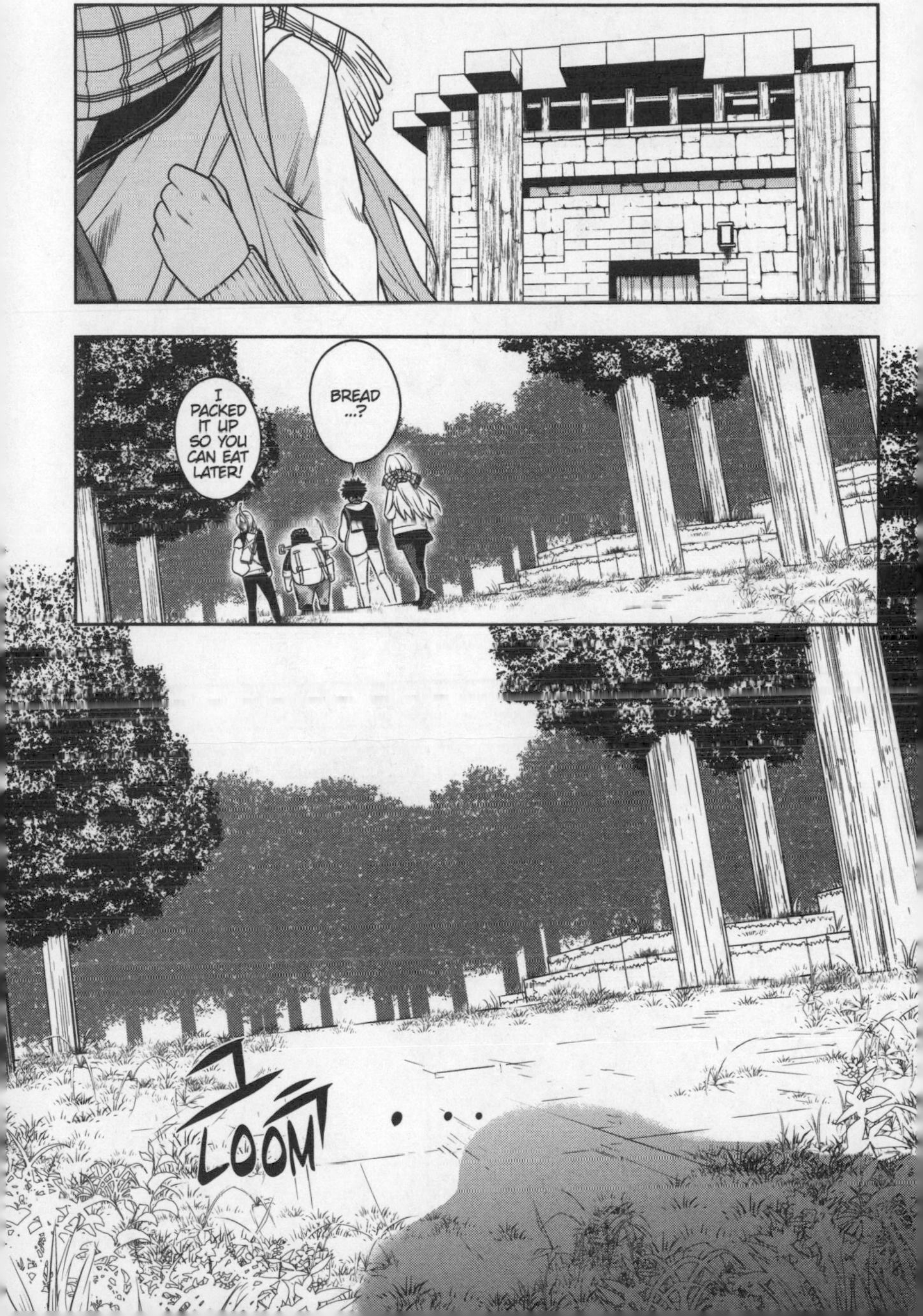
BREAD ...?
I PACKED IT UP SO YOU CAN EAT LATER!
LOOM
...

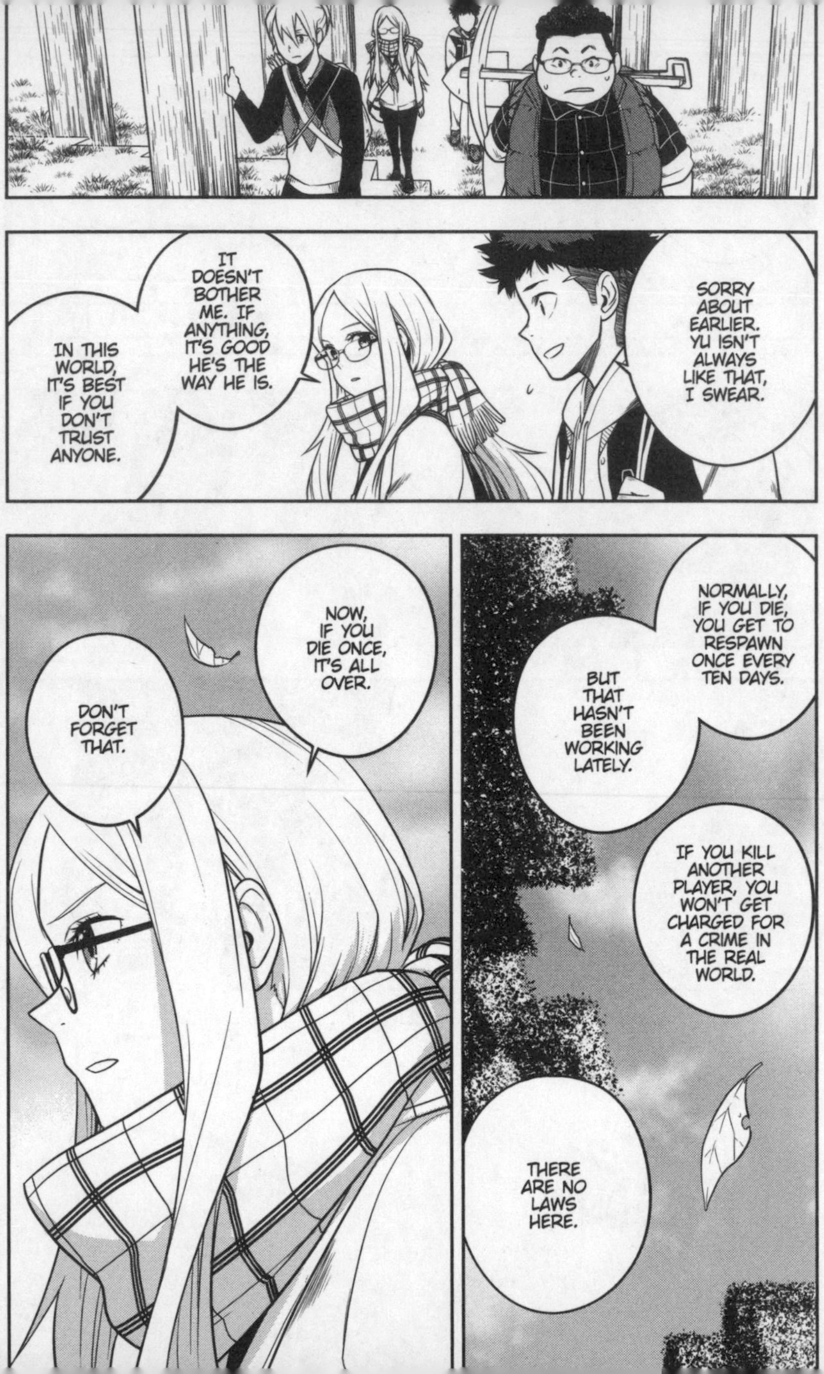
SORRY ABOUT EARLIER. YU ISN'T ALWAYS LIKE THAT, I SWEAR.
IT DOESN'T BOTHER ME. IF ANYTHING, IT'S GOOD HE'S THE WAY HE IS.
IN THIS WORLD, IT'S BEST IF YOU DON'T TRUST ANYONE.
NORMALLY, IF YOU DIE, YOU GET TO RESPAWN ONCE EVERY TEN DAYS.
BUT THAT HASN'T BEEN WORKING LATELY.
IF YOU KILL ANOTHER PLAYER, YOU WON'T GET CHARGED FOR A CRIME IN THE REAL WORLD.
THERE ARE NO LAWS HERE.
NOW, IF YOU DIE ONCE, IT'S ALL OVER.
DON'T FORGET THAT.

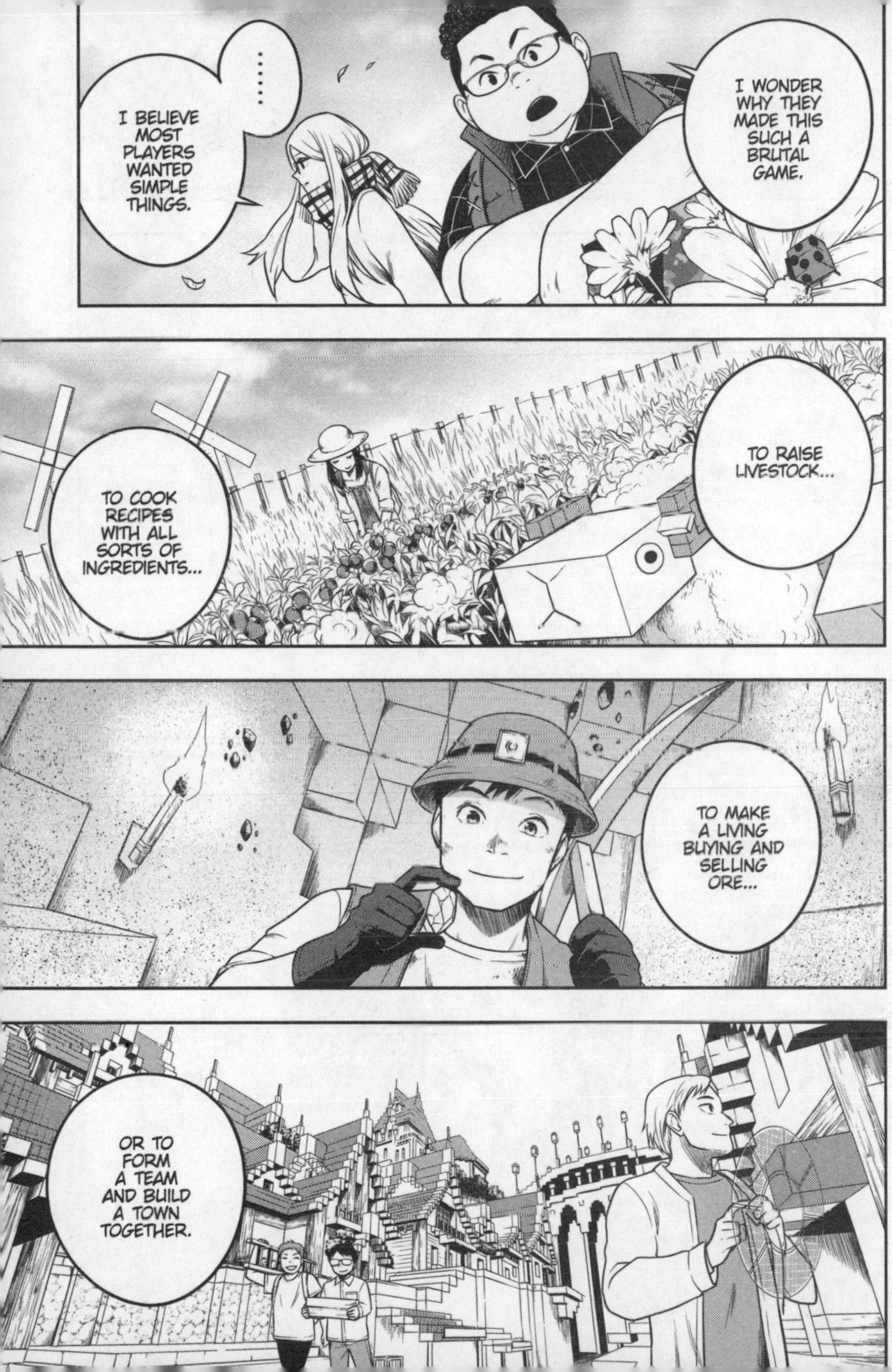
I WONDER WHY THEY MADE THIS SUCH A BRUTAL GAME.
......
I BELIEVE MOST PLAYERS WANTED SIMPLE THINGS.
TO RAISE LIVESTOCK...
TO COOK RECIPES WITH ALL SORTS OF INGREDIENTS...
TO MAKE A LIVING BUYING AND SELLING ORE...
OR TO FORM A TEAM AND BUILD A TOWN TOGETHER.

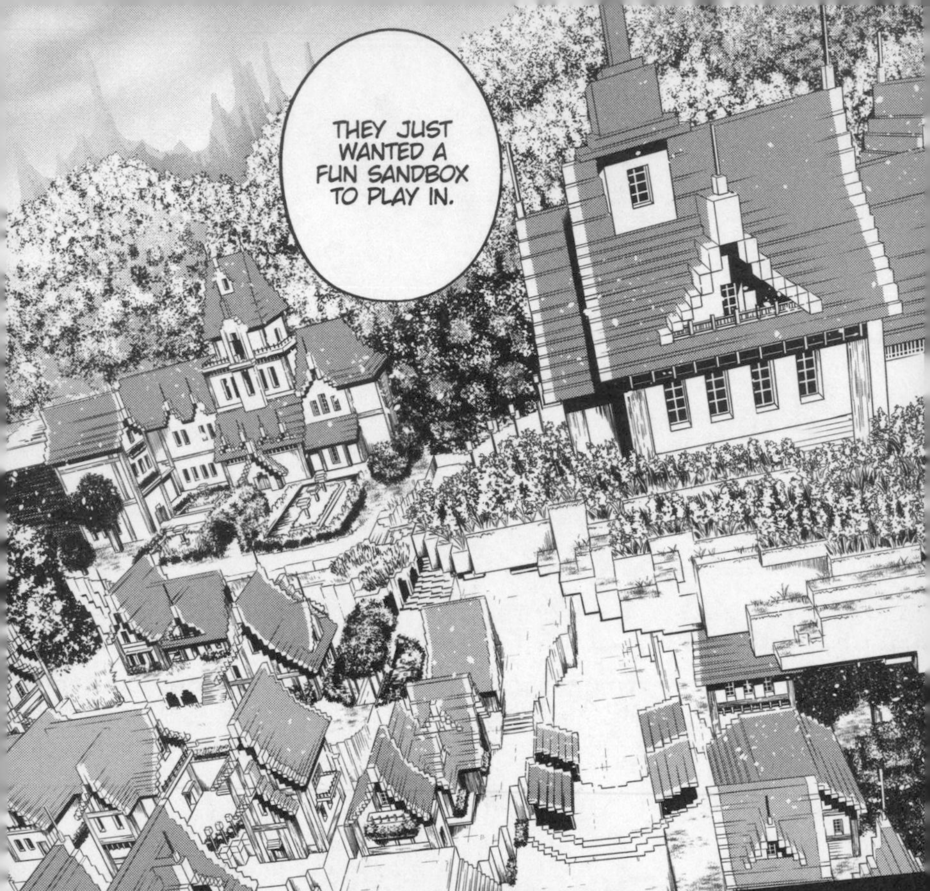
THEY JUST WANTED A FUN SANDBOX TO PLAY IN.
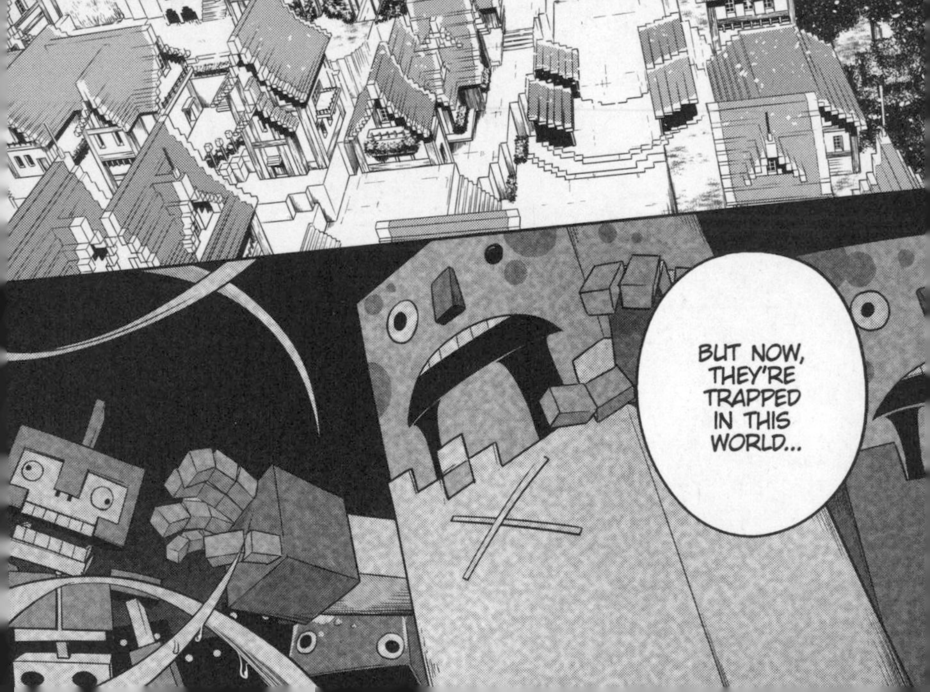
BUT NOW, THEY'RE TRAPPED IN THIS WORLD...

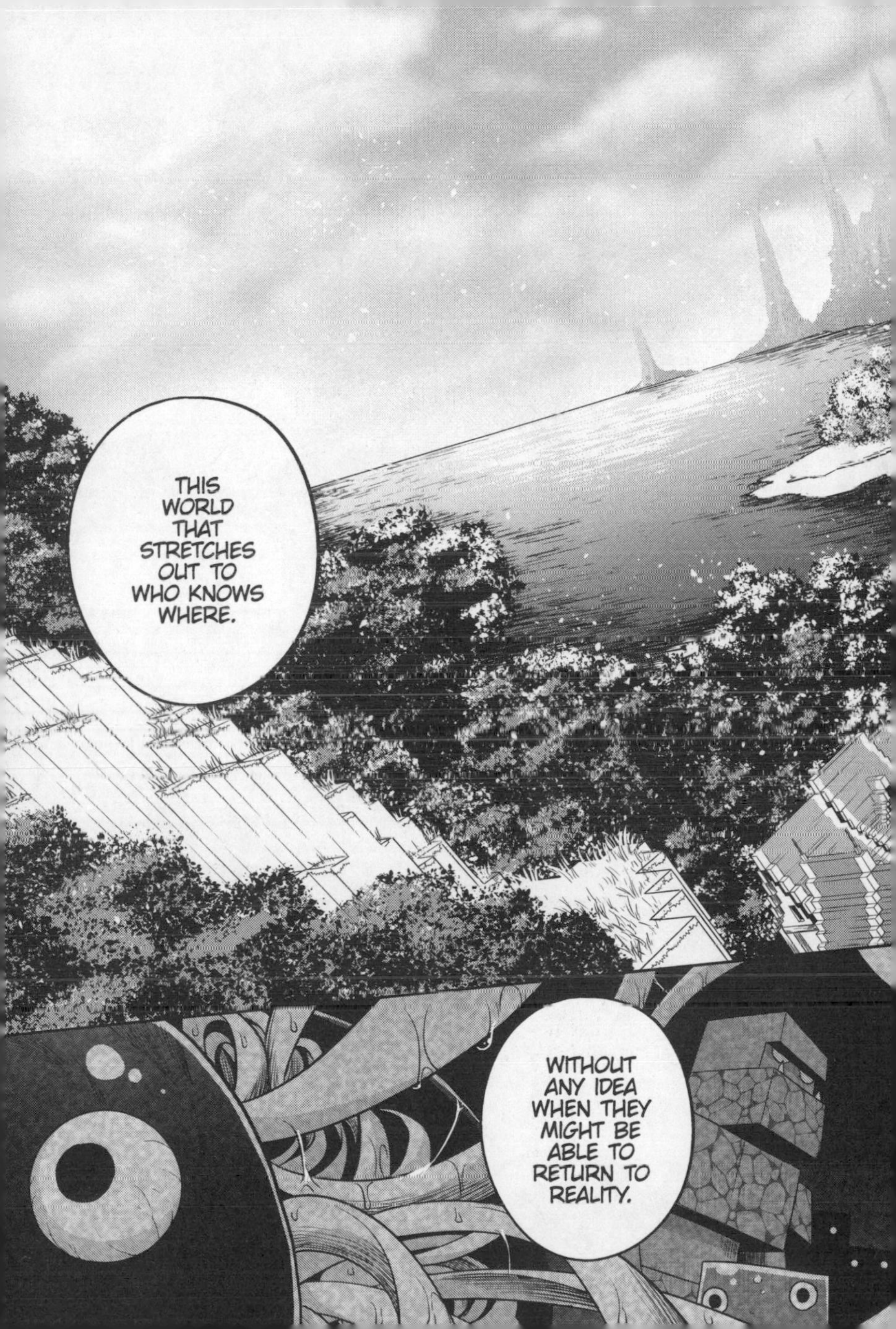
THIS WORLD THAT STRETCHES OUT TO WHO KNOWS WHERE.
WITHOUT ANY IDEA WHEN THEY MIGHT BE ABLE TO RETURN TO REALITY.

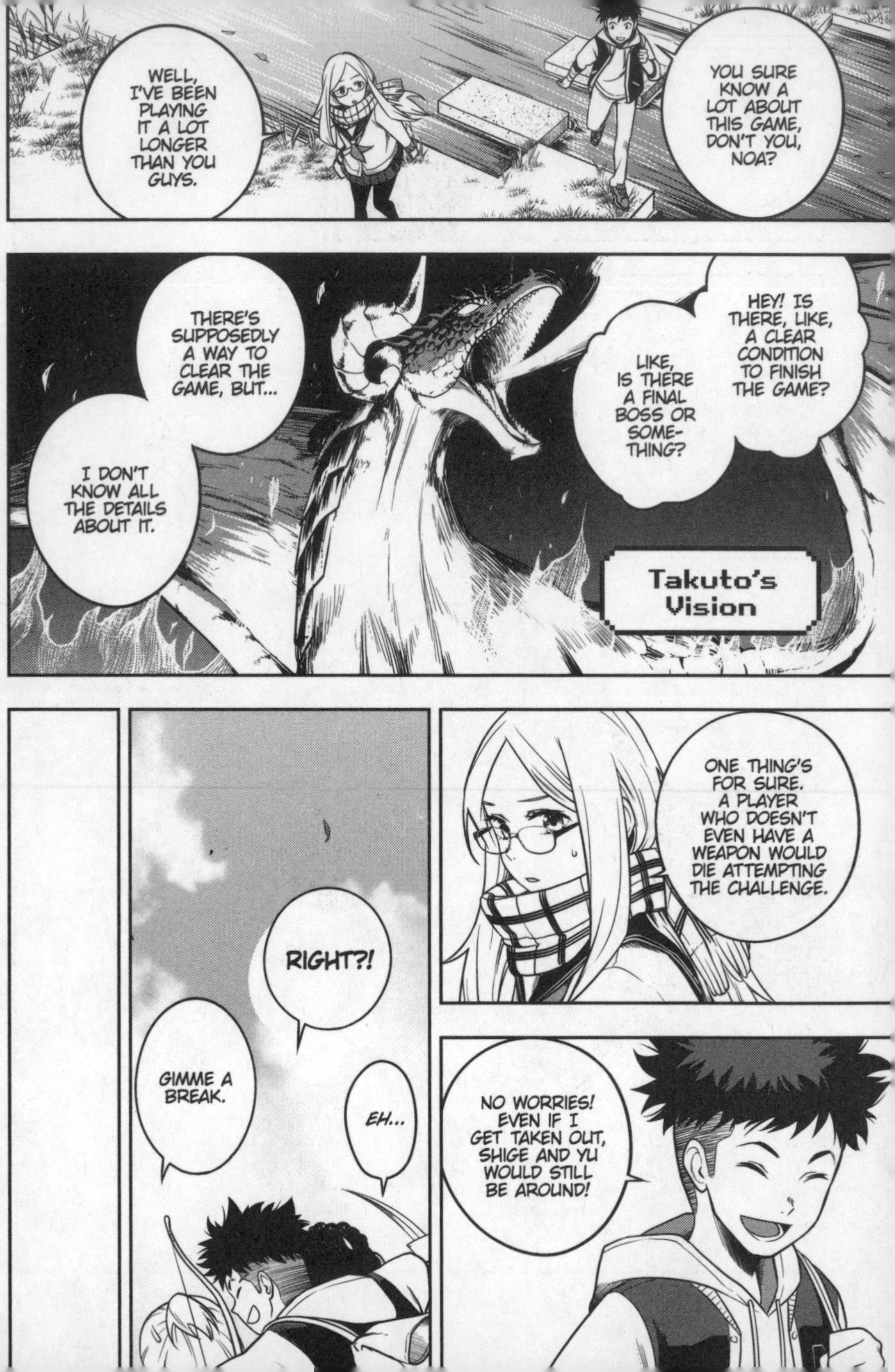
YOU SURE KNOW A LOT ABOUT THIS GAME, DON'T YOU, NOA?
WELL, I'VE BEEN PLAYING IT A LOT LONGER THAN YOU GUYS.
HEY! IS THERE, LIKE, A CLEAR CONDITION TO FINISH THE GAME?
LIKE, IS THERE A FINAL BOSS OR SOME-THING?
THERE'S SUPPOSEDLY A WAY TO CLEAR THE GAME, BUT...
I DON'T KNOW ALL THE DETAILS ABOUT IT.
Takuto's Vision
ONE THING'S FOR SURE. A PLAYER WHO DOESN'T EVEN HAVE A WEAPON WOULD DIE ATTEMPTING THE CHALLENGE.
NO WORRIES! EVEN IF I GET TAKEN OUT, SHIGE AND YU WOULD STILL BE AROUND!
RIGHT?!
EH...
GIMME A BREAK.

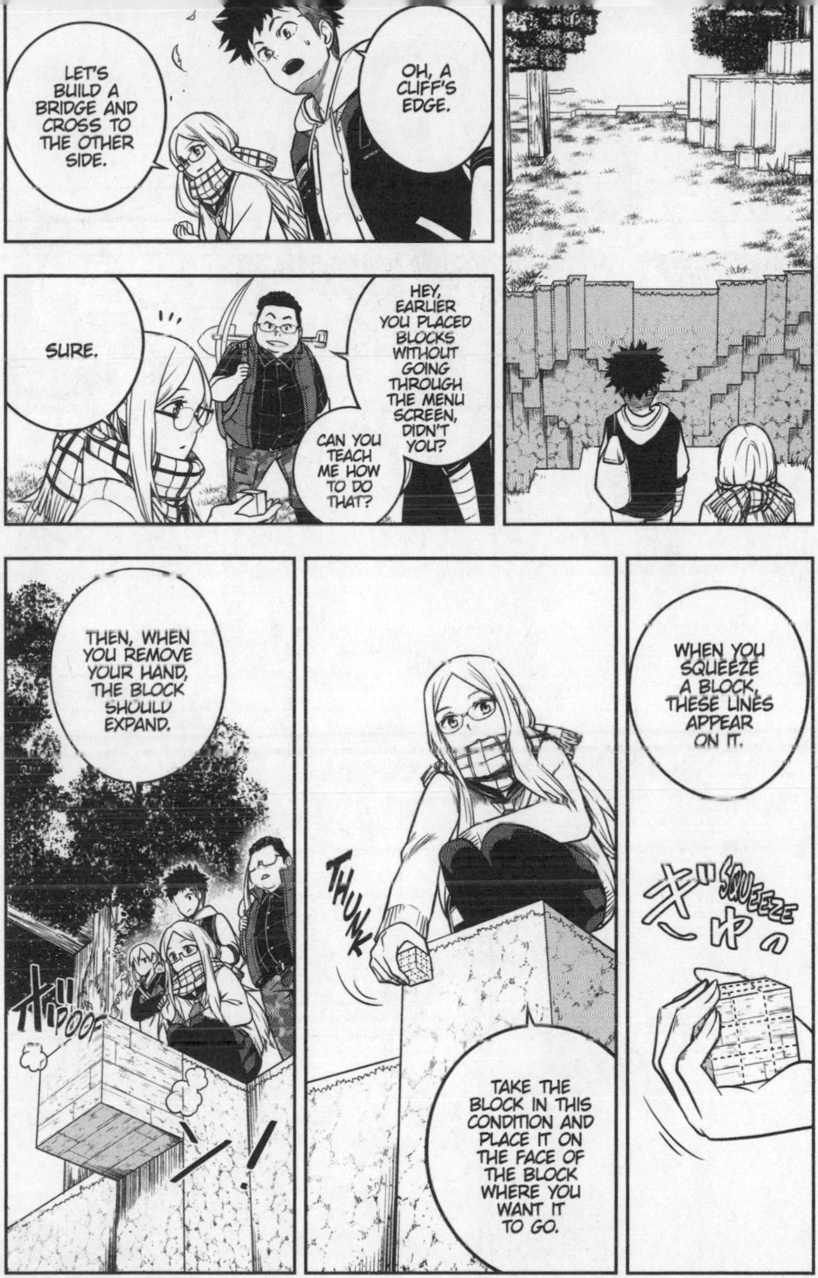
OH, A CLIFF'S EDGE.
LET'S BUILD A BRIDGE AND CROSS TO THE OTHER SIDE.
HEY, EARLIER YOU PLACED BLOCKS WITHOUT GOING THROUGH THE MENU SCREEN, DIDN'T YOU?
CAN YOU TEACH ME HOW TO DO THAT?
SURE.
WHEN YOU SQUEEZE A BLOCK, THESE LINES APPEAR ON IT.
ぎゅっ
SQUEEZE
TAKE THE BLOCK IN THIS CONDITION AND PLACE IT ON THE FACE OF THE BLOCK WHERE YOU WANT IT TO GO.
THUNK
THEN, WHEN YOU REMOVE YOUR HAND, THE BLOCK SHOULD EXPAND.
POOF

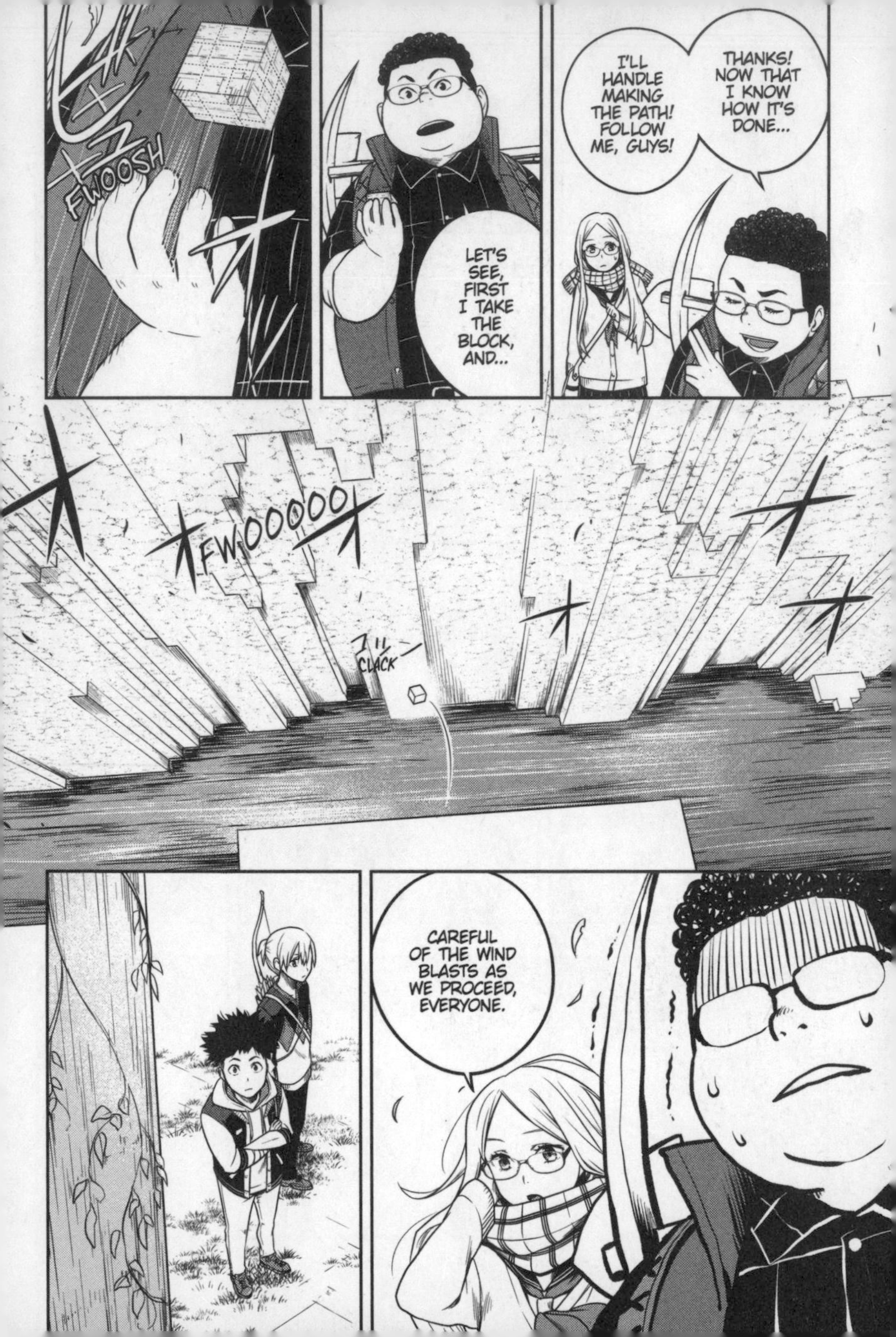
THANKS! NOW THAT I KNOW HOW IT'S DONE...
I'LL HANDLE MAKING THE PATH! FOLLOW ME, GUYS!
LET'S SEE, FIRST I TAKE THE BLOCK, AND...
FWOOSH
FWOOOOO
CLACK
CAREFUL OF THE WIND BLASTS AS WE PROCEED, EVERYONE.

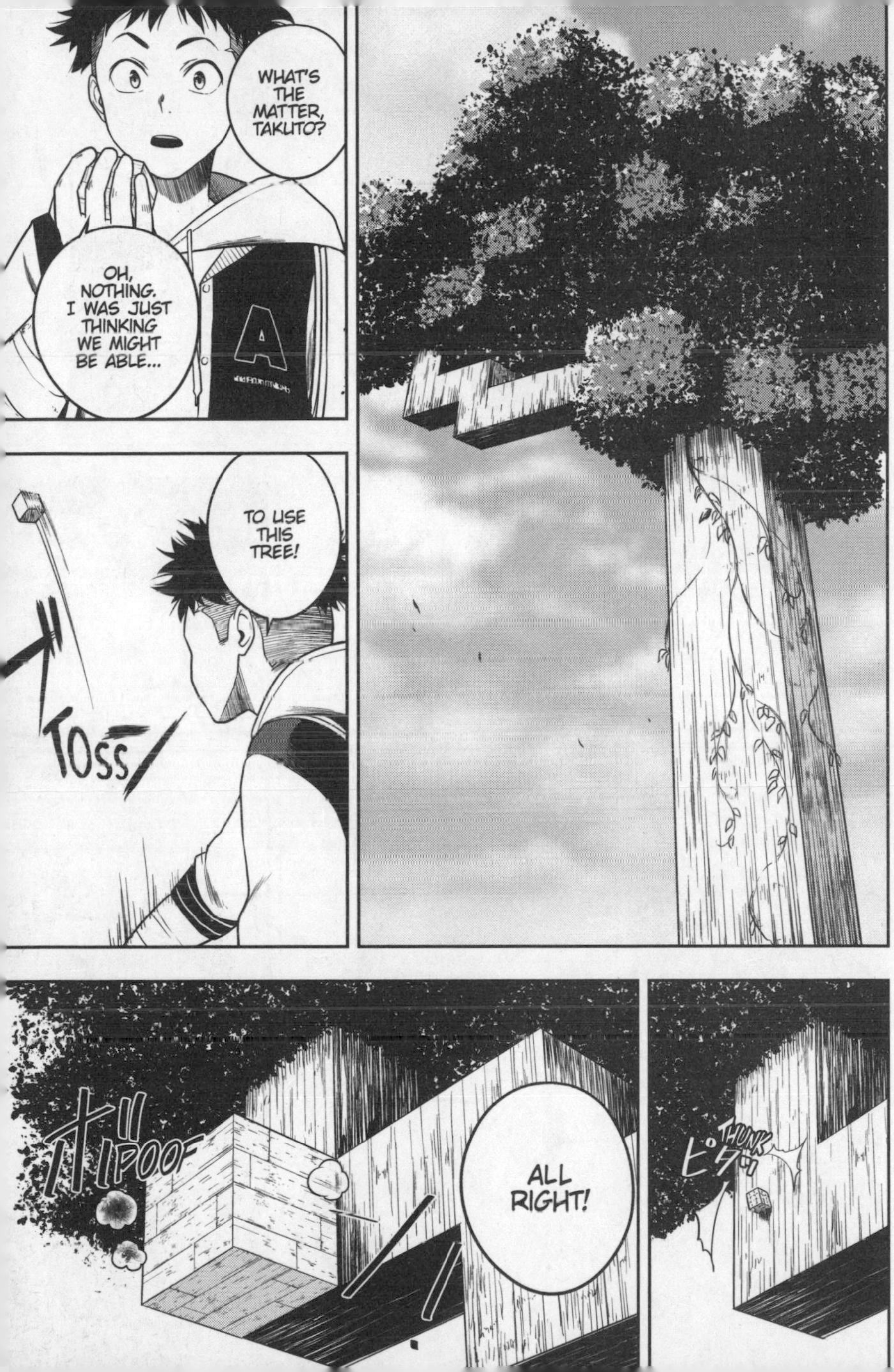
WHAT'S THE MATTER, TAKUTO?
OH, NOTHING. I WAS JUST THINKING WE MIGHT BE ABLE...
TO USE THIS TREE!
TOSS
THUNK
ALL RIGHT!
POOF

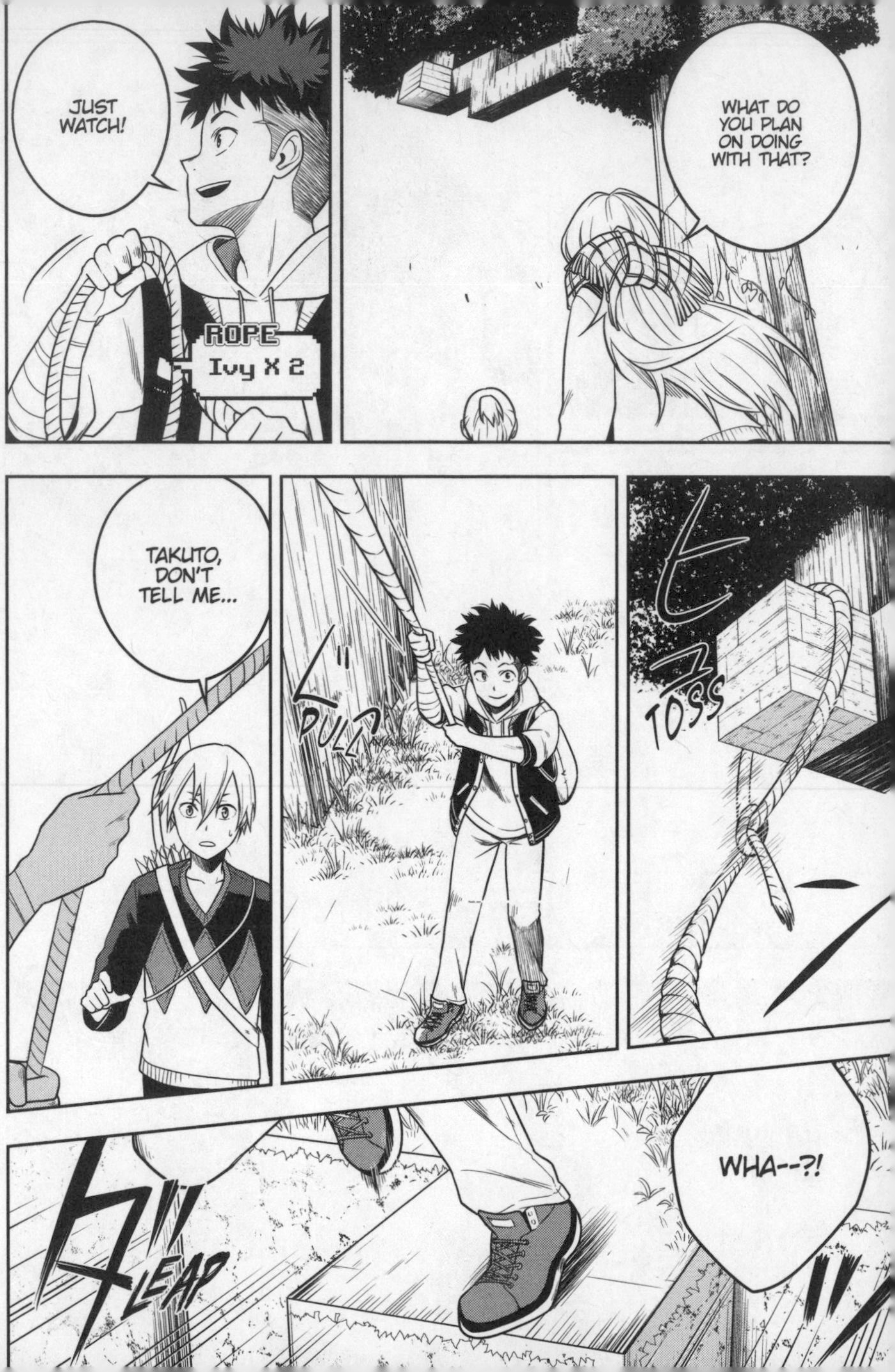
WHAT DO YOU PLAN ON DOING WITH THAT?
JUST WATCH!
ROPE
Ivy X 2
TOSS
PULL
TAKUTO, DON'T TELL ME...
WHA--?!
LEAP

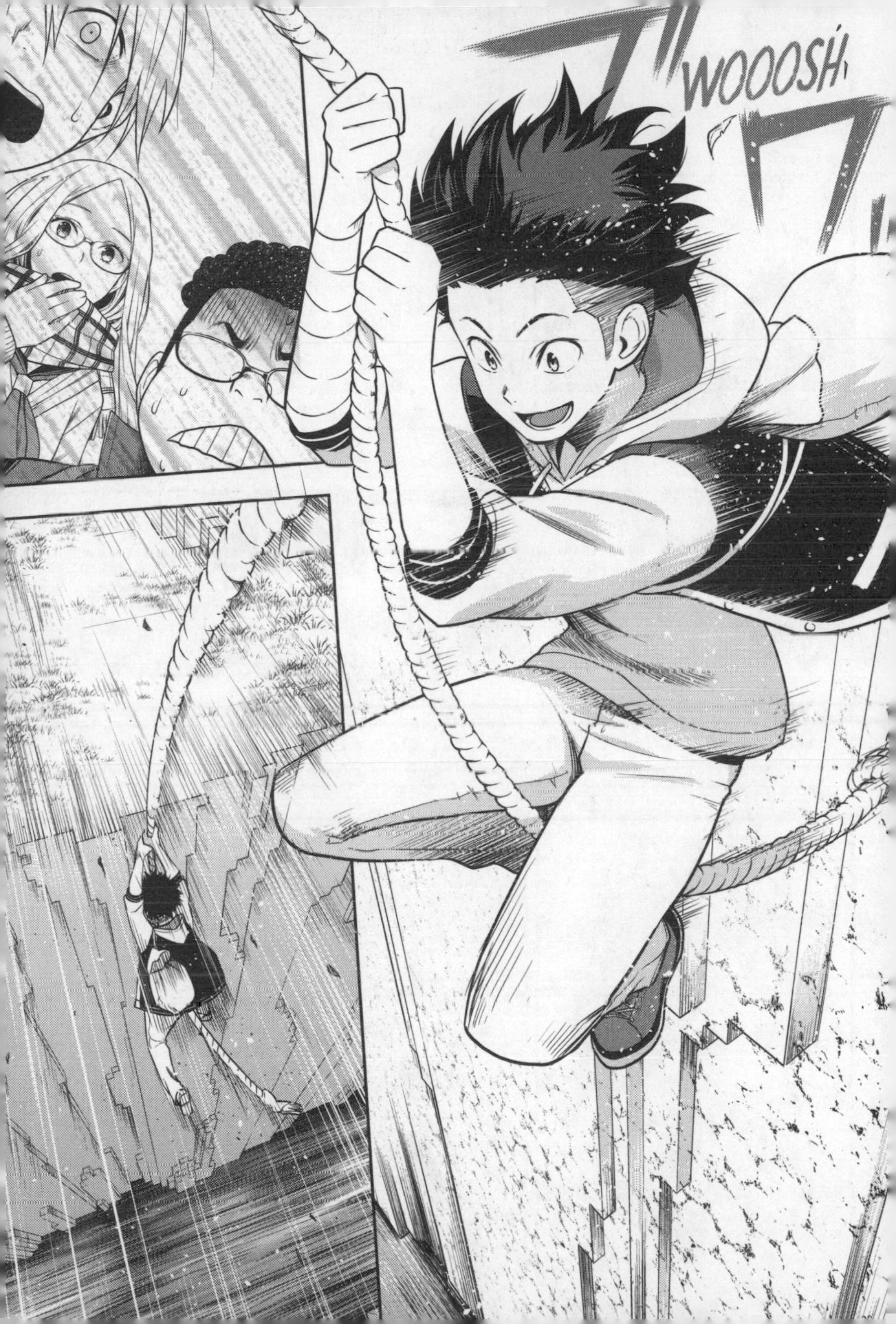
WOOOSH

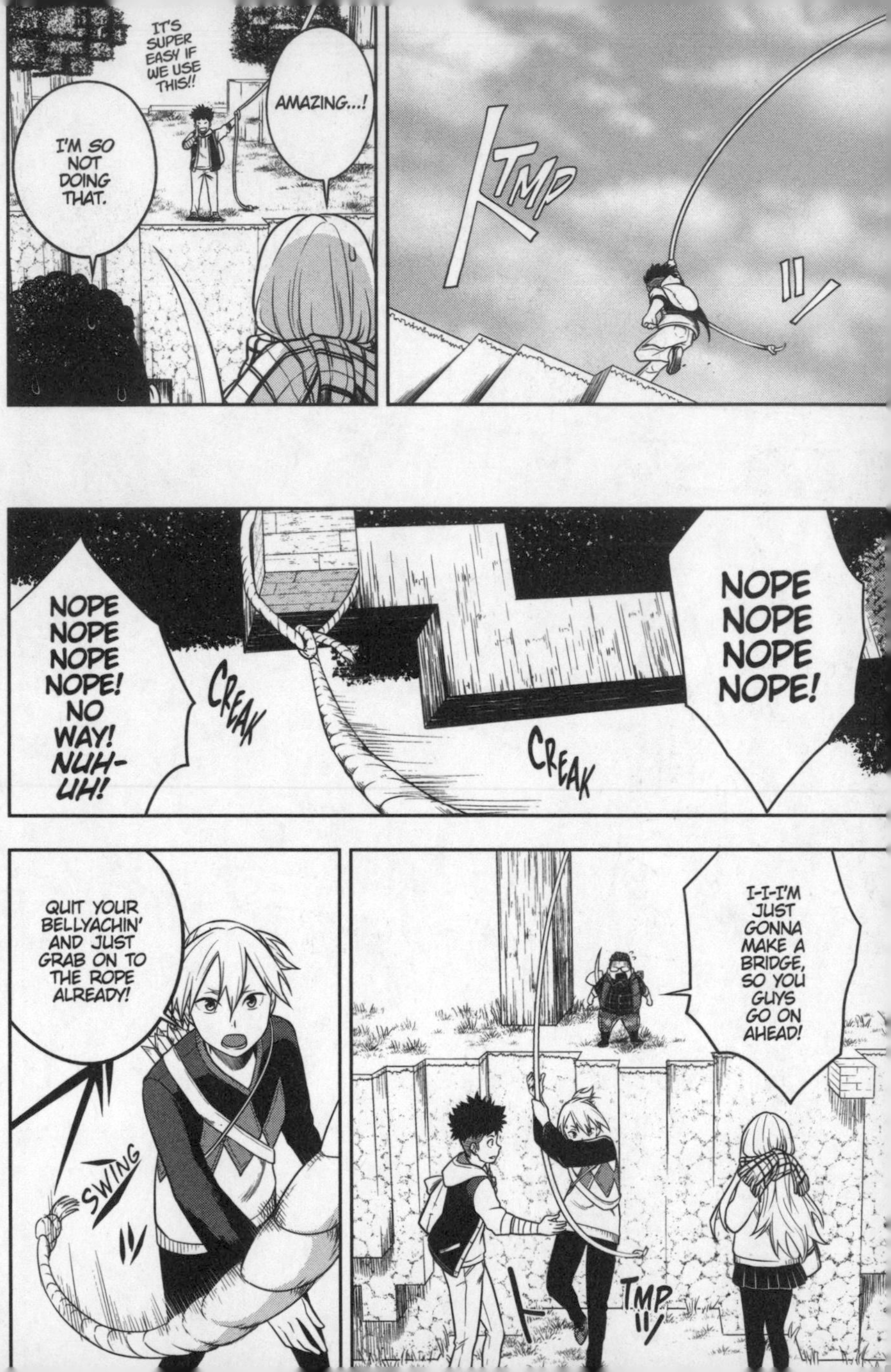
TMP
!!
IT'S SUPER EASY IF WE USE THIS!!
AMAZING...!
I'M SO NOT DOING THAT.
NOPE NOPE NOPE NOPE!
CREAK
CREAK
NOPE NOPE NOPE NOPE! NO WAY! NUH-UH!
I-I-I'M JUST GONNA MAKE A BRIDGE, SO YOU GUYS GO ON AHEAD!
TMP
QUIT YOUR BELLYACHIN' AND JUST GRAB ON TO THE ROPE ALREADY!
SWING

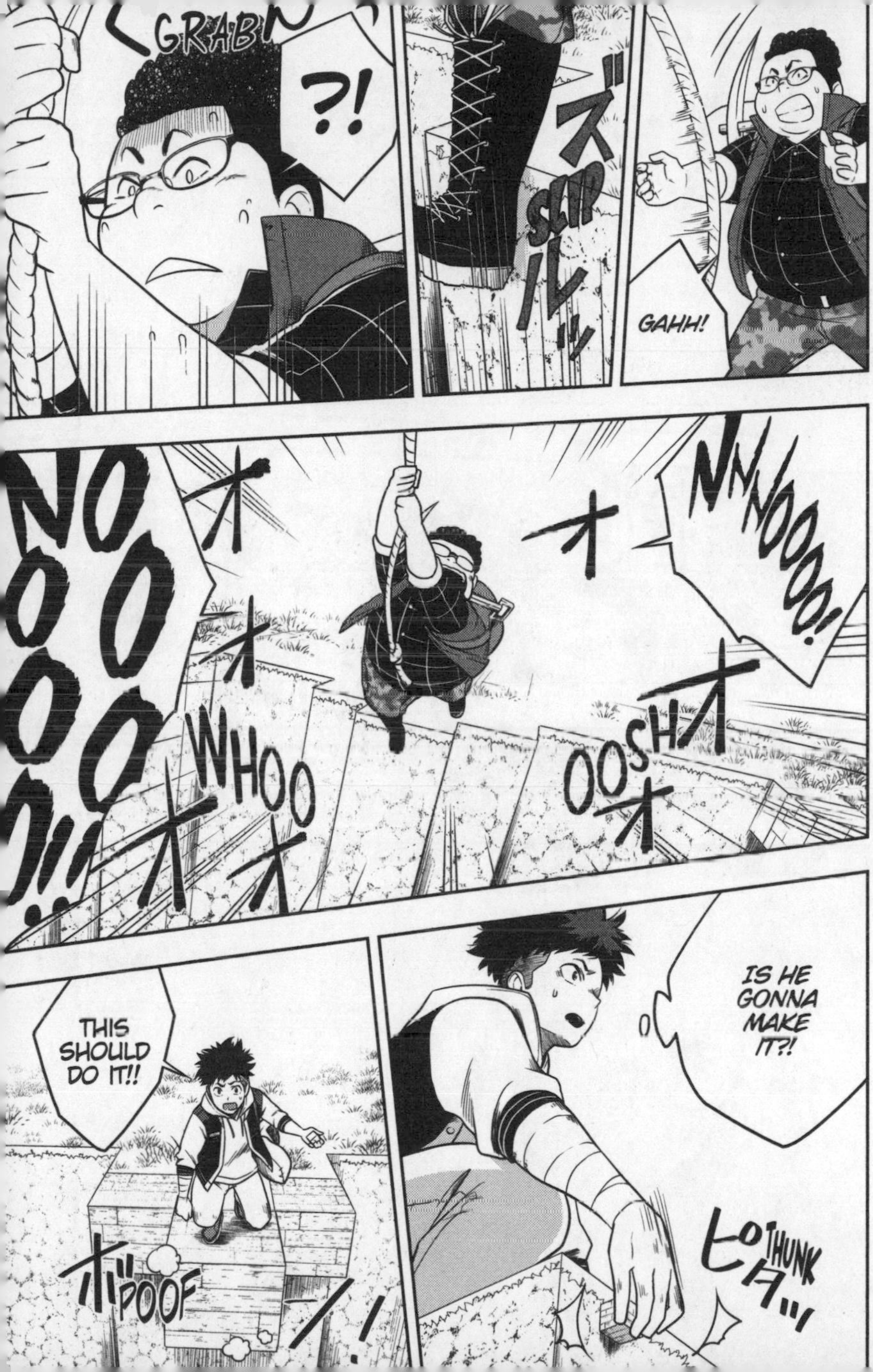
GAHH!
SLIP
GRAB
?!
NNNOOOOO!!
WHOOOSH
NOOOOOOO!!!
IS HE GONNA MAKE IT?!
THUNK
THIS SHOULD DO IT!!
POOF

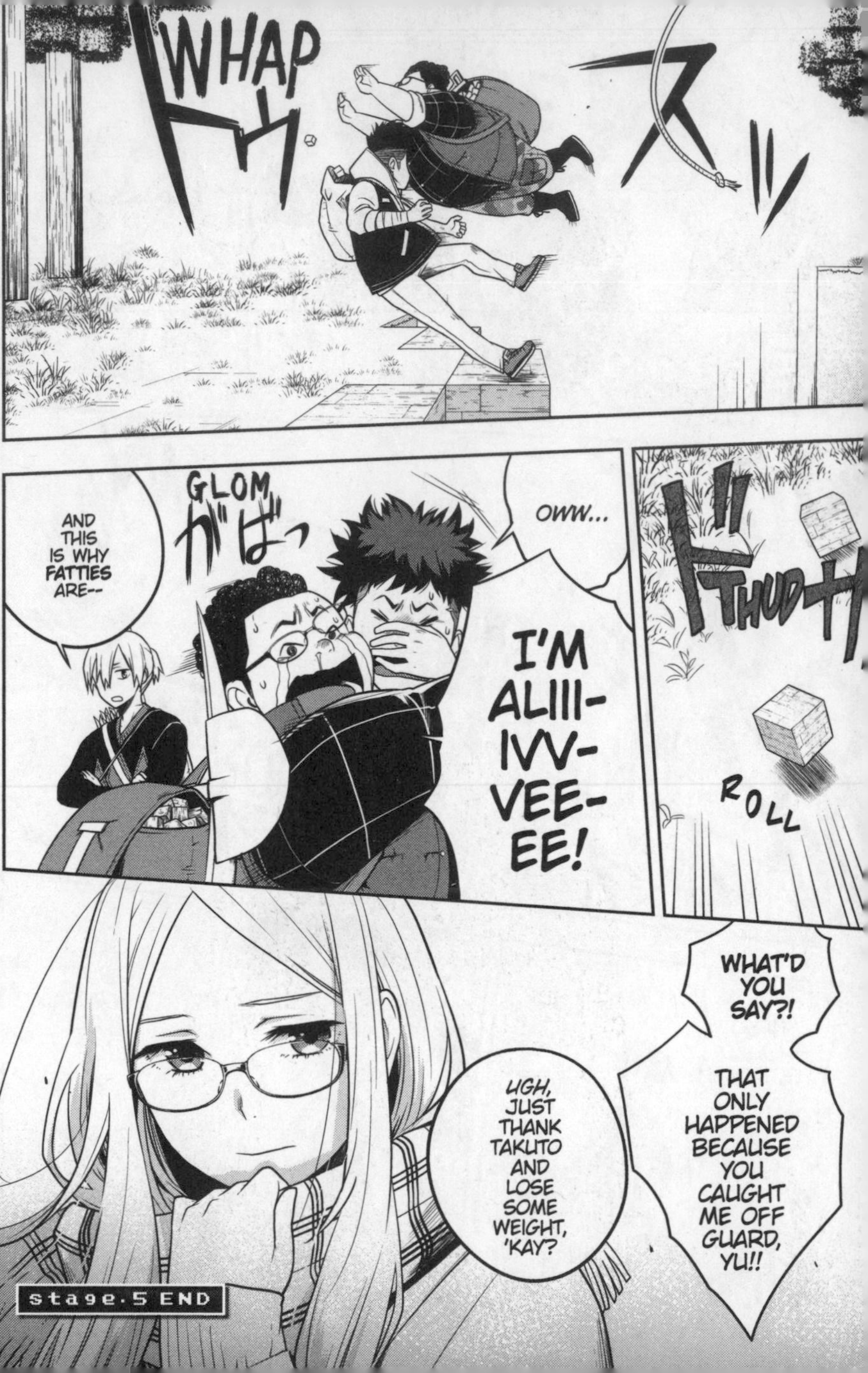
スッ
WHAP
ドゥ
THUD
ドッ
ROLL
OWW...
I'M ALIIII-IVV-VEE-EE!
GLOM
がばっ
AND THIS IS WHY FATTIES ARE--
WHAT'D YOU SAY?!
THAT ONLY HAPPENED BECAUSE YOU CAUGHT ME OFF GUARD, YU!!
UGH, JUST THANK TAKUTO AND LOSE SOME WEIGHT, 'KAY?
stage.5 END

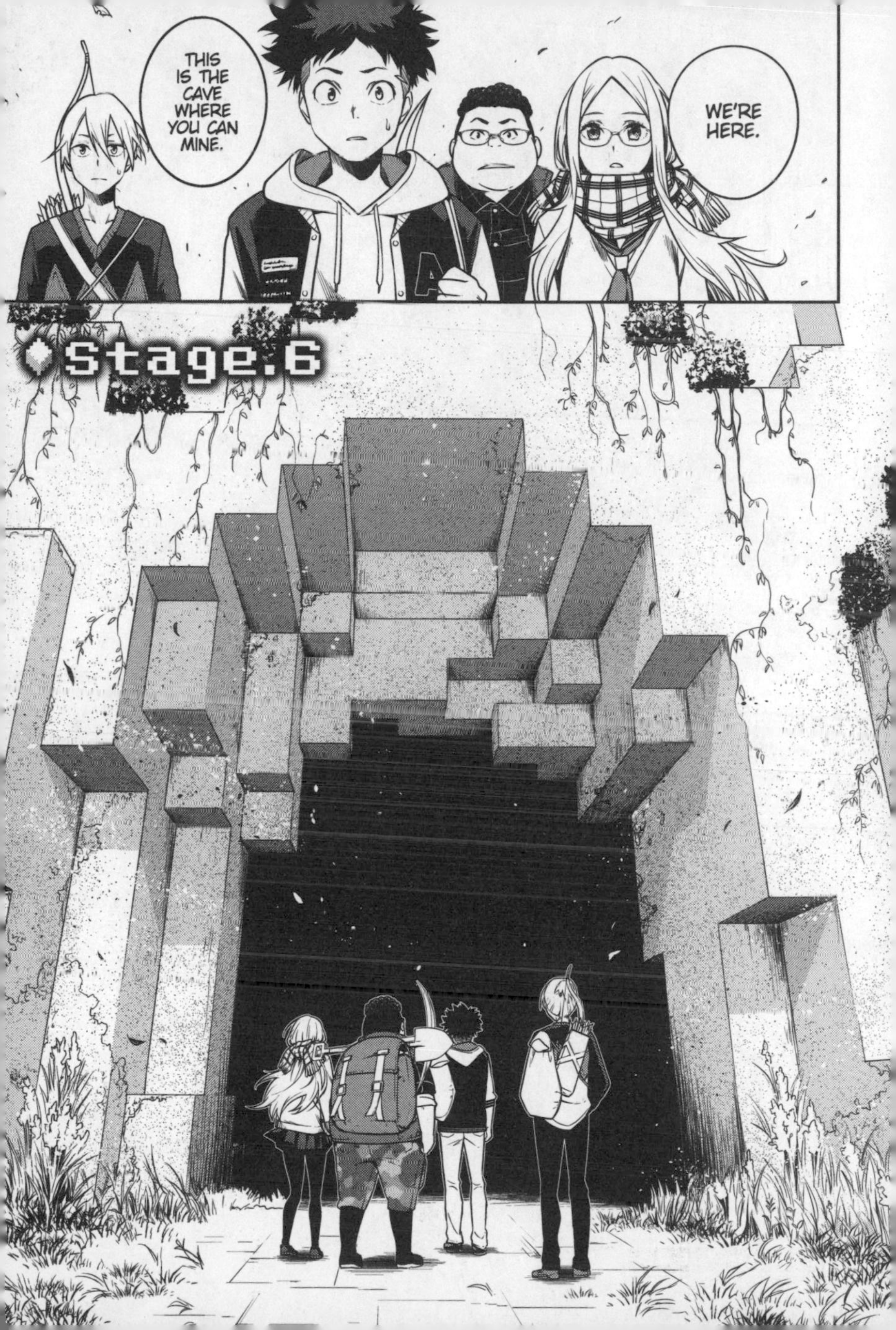
WE'RE HERE.
THIS IS THE CAVE WHERE YOU CAN MINE.
Stage.6

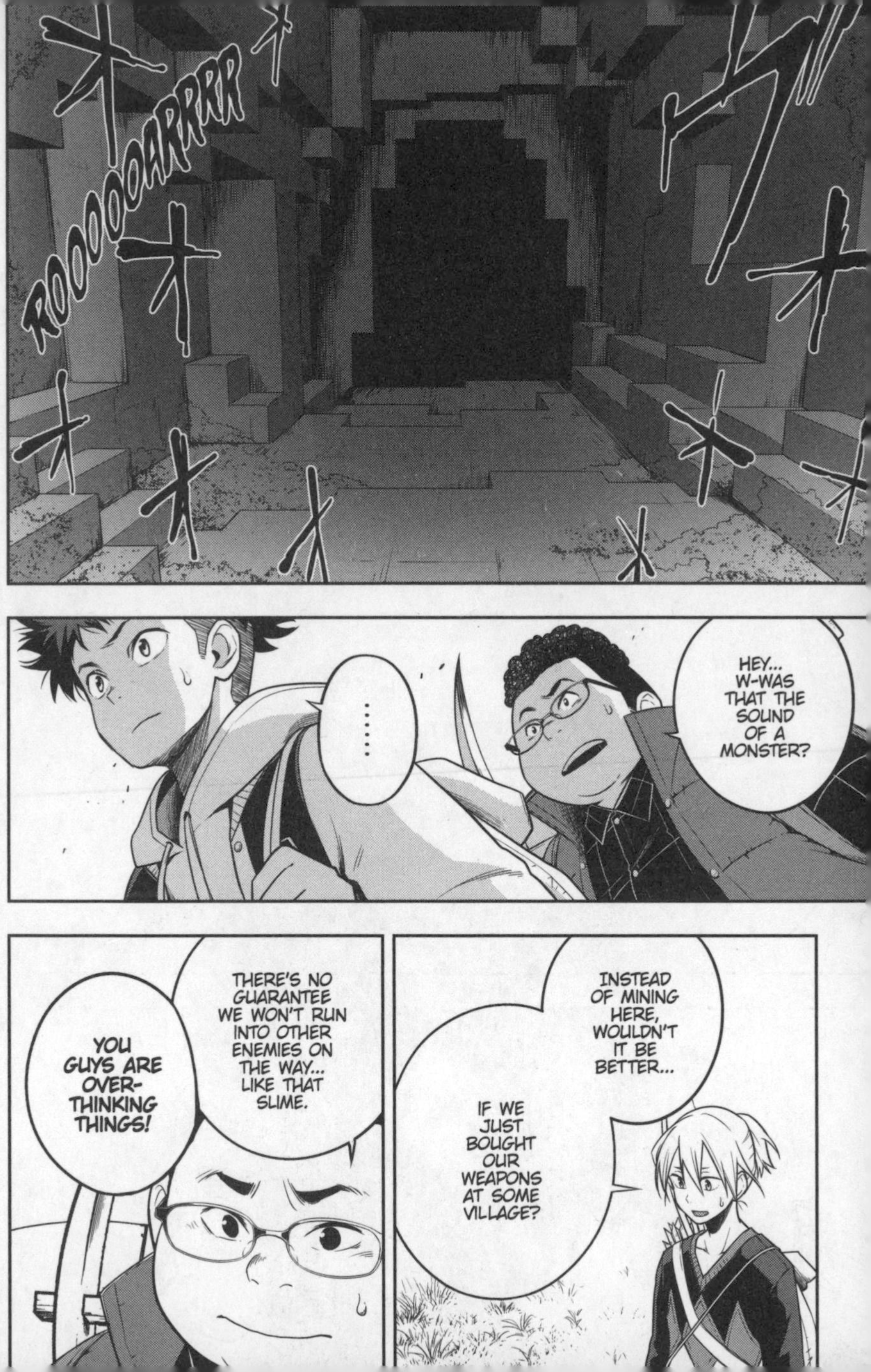
ROOOOOARRRR
HEY... W-WAS THAT THE SOUND OF A MONSTER?
......
INSTEAD OF MINING HERE, WOULDN'T IT BE BETTER...
IF WE JUST BOUGHT OUR WEAPONS AT SOME VILLAGE?
THERE'S NO GUARANTEE WE WON'T RUN INTO OTHER ENEMIES ON THE WAY... LIKE THAT SLIME.
YOU GUYS ARE OVER-THINKING THINGS!

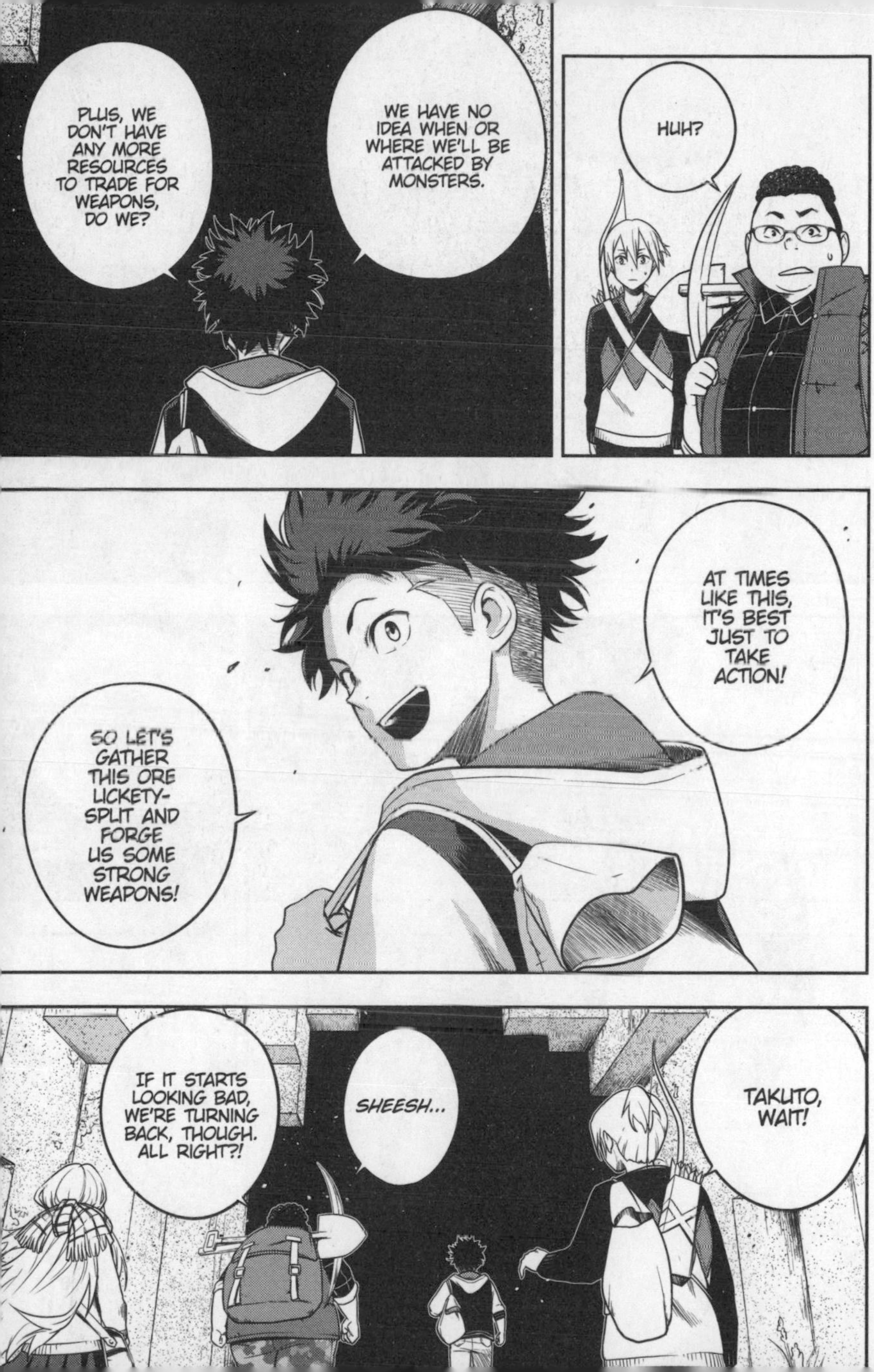
HUH?
WE HAVE NO IDEA WHEN OR WHERE WE'LL BE ATTACKED BY MONSTERS.
PLUS, WE DON'T HAVE ANY MORE RESOURCES TO TRADE FOR WEAPONS, DO WE?
AT TIMES LIKE THIS, IT'S BEST JUST TO TAKE ACTION!
SO LET'S GATHER THIS ORE LICKETY-SPLIT AND FORGE US SOME STRONG WEAPONS!
TAKUTO, WAIT!
SHEESH...
IF IT STARTS LOOKING BAD, WE'RE TURNING BACK, THOUGH. ALL RIGHT?!

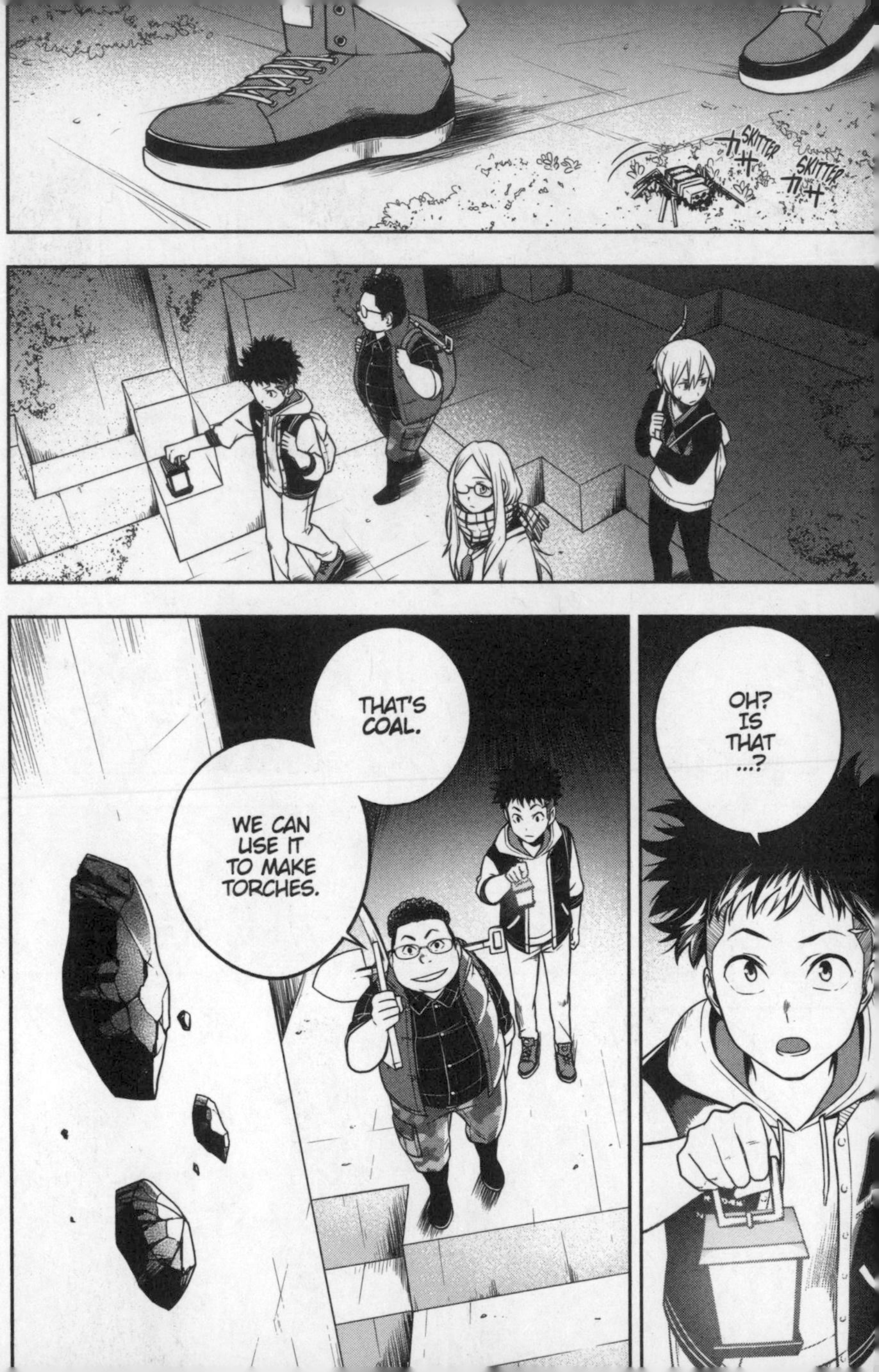
SKITTER
SKITTER
OH? IS THAT ...?
THAT'S COAL.
WE CAN USE IT TO MAKE TORCHES.

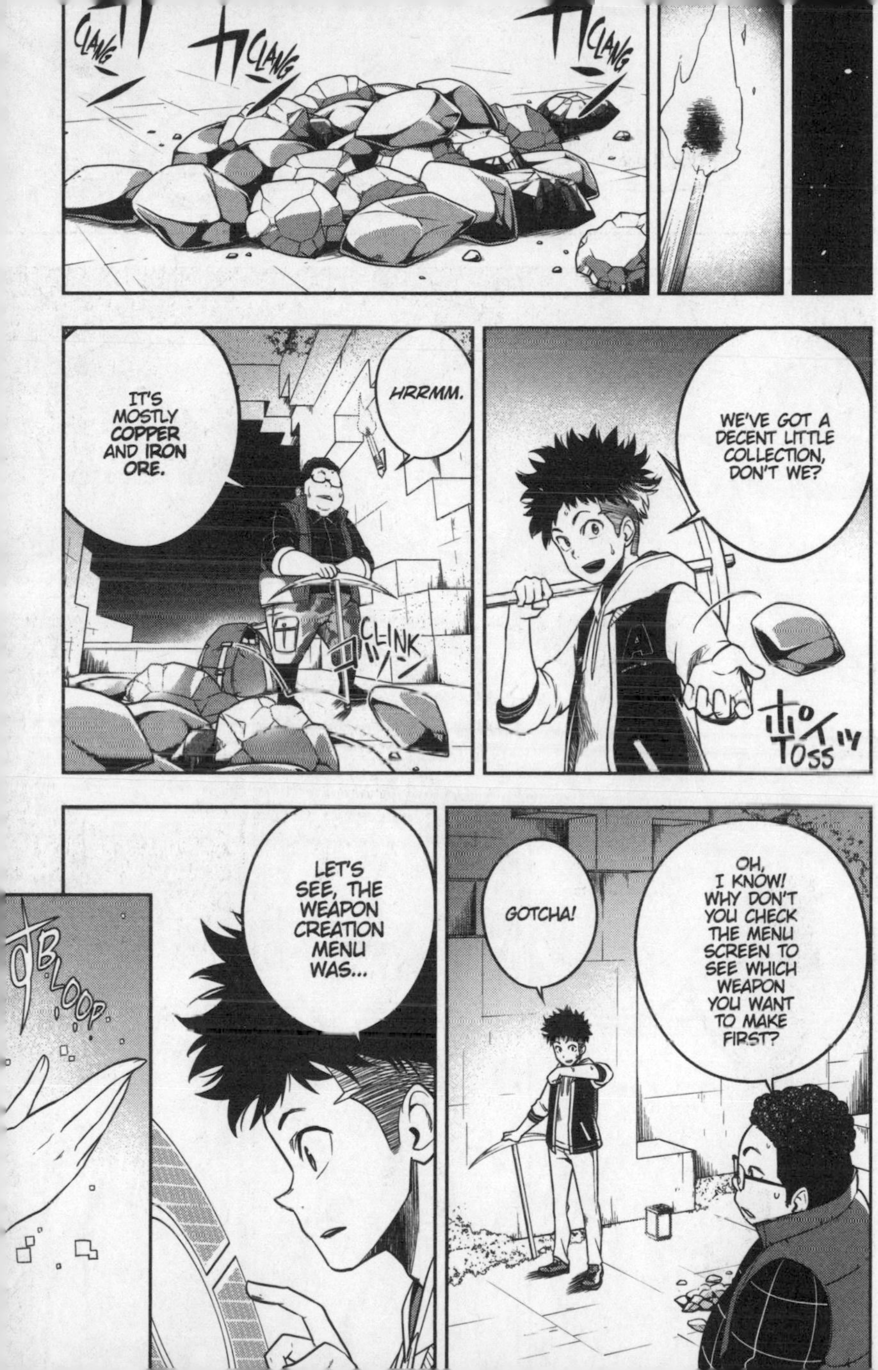
CLANG
CLANG
CLANG
WE'VE GOT A DECENT LITTLE COLLECTION, DON'T WE?
TOSS
HRRMM.
IT'S MOSTLY COPPER AND IRON ORE.
CL-INK
OH, I KNOW! WHY DON'T YOU CHECK THE MENU SCREEN TO SEE WHICH WEAPON YOU WANT TO MAKE FIRST?
GOTCHA!
LET'S SEE, THE WEAPON CREATION MENU WAS...
BLOOP

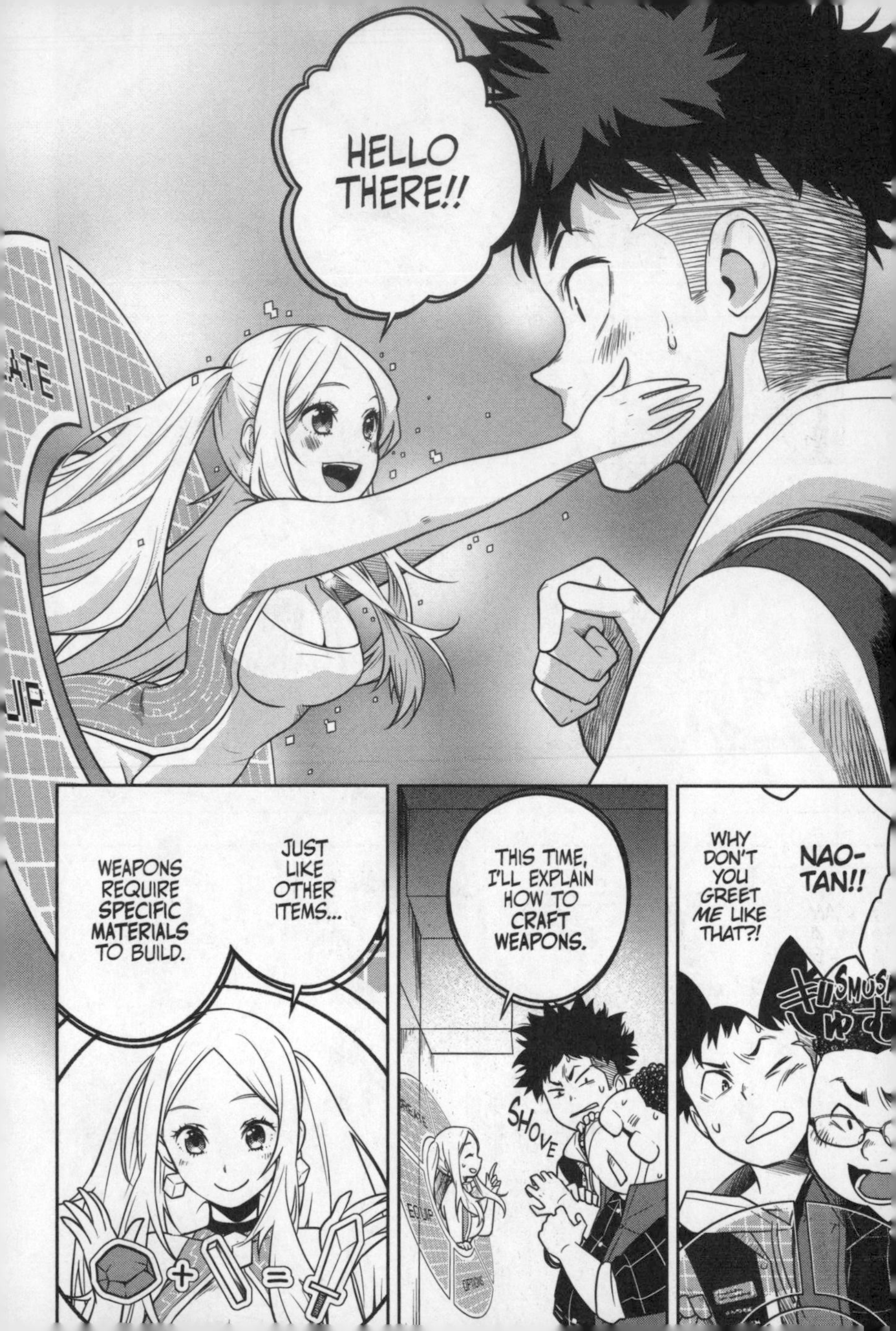
HELLO THERE!!
NAO-TAN!!
WHY DON'T YOU GREET ME LIKE THAT?!
SMUSH
THIS TIME, I'LL EXPLAIN HOW TO CRAFT WEAPONS.
SHOVE
EQUIP
JUST LIKE OTHER ITEMS...
WEAPONS REQUIRE SPECIFIC MATERIALS TO BUILD.

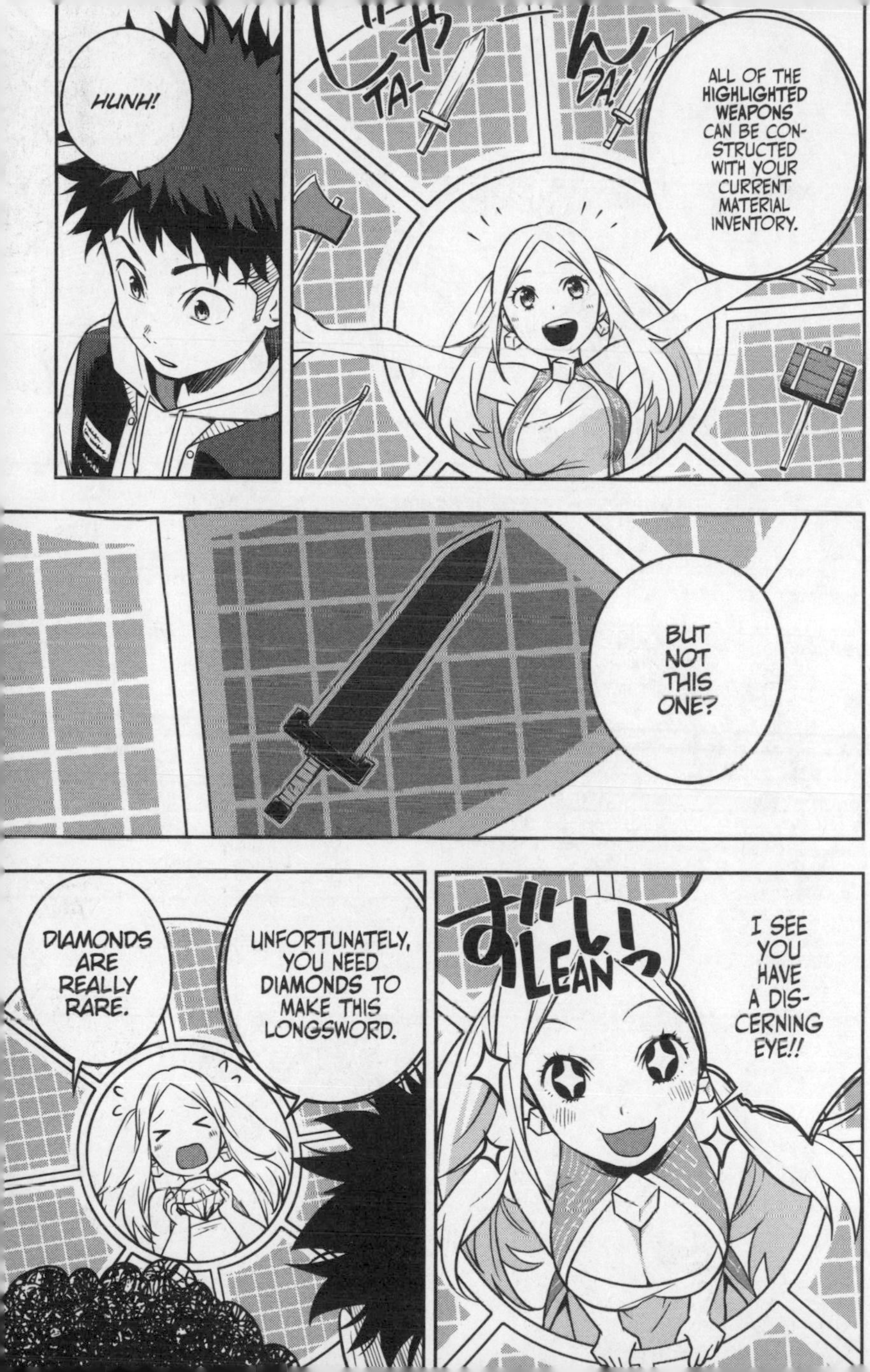
じゃーん
TA-DA!
ALL OF THE HIGHLIGHTED WEAPONS CAN BE CON-STRUCTED WITH YOUR CURRENT MATERIAL INVENTORY.
HUNH!
BUT NOT THIS ONE?
ずいっ
LEAN
I SEE YOU HAVE A DIS-CERNING EYE!!
UNFORTUNATELY, YOU NEED DIAMONDS TO MAKE THIS LONGSWORD.
DIAMONDS ARE REALLY RARE.

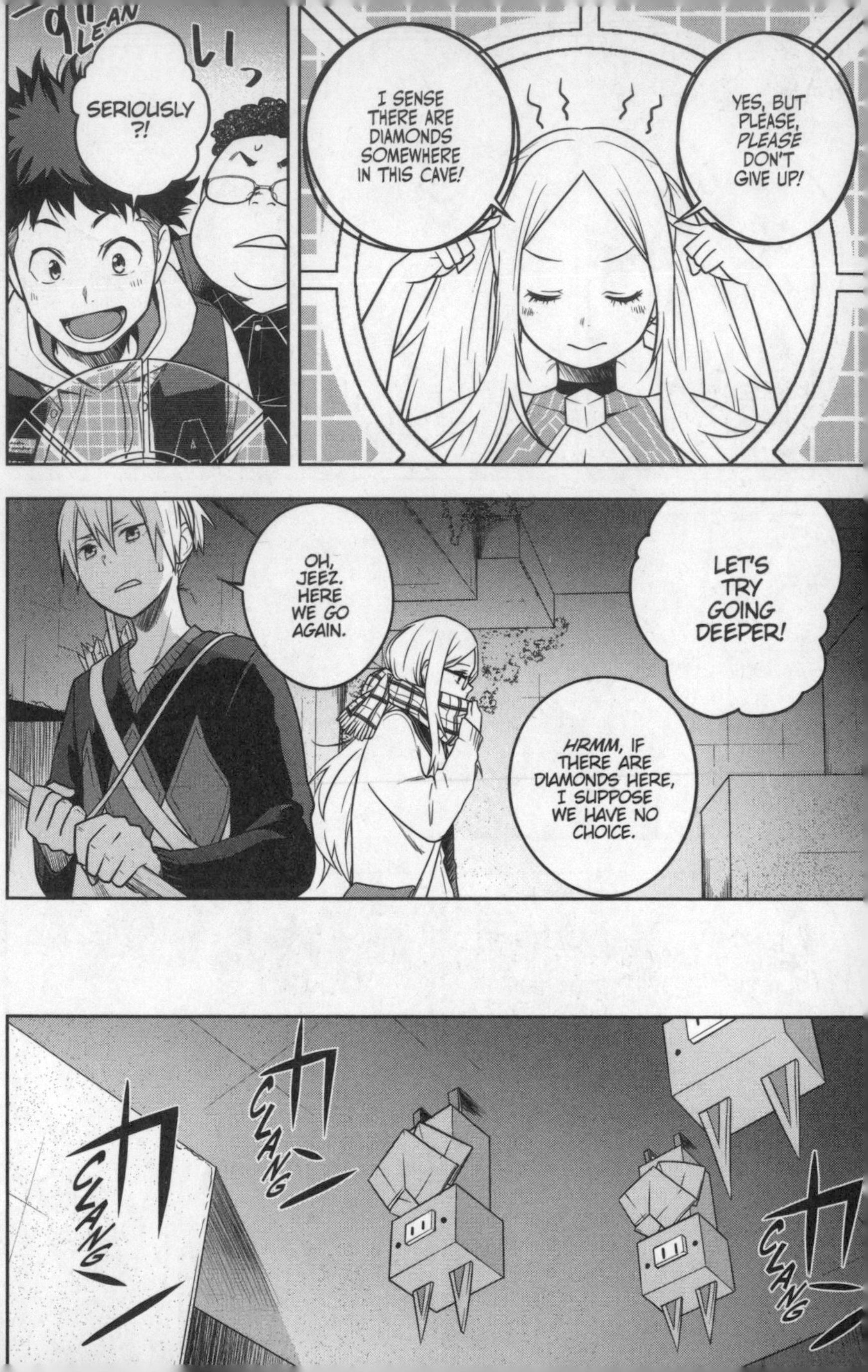
YES, BUT PLEASE, *PLEASE* DON'T GIVE UP!
I SENSE THERE ARE DIAMONDS SOMEWHERE IN THIS CAVE!
LEAN
SERIOUSLY ?!
LET'S TRY GOING DEEPER!
HRMM, IF THERE ARE DIAMONDS HERE, I SUPPOSE WE HAVE NO CHOICE.
OH, JEEZ. HERE WE GO AGAIN.
CLANG
CLANG
CLANG
CLANG

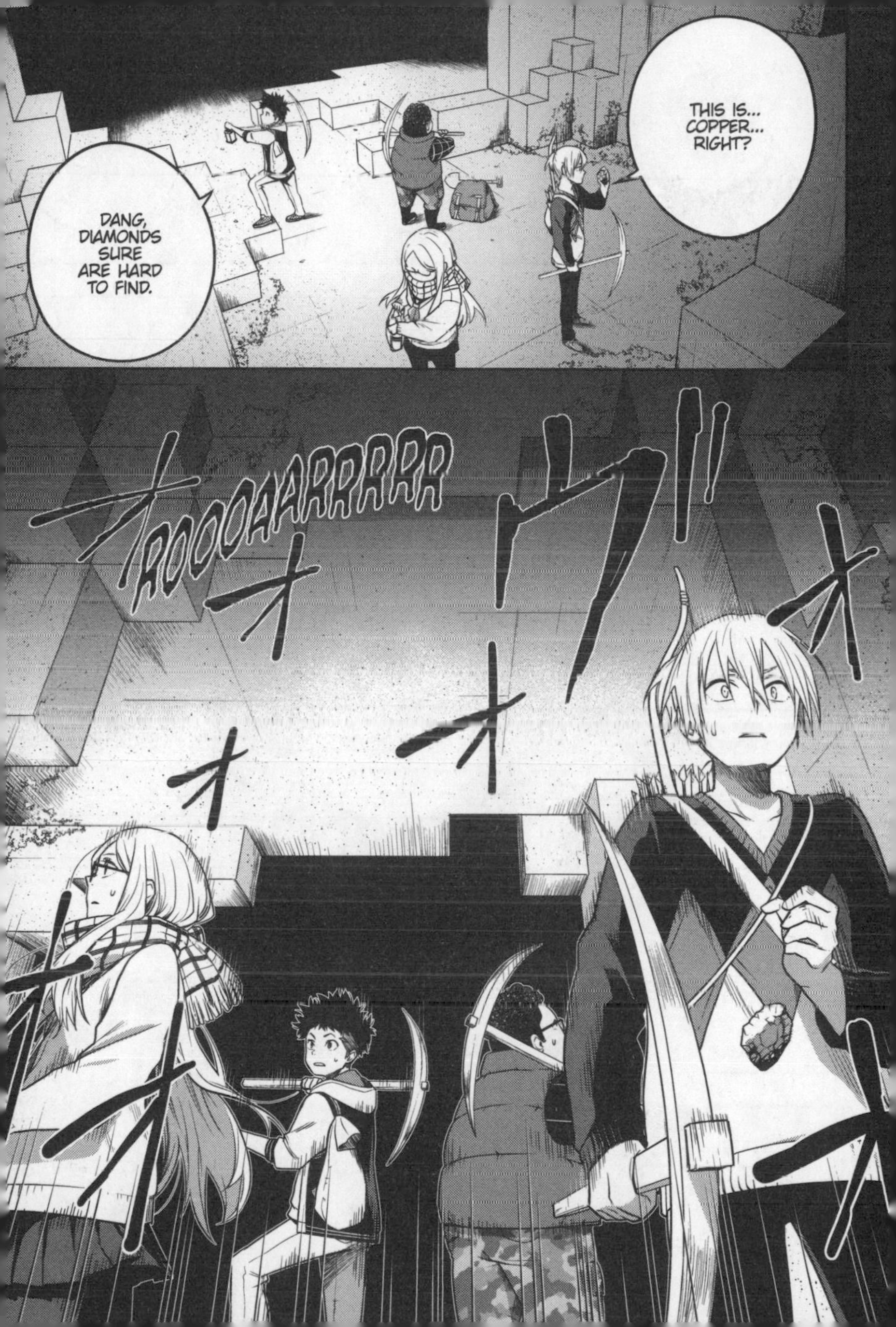
THIS IS... COPPER... RIGHT?
DANG, DIAMONDS SURE ARE HARD TO FIND.
ROOOAARRRRR

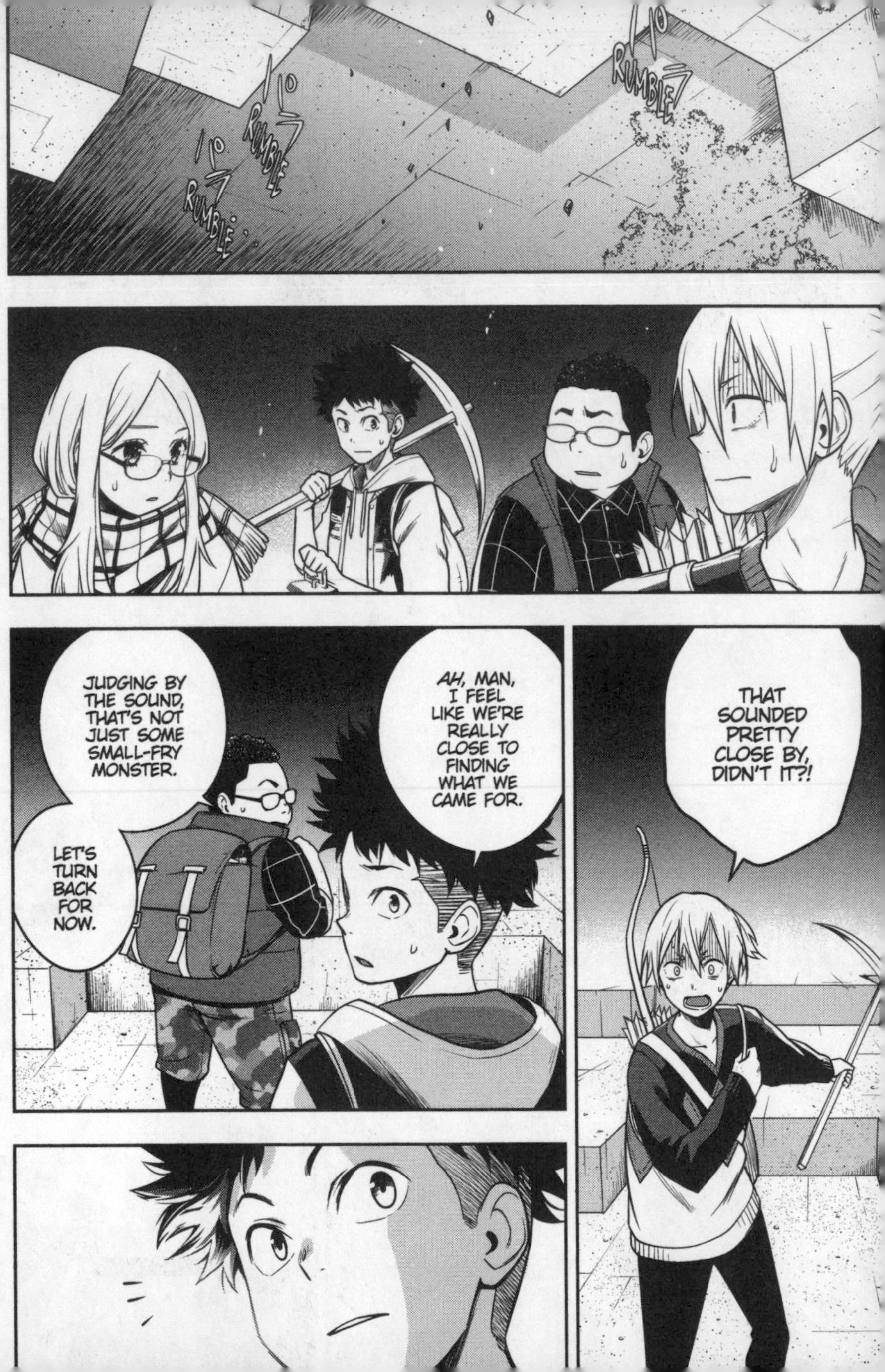
RUMBLE
RUMBLE
RUMBLE...
THAT SOUNDED PRETTY CLOSE BY, DIDN'T IT?!
AH, MAN, I FEEL LIKE WE'RE REALLY CLOSE TO FINDING WHAT WE CAME FOR.
JUDGING BY THE SOUND, THAT'S NOT JUST SOME SMALL-FRY MONSTER.
LET'S TURN BACK FOR NOW.

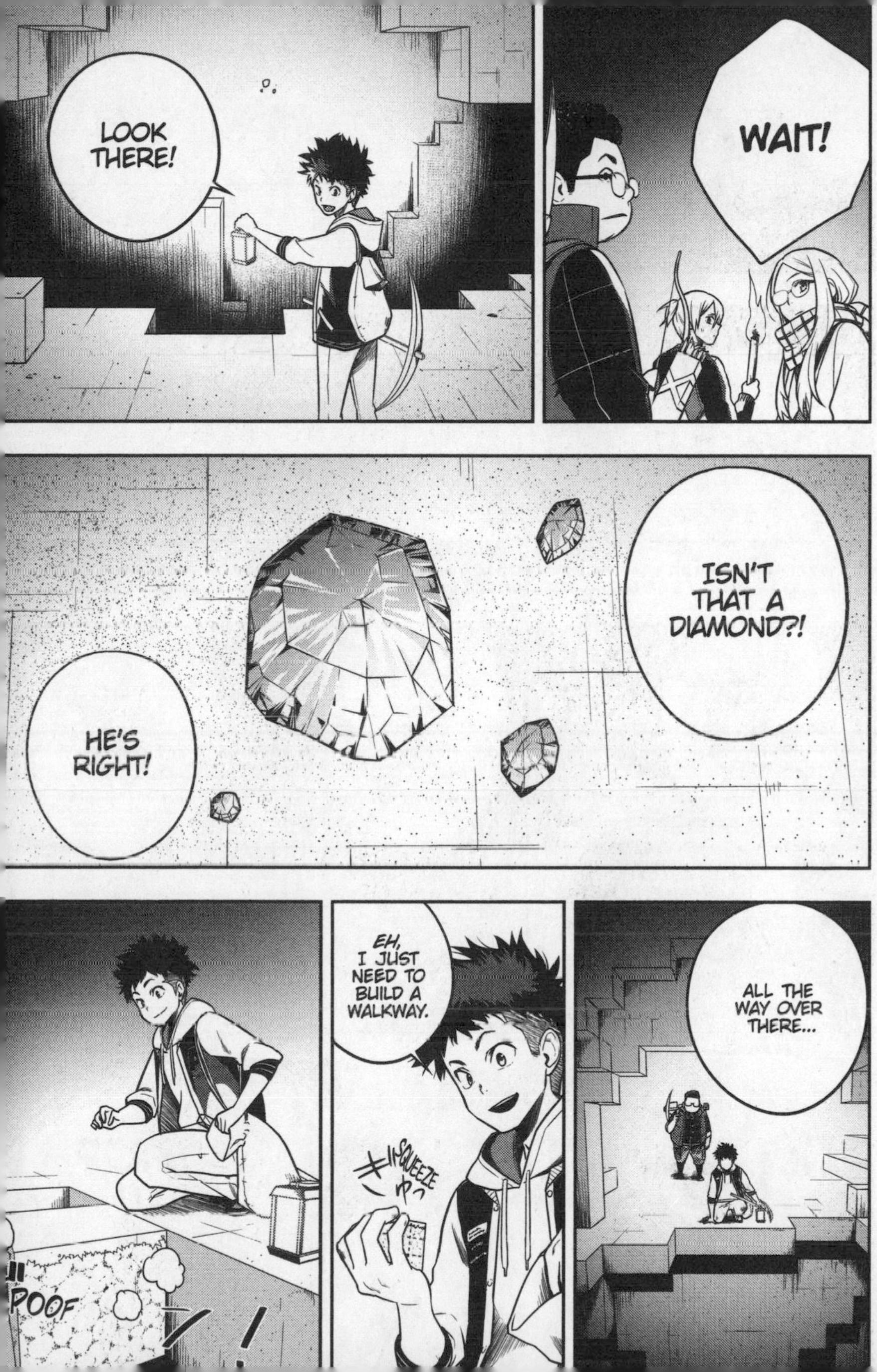
WAIT!
LOOK THERE!
ISN'T THAT A DIAMOND?!
HE'S RIGHT!
ALL THE WAY OVER THERE...
EH, I JUST NEED TO BUILD A WALKWAY.
SQUEEZE
POOF

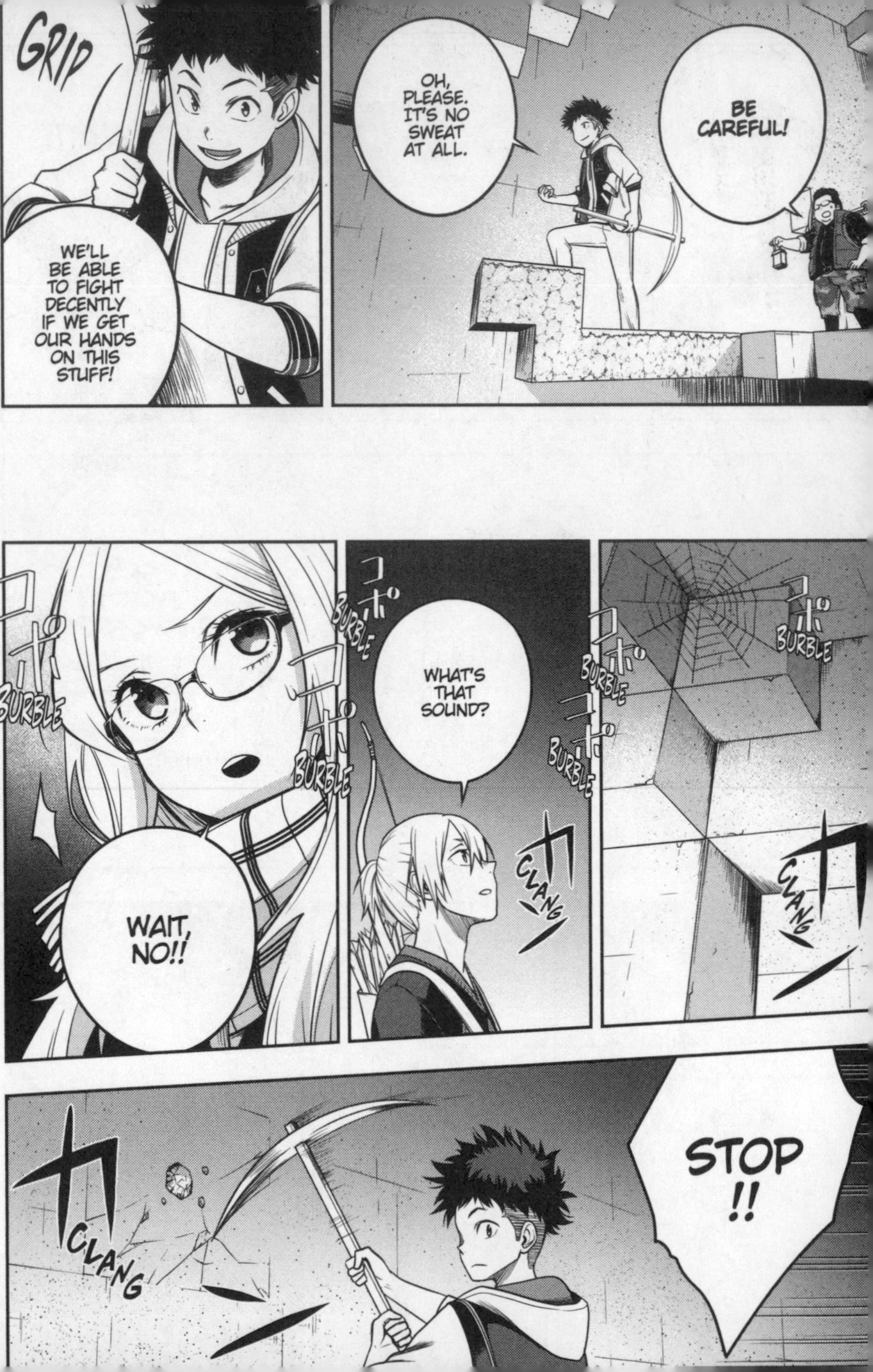
BE CAREFUL!
OH, PLEASE. IT'S NO SWEAT AT ALL.
GRIP
WE'LL BE ABLE TO FIGHT DECENTLY IF WE GET OUR HANDS ON THIS STUFF!
コポ
BURBLE
コポ
BURBLE
コポ
BURBLE
CLANG
コポ
BURBLE
WHAT'S THAT SOUND?
CLANG
コポ
BURBLE
コポ
BURBLE
WAIT, NO!!
STOP!!
CLANG

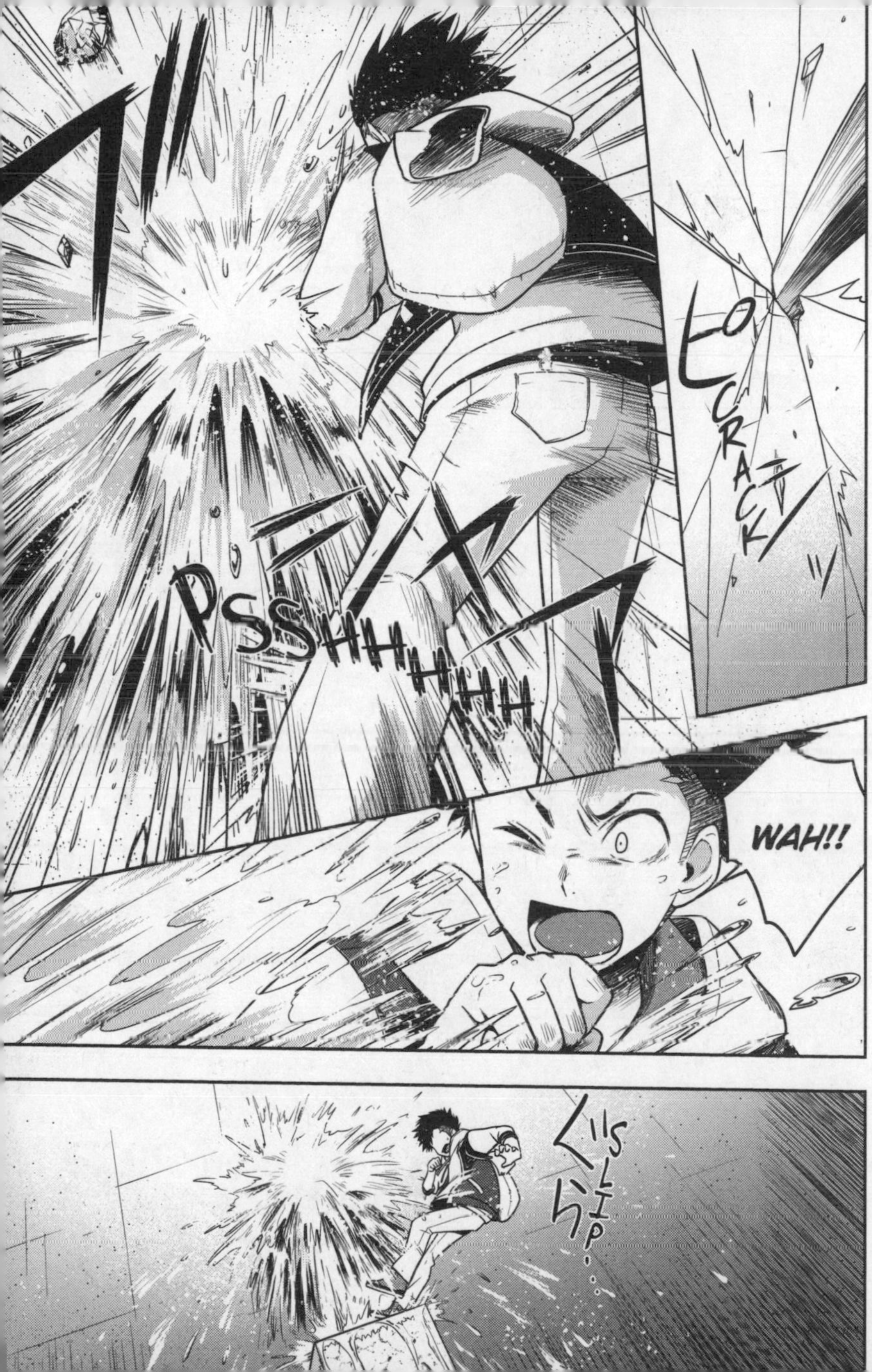
CRACK
PSSHHHHHHHH
WAH!!
SLIP...

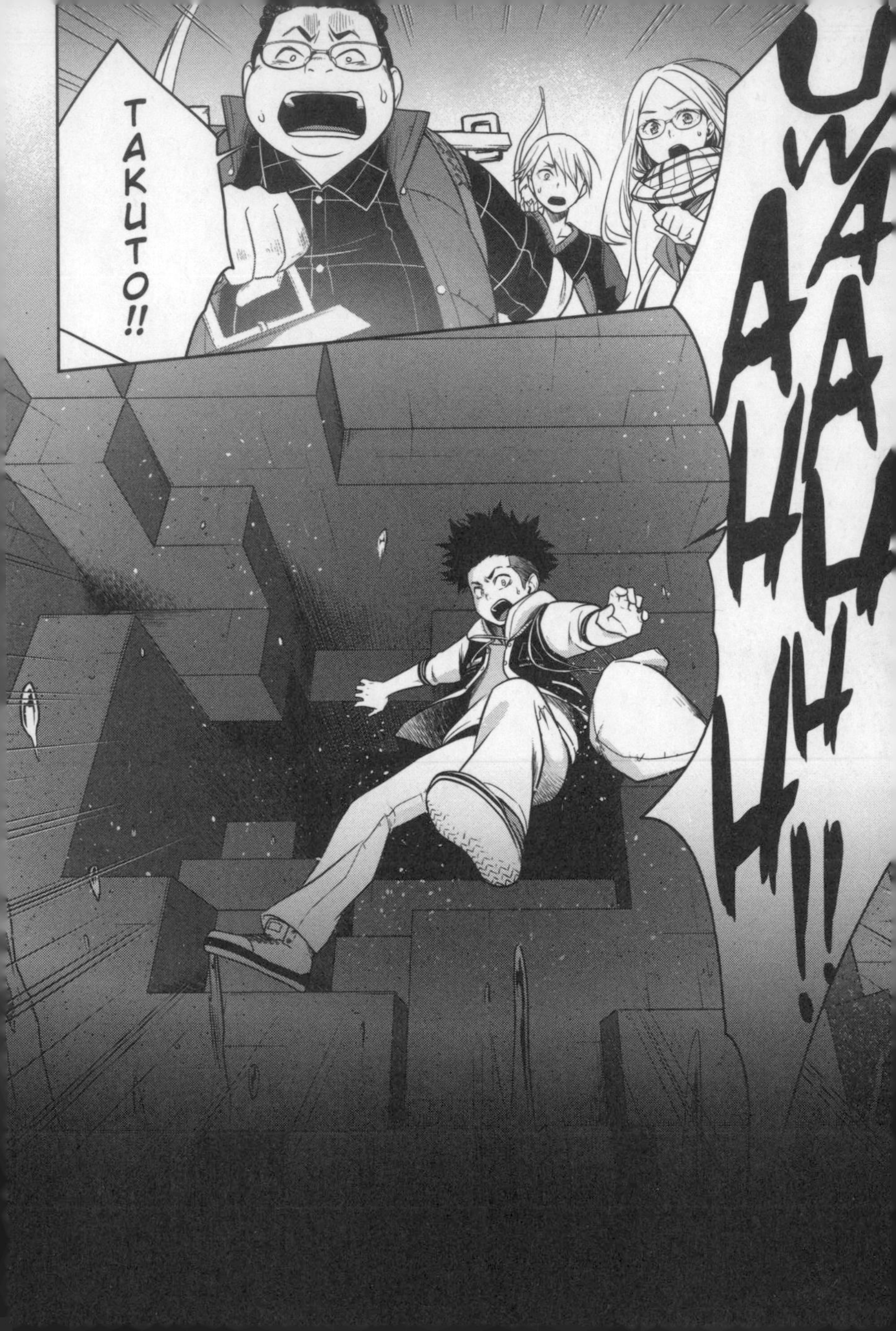
TAKUTO!!
UWAAAAHHHH!!

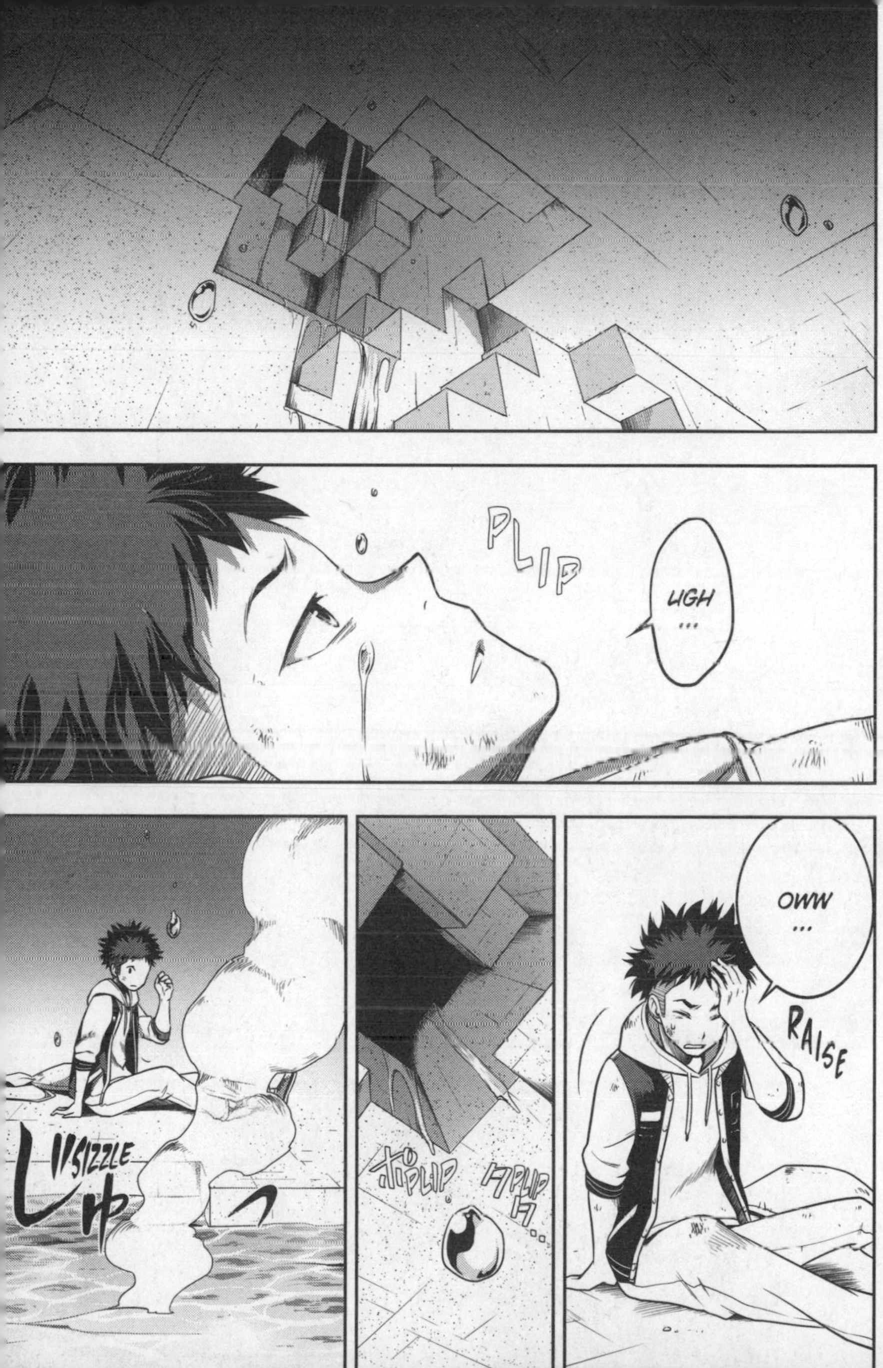
UGH ...
PLIP
OWW ...
RAISE
PLIP
PLIP
SIZZLE

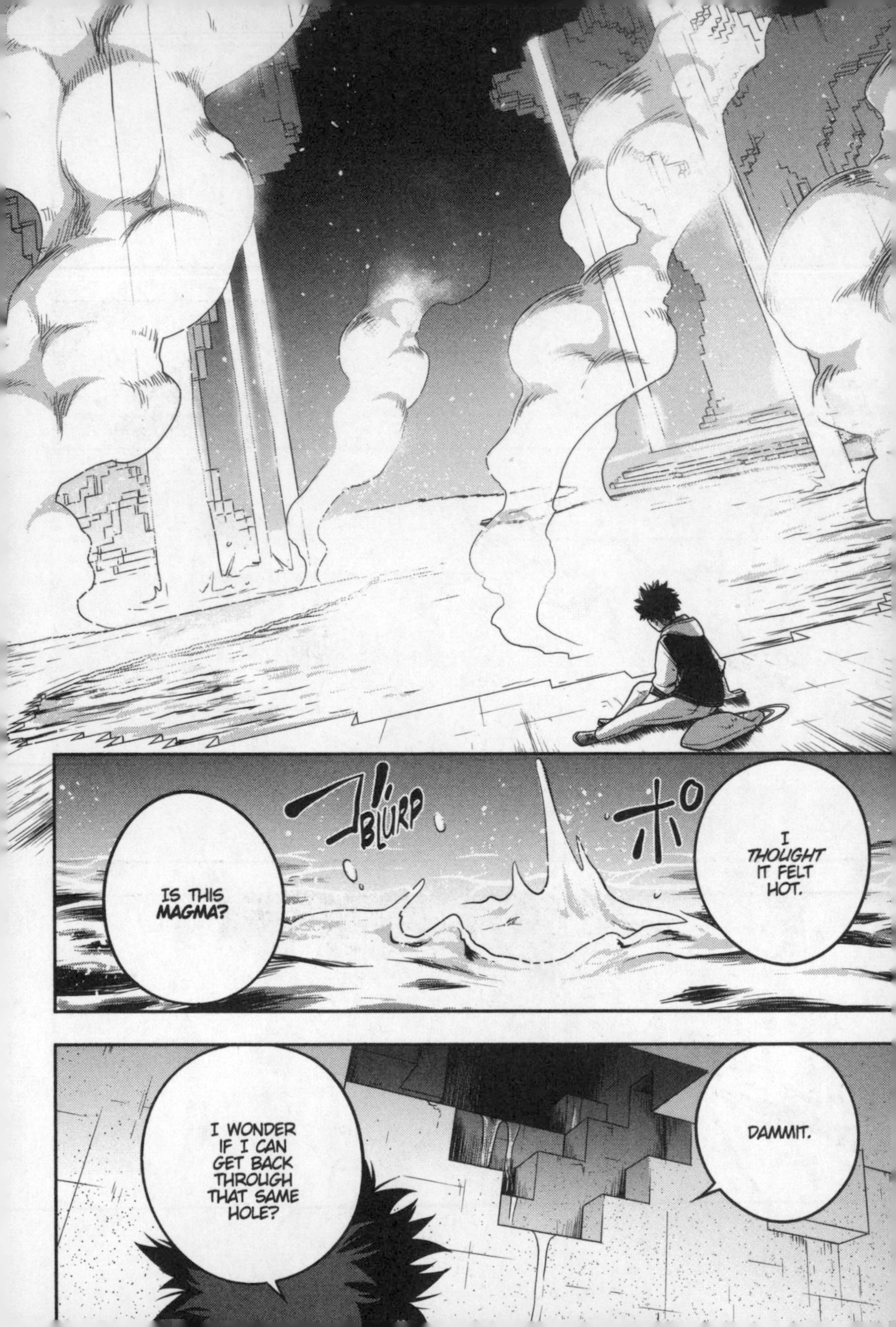

I THOUGHT IT FELT HOT.
ポ
BLURP
IS THIS MAGMA?
DAMMIT.
I WONDER IF I CAN GET BACK THROUGH THAT SAME HOLE?

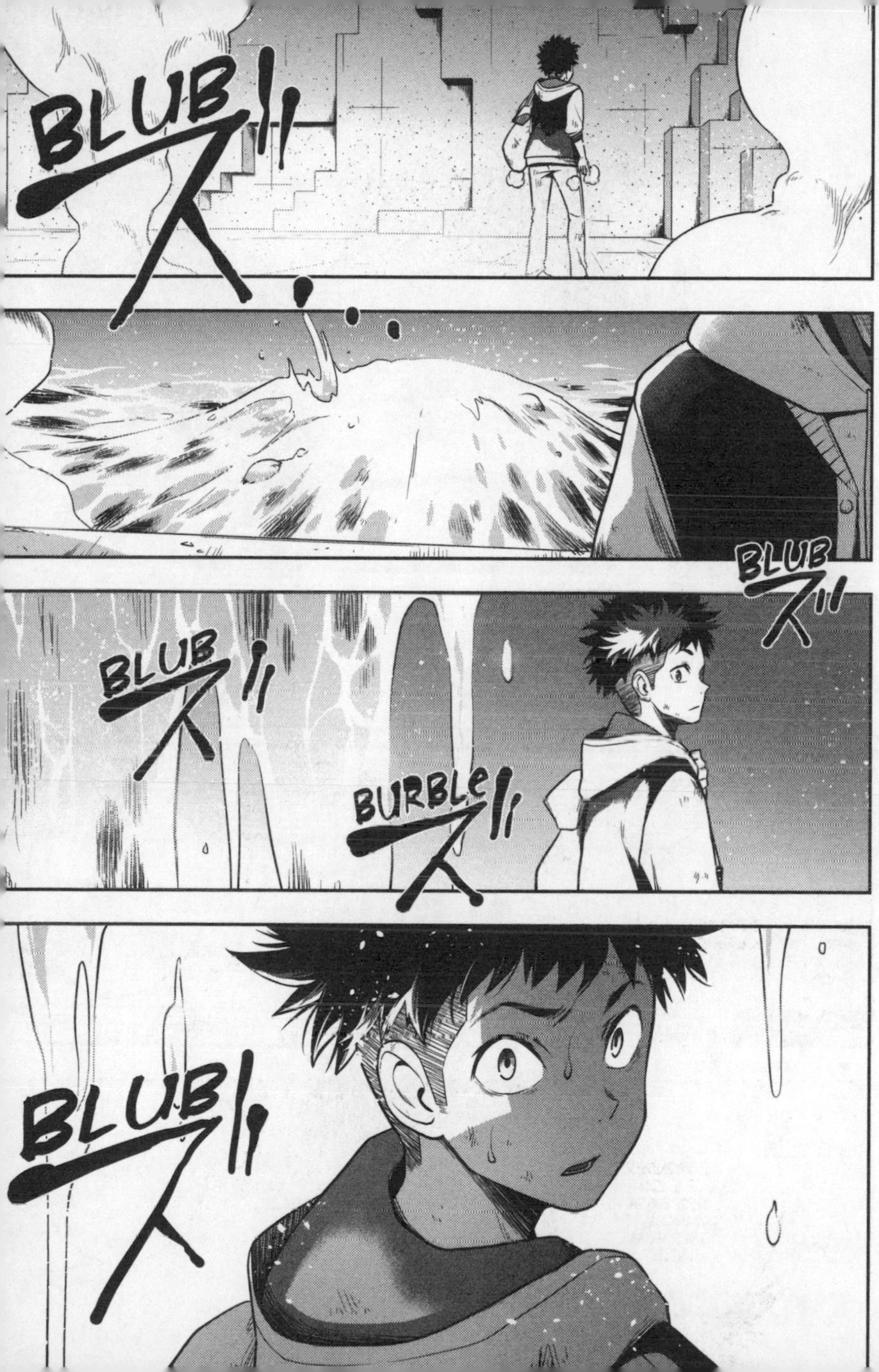
BLUB ズ
BLUB ズ
BURBLE ズ
BLUB ズ
BLUB ズ

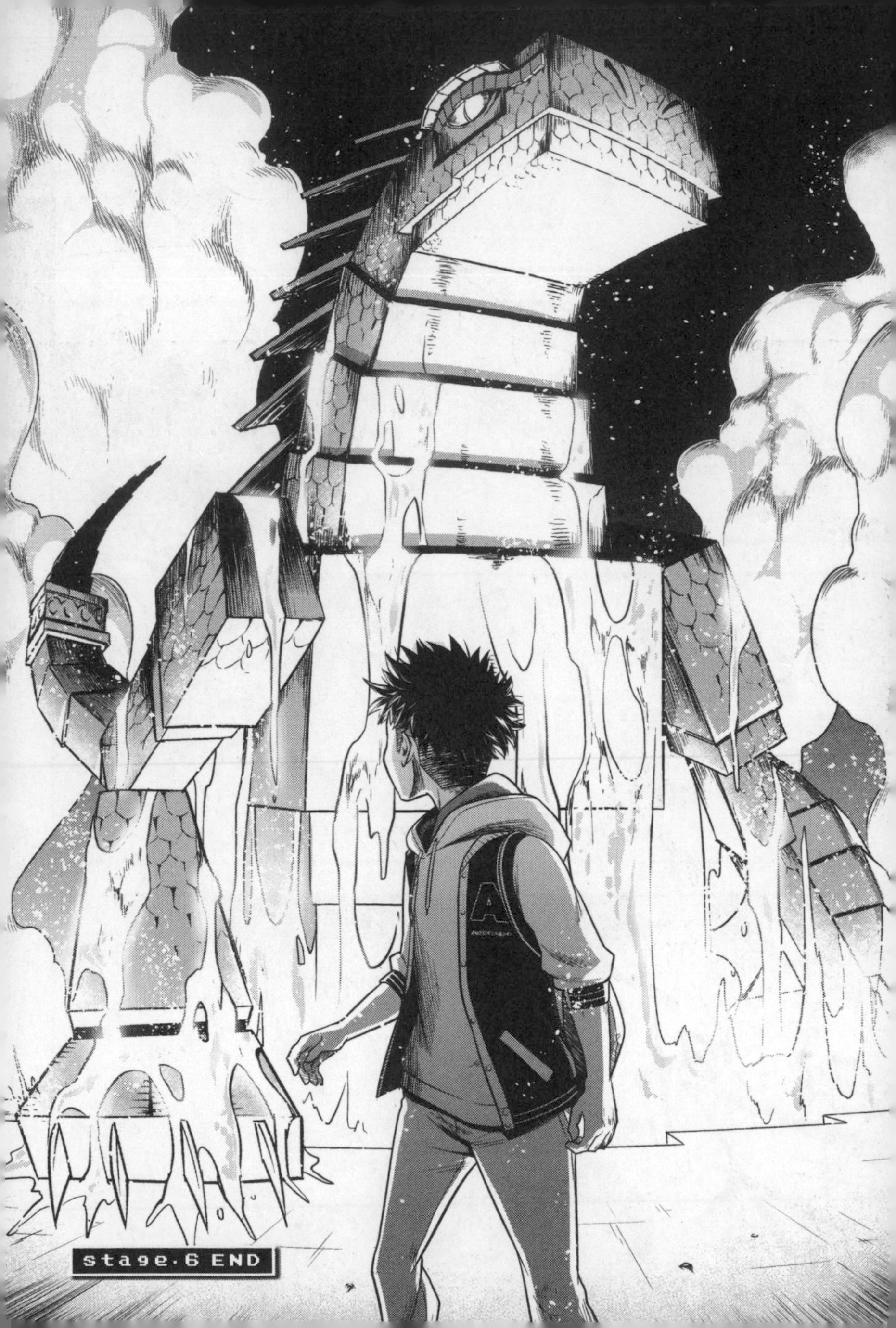
stage.6 END

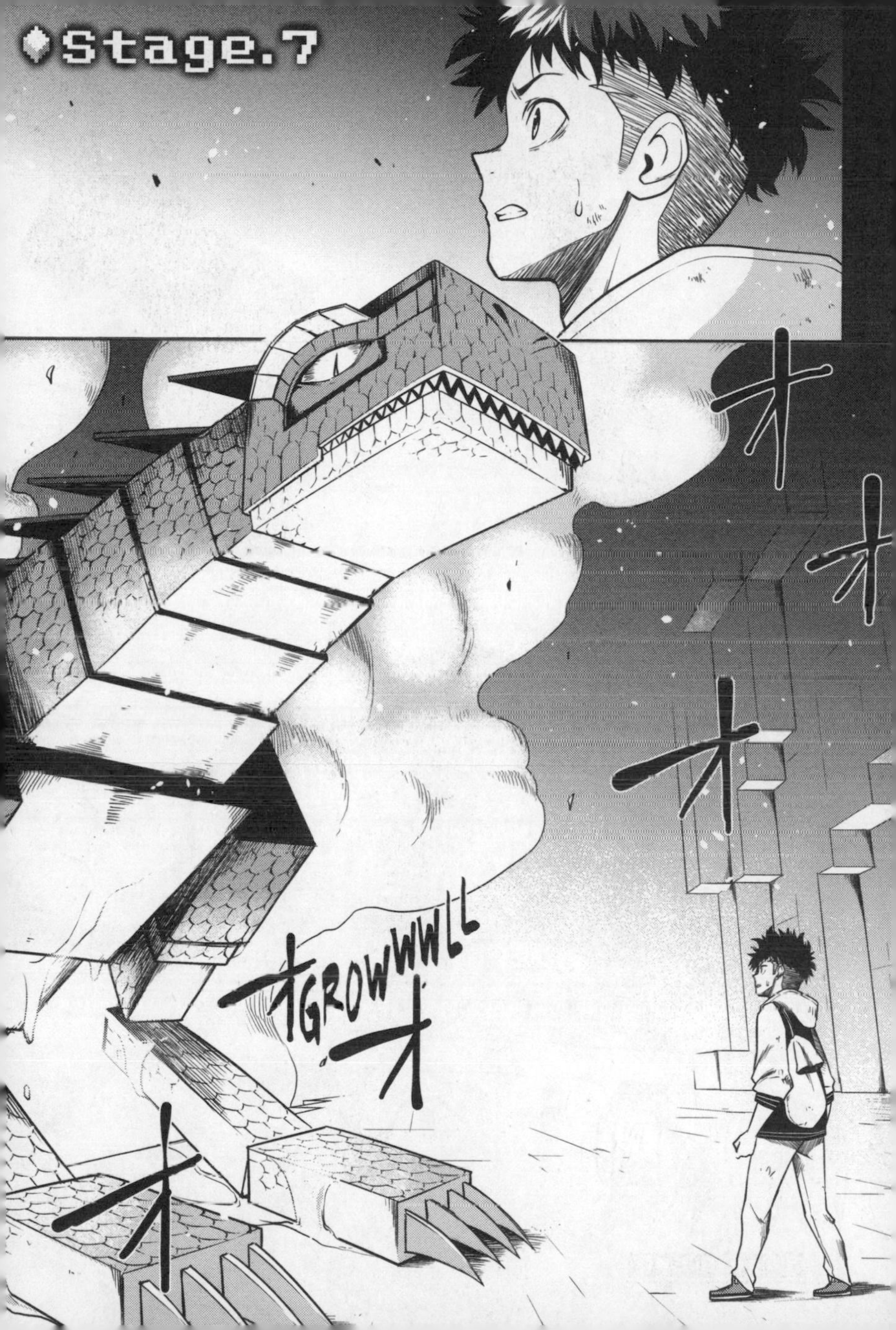
Stage.7
オオオ
GROWWWLL
オオオ

WHAT IS THAT THING?!

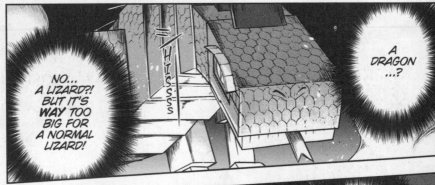

A DRAGON...?

NO... A LIZARD?! BUT IT'S WAY TOO BIG FOR A NORMAL LIZARD!

HISSSS

THERE'S ONLY ONE THING I CAN DO.

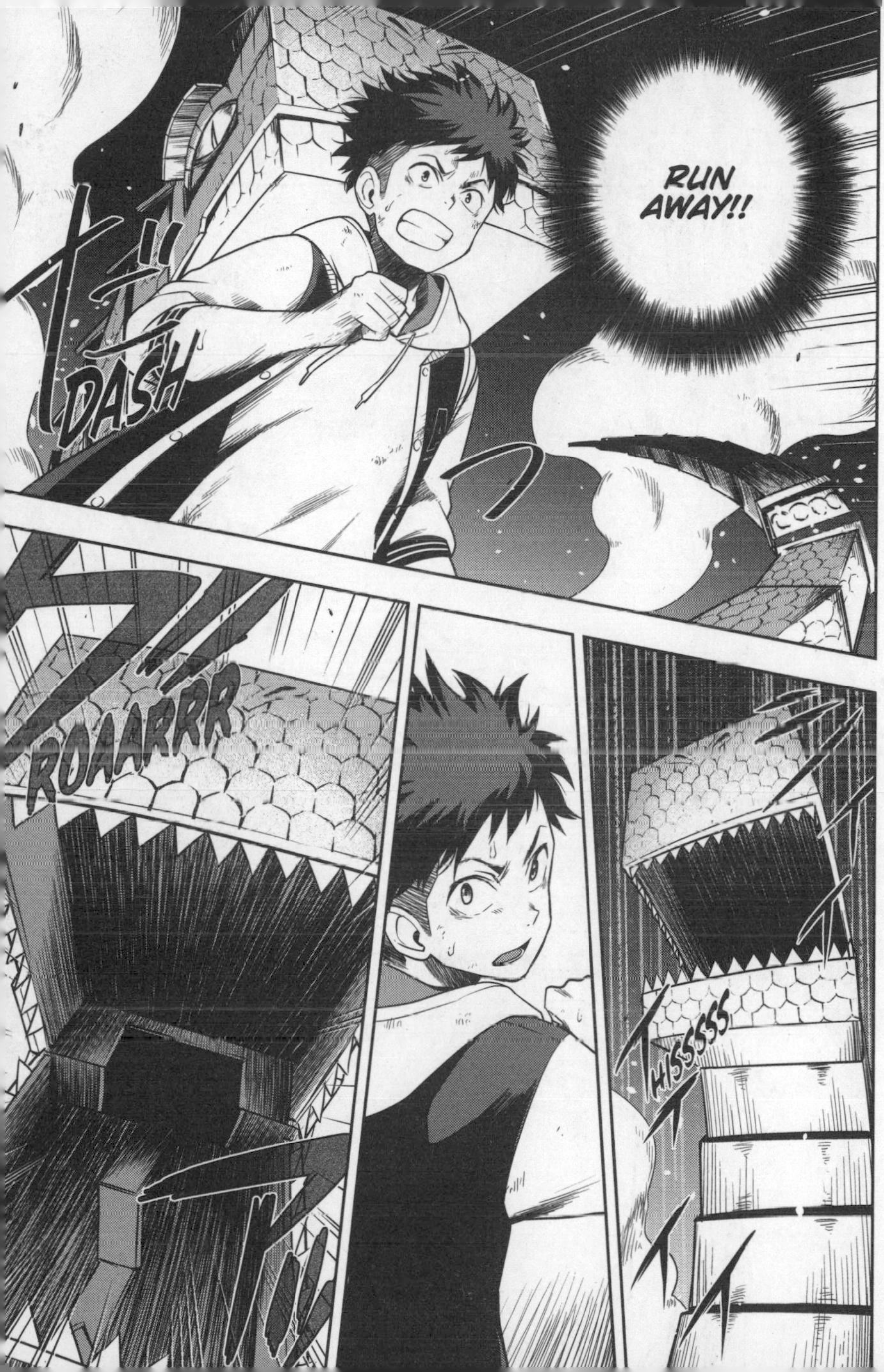
RUN AWAY!!
DASH
HISSSSS
ROAARRR

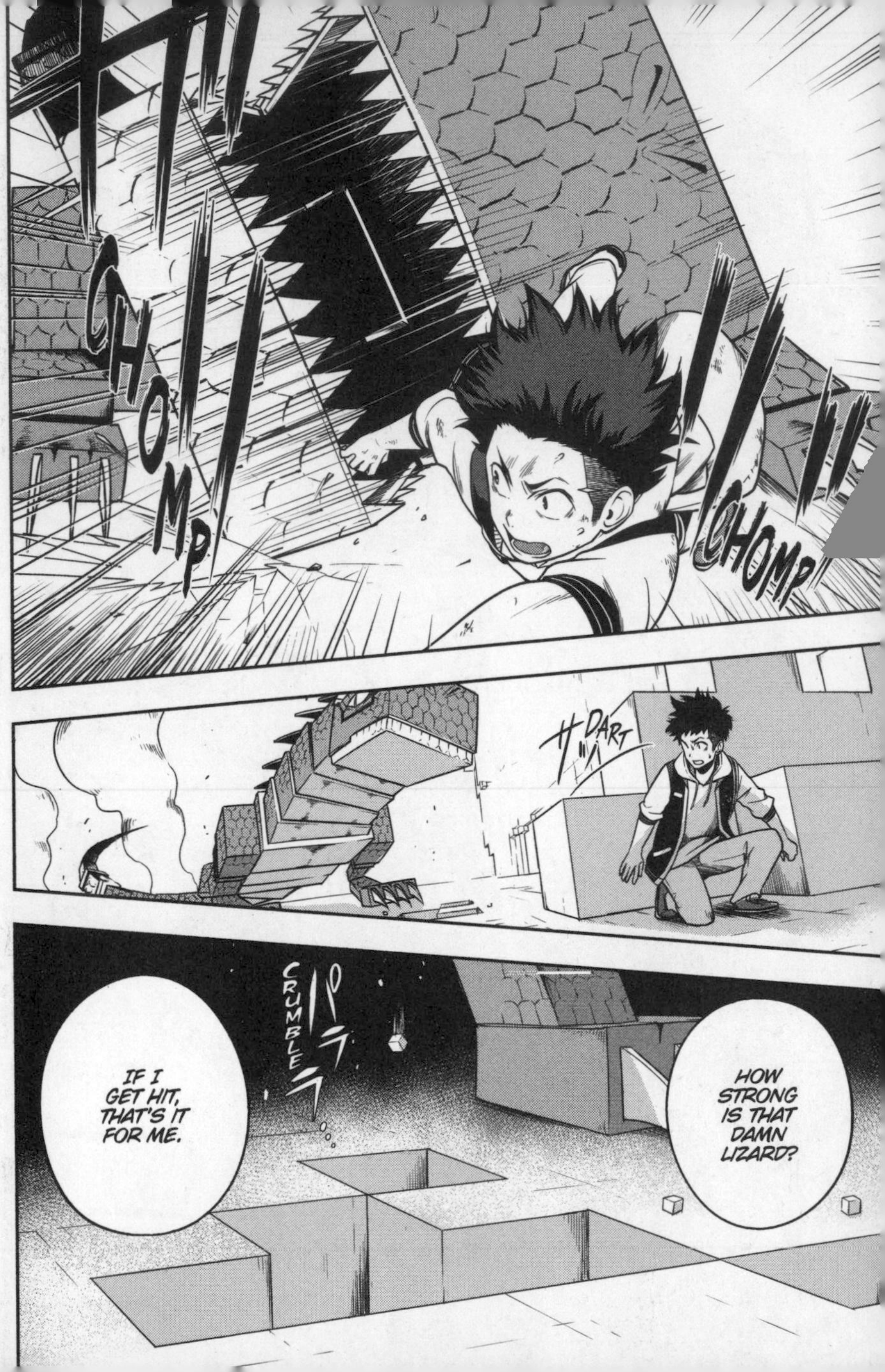
CHOMP
CHOMP
DART
HOW STRONG IS THAT DAMN LIZARD?
CRUMBLE
IF I GET HIT, THAT'S IT FOR ME.

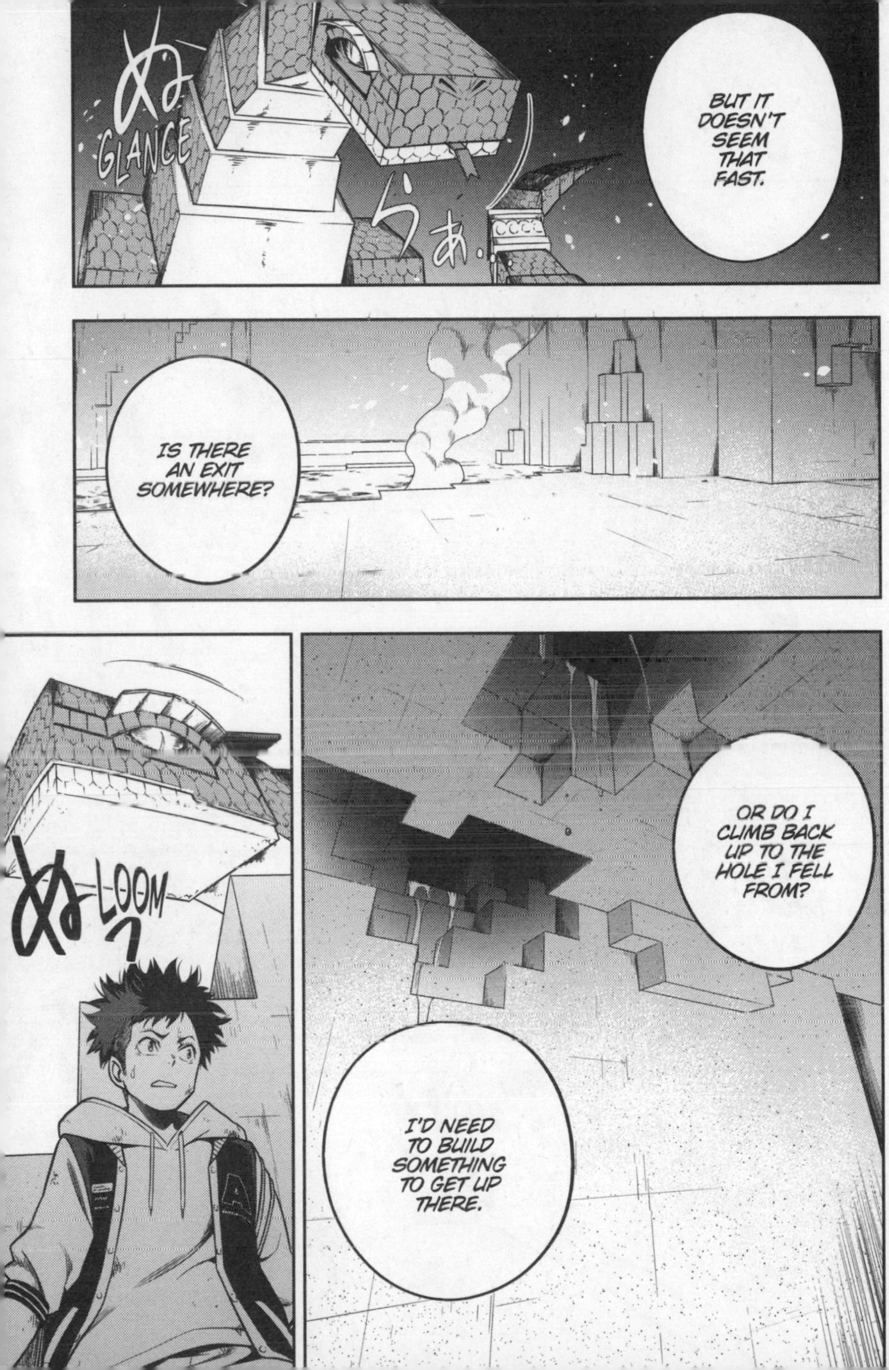
BUT IT DOESN'T SEEM THAT FAST.
らぁ..
ぬ GLANCE
IS THERE AN EXIT SOMEWHERE?
OR DO I CLIMB BACK UP TO THE HOLE I FELL FROM?
I'D NEED TO BUILD SOMETHING TO GET UP THERE.
ぬ LOOM

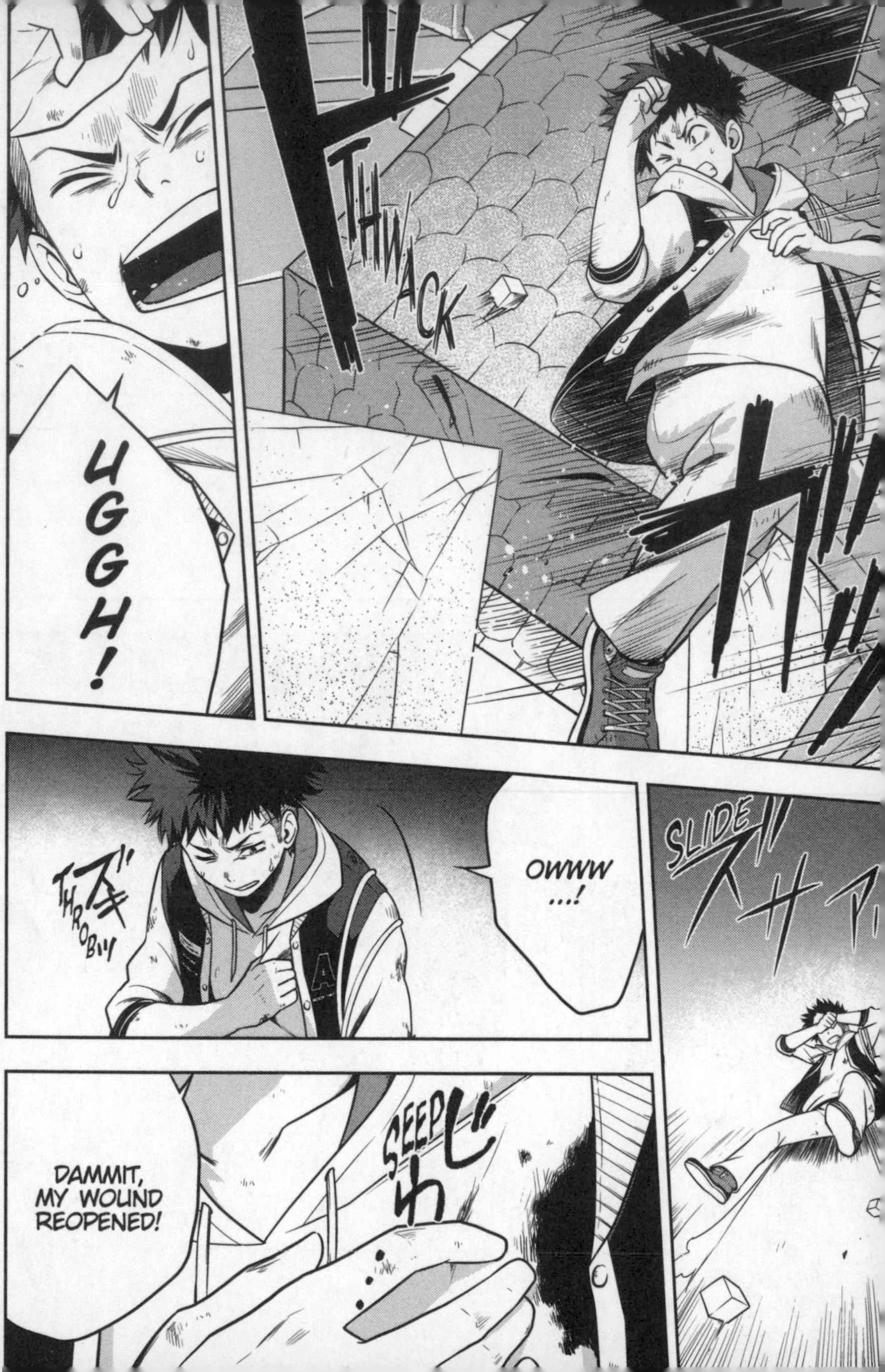
THWACK
ガッ
UGGGH!
SLIDE
ズサァ
OWWW ...!
THROB
ズキ
SEEP
じわ
DAMMIT, MY WOUND REOPENED!

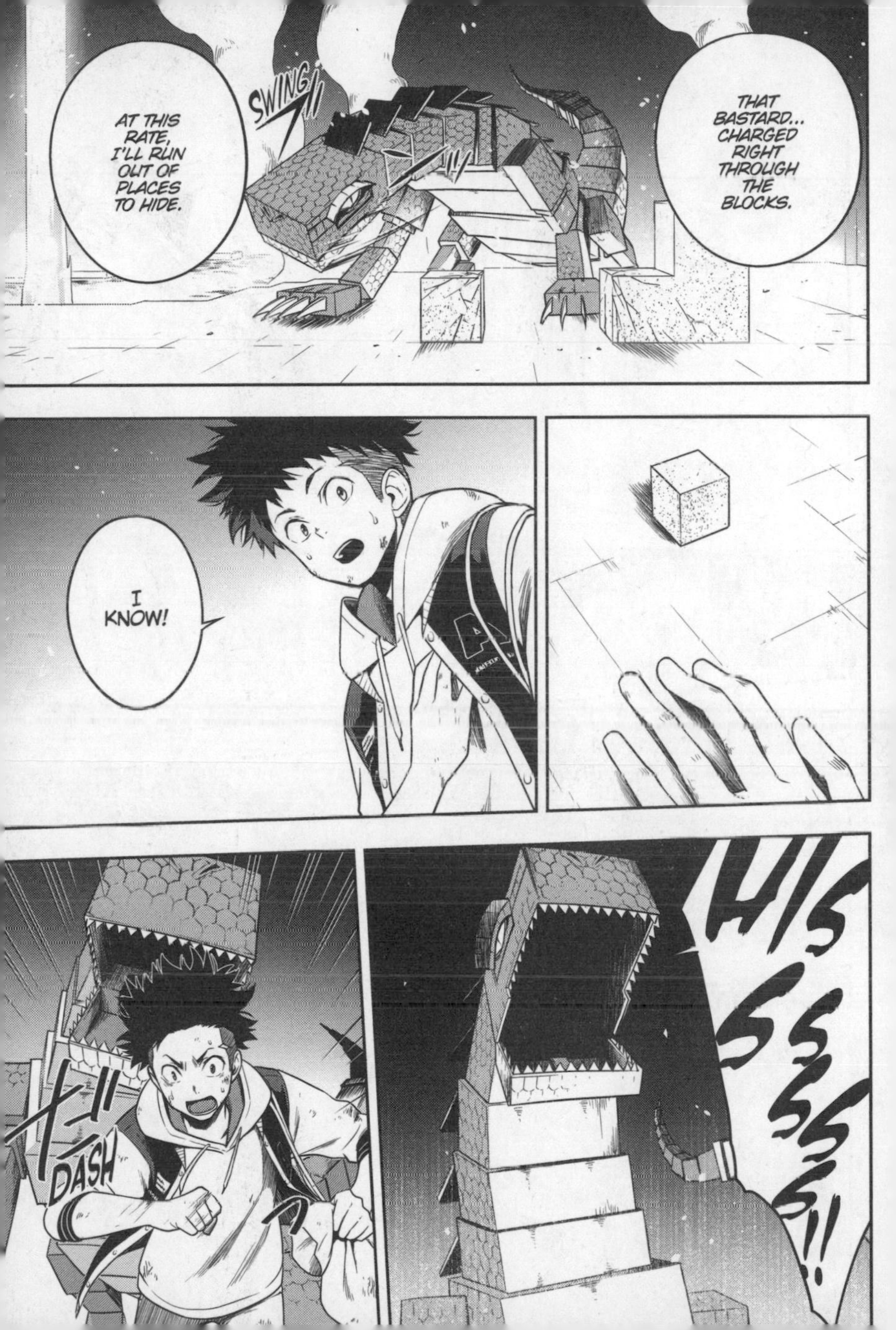
THAT BASTARD... CHARGED RIGHT THROUGH THE BLOCKS.
SWING!!
AT THIS RATE, I'LL RUN OUT OF PLACES TO HIDE.
I KNOW!
HISSSSSS!!
DASH

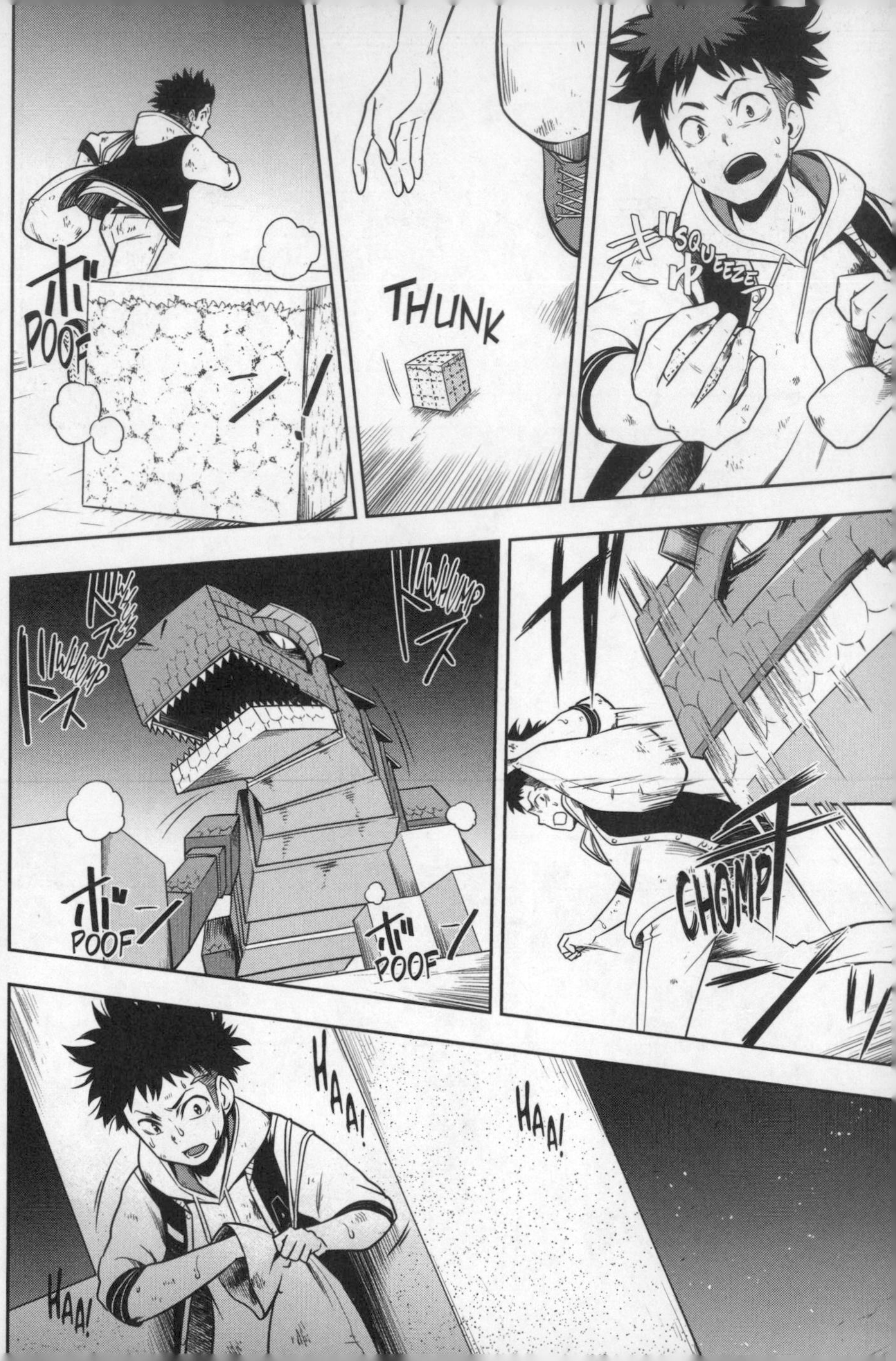
SQUEEZE
THUNK
POOF
CHOMP
WHUMP
WHUMP
WHUMP
POOF
POOF
HAA!
HAA!
HAA!

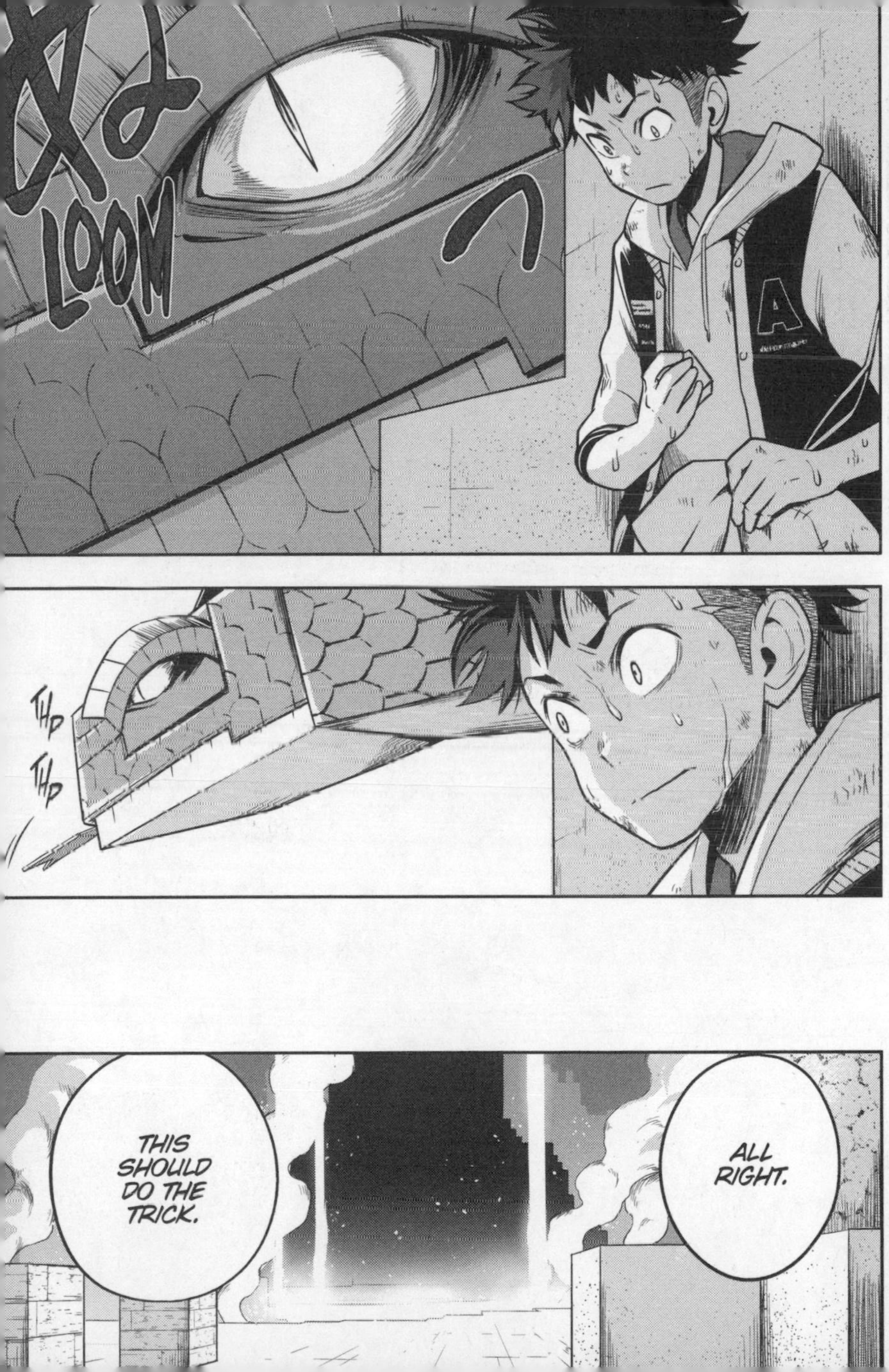
LOOM
THP THP
ALL RIGHT.
THIS SHOULD DO THE TRICK.

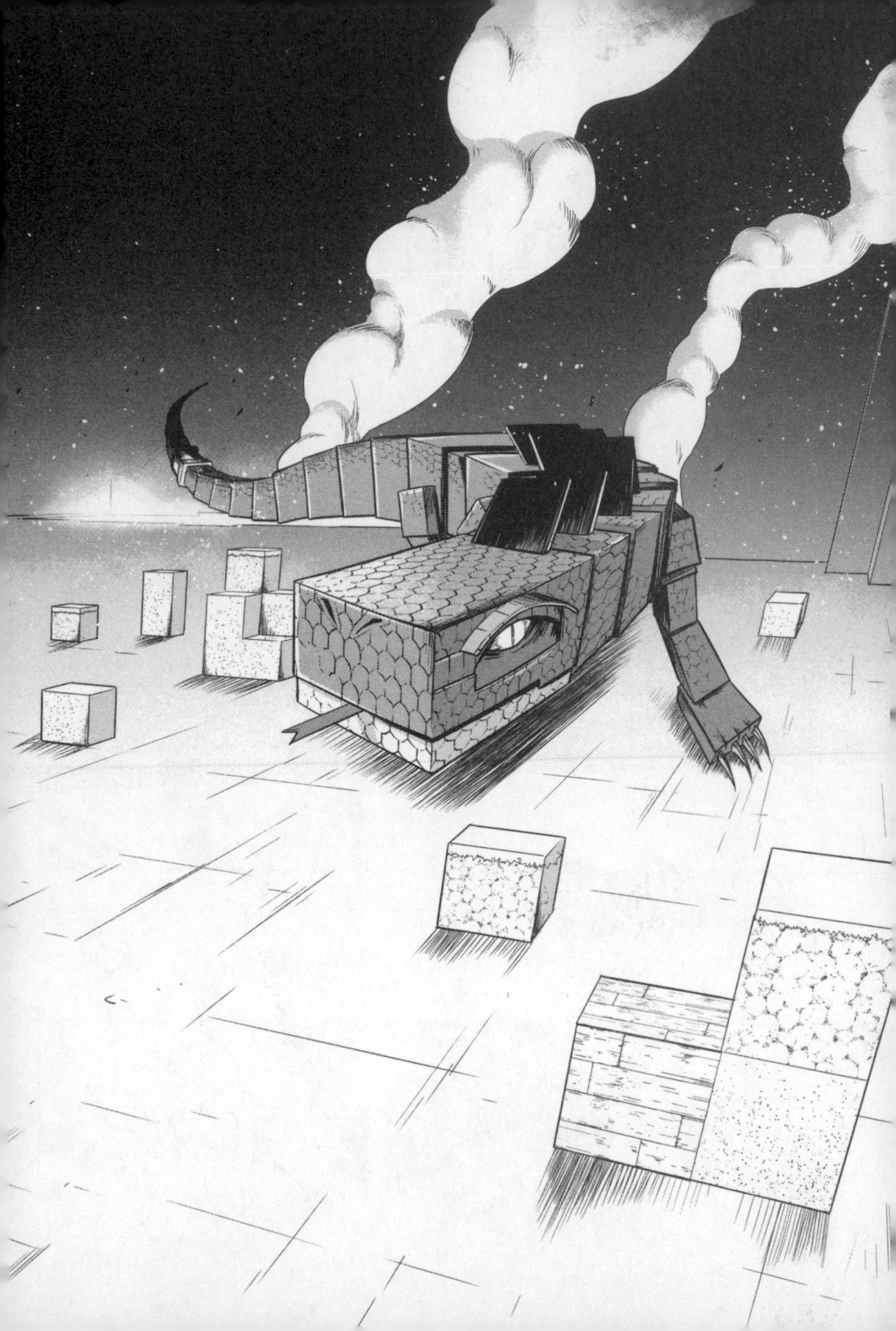

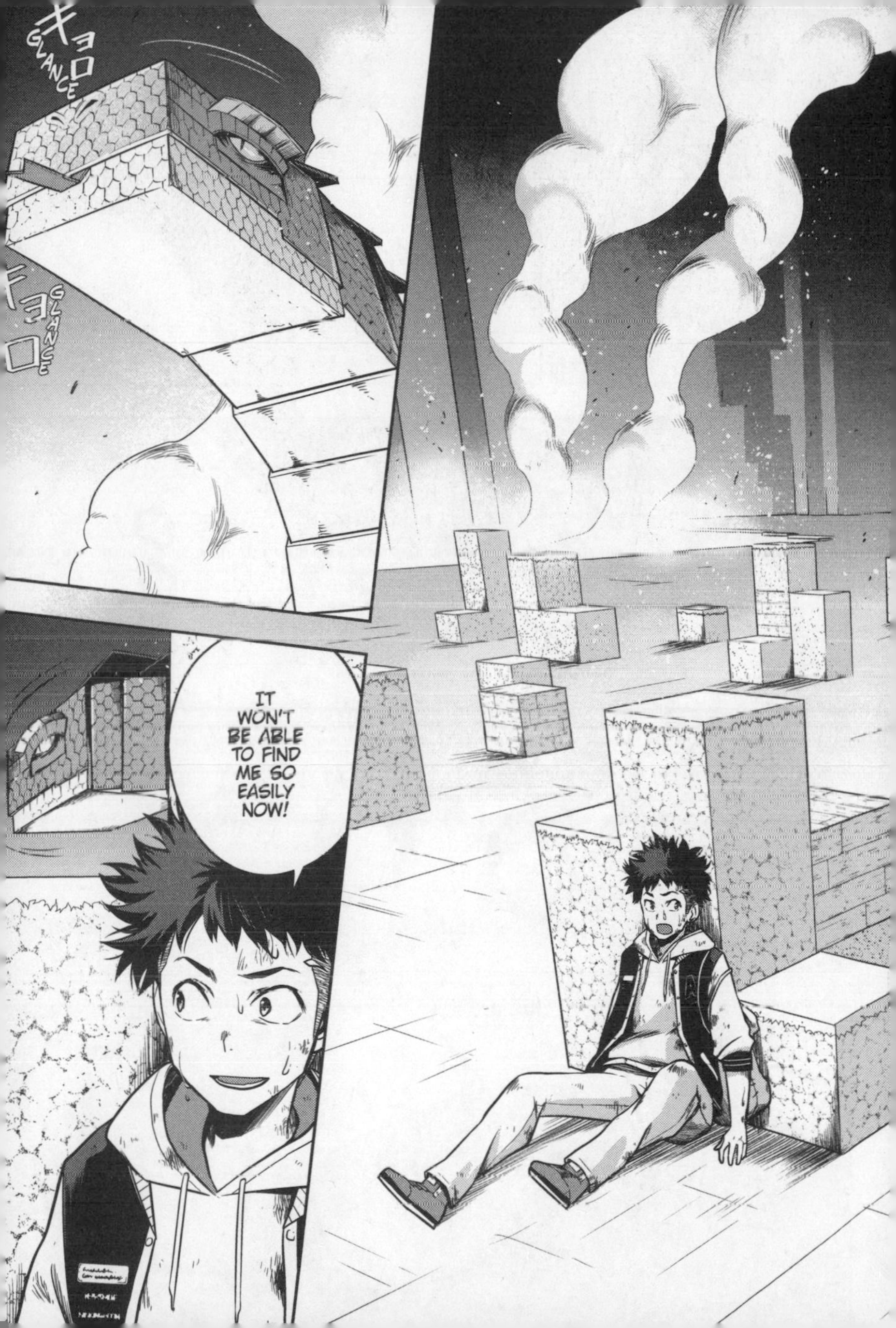
キョロ
GLANCE
キョロ
GLANCE
IT WON'T BE ABLE TO FIND ME SO EASILY NOW!

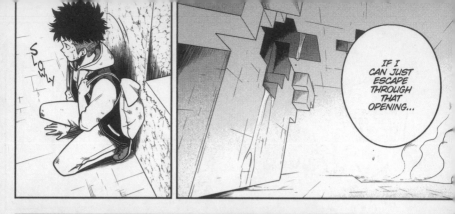

IF I CAN JUST ESCAPE THROUGH THAT OPENING...

THUMP

?!

OOF!!

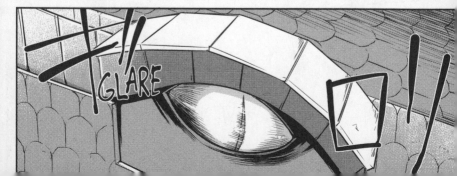

GLARE

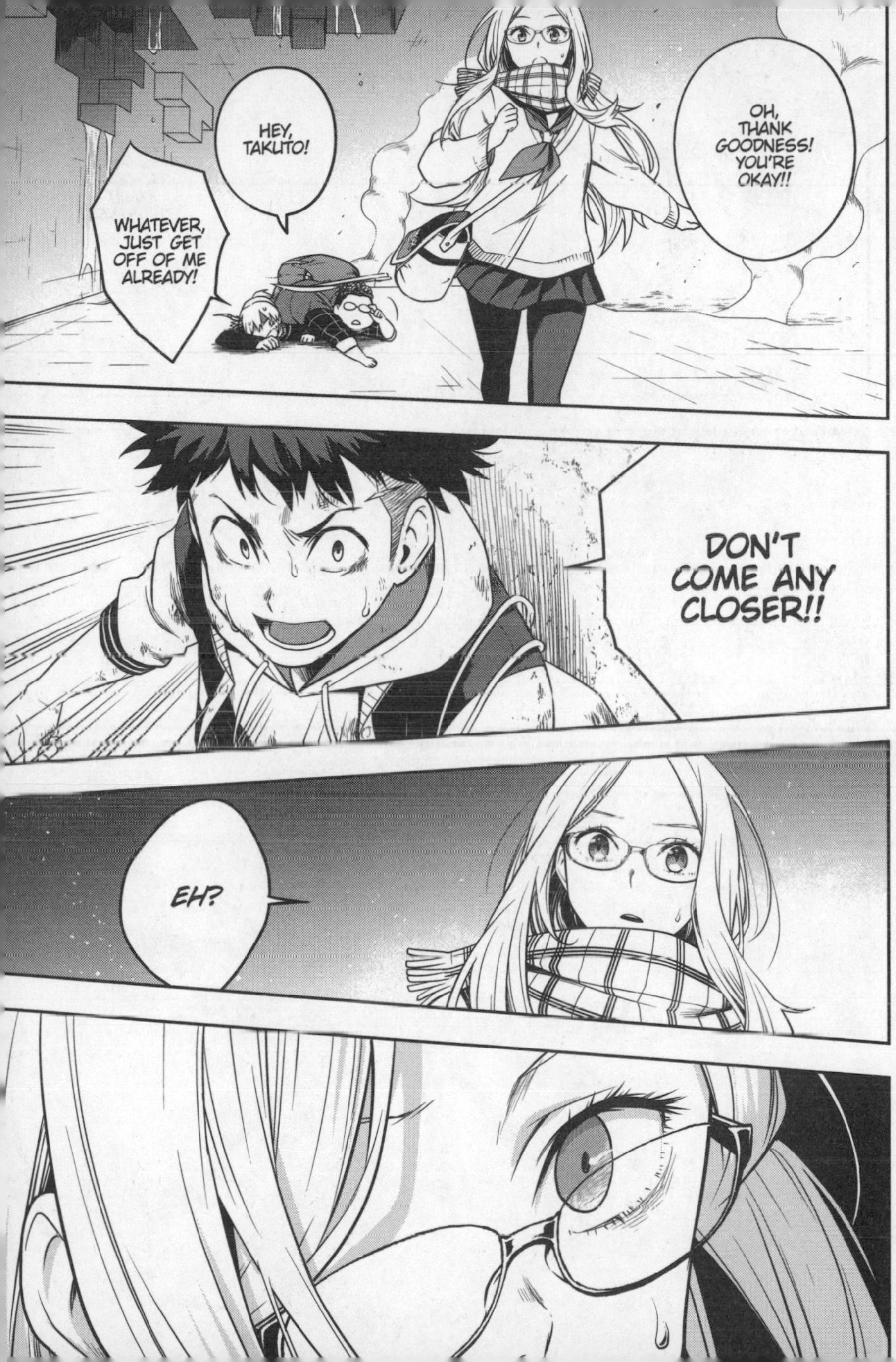
OH, THANK GOODNESS! YOU'RE OKAY!!
HEY, TAKUTO!
WHATEVER, JUST GET OFF OF ME ALREADY!
DON'T COME ANY CLOSER!!
EH?

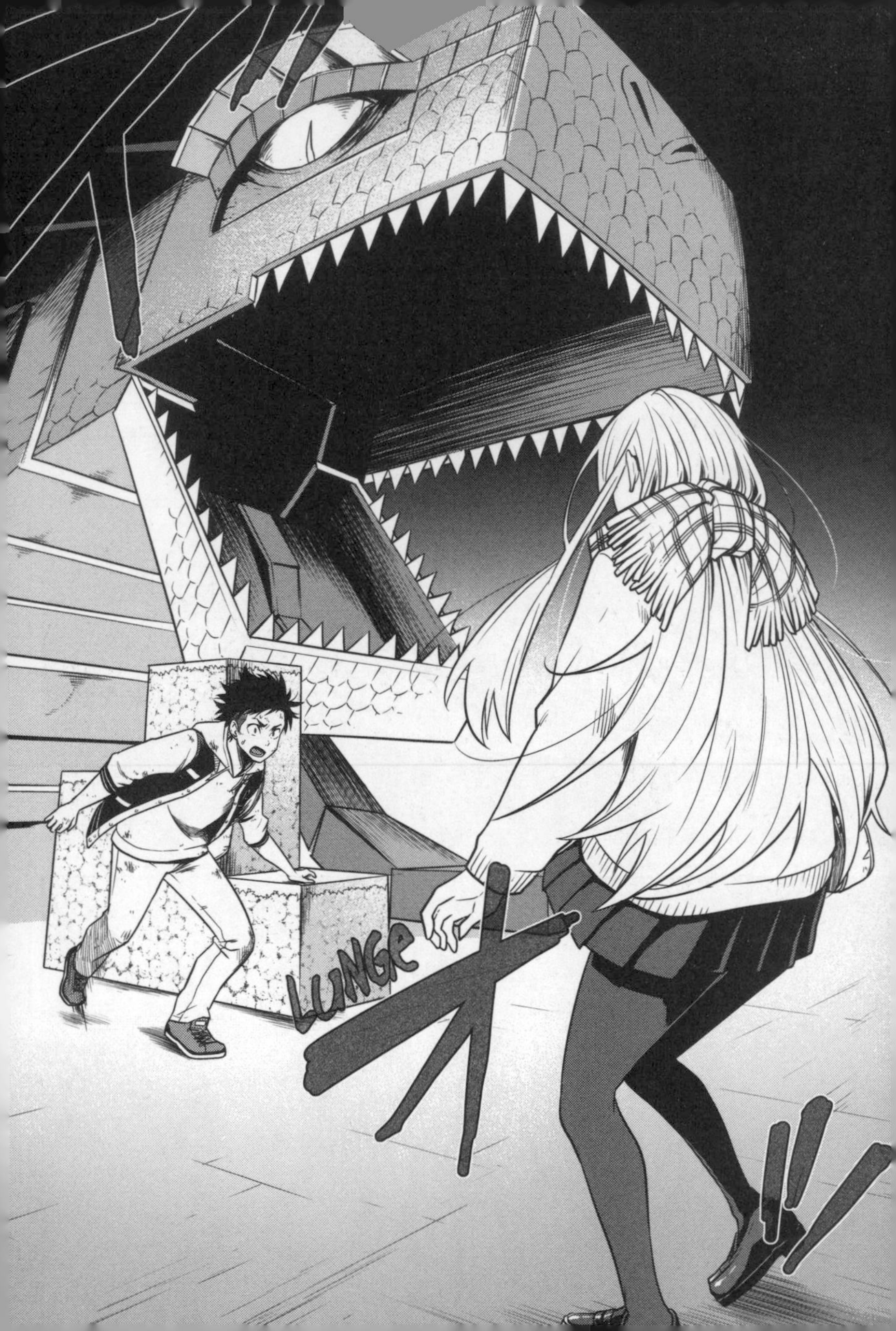
LUNGE

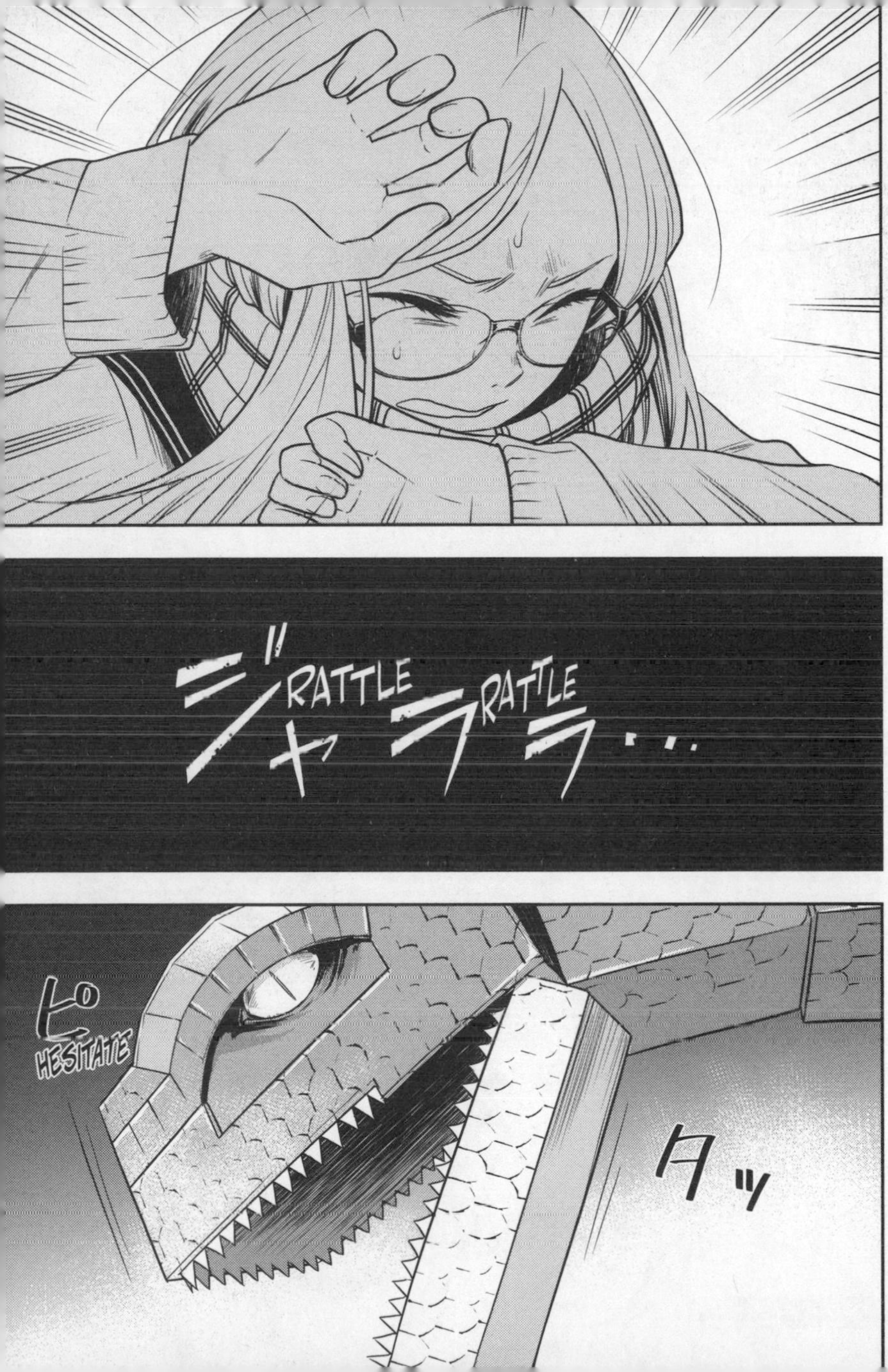
ジャララ…
RATTLE RATTLE
ピ
HESITATE
タッ

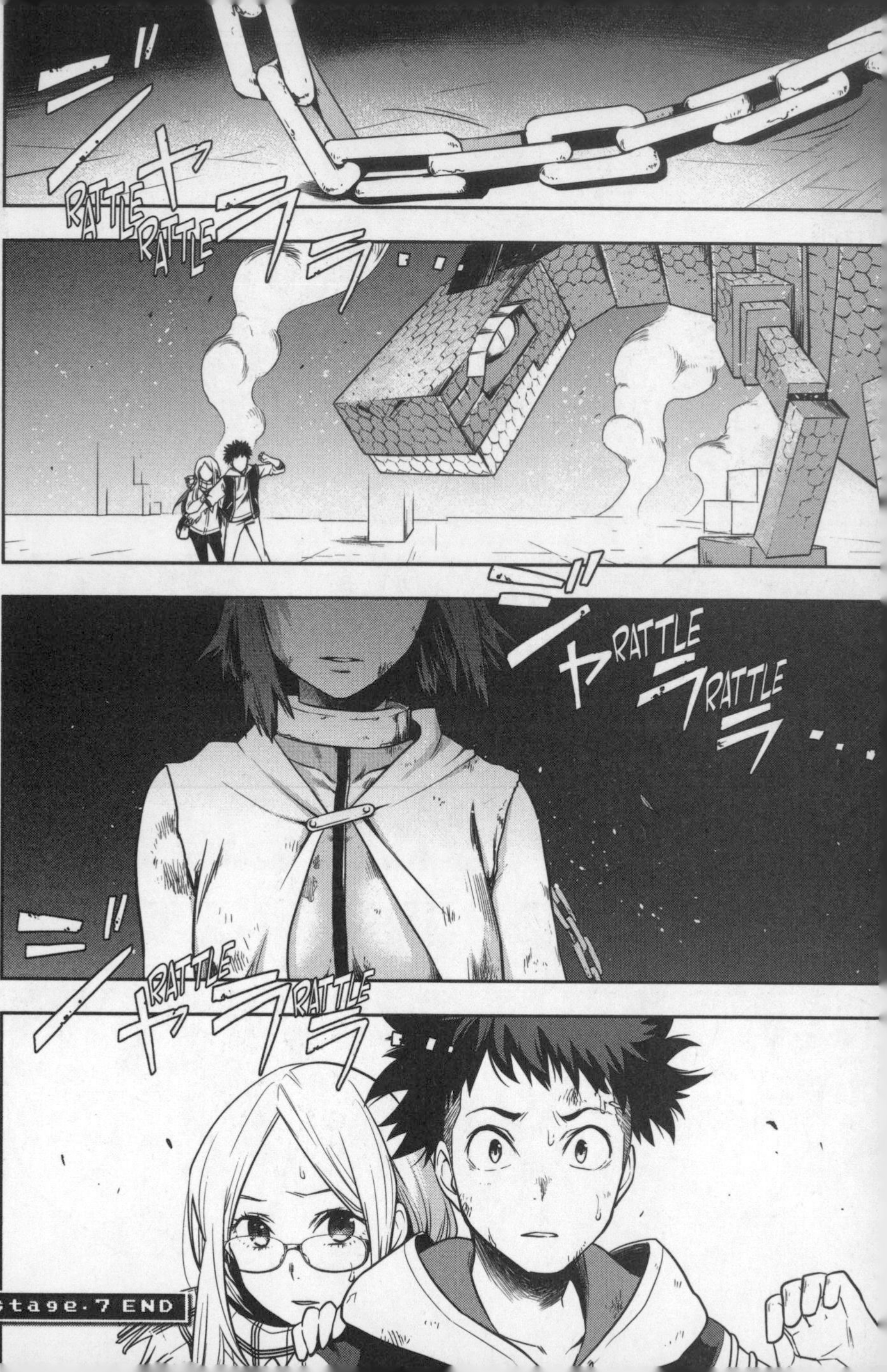
RATTLE RATTLE
RATTLE RATTLE
RATTLE RATTLE
stage.7 END

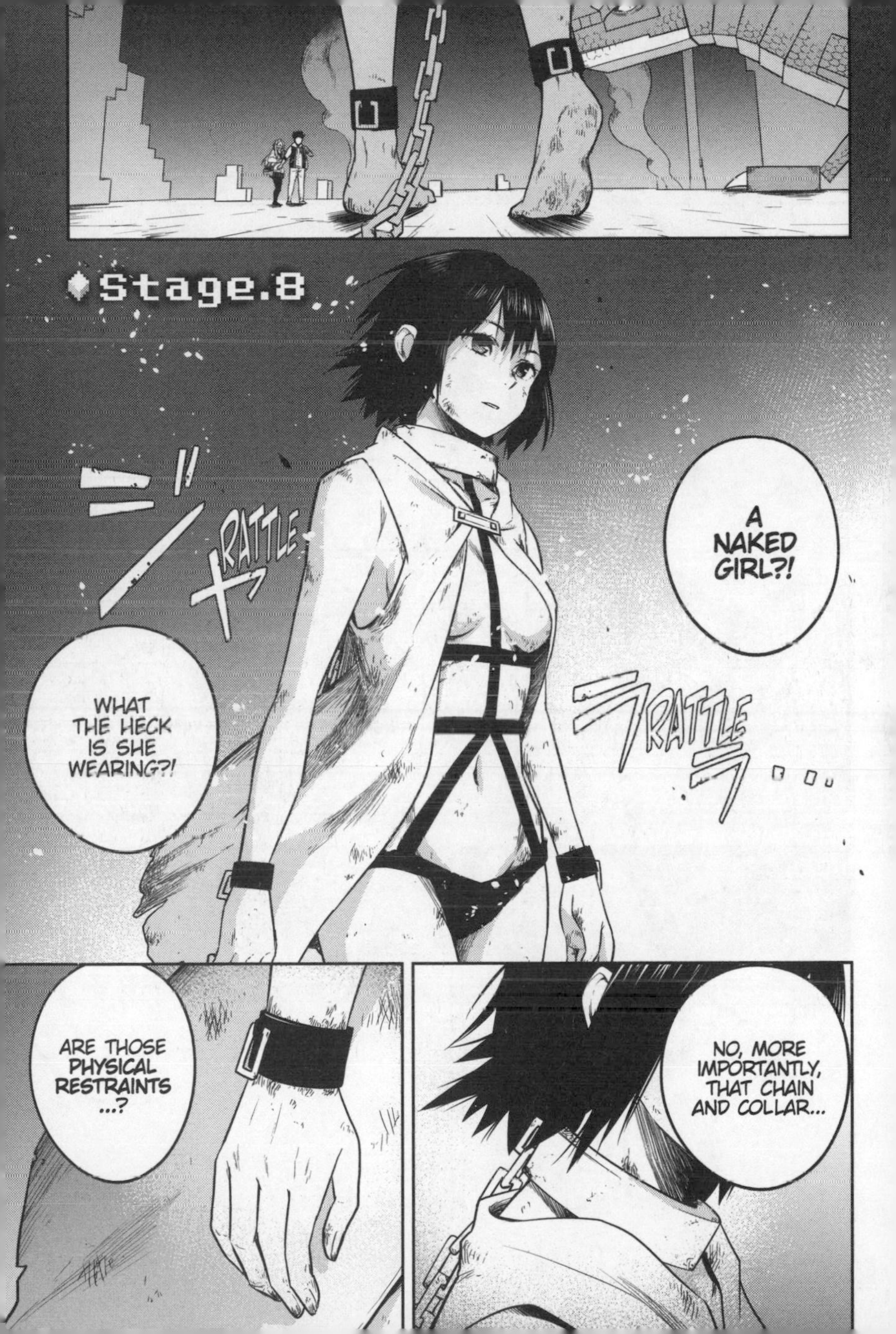
Stage.8
A NAKED GIRL?!
RATTLE
RATTLE...
WHAT THE HECK IS SHE WEARING?!
NO, MORE IMPORTANTLY, THAT CHAIN AND COLLAR...
ARE THOSE PHYSICAL RESTRAINTS ...?

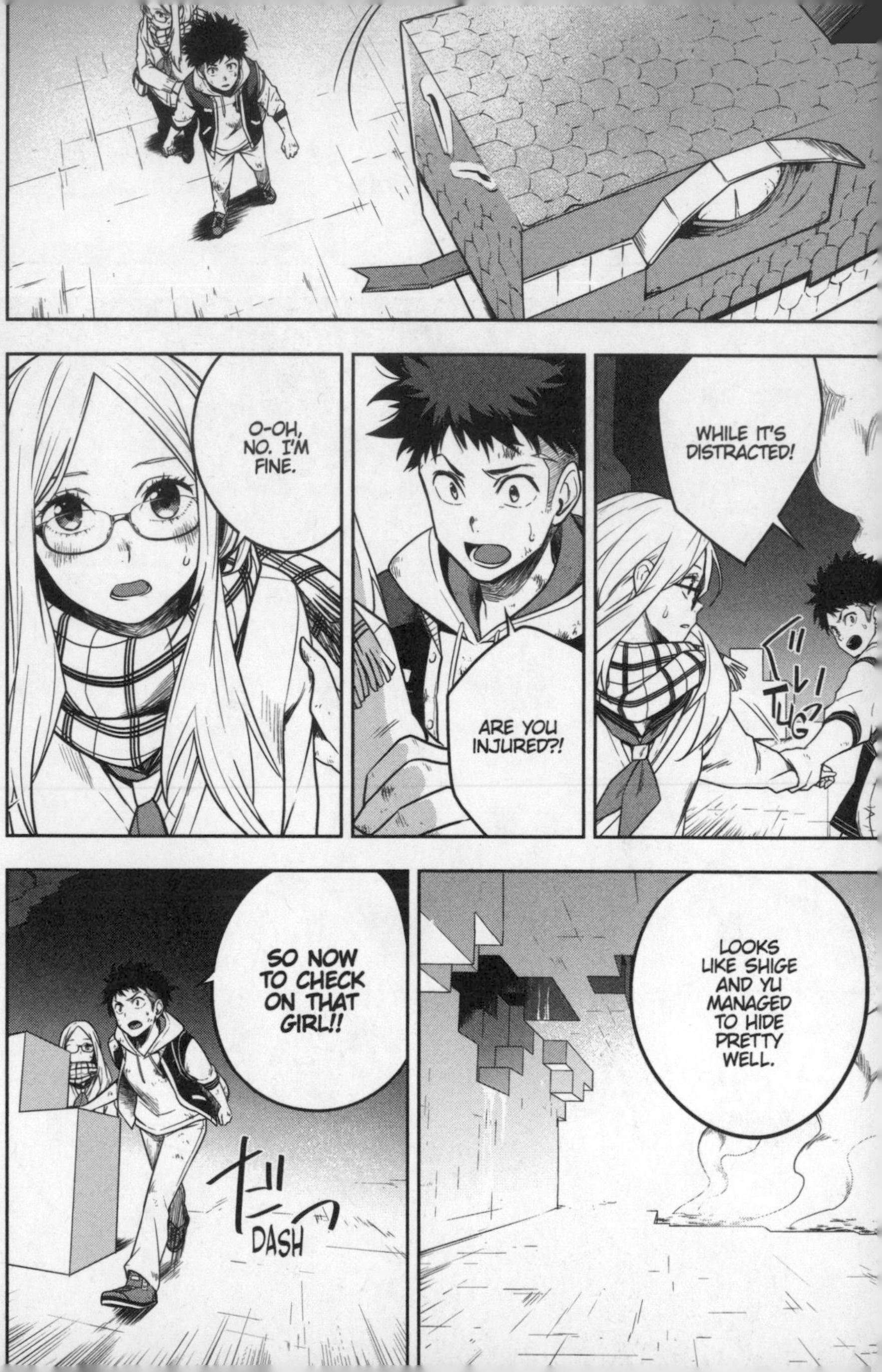
WHILE IT'S DISTRACTED!
TUG
ARE YOU INJURED?!
O-OH, NO. I'M FINE.
LOOKS LIKE SHIGE AND YU MANAGED TO HIDE PRETTY WELL.
SO NOW TO CHECK ON THAT GIRL!!
DASH

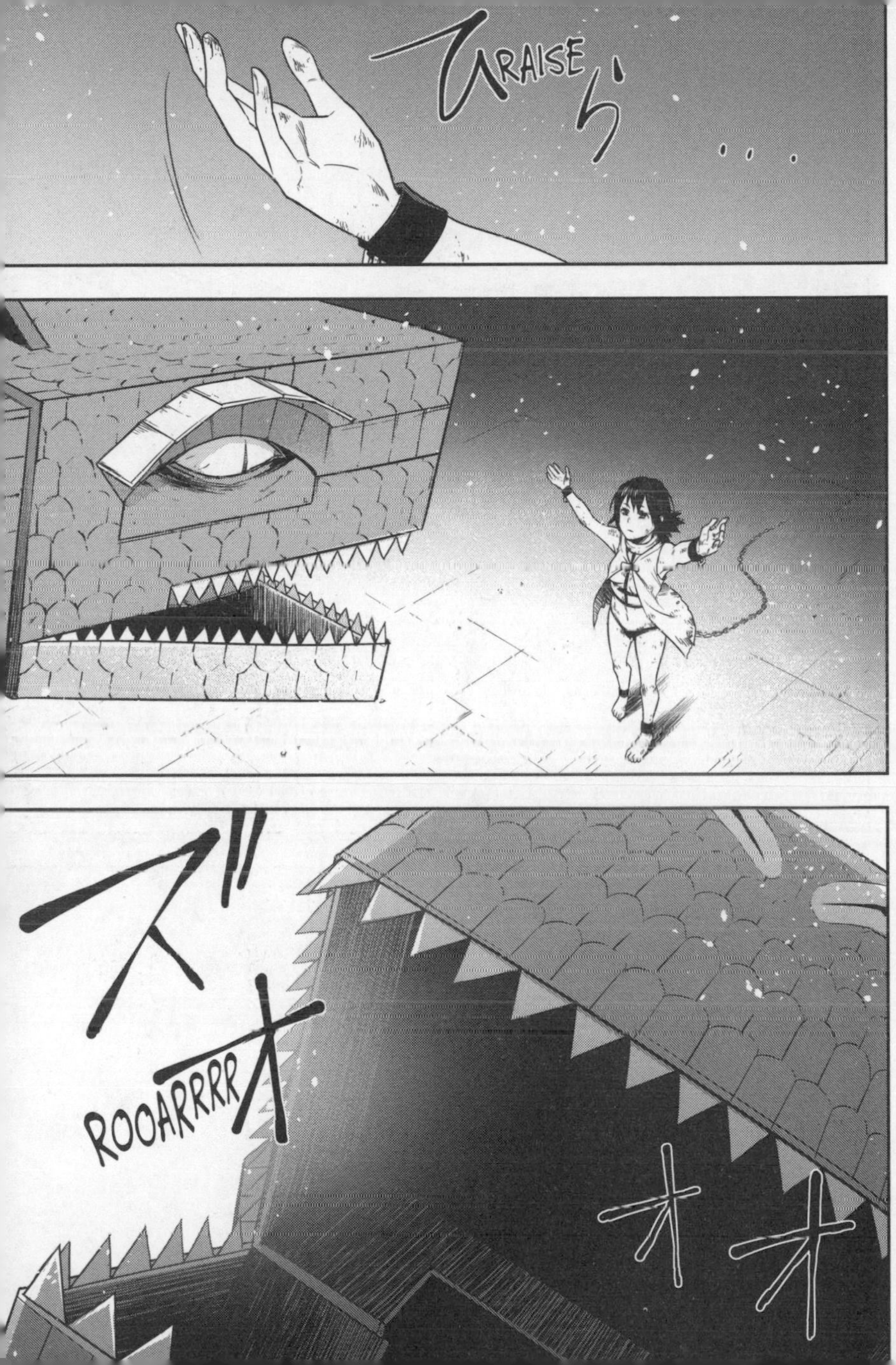

RAISE
...
ROOARRRR

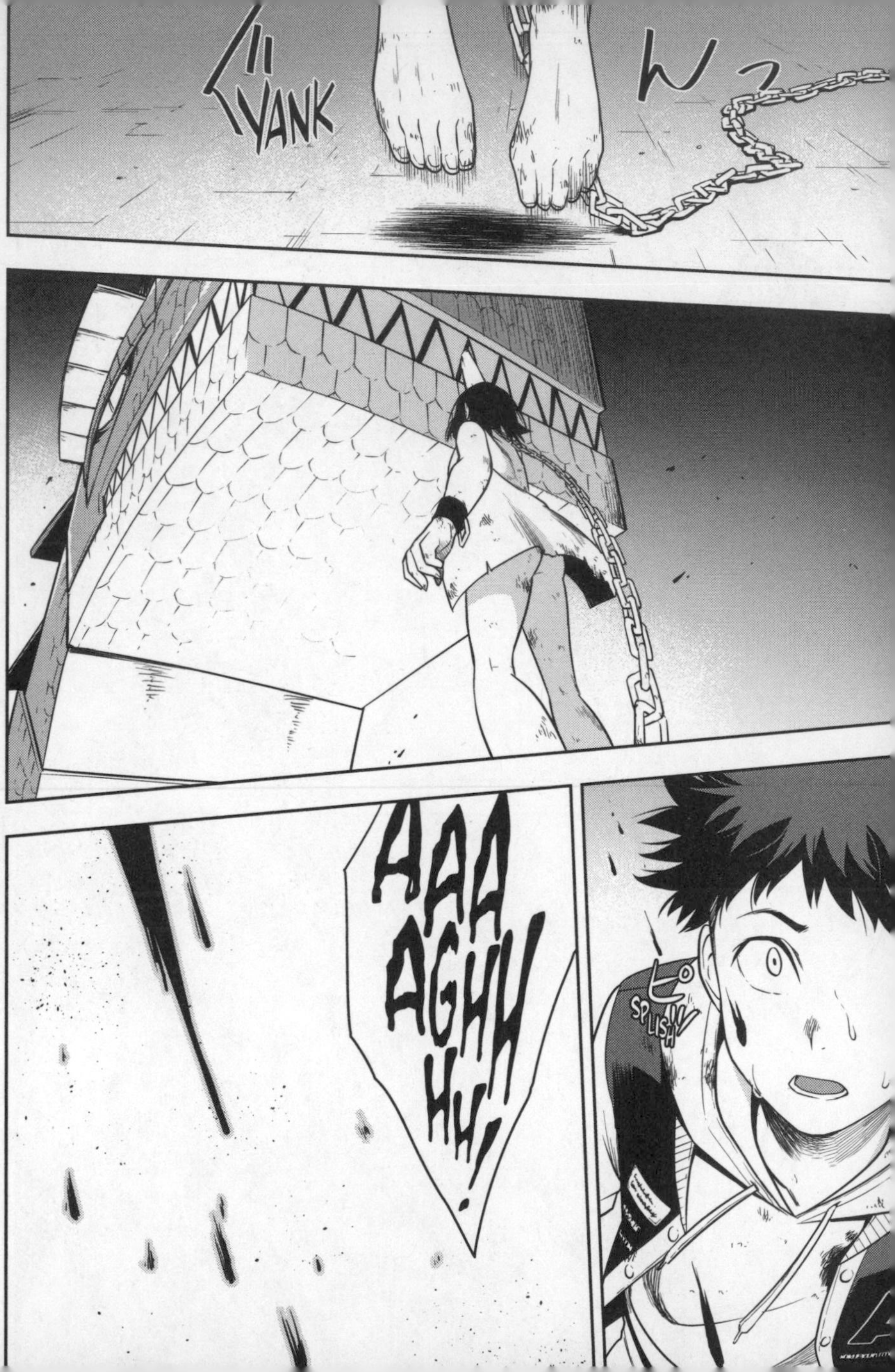

んっ
YANK
SPLISH
AAAAGHHHH!

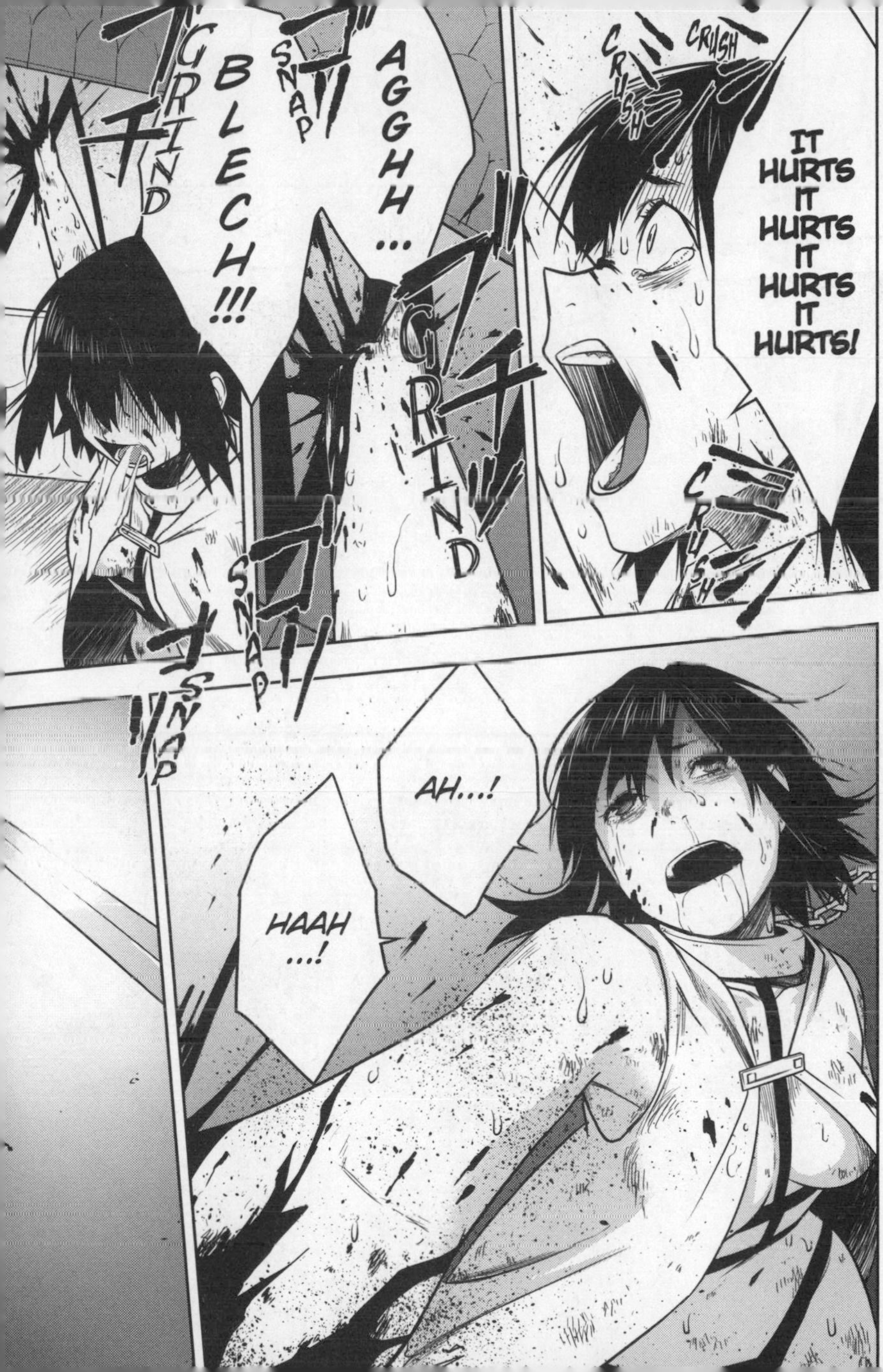
CRUSH
CRUSH
IT HURTS IT HURTS IT HURTS IT HURTS!
CRUSH
AGGHH...
SNAP
GRIND
SNAP
GRIND
BLECH!!!
SNAP
AH...!
HAAH ...!

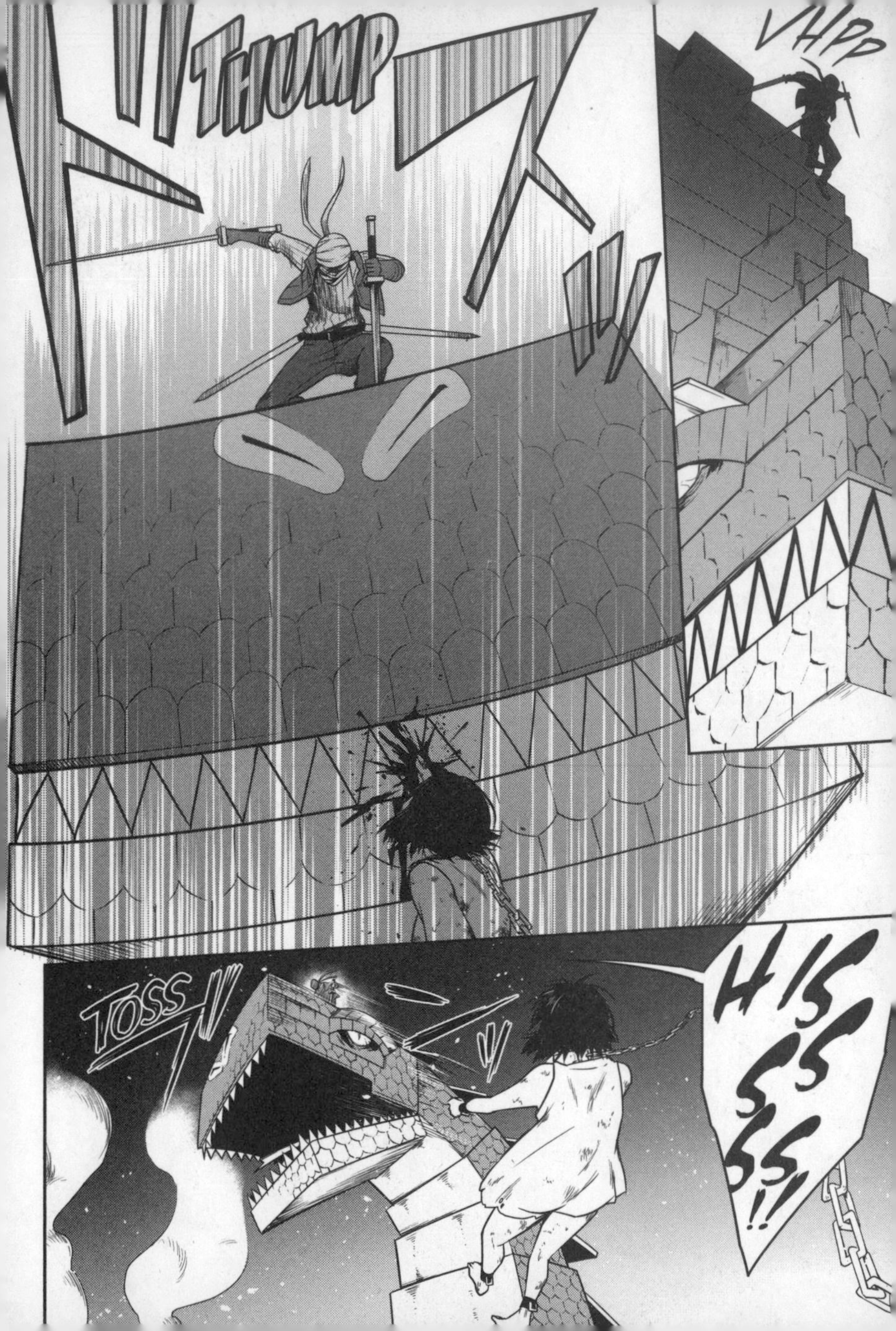
VHPP
THUMP
HISSSSSSS!!
TOSS

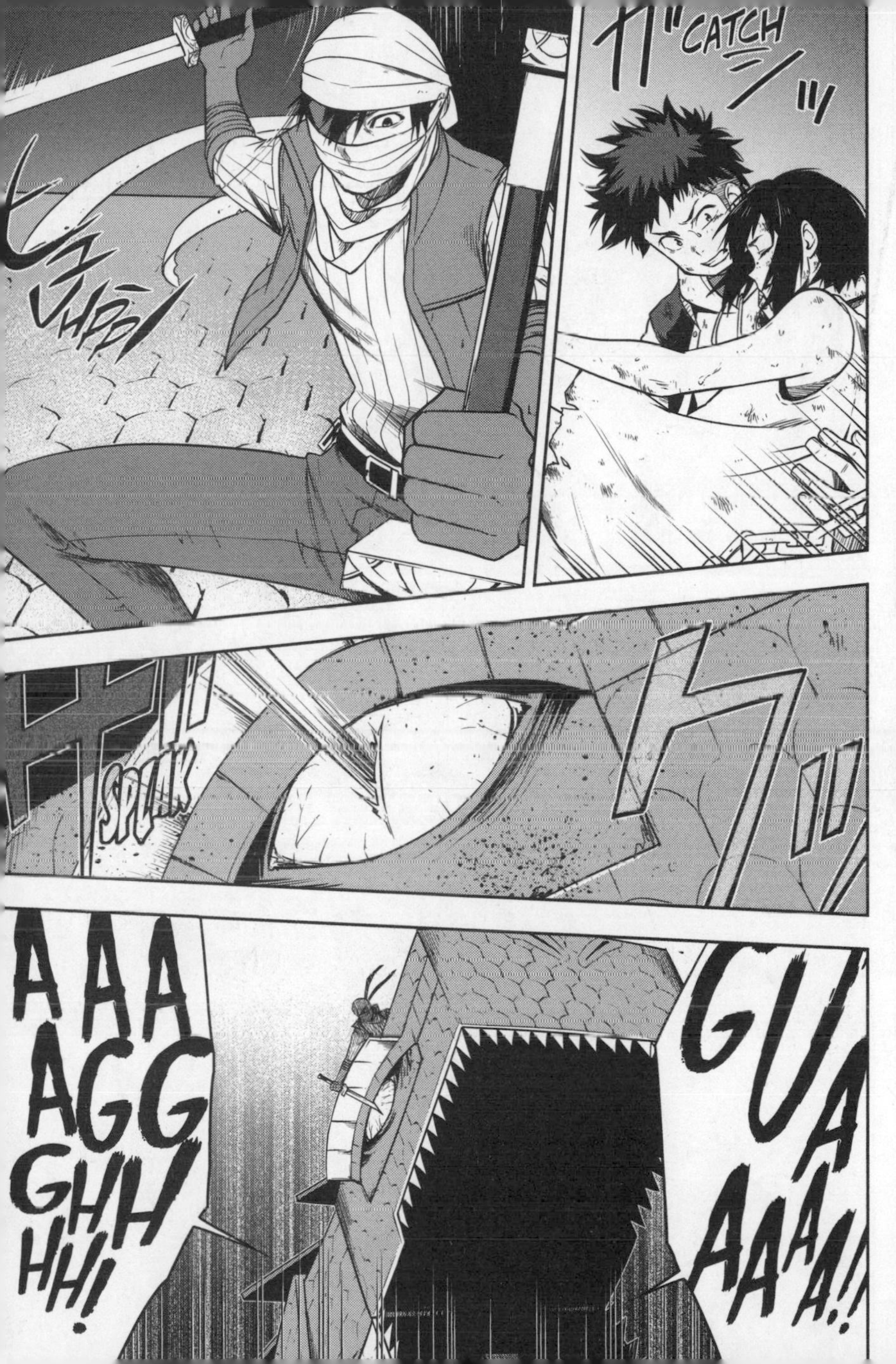
CATCH
SPLAK
GUAAAAAA!!
AAAAGGGHHHH!

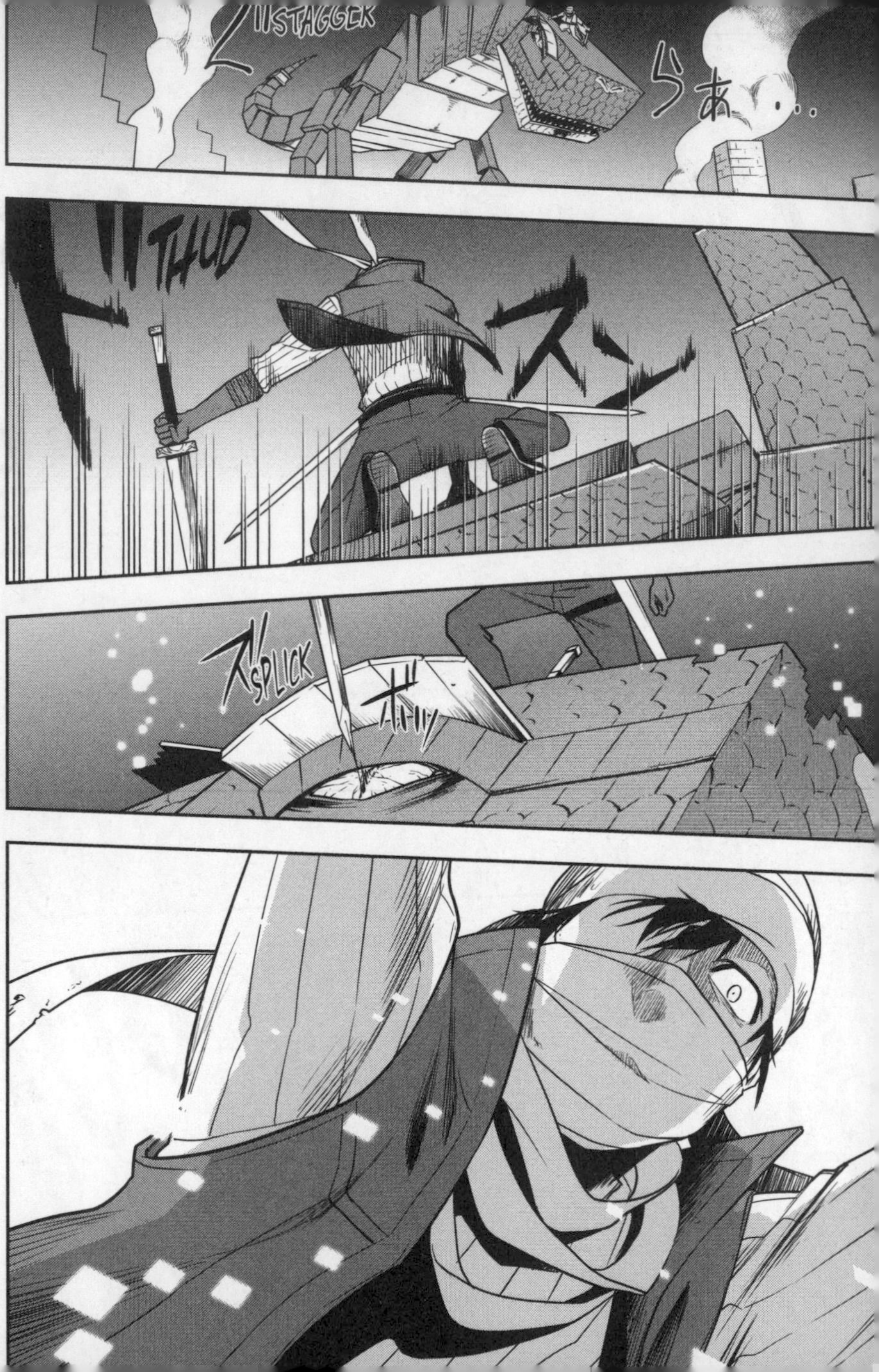
Z!! STAGGER
らあ...
THUD
SPLICK

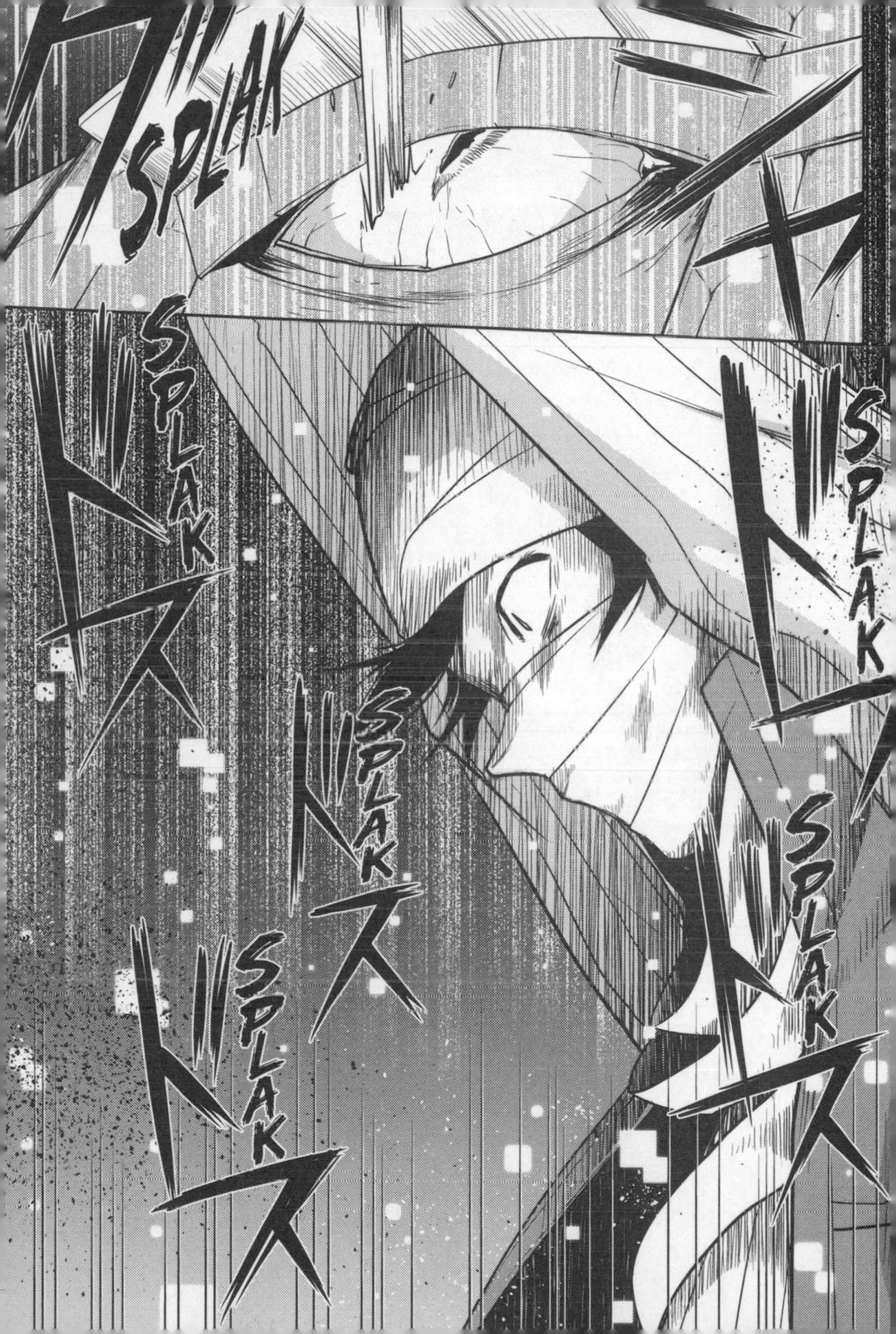
SPLAK
SPLAK
SPLAK
SPLAK
SPLAK
SPLAK

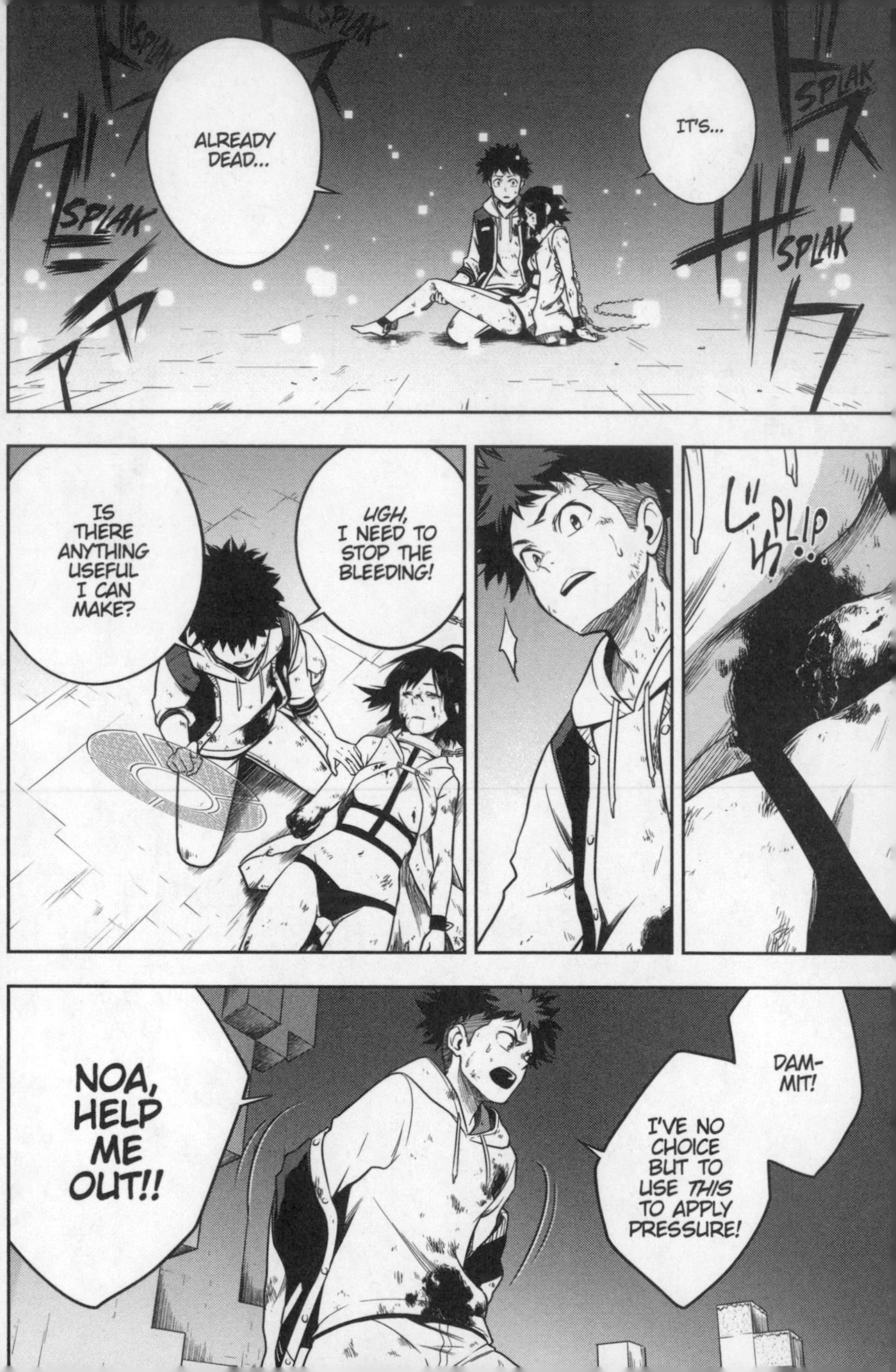
SPLAK
SPLAK
IT'S...
ALREADY DEAD...
SPLAK
SPLAK
PLIP
UGH, I NEED TO STOP THE BLEEDING!
IS THERE ANYTHING USEFUL I CAN MAKE?
DAM-MIT!
I'VE NO CHOICE BUT TO USE *THIS* TO APPLY PRESSURE!
NOA, HELP ME OUT!!

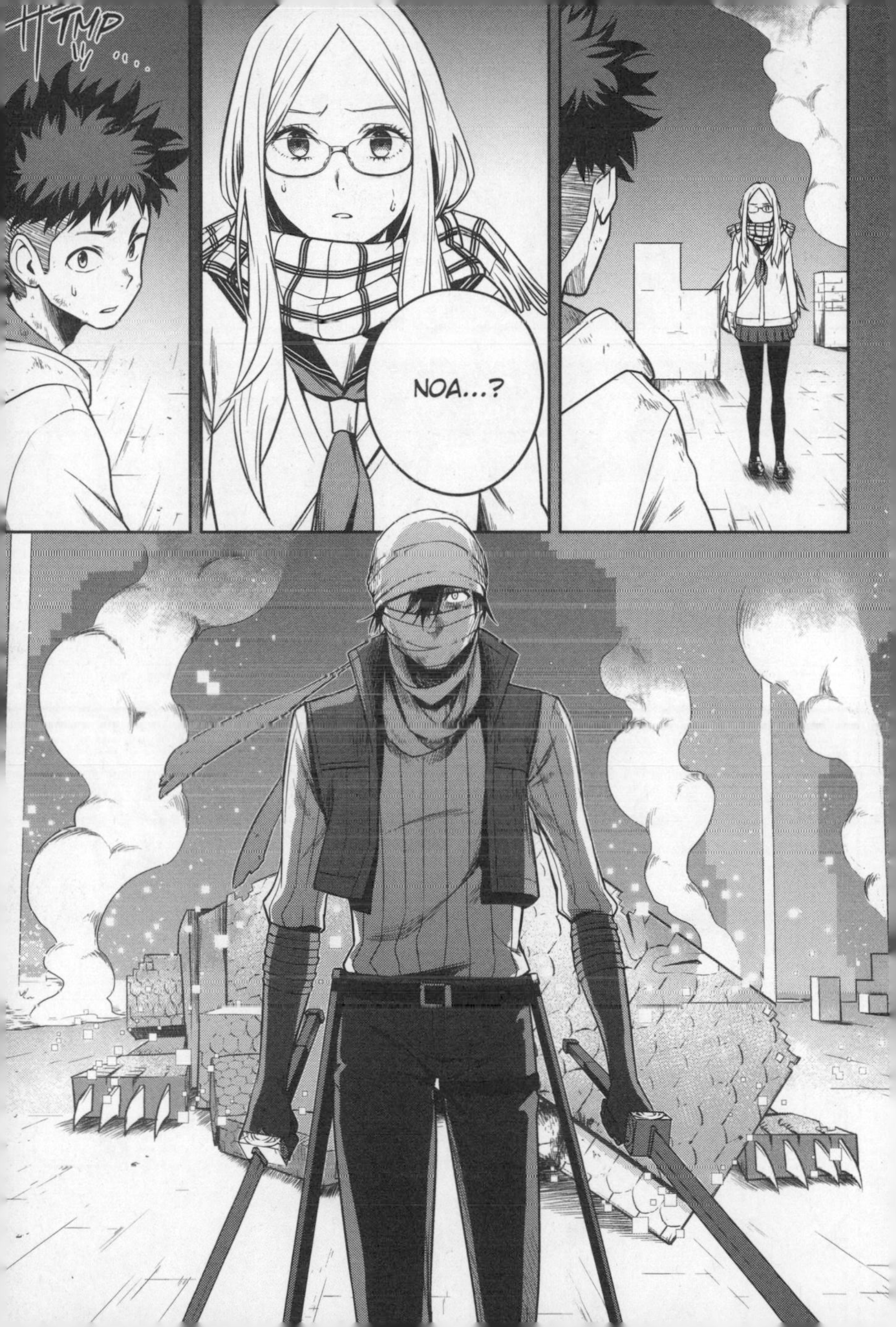
HTMP
...
NOA...?

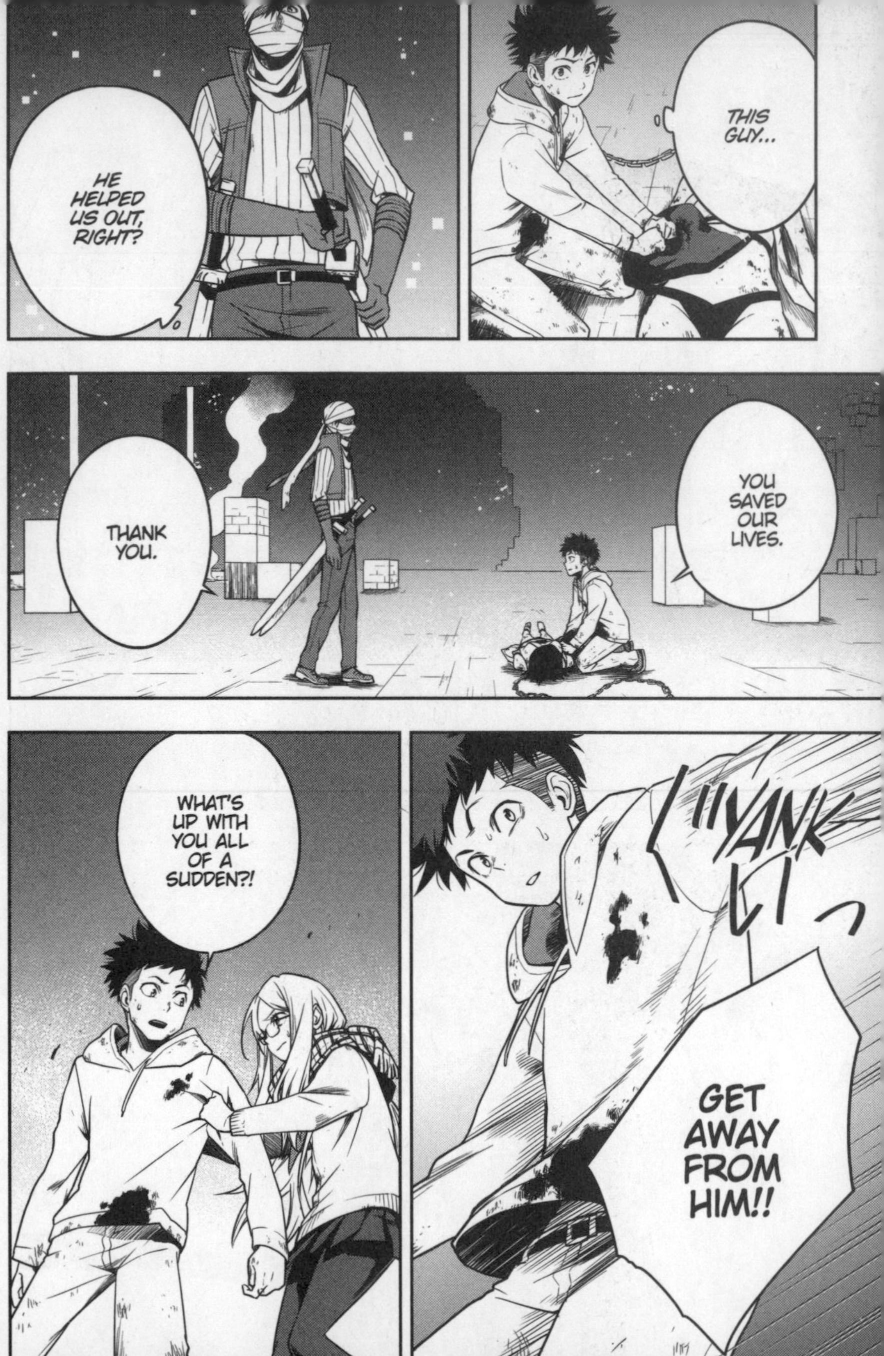
THIS GUY...
HE HELPED US OUT, RIGHT?
YOU SAVED OUR LIVES.
THANK YOU.
YANK
GET AWAY FROM HIM!!
WHAT'S UP WITH YOU ALL OF A SUDDEN?!

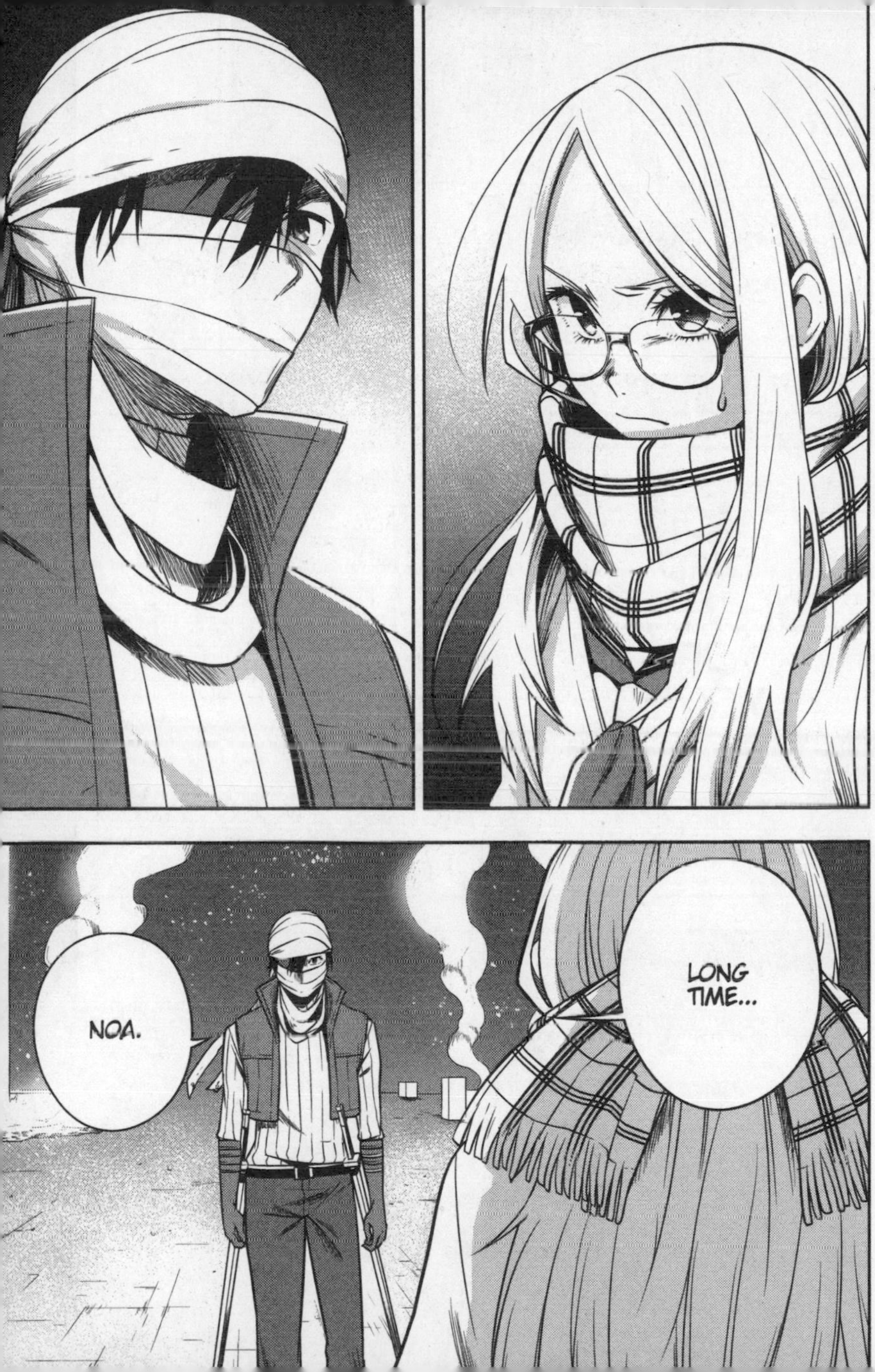
LONG TIME...
NOA.

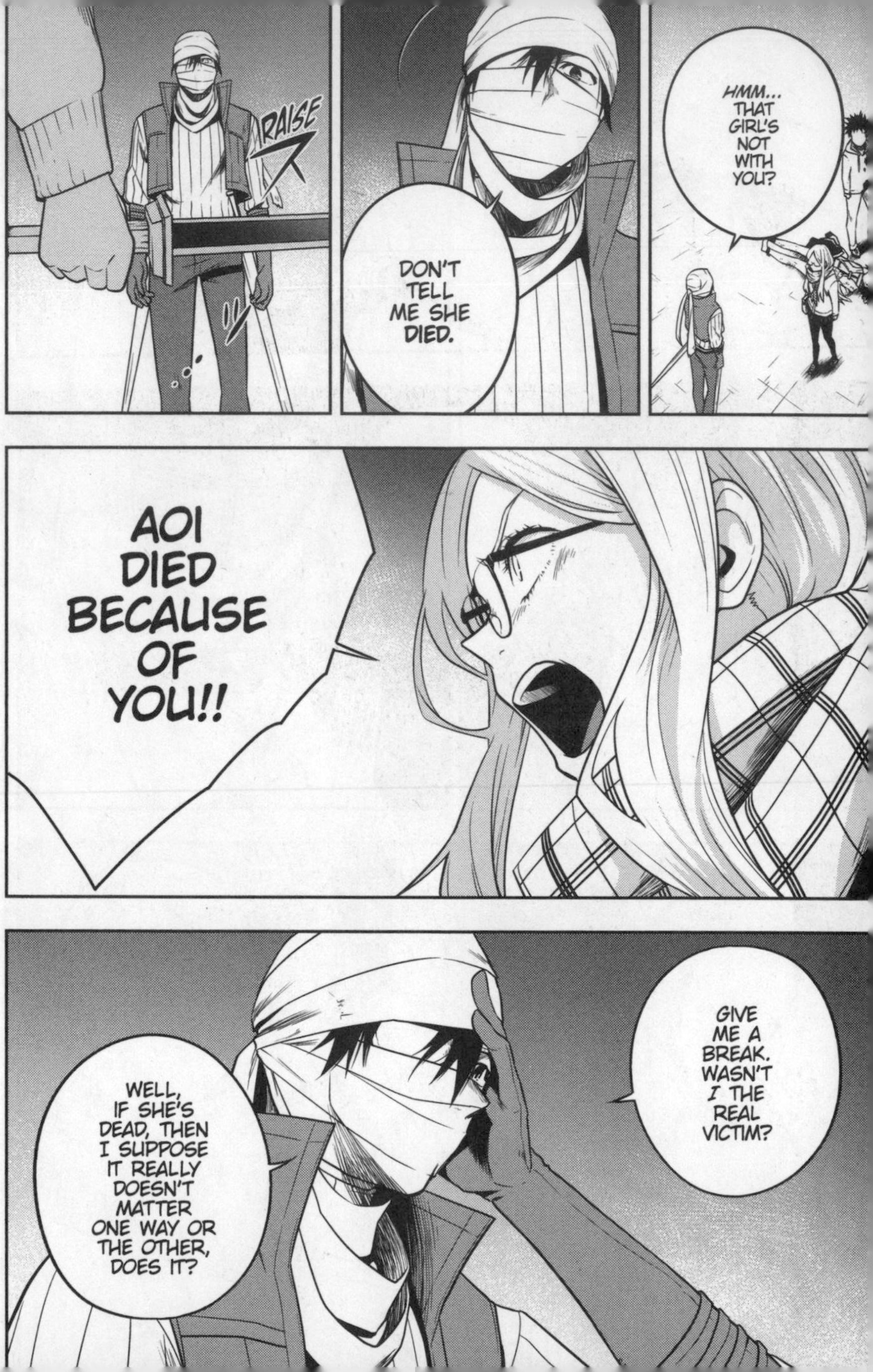
HMM... THAT GIRL'S NOT WITH YOU?
DON'T TELL ME SHE DIED.
RAISE
AOI DIED BECAUSE OF YOU!!
GIVE ME A BREAK. WASN'T I THE REAL VICTIM?
WELL, IF SHE'S DEAD, THEN I SUPPOSE IT REALLY DOESN'T MATTER ONE WAY OR THE OTHER, DOES IT?

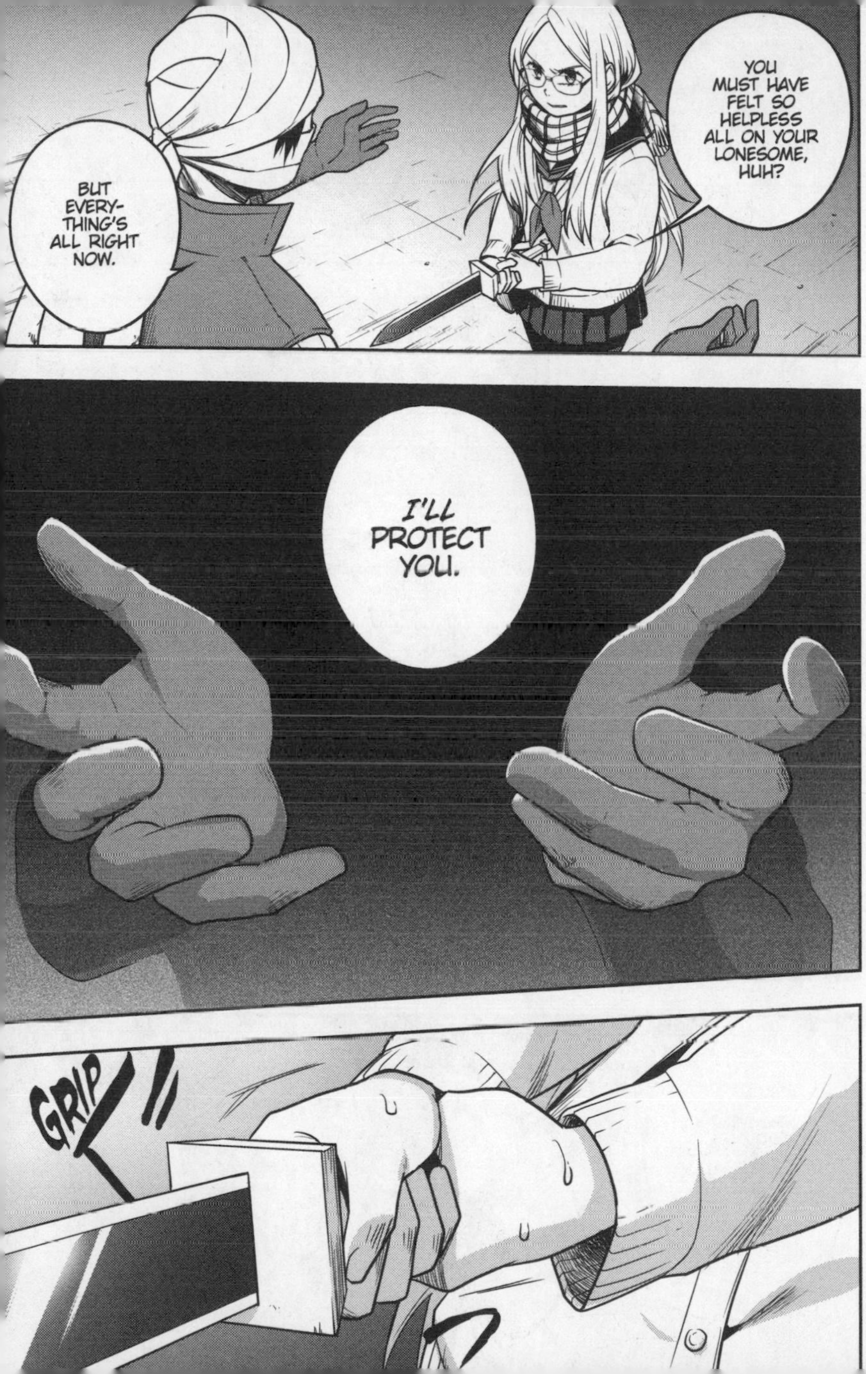
YOU MUST HAVE FELT SO HELPLESS ALL ON YOUR LONESOME, HUH?
BUT EVERY-THING'S ALL RIGHT NOW.
I'LL PROTECT YOU.
GRIP

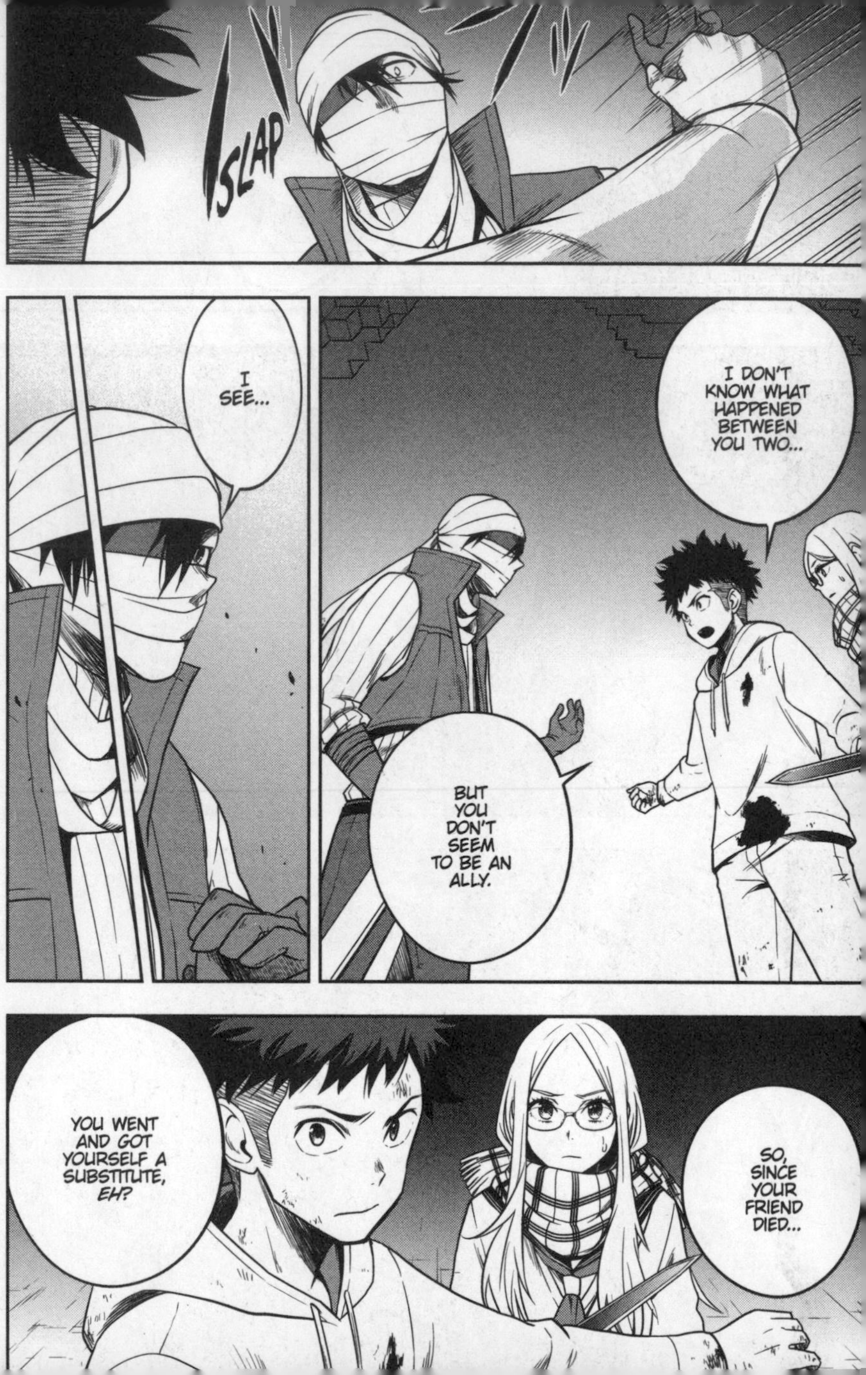
SLAP
I DON'T KNOW WHAT HAPPENED BETWEEN YOU TWO...
BUT YOU DON'T SEEM TO BE AN ALLY.
I SEE...
SO, SINCE YOUR FRIEND DIED...
YOU WENT AND GOT YOURSELF A SUBSTITUTE, EH?

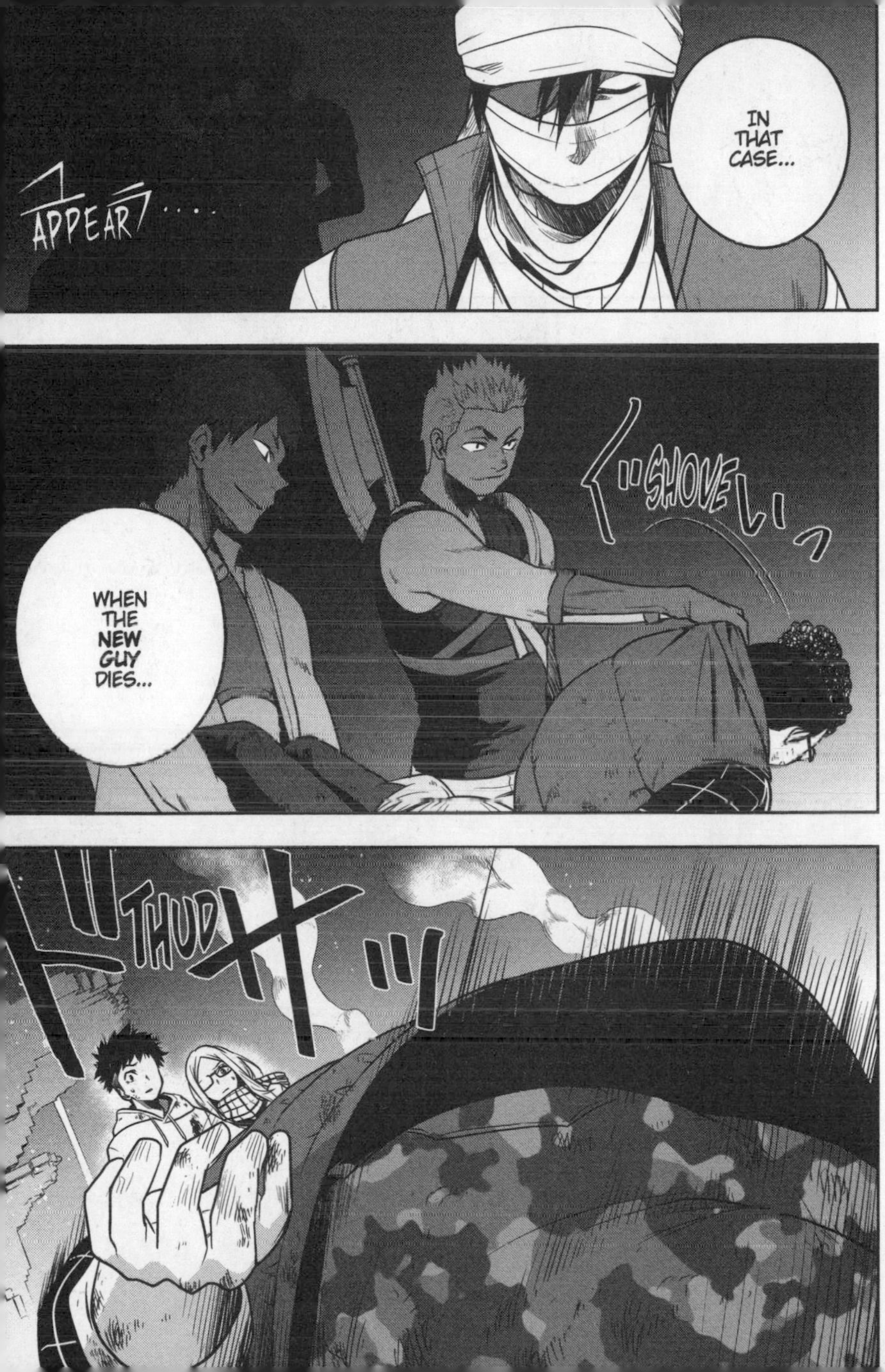
IN THAT CASE...
APPEAR
SHOVE
WHEN THE NEW GUY DIES...
THUD

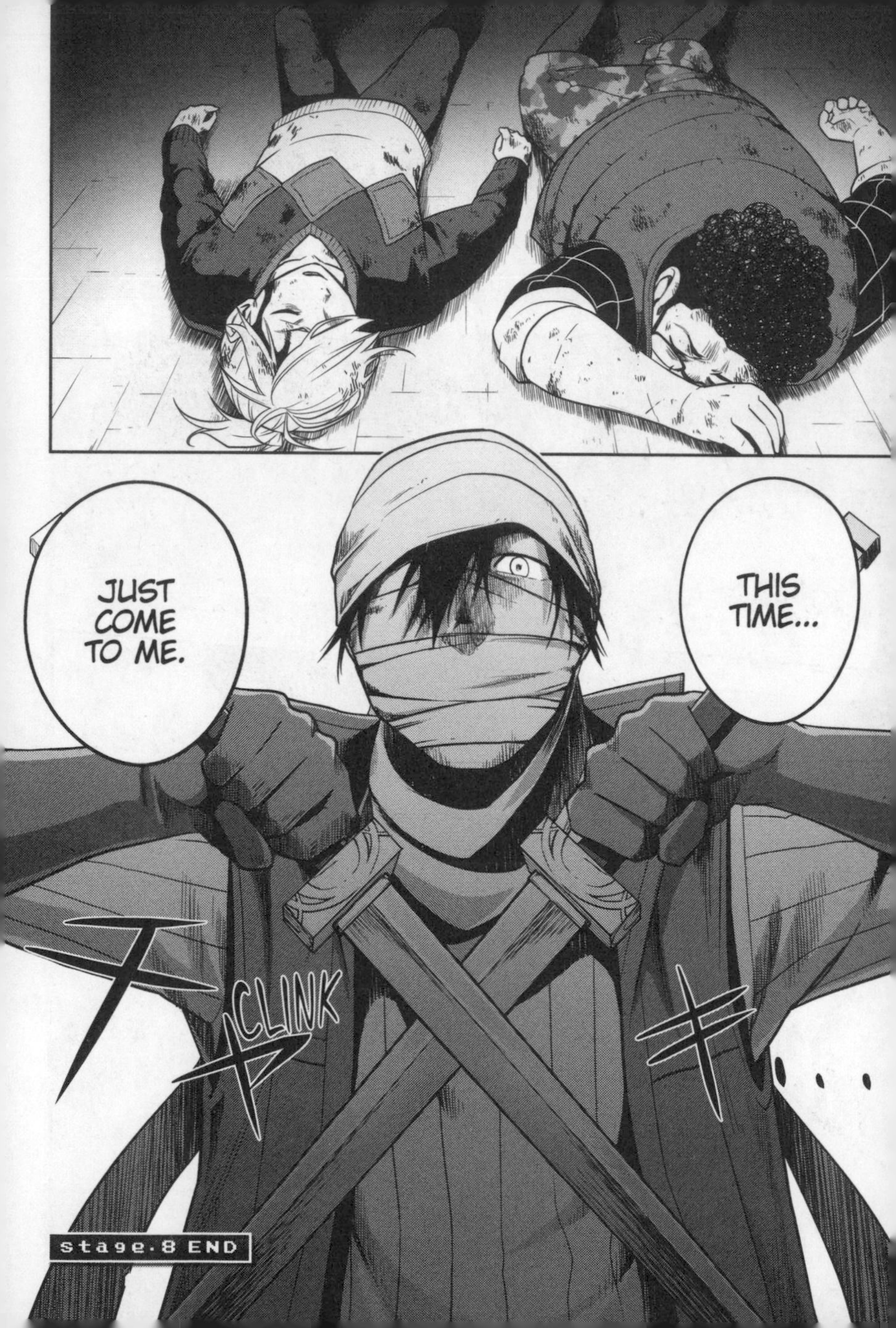
THIS TIME...
JUST COME TO ME.
...
CLINK
stage.8 END

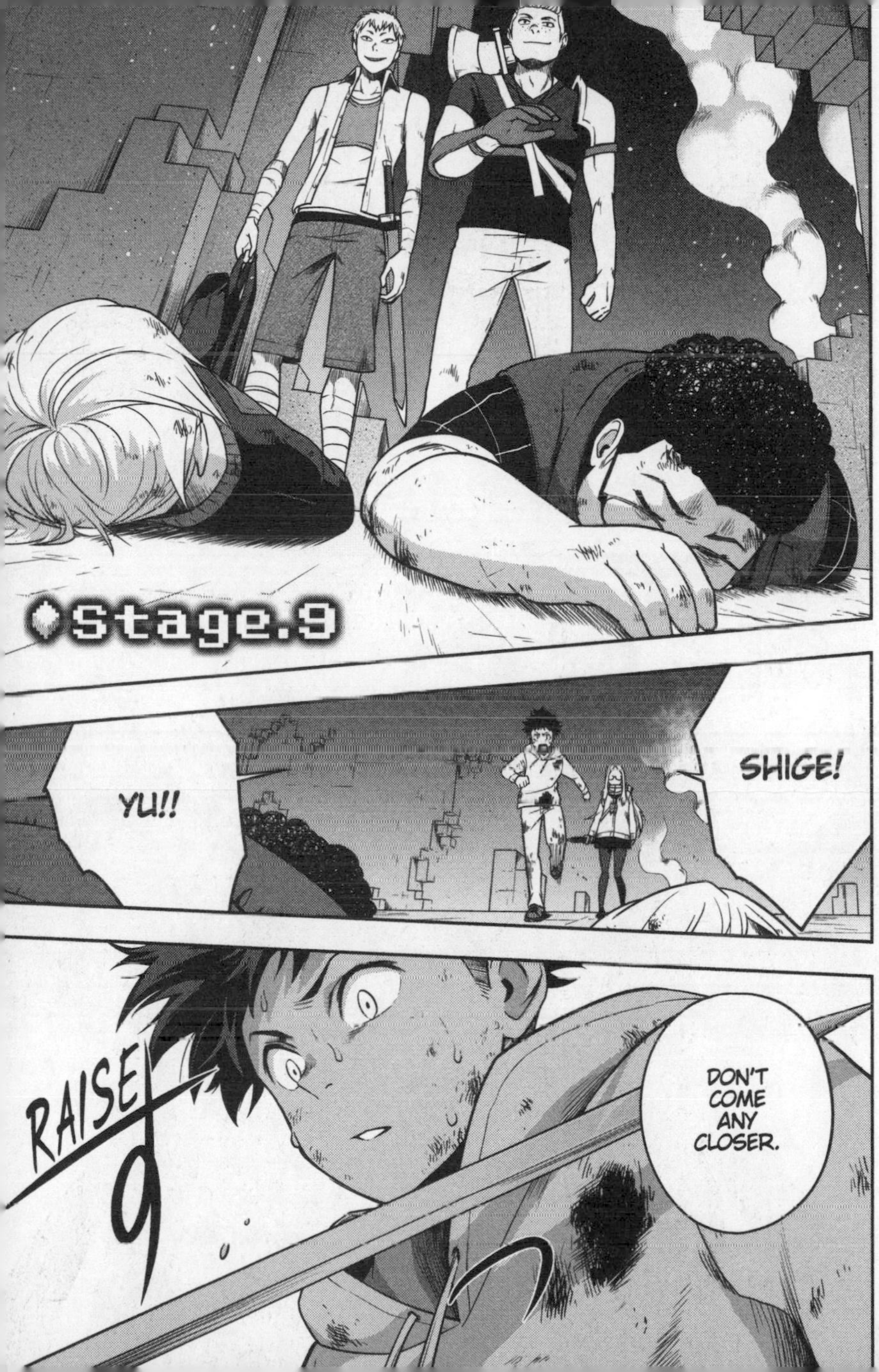
Stage.9
SHIGE!
YU!!
DON'T COME ANY CLOSER.
RAISE
9

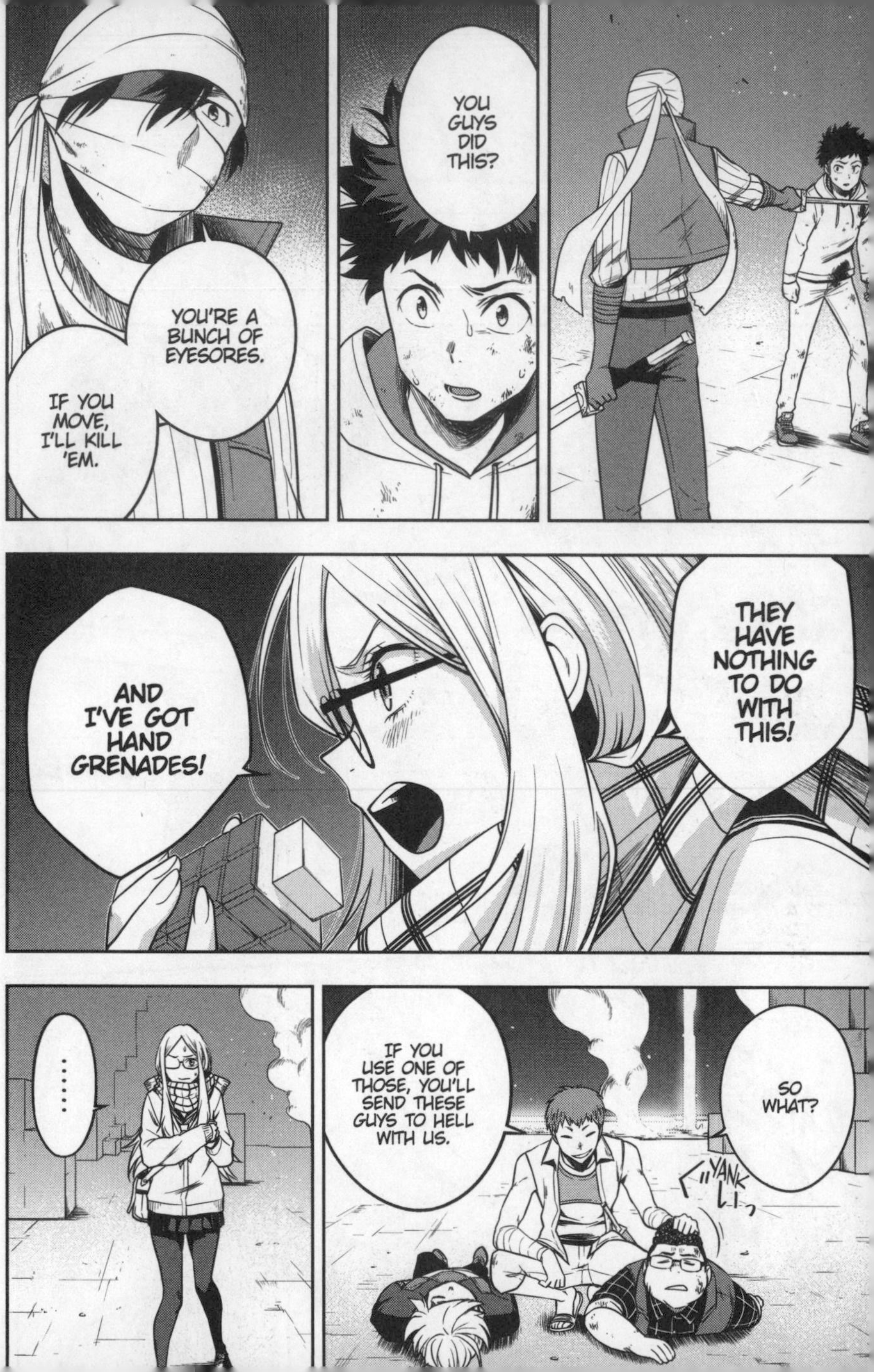
YOU GUYS DID THIS?
YOU'RE A BUNCH OF EYESORES.
IF YOU MOVE, I'LL KILL 'EM.
THEY HAVE NOTHING TO DO WITH THIS!
AND I'VE GOT HAND GRENADES!
IF YOU USE ONE OF THOSE, YOU'LL SEND THESE GUYS TO HELL WITH US.
SO WHAT?
YANK
......

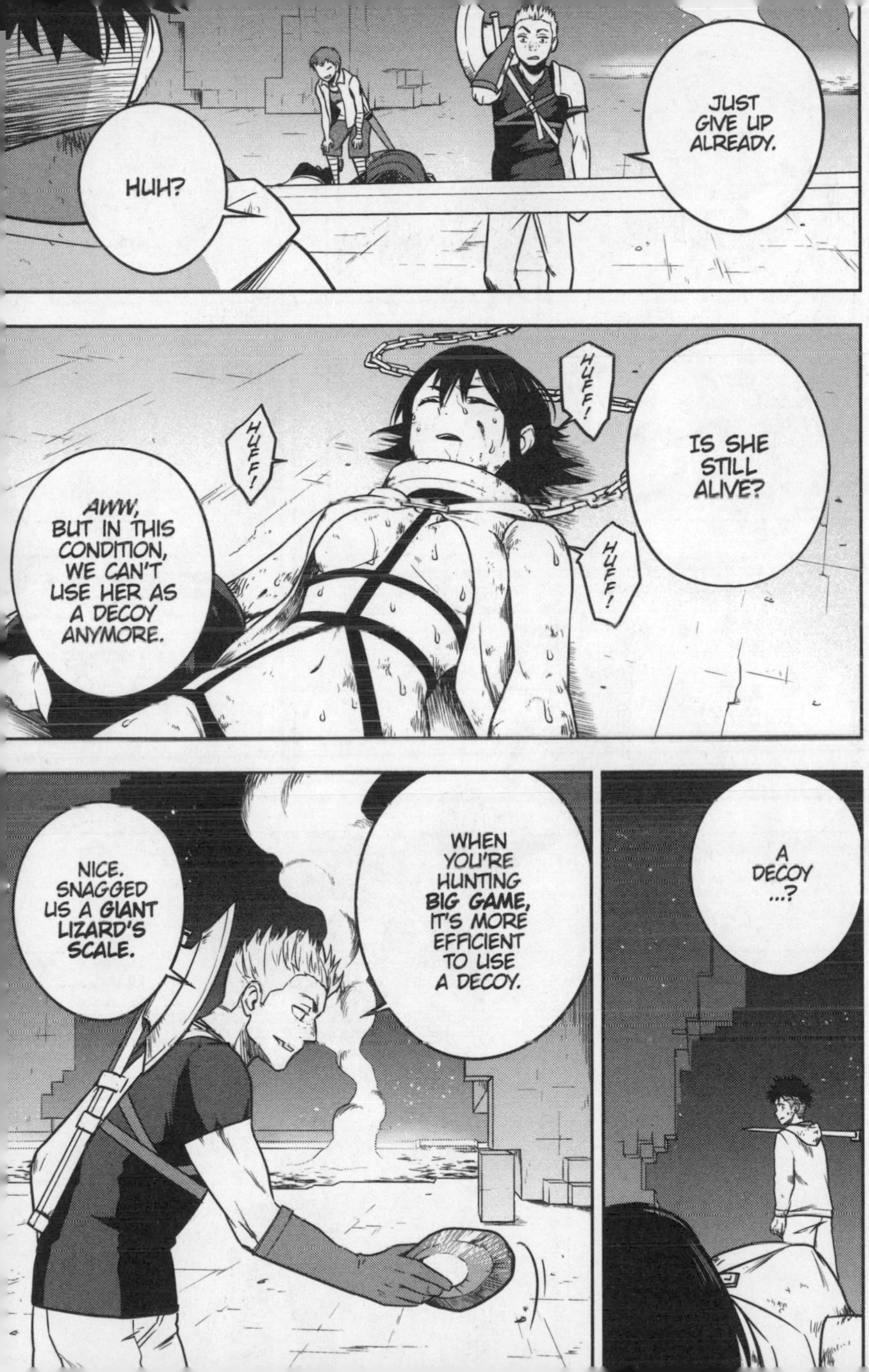
JUST GIVE UP ALREADY.
HUH?
HUFF!
IS SHE STILL ALIVE?
HUFF!
HUFF!
AWW, BUT IN THIS CONDITION, WE CAN'T USE HER AS A DECOY ANYMORE.
A DECOY ...?
WHEN YOU'RE HUNTING BIG GAME, IT'S MORE EFFICIENT TO USE A DECOY.
NICE. SNAGGED US A GIANT LIZARD'S SCALE.

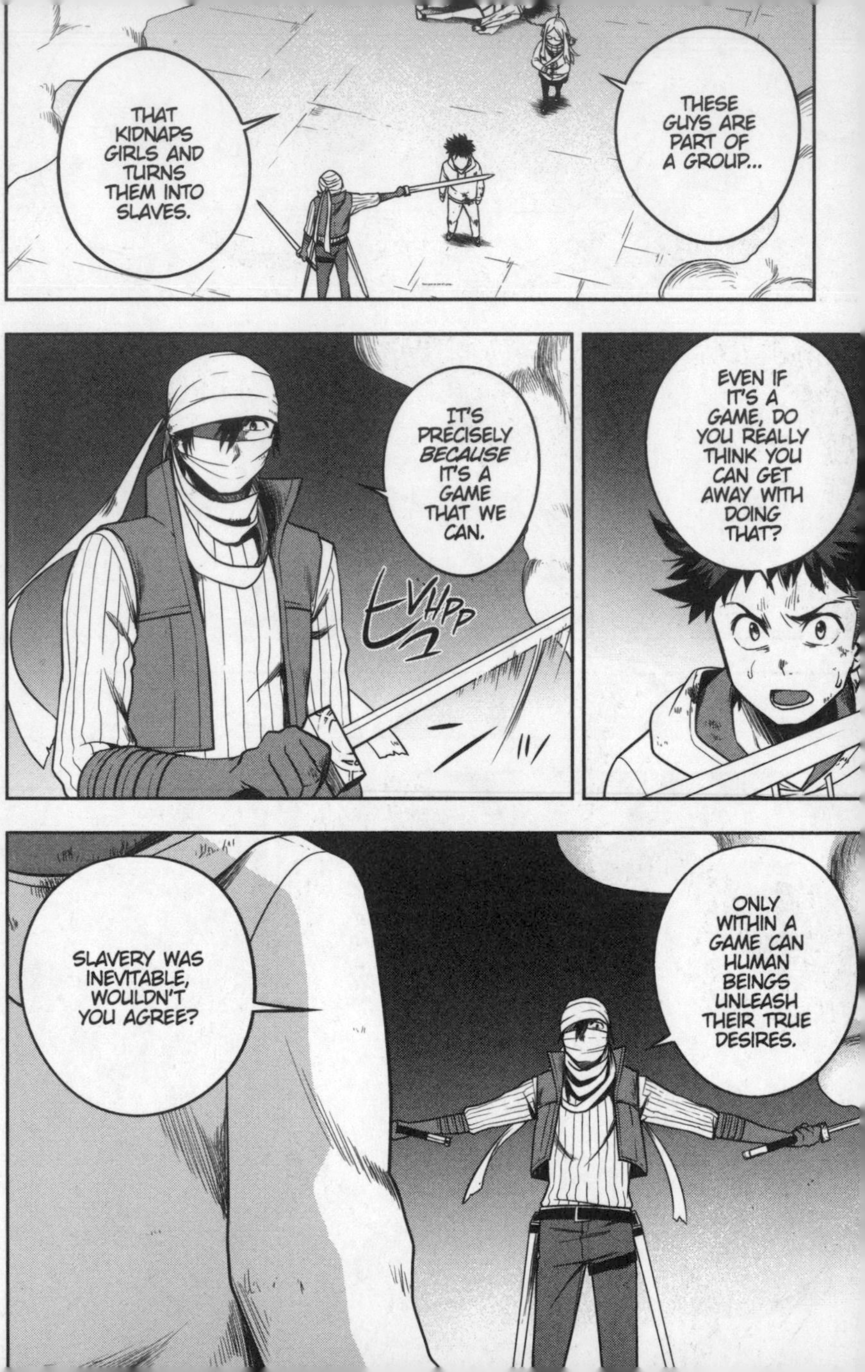
THESE GUYS ARE PART OF A GROUP...
THAT KIDNAPS GIRLS AND TURNS THEM INTO SLAVES.
EVEN IF IT'S A GAME, DO YOU REALLY THINK YOU CAN GET AWAY WITH DOING THAT?
IT'S PRECISELY *BECAUSE* IT'S A GAME THAT WE CAN.
VHPP
ONLY WITHIN A GAME CAN HUMAN BEINGS UNLEASH THEIR TRUE DESIRES.
SLAVERY WAS INEVITABLE, WOULDN'T YOU AGREE?

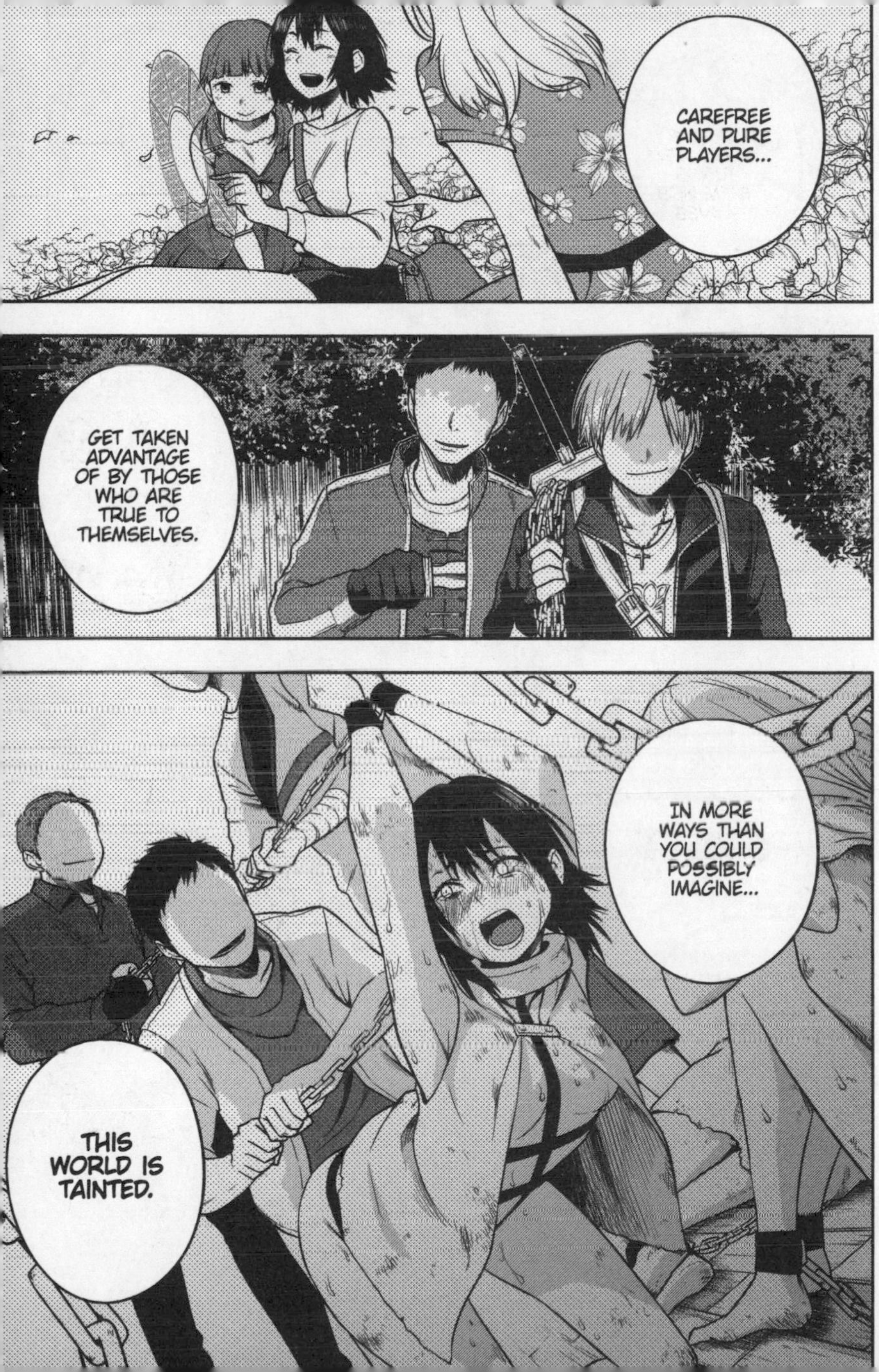
CAREFREE AND PURE PLAYERS...
GET TAKEN ADVANTAGE OF BY THOSE WHO ARE TRUE TO THEMSELVES.
IN MORE WAYS THAN YOU COULD POSSIBLY IMAGINE...
THIS WORLD IS TAINTED.

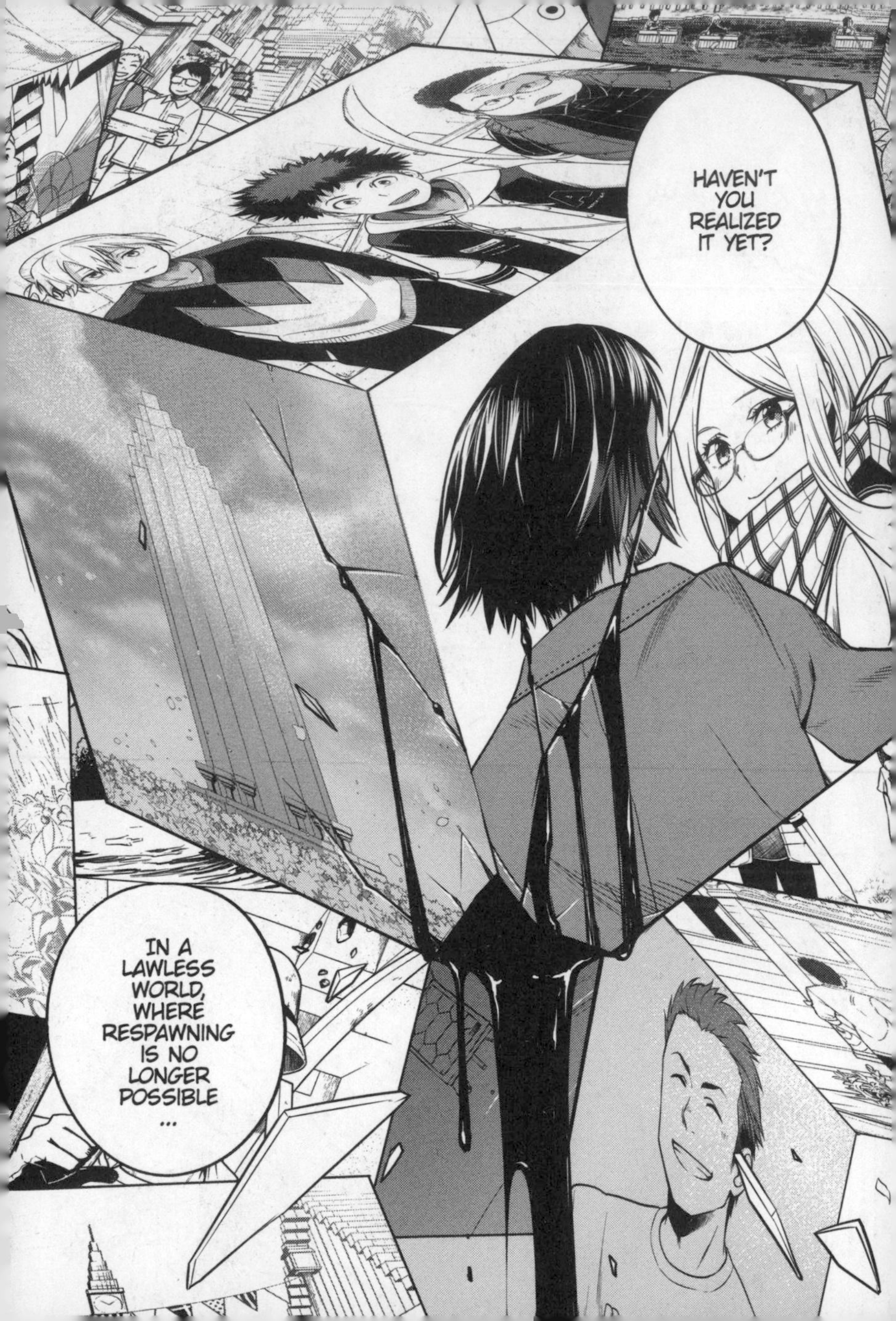
HAVEN'T YOU REALIZED IT YET?
IN A LAWLESS WORLD, WHERE RESPAWNING IS NO LONGER POSSIBLE ...

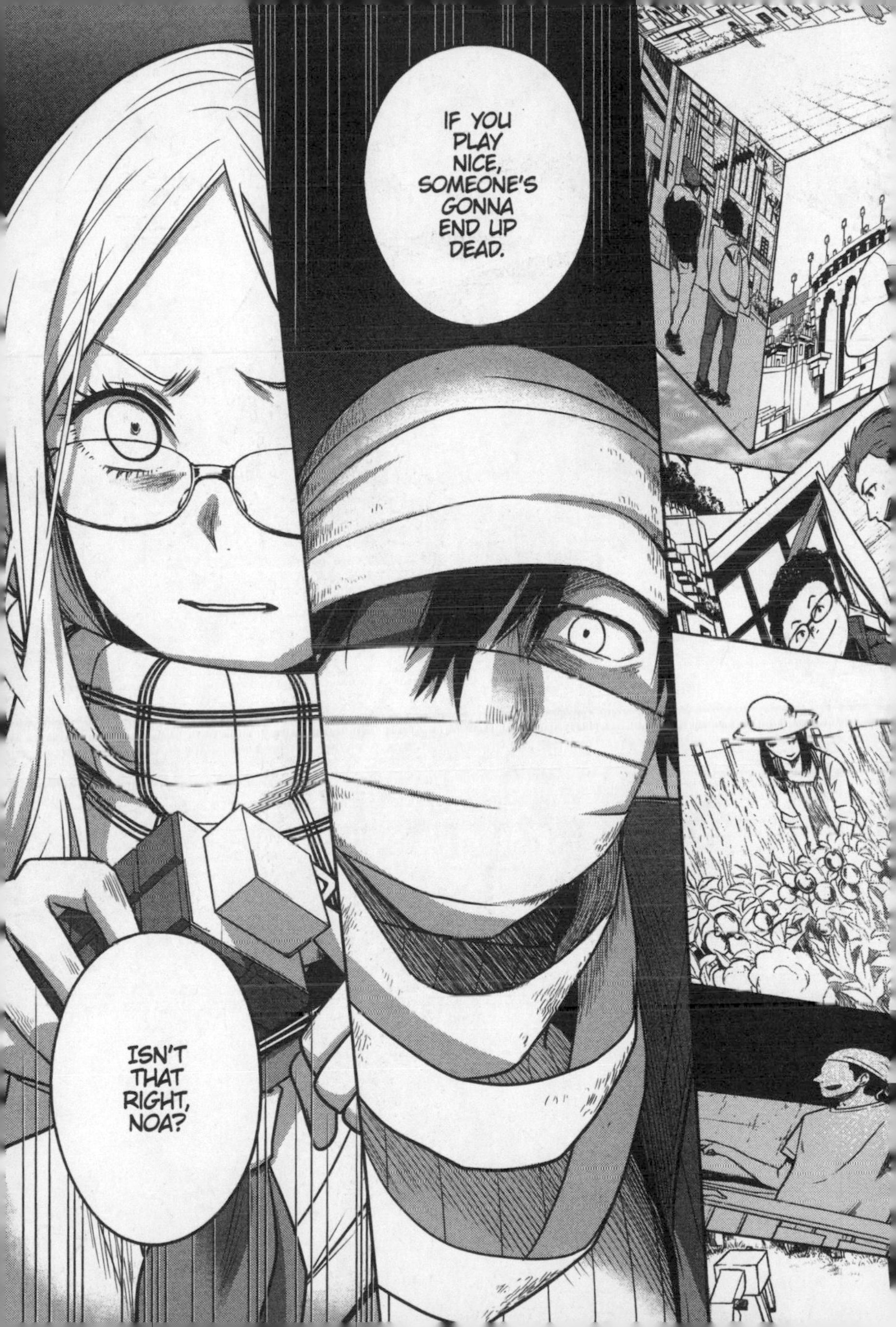
IF YOU PLAY NICE, SOMEONE'S GONNA END UP DEAD.
ISN'T THAT RIGHT, NOA?

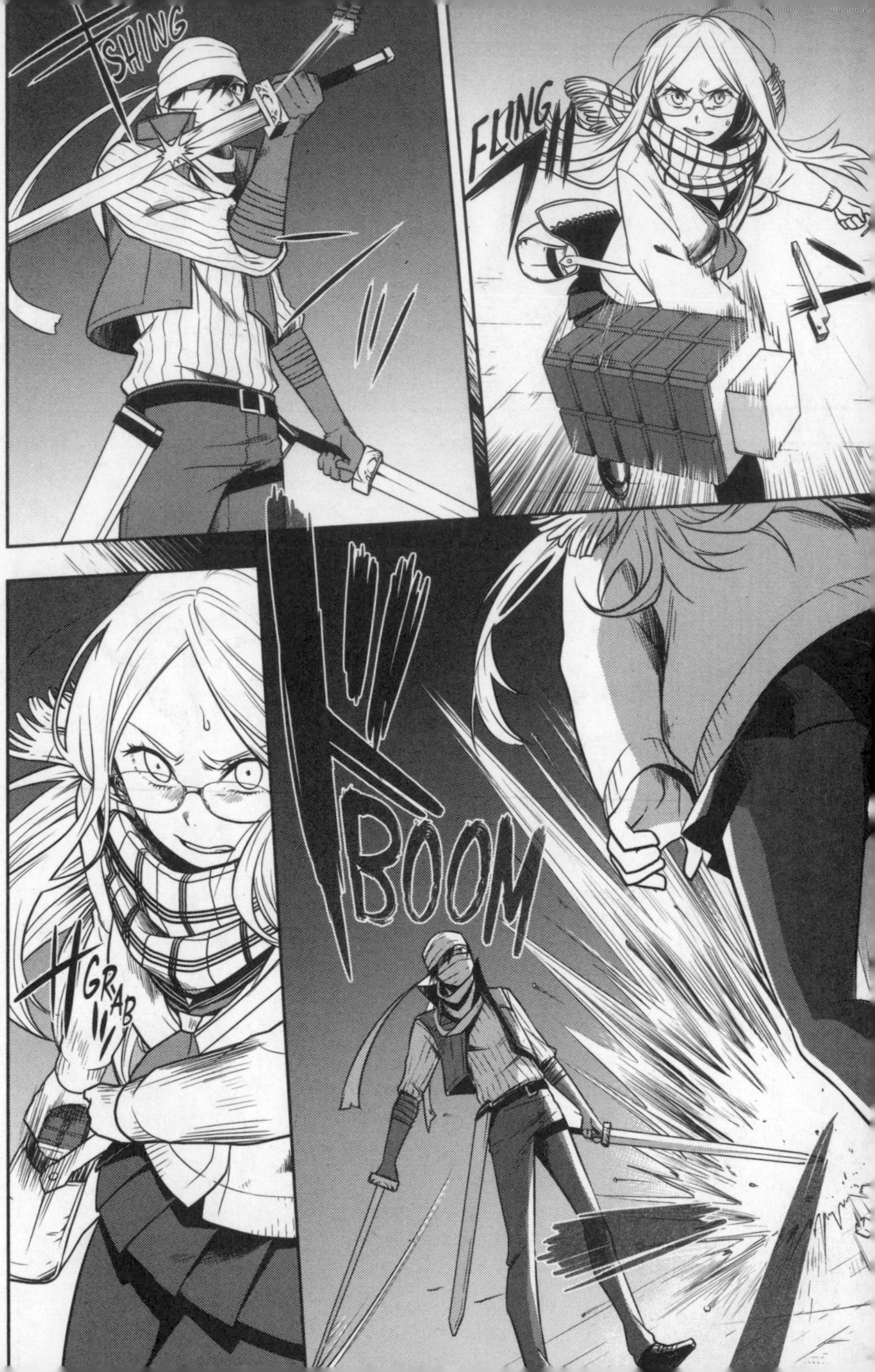
FLING
SHING
BOOM
GRAB

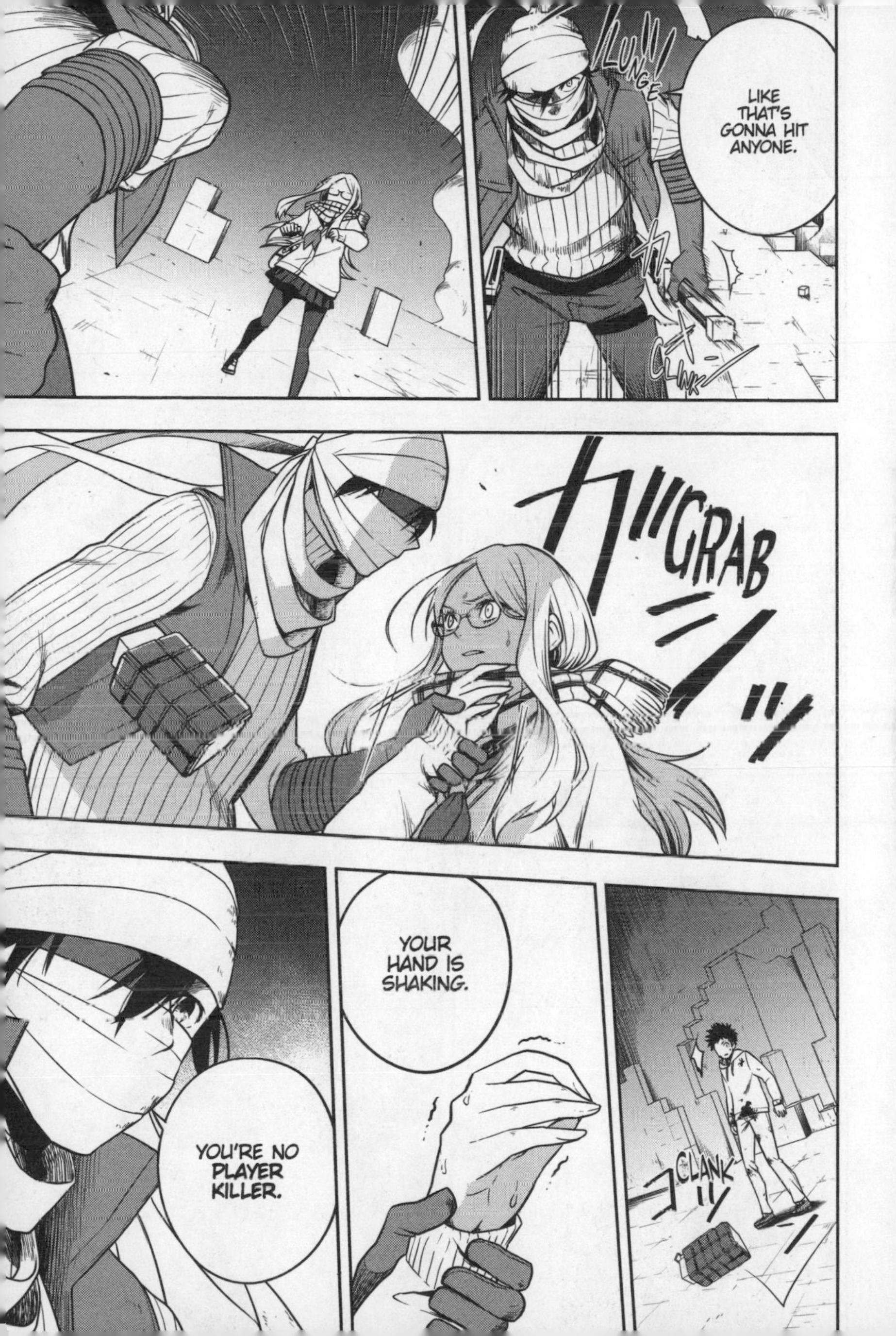
LUNGE
LIKE THAT'S GONNA HIT ANYONE.
CLINK
GRAB
CLANK
YOUR HAND IS SHAKING.
YOU'RE NO PLAYER KILLER.

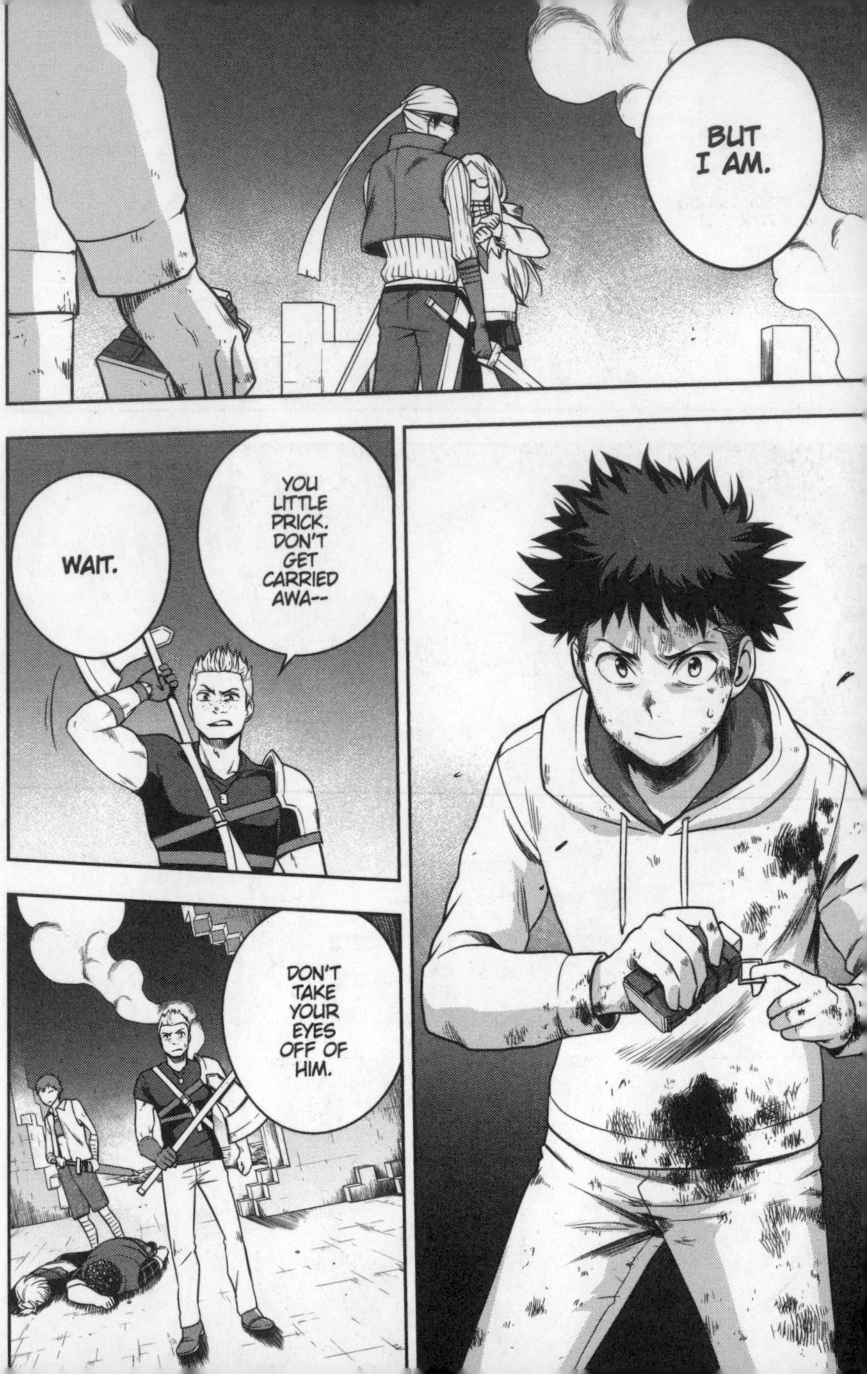
BUT I AM.
YOU LITTLE PRICK. DON'T GET CARRIED AWA--
WAIT.
DON'T TAKE YOUR EYES OFF OF HIM.

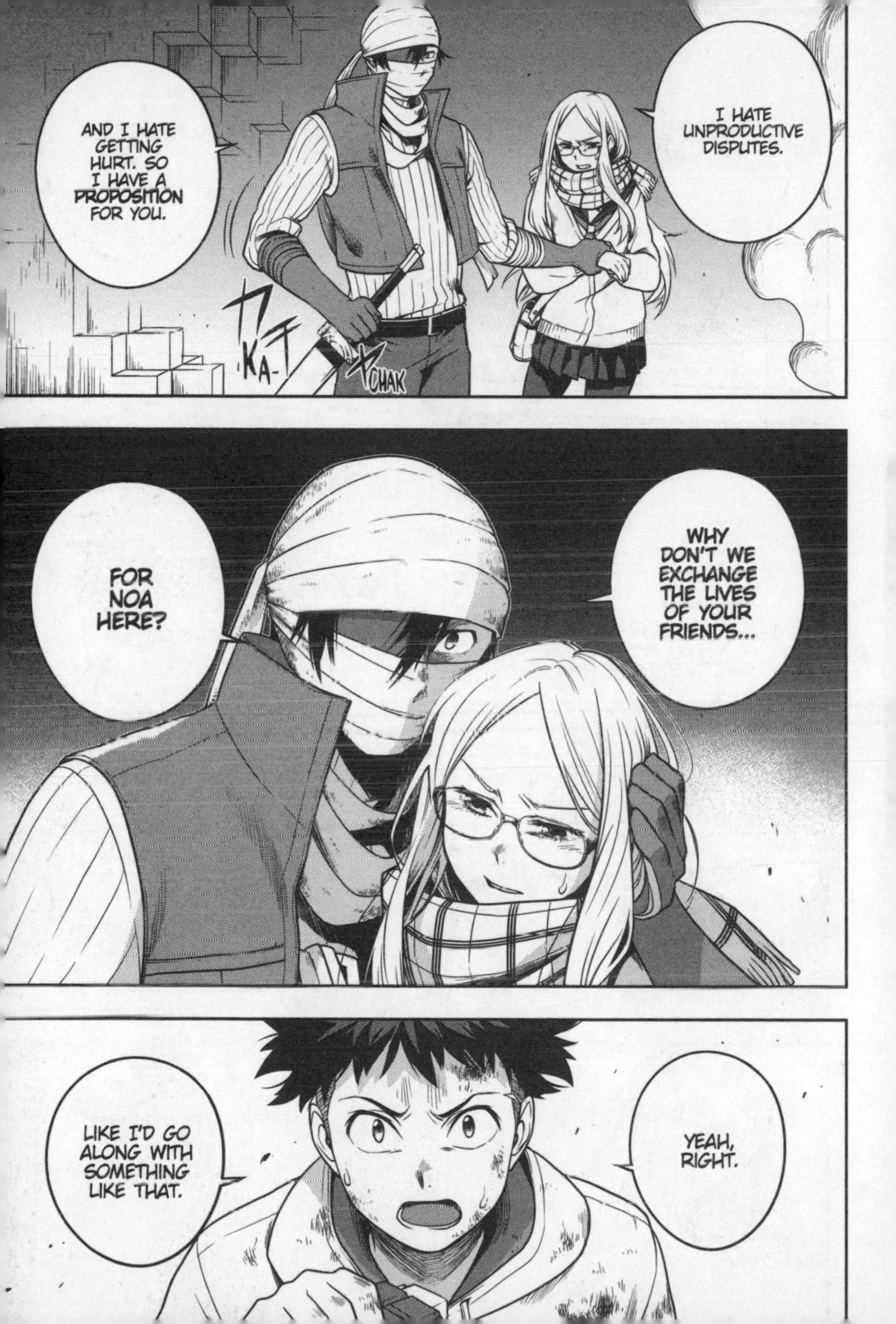
I HATE UNPRODUCTIVE DISPUTES.
AND I HATE GETTING HURT. SO I HAVE A PROPOSITION FOR YOU.
CHAK
KA-
WHY DON'T WE EXCHANGE THE LIVES OF YOUR FRIENDS...
FOR NOA HERE?
YEAH, RIGHT.
LIKE I'D GO ALONG WITH SOMETHING LIKE THAT.

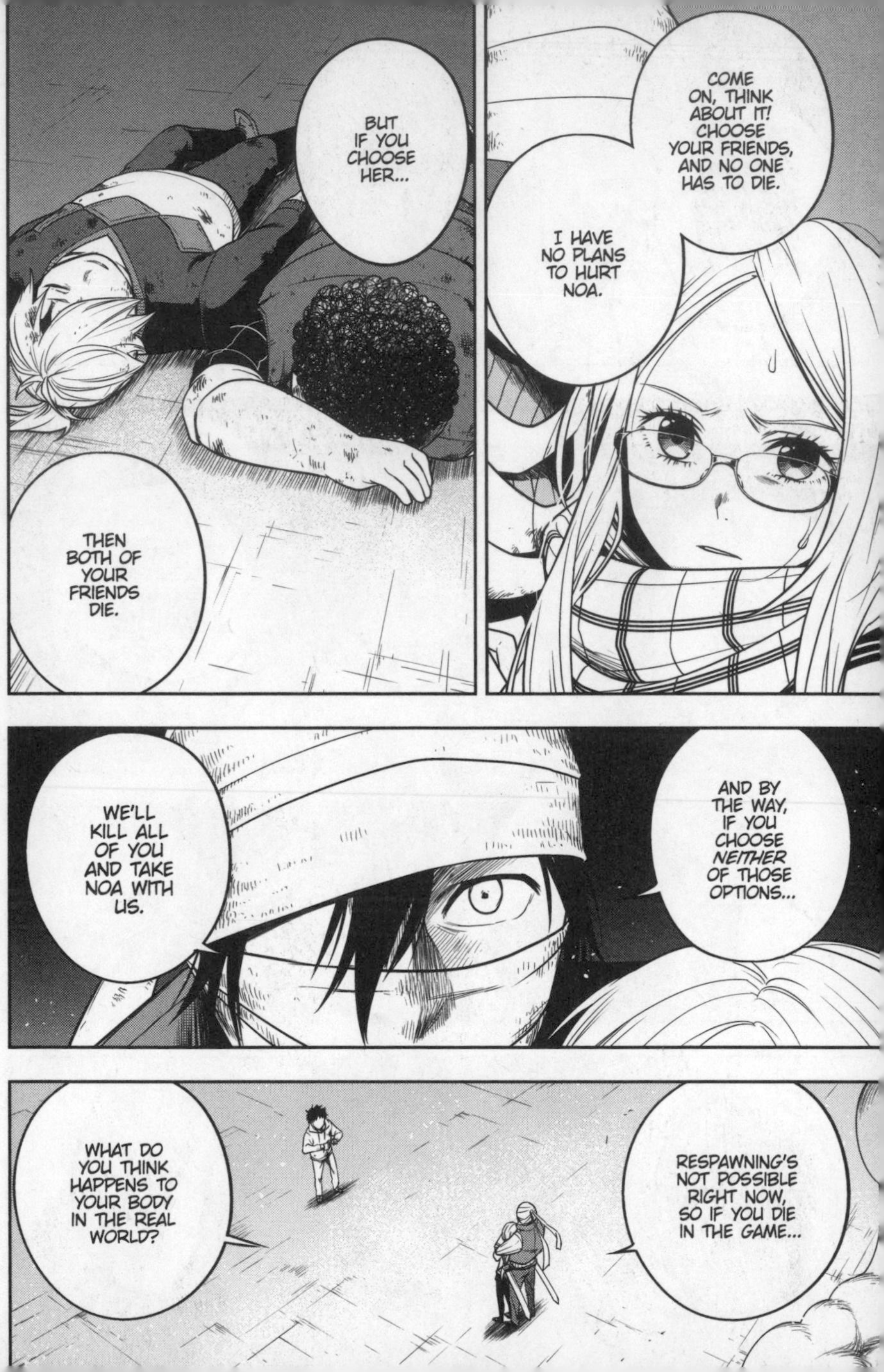
COME ON, THINK ABOUT IT! CHOOSE YOUR FRIENDS, AND NO ONE HAS TO DIE.
I HAVE NO PLANS TO HURT NOA.
BUT IF YOU CHOOSE HER...
THEN BOTH OF YOUR FRIENDS DIE.
AND BY THE WAY, IF YOU CHOOSE *NEITHER* OF THOSE OPTIONS...
WE'LL KILL ALL OF YOU AND TAKE NOA WITH US.
RESPAWNING'S NOT POSSIBLE RIGHT NOW, SO IF YOU DIE IN THE GAME...
WHAT DO YOU THINK HAPPENS TO YOUR BODY IN THE REAL WORLD?

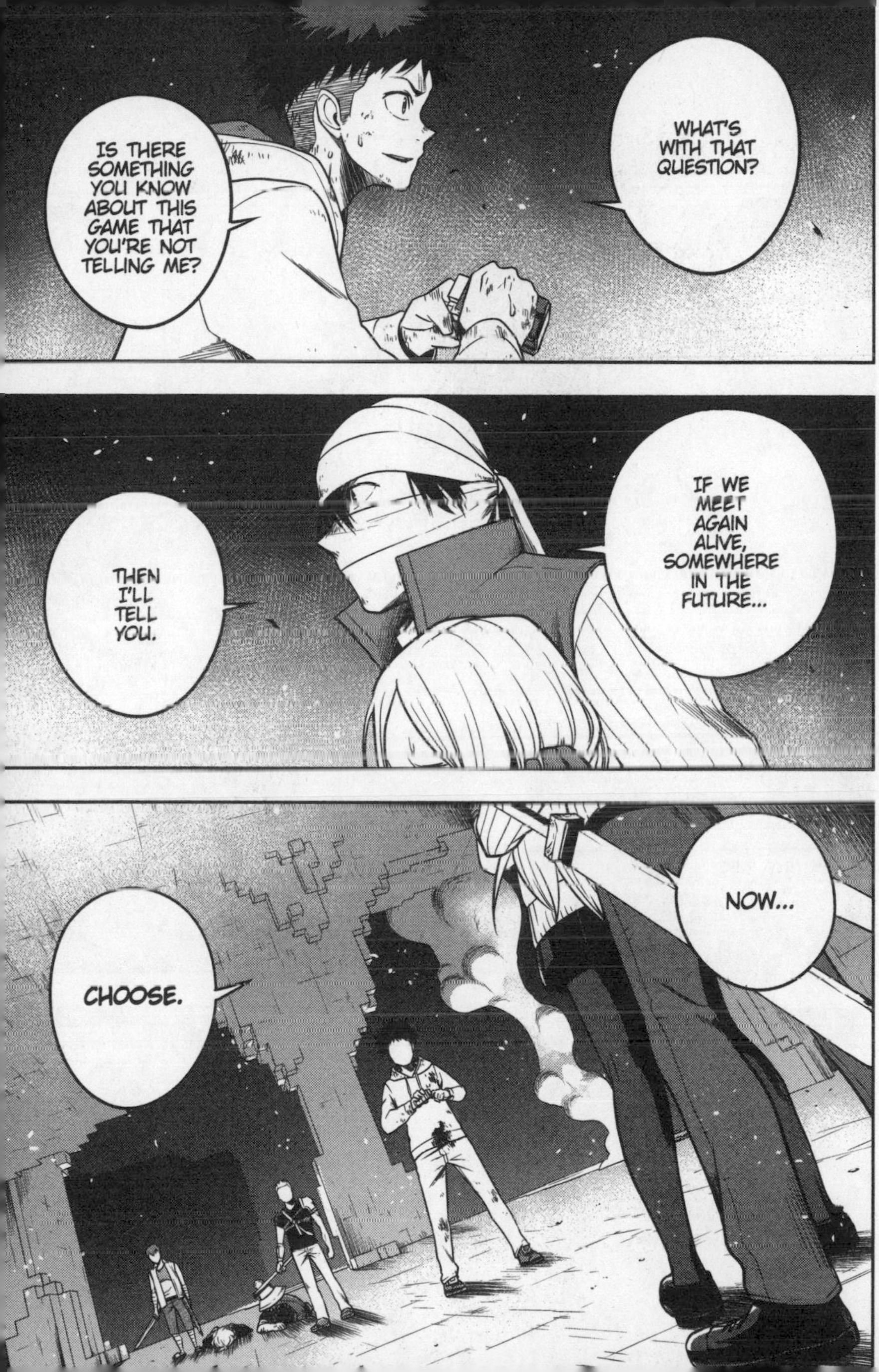
WHAT'S WITH THAT QUESTION?
IS THERE SOMETHING YOU KNOW ABOUT THIS GAME THAT YOU'RE NOT TELLING ME?
IF WE MEET AGAIN ALIVE, SOMEWHERE IN THE FUTURE...
THEN I'LL TELL YOU.
NOW...
CHOOSE.

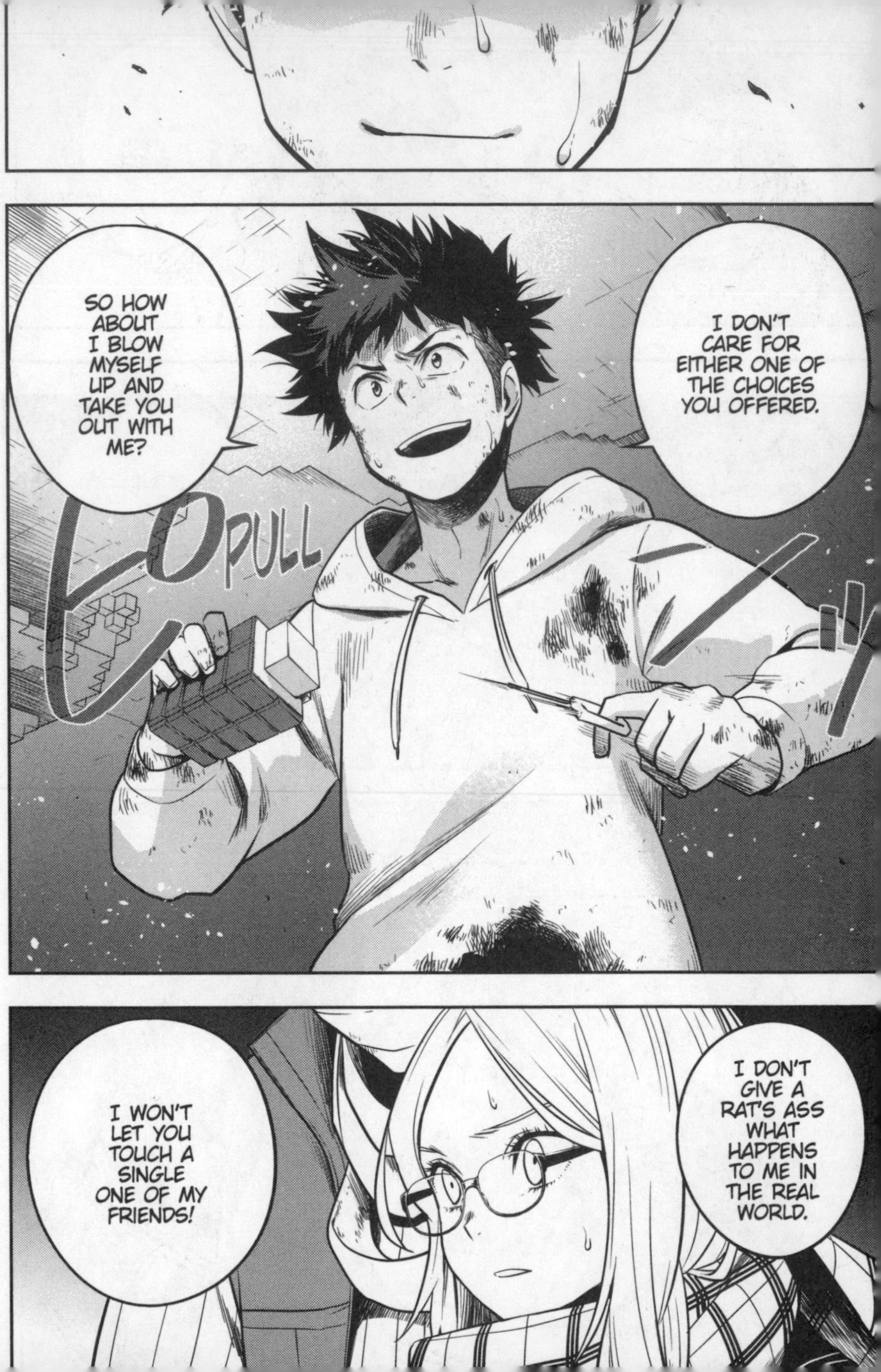
I DON'T CARE FOR EITHER ONE OF THE CHOICES YOU OFFERED.
SO HOW ABOUT I BLOW MYSELF UP AND TAKE YOU OUT WITH ME?
PULL
I DON'T GIVE A RAT'S ASS WHAT HAPPENS TO ME IN THE REAL WORLD.
I WON'T LET YOU TOUCH A SINGLE ONE OF MY FRIENDS!

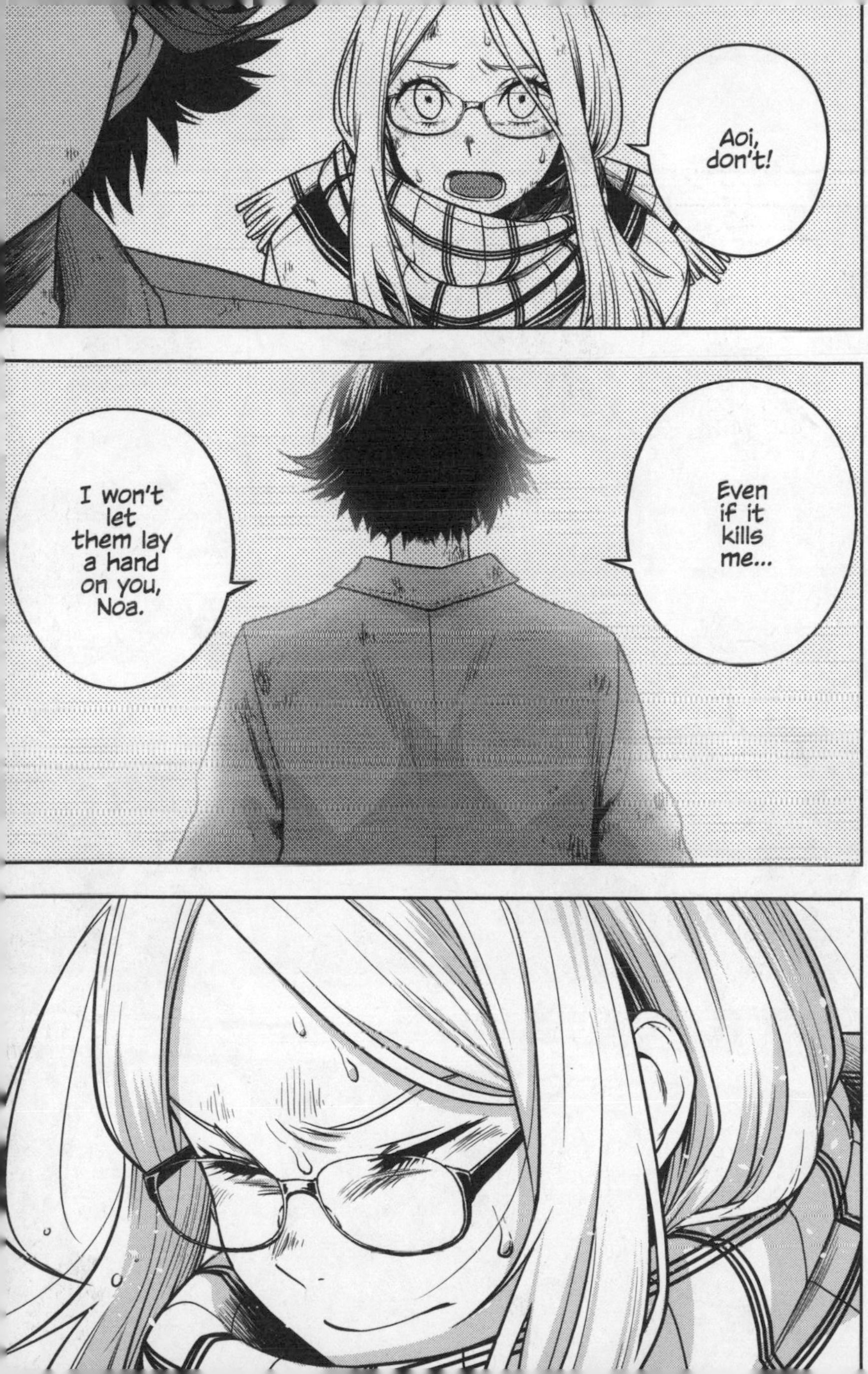
Aoi, don't!
Even if it kills me...
I won't let them lay a hand on you, Noa.

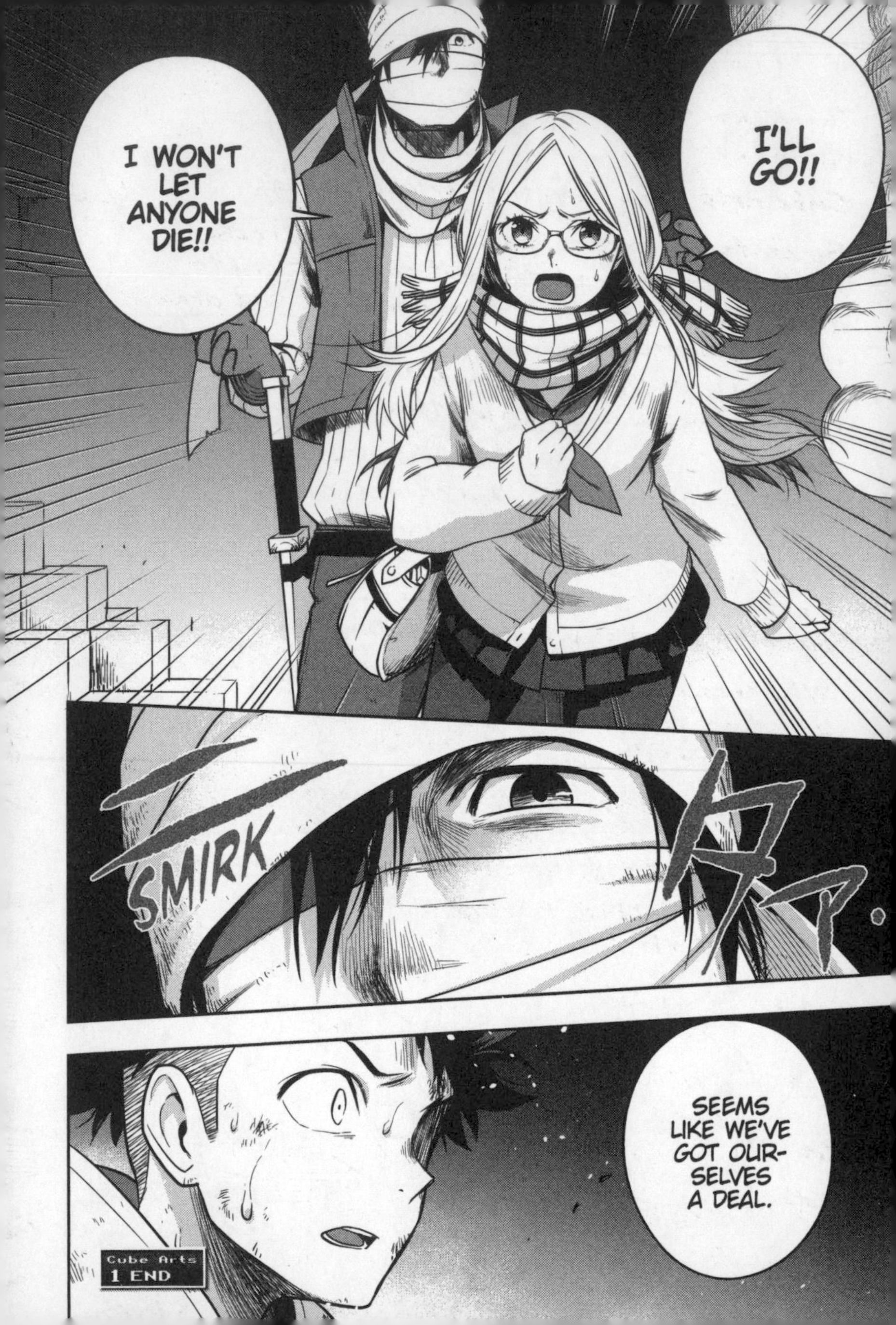
I'LL GO!!
I WON'T LET ANYONE DIE!!
SMIRK
SEEMS LIKE WE'VE GOT OURSELVES A DEAL.
Cube Arts 1 END

Afterword

Thank you so, so much for picking up this book!

Cube Arts is my very first original manga.

Since it's my first original work, I truly racked my brain coming up with what sort of story to draw. My editor asked, "Why don't you just draw what you want to draw, Usui-san?" And since I'm always playing games in my everyday life, I decided to use games as my manga's theme.

At the time, I was totally into a game called **M—craft**, and I was intently building cities I wanted to live in. I also like games like **Portal Kn—ts** and **A-K**. I just love adventuring and building a base anywhere I want to. I still play **M—craft**, and I'm currently, slowly but surely, building a giant, floating city on the water.

Who knows...you may see a village similar to ones I constructed in the past show up in **Cube Arts!**

I strived to create a story that those who like this sort of game, those who don't like this sort of game, and those who don't play games at all will equally enjoy, so please continue to support **Cube Arts!**

Tomomi Usui
臼井ともみ

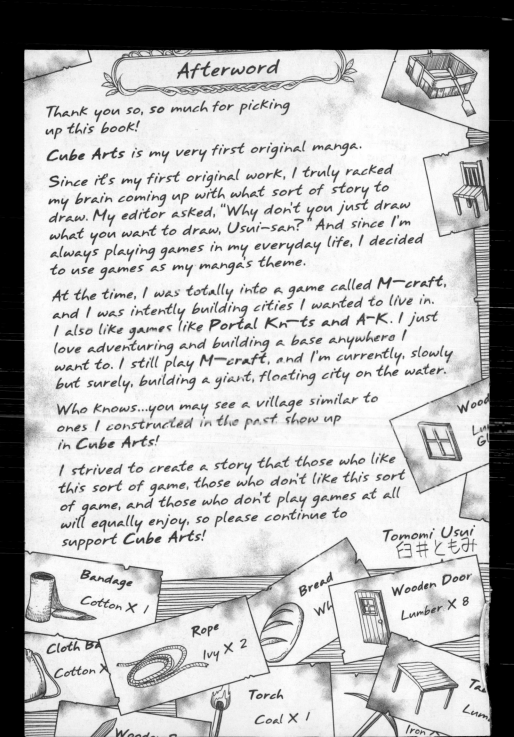

Wood

Lu
Gl

Bandage

Cotton X 1

Bread
Wh

Wooden Door

Lumber X 8

Cloth Ba

Cotton X

Rope

Ivy X 2

Torch

Coal X 1

Ta
Lum

Iron

SEVEN SEAS ENTERTAINMENT PRESENTS

CUBE ARTS

story and art by TOMOMI USUI   VOLUME 1

TRANSLATION
Nan Rymer

ADAPTATION
Patrick King

LETTERING AND RETOUCH
James Gaubatz

COVER DESIGN
Kris Aubin

PROOFREADER
B. Lana Guggenheim

EDITOR
Peter Adrian Behravesh

PREPRESS TECHNICIAN
Rhiannon Rasmussen-Silverstein

PRODUCTION MANAGER
Lissa Pattillo

MANAGING EDITOR
Julie Davis

ASSOCIATE PUBLISHER
Adam Arnold

PUBLISHER
Jason DeAngelis

Seven Seas press and purchase enquiries can be sent to Marketing Manager
Lianne Sentar at press@gomanga.com. Information regarding the distribution
and purchase of digital editions is available from Digital Manager CK Russell
at digital@gomanga.com.

Seven Seas and the Seven Seas logo are trademarks of
Seven Seas Entertainment. All rights reserved.

ISBN: 978-1-64505-638-6

Printed in Canada

First Printing: September 2020

10 9 8 7 6 5 4 3 2 1

FOLLOW US ONLINE: *www.sevenseasentertainment.com*

READING DIRECTIONS

This book reads from ***right to left***, Japanese style.
If this is your first time reading manga, you start
reading from the top right panel on each page and
take it from there. If you get lost, just follow the
numbered diagram here. It may seem backwards at
first, but you'll get the hang of it! Have fun!!

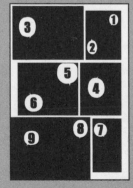